KT-198-833

THE SOUND
OF HISTORY

Songs and Social Comment

ROY PALMER

PIMLICO

PIMLICO
An imprint of Random House
20 Vauxhall Bridge Road,
London SW1V 2SA

Random House Australia (Pty) Limited
16 Dalmore Drive, Scoresby,
Victoria 3179, Australia

Random House New Zealand Limited
18 Poland Road, Glenfield, Auckland 10, New Zealand

Random House South Africa (Pty) Limited
Box 2263, Rosebank 2121, South Africa

Random House UK Ltd Reg. No. 954009

First published by Oxford University Press 1988
Pimlico edition 1996

1 3 5 7 9 10 8 6 4 2

© Roy Palmer 1988

The right of Roy Palmer to be identified as the
Author of this work has been asserted by him in accordance
with the Copyright, Designs and Patents Act 1988

This book is sold subject to the condition that it shall not, by way
of trade or otherwise, be lent, resold, hired out, or otherwise circulated
without the publisher's prior consent in any form of binding or cover
other than that in which it is published and without a similar condition
including this condition being imposed on the subsequent purchaser

Papers used by Random House UK Limited are natural,
recyclable products made from wood grown in sustainable forests.
The manufacturing processes conform to the environmental
regulations of the country of origin.

Printed and bound in Great Britain
by Mackays of Chatham PLC

ISBN 0-7126-7316-4

for Simon, Adam, Thomas

Le peuple a ses archives: ce sont les chansons.

Sylvain Trébucq, *La Chanson populaire et la Vie rurale des Pyrénées à la Vendée* (Bordeaux, 1912), p. 30

I shall not expatiate upon the importance of folk songs. They are a people's history, vital, vivid, full of colours and truth, laying bare all the life of a people. ... a historical inscription is nothing against this living, talking chronicle, resonant with the past.

Nikolai Gogol, 'About Ukrainian Songs' (1834), *Soviet Literature*, 4 (Moscow, 1984), 113

Our modern Political Songs and Ballads—the best popular illustrations of history.

W. W. Wilkins, *Political Ballads of the Seventeenth and Eighteenth Centuries* (1860), vol. 1, p. vi

PREFACE TO THE PIMLICO EDITION

ONE of my motives in writing *The Sound of History* was to argue that ballads can illuminate, in Selden's phrase, 'the Complexion of the Times', and are therefore worthy of consideration by historians. If historians often remain sceptical, makers of documentary radio programmes and films about the past seem to accept the thesis readily enough, though they sometimes fall into grotesque anachronism. One television film on the Civil War had Cromwell's troopers singing 'He Who Would Valiant Be', to a tune composed by Ralph Vaughan Williams in the 1920s and words written by John Bunyan in 1684. Other producers are more careful with chronology, though some fall into a besetting literalness: so, for example, a sequence on the hard life of a ploughman has to be accompanied by a song along the same lines, whereas a more idyllic piece might have set up a creative tension between perception and reality.

A historian who has not only explored ballads as source material (in addition, of course, to a wide range of other evidence) but has also written an outstanding, indeed prize-winning, book in the process is Dr V.A.C. Gatrell. When I wrote to congratulate him on *The Hanging Tree: Execution and the English People, 1770–1868* (Oxford, 1994), I was delighted to receive this reply, which I quote with Dr Gatrell's permission: 'It was your *Sound of History* with its lament that so few academic historians took ballads and music seriously, that was one of the first things on the subject which I read and was excited by—a fine book'. The exigencies of reprinting were such that I have not been able to do any radical updating, but I have taken the opportunity of correcting some errors and of making some very minor changes. I am grateful for the comments of Hamish Henderson, N.A. Hudleston and Michael Grosvenor Myer.

Roy Palmer
Dymock, 1996

FOREWORD

THIS is an examination of songs and the social comment they make. The narrative attempts to tell the history of the songs and to situate them in the context from which they came. The commentary is not exhaustive, and in some cases readers are left to draw their own conclusions from the material presented. The book is an anthology, in that 54 songs are given in full (40 with music), and also a guide, in that many others are mentioned or are quoted briefly. All the songs discussed or cited, together with other quotations and allusions, are carefully identified, and a select bibliography and a discography are also included.

Consideration is limited to the overlapping categories of oral songs, street ballads, and the work of singer/song-writers who employ a largely traditional idiom. Even so, the field remains enormous, and coverage of the broad themes chosen must inevitably be impressionistic. No attempt has been made to provide exhaustive coverage or to follow a relentlessly chronological pattern. The topics adopted are those on which songs have something to say: it would have been pointless to have chosen others. Nevertheless, I have necessarily had to be selective. The examples cover a span of some four hundred years up to and including the present day, though the bulk come from the second half of this period. It would be perfectly possible to cover the same ground with a different choice of songs, but I believe that similar trends would emerge.

Balladry was once favoured as a vehicle for the views of a wide social cross-section, but it increasingly became the voice of those who felt themselves to be excluded from other means of public self-expression. The element of opposition to the great and powerful which had always been there tended to increase as those in power adopted other means of putting across their views. British Coal did not commission songs during the miners' strike of 1984–5; nor did the Central Electricity Generating Board during the public debate on the projected Sizewell B power-station. Those opposing the coal and electricity boards (and behind them, the Government) did choose songs, partly in deference to tradition, partly for reasons of style and accessibility, partly for economic reasons, and partly because they felt that their share of the conventional media was minimal. The songs so written, like many before them, make no claim to fairness or objectivity, but are perhaps the more interesting and significant for that.

The wide-ranging survey of song and social comment which is offered here is intended for the non-specialist, though the historian and the student of popular culture should find much of interest. Tender or harsh, fleeting or long-remembered, these ballads have the sound of history.

CONTENTS

LIST OF ILLUSTRATIONS   XV

ACKNOWLEDGEMENTS   xix

INTRODUCTION   I

1. The Country   30

2. The Town   61

3. Industry   84

4. Crime   121

5. Pastime   160

6. The Sexes   197

7. Politics   235

8. War and Peace   271

ABBREVIATIONS   303

NOTES   304

SELECT BIBLIOGRAPHY   336

DISCOGRAPHY   344

INDEX OF TITLES, TUNES, AND FIRST LINES   347

GENERAL INDEX   355

ILLUSTRATIONS

'Jack the Chimney Sweep'   9
The Master and Fellows of Trinity College, Cambridge

Lord Macaulay taken for a ballad vendor   10
Leslie Shepard Collection

Street Scene by Thomas Rowlandson (1756–1827)   10
*Watercolour 6¹/₄" x 8¹/₄". Vassar College Art Gallery, Poughkeepsie, N.Y. Gift of Francis
Fitz Randolph, 7.10.53. (Vassar College Art Gallery, Poughkeepsie, New York)*

Tommy Armstrong, one of only two known photographs   11

'W——'s Thirteens'   11
Sheffield City Libraries

'A New Song, entitled No Inclosure!'   43
*Ballads, 1, pt 2, no. 18, University of Nottingham Library. Special Collections.
Reproduced by permission of the Librarian*

'My Master & I'   44
Mitchell Library, Glasgow District Libraries

Bothy Musicians   45
Scottish Ethnological Archive, National Museums of Scotland

A Westmorland shepherd   45
Museum of Lakeland Life & Industry, Abbot Hall, Kendal, Cumbria

'The Skeleton at Plough'. Engraving from book of the same title by
G. Mitchell, 1874   46

Ploughing: four oxen at wheel-plough. Engraving from W. H. Pyne,
Microcosm, 1808   46

'A New Touch of the Times'   77
Bodleian Library, Firth b 22, p. 107

Public Clock, West Dial, Manchester Royal Infirmary, 1899   78
Manchester Public Libraries

Victoria Bridge, Manchester, 1859   79
Manchester Public Libraries

Manchester Royal Infirmary, c.1853   79
Manchester Public Libraries

George Dunn revisiting Noah Bloomer's chainshop, 1974   111
Photograph: Janet Kerr. Author's Collection

Leicestershire stocking-weaver of the 1850s   111
Leicestershire Museums

'The Cloth-dresser'. A cropper at work in 1814. From George Walker,
The Costumes of Yorkshire, 1814   112

Brian Deacon of Leicester, 'Getting Married Tomorrow', 1984   112
Photograph: Theodore Sturge

'The Submissive Petition of the Distressed Hugh Boyd'   113
Bodleian Library, John Johnson Street Ballads, 23

Women chainmakers on strike in 1910   114
Author's Collection

Notice from the Civil Authorities to the Keelmen and Inhabitants of
Newcastle, 1822   114
Newcastle upon Tyne City Libraries

'The Strike Alphabet'   115
Bodleian Library, Firth c. 16, p. 211, item 260

'The Golden Farmer's Last Farewell'   137
The British Library

'Manners and Customs of Ye Englyshe in 1849'. *Punch* cartoon   137
Bodleian Library, N. 2706 d 10. 1849 No. 1, p. 114

'God's Revenge Against Murder'   138

'Confession and Execution of William Corder'   139

'William Burk's Execution'   140
Central Library, City of Edinburgh

'The Lads of Virginia'   141
Leslie Shepard Collection

The Treadmill, Old Boro' Gaol in Highcross Street, Leicester.   142
Watercolour by H. Goddard, 1823
Leicestershire Museums, Art Galleries and Records Service

The Execution of Mary Evans at York, 10 August 1799. Watercolour by
Thomas Rowlandson   143
York City Art Gallery

'Poor Old Greenwich Fair'   177
Bodleian Library, Firth c 19, p. 60v, item 138

'The Fox Chase'   178
Chetham's Library, Manchester

'The Great North Run'   179
    Keith Gregson

'Rural Sports or a Cricket Match Extraordinary'. Etching by Thomas
Rowlandson, 1811 12   180
    Marylebone Cricket Club

The fight between John Heenan and Tom Sayers, 17 April 1860   180
    BBC Hulton Picture Library

'Bull Baiting, Cock Fighting, and Dog Fighting, at an End'   181
    William Salt Library, Stafford County Record Office

Shrove Tuesday Football at Ashbourne, 1987   182
    Photograph: Michael Steele. The Independent

Lewbelling: A Survival in Shakespeare's Country   205
    London Illustrated News, 14 August 1909. Photograph by permission of Birmingham City
    Library

'Sale of a Wife'   206
    The British Library

'The Fright'ned Yorkshire Damosel'   207
    By permission of the Master and Fellows, Magdalene College, Cambridge

'The Ranting Whore's Resolution'   208
    By permission of the Master and Fellows, Magdalene College, Cambridge

'There's Bound to be a Row/'Shy! Shy!! Dreadfully Shy!'   209
    Manchester Public Libraries

'The Map of Mock-beggar Hall'. From *Roxburghe Ballads*, vol. 2,
p. 132   210

'Stick Up for the Women'   211
    Bodleian Library, Firth c 16, p. 215, item 262

'The Woman to the Plow'   212
    Bodleian Library, Douce Ballads 2, fol. 2476

'Monde à l'Envers'   212
    Editions G.-P. Maisonneuve et Larose

'The Irish Emigrant/Noble Sportsmen'   247
    Norfolk County Library

'They are all sliding in Bobby's Sliding Scale'   248
    The British Library

'A New Song on the Great Demonstration'   249
    Bodleian Library, Firth c 16

'The Poor Law Catechism'   250
    Crawford Broadside 1737. By permission of Lord Crawford

Sale of Ballads   251
Guildhall Library, City of London

'You noble diggers all stand up now'   251
Clarke Papers, Worcester College, Oxford

'The Pressed Man's Lamentation'   293
Derby Local Studies Library

'Never Flog our Soldiers'/'You would not leave your Norah?'   294
Bodleian Library, Ballad 2626

'An Appeal by Unemployed ex-Service Men'   295
Bodleian Library, N. 1037 Street ballads 8

Sapper Dorothy Lawrence. From the book of the same name   296

Hannah Snell   296
Royal Warwickshire Regimental Museum

ACKNOWLEDGEMENTS

FOR advice and assistance I should like to thank Harry Boardman, Gordon Brown, MP, Alan Bruford, Jim Carroll, Penelope Corfield, Philip Donnellan, Edmund and Ruth Frow, Vic Gammon, Tony Green, H. W. Gwilliam, Robert Leach, Peter Linebaugh, Norman Longmate, Pat Mackenzie, Adrian May, Geordie McIntyre, Ailie Munro, Michael Grosvenor Myer, Pat Palmer, Alan Plater, Frank Purslow, Philip Reed, Peter Shellard, Malcolm Taylor, Edward Thompson, Katharine Thomson, R.S. Thomson, and Tony Wales, together with all those listed in the Notes. I should also like to thank all the singers, collectors, editors, and authors listed, and also the staffs of the various institutions. I am grateful to Dorothy Thompson for her comments on the typescript.

For permission to include the following songs (words and music unless otherwise stated) I should like to thank those listed:

'Aherlow' and 'Love Song': Henry Glassie.

'At Turners Hill': Steve Roud.

'Burke and Hare': Peter Cooke, Mrs C. R. Russell and the Director, School of Scottish Studies. Copyright © Mrs C. R. Russell.

'Derry Gaol': Jim Eldon and Topic Records Ltd.

'Dockers' Strike': Norman Buchan (words).

'The Great North Run': Keith Gregson.

'Henry Dubb': John Maxton.

'The Jeelie Piece Song': Adam McNaughton.

'It's a Mean Old Scene': Peter Coe.

'The Maiden's Lamentation': University of Massachusetts Press. Reprinted from *A Sailor's Songbag: An American Rebel in an English Prison 1777–1779*, by George G. Carey (Amherst: University of Massachusetts Press, 1976), copyright © by the University of Massachusetts Press, 1976.

'O Dear O': the Administrator, Cecil Sharp Estate.

'Our Bill': Bernard Wrigley.

'Shiny Dew': Anton R. Lagzdins.

'Snuff Box Song': Betty Messenger, from *Picking up the Linen Threads* (pp. 67–8) (words).

'Sizewell ABC': Tim Laycock.

'Starlaw Disaster': Hamish Henderson and the School of Scottish Studies.

'A Stitch in Time': © Looking Glass Music.

'The Sun is Burning': Ian Campbell and TRO Essex Music Ltd. © 1963 TRO

Essex Music Ltd, 19/20 Poland Street, London WIV 3DD. International Copyright secured. All Rights Reserved.
'When this Old Hat was New': English Folk Dance and Song Society.
'Who Owns the Game?': Mike Yates.

INTRODUCTION

'MORE solid things do not shew the Complexion of the Times, so well as Ballads and Libells,' said John Selden (1584–1654).[1] He preserved a great many ballads himself, and these were later acquired by Samuel Pepys, forming the basis of the latter's famous collection. To Selden and Pepys a ballad meant a sheet printed for sale by street singers. Hardy's Dorset countrymen and women used the same term, 'a ballet'. The earliest extant seems to be that of a song on the downfall of Thomas Cromwell, in 1540.[2] One of the last ballad-printers, Charles Sanderson of Edinburgh, was publishing until 1944; but in many areas the trade had been superseded some fifty years earlier by the spread of cheap newspapers for information and music-hall songs for entertainment.

Of course, there were other ways in which ballads, defined as verse narratives intended for singing, were circulated. Some writers preferred the song-book to the broadsheet, and their modern successors have used tape and record, television and radio. Manuscript was, and is, another form of transmission; so, too, is word of mouth. Not that such categories are mutually exclusive: a manuscript can easily be printed, or a broadside text achieve oral currency, and there is often a complex interrelationship between print and oral transmission.

Musical narratives of all kinds have reflected historical and social movements, and have sometimes influenced them in turn. In Verdi's *Nabucco* (1842) the captive Jewish people's song of their lost homeland was immediately adopted by Italians struggling against Austrian rule in their own country. More recently the songs of Mikis Theodorakis, even those that were apparently innocuous, were banned in Greece after the colonels' coup in 1967, because they inspired opposition to the illiberal regime. However, in order to reduce the amount of material under consideration from monstrous to merely enormous proportions, the present book will examine only historical ballads on broadly traditional lines from England and to some extent Ireland, Scotland, and Wales.

Oral Tradition

The oral tradition seems to arouse in historians suspicion at best, loathing at worst. As recently as 1986 a chorus of critics accused the television series *The Monocled Mutineer* and the book of the same title by William Allison and John Fairley (1979) on which it was based of inventing history. The series, by Alan Bleasdale, was avowedly 'a dramatic evocation', but the book, as Fairley pointed out in the *Listener*, relied on 'entirely accurate source material' obtained through correspondence and interviews from 'men who were there'. 'The mutiny at Etaples', he continued, 'does not fit into the academic picture of the First World War.'[3] Differences of both opinion and fact between historians and eye-witnesses are intriguing; I have seen them myself in the case of veterans of the Spanish Civil War and those writing about it without the benefit of firsthand experience.

Historians point to the fallibility of memory even in the short term, and all the more when people recall long-past events. Furthermore, oral tradition may well relate happenings which long pre-date the speaker's personal knowledge. On the other hand, evidence from oral sources is open to checking like any other, and there are remarkable examples of its reliability. An Oxfordshire gardener of the twentieth century astounded a gentleman once by saying, 'I've 'eard my granddad say as 'is granddad said that Mr Chaucer, the king's poet, used to walk this way.' He added that Chaucer was going to visit his son at Ewelme: 'Mr Chaucer's son's buried there, where old Henry the Eight 'ad 'is 'oneymoon—one of them.'[4] On checking, it was found that Thomas Chaucer, son of the poet, indeed owned the manor of Ewelme and was buried in the church there, and that Henry VIII spent his honeymoon with Jane Seymour in the manor house.

In the 1950s Roger J. McHugh set out to make a painstaking examination of the contribution of oral tradition, in the shape of both recollections and ballads, to knowledge of the Great Famine in Ireland. He was well aware that 'only accounts at second and third hand are by now available', and asked himself these questions:

Could anything of value result from a survey of oral tradition? Had oral tradition anything to add to the newspaper reports, the travellers' accounts, the official documents of the period? Or could it supply anything more than a vague and distorted outline to place beside the clear picture presented by the historian?

This was his conclusion:

It seems clear that oral tradition, by the way in which it relates experience to daily life, can play its part in adding something human and vivid to our understanding of the past and can also bring new information to light. It would be easy to over-estimate the value of oral tradition, which is not always subject to the exact checks required by the historians; but one cannot ignore the contribution, both factual and psychological, which it has to offer.[5]

Problems undoubtedly arise in considering ballads which have come to light after long periods in oral circulation. One has to ask how they might have evolved between their origin and their first fixation in print or manuscript (or, latterly, on tape), and whether their message is the same for later generations as it was for the original singers and listeners. Unfortunately, these questions are often unanswerable. What is clear, however, is that these ballads were cherished and handed on by ordinary people. A subterranean stream may run along silently for centuries, and then bubble to the surface, where it is noticed fleetingly by some literate observer. It may then disappear for ever, or survive to be recorded, preserved like an archaeological specimen, or given fresh life, albeit by new means of transmission.

A British admiral, John Benbow, and a housebreaker, Jack Hall, both died in the early years of the eighteenth century, the first from battle wounds, the second by hanging. Each was commemorated in song, the same metre and tune family serving for both:

> Come all ye seamen bold, lend an ear, lend an ear,
> Come all ye seamen bold, lend an ear:
> 'Tis of our admiral's fame,
> Brave Benbow called by name,
> How he fought all on the main you shall hear, you shall hear,
> How he fought all on the main you shall hear.

> O my name it is Jack Hall, chimney sweep, chimney sweep,
> O my name it is Jack Hall, chimney sweep.
> Oh my name it is Jack Hall
> and I've robbed both great and small,
> But my neck shall pay for all when I die, when I die,
> But my neck shall pay for all when I die.

A printed version of the Benbow song, including, very unusually, a tune, was produced immediately after his death. Chappell reprints it, without giving its exact source in the British Library.[6] There were several later editions, and a copy of one of these was given to a German visitor, Carl Philip Moritz, in 1782, by the son of his London landlord. It occasioned this comment:

Love of their homeland and warlike valour are the common themes of their ballads and folksongs, sung in the streets by women selling them for a few farthings. Only lately our Jacky brought one home telling the story of a courageous admiral who continued in command even though he had both legs shot away and had to be supported. Yet the scorn of the people for their king goes to astonishing lengths.[7]

Further printed sheets on Benbow appeared until at least the early nineteenth century, but it was a hundred years more before oral versions were noted. All bear comparison with the historical record, but their special quality is their expression of feeling.

Jack Hall's 'goodnight' ballad, ostensibly his testament before being launched into eternity, first appears as a two-verse fragment in Francis Place's little collection of 'Songs sung about the Streets' of London in the 1780s.[8] The earliest full text extant dates from between 1820 and 1844, when it was issued by J. Pitts with the title 'Jack the Chimney Sweep' (see illustration), a copy of which has survived in Macaulay's scrap-book of ballads.[9] The words are unlike those of most gallows songs, which tend to be maudlin and moralistic, and its bold, defiant, sardonic hero, who is in the highwayman tradition, is completely different from the squalid, compulsive thief of near-contemporary accounts. The attitude adopted in this case towards crime and the criminal is significant, as is the long history of the song.

Sometimes the gap between the emergence in print of a song and the events which it relates is relatively short. Frank Peel, researching in the late 1870s for his book on the Luddites of 1811–12, came across 'rude home-spun songs' some of which were 'remembered only in disjointed fragments by the few old people who have a personal knowledge of those unhappy days'.[10] Two of his informants remembered a song which celebrates the occasion of 9 April 1812 when a crowd of between three hundred and six hundred people destroyed gig mills, shear-frames, and cloth at a factory between Horbury and Ossett in Yorkshire. One of them, John Hirst of Liversedge, helped to guide the force of croppers to the attack on Cartwright's Mill in 1812. He stood trial at York, but was acquitted. Peel writes:

Knowing that he had escaped the hangman by the skin of his teeth and conscious that he was more blameworthy than some of the men who had been hanged, he would never discuss Luddism nor give any information respecting it; but years after when he came to be an old man and fell into dotage he seemed to live over again that period of his eventful life, and was constantly muttering mysterious pass words, administering secret oaths, or going through imaginary drills. During the last few years of his life he lived with a married daughter, and when engaged in rocking his grandchildren to sleep, he invariably crooned out some Luddite ditty, generally the following:

[HORSFALL'S MILL]

Come all you croppers, stout and bold,
Let your faith grow stronger still,
These cropping lads in the County of York,
Broke the shears at Horsfall's mill.
They broke the shears and the windows too,
Set fire to the tazzling mill;
They formed themselves all in a line,
Like soldiers at the drill.

The wind it blew, and the sparks they flew,
And awoke the the town full soon.
People got up in the middle of the night,
And they ran by the light of the moon;
When these lads around the mill did stand,
And they all did vow and swear,
Neither blanket nor can, nor any such thing,
Should be of service there.[11]

Peel, in effect practising oral history before the technique was invented, was fascinated by these 'home-spun songs', of which he printed another in full, 'The Cropper Lads'. 'Most of these ballads', he writes, 'are triumphant paeans on the glorious deeds of the "cropper lads", like that sung by Walker, at the Shears Inn, Hightown, but some are full of expressions of bitter hatred for Cartwright, who, under a thinly disguised cognomen, is likened to a bloodhound delighting in hunting to death those who opposed his arbitrary will.' He concludes:

Anyone who has studied the history of his country will be well aware what great effects have been produced by ballads in which uncultured minstrels of the time enshrined the records of notable deeds of some great leader, or of some movement, and there are evidences that the Luddite rebellion was not destitute of poets who celebrated in rough but vigorous rhyme the progress of the triumphant croppers in their crusades against the machines that robbed their children of their food; or appealed solemnly to the God of Heaven to smite with swift vengeance the oppressors who despised the cries of the poor and needy and ground them down to the dust.[12]

The Luddites appear in history largely in newspapers and in courts of law, where they were aliens and outsiders. Their own voices are heard in the occasional anonymous letter, otherwise only in a few songs and fragments of song. I believe this song source to be unique and precious, but some are prepared to ignore such evidence. One historian of the Luddites told me that he was 'not interested' in their ballads.

Like the Luddites, the labourers of 1830–2 have been seen largely through the eyes of their enemies, but at least one song gives the viewpoint of those taking part in the riots. 'The Owlesbury Lads' was taken down in 1896, from a man who had been involved in the events it evokes. He had earlier received 'many a pot of beer' for singing the song, which had been written by his brother before he was transported to Van Diemen's Land (Tasmania).

Other songs from oral tradition were noted during or shortly after the circumstances which gave rise to them. Sailors' songs written down in the backs of ships' log-books for the use of shipmates help us to understand their preoccupations. One fine collection, Gale Huntington's *Songs the Whalemen Sang* (New York, 1964), reprints items originally noted between 1767 and 1879. The vigorous flowering of sea-shanties and forebitters (respectively work and recreational songs) during the apogee and decline of commercial sail in the second half of the nineteenth century gives an unforgettable insight into the lives of the iron men who worked the wooden ships. *Shanties from the Seven Seas* (1961), by Stan Hugill, is the outstanding work on the subject.

On land the shanties were paralleled by the bothy songs of north-east Scotland, though these were songs not *of* work but *about* work and the men and women engaged in it. For the most part, they stem from between the 1880s and the 1910s, and they provide an invaluable picture of people now gone for ever (see Chapter 1). Their power has ensured that they are still sung, but now the singers are outsiders looking in, rather than insiders expressing their own joy, sorrow, and anger.

Street Ballads

The same is true of other genuinely popular forms, including printed street ballads. Among the purchasers were the sailors, soldiers, labourers, and women workers just mentioned. Macaulay's comment regarding the common people of the time of Charles II is applicable to many other periods: 'It was in rude rhyme that their love and hatred, their exultation and their distress found utterance. A great part of their history is to be learned only from their ballads.'[13]

In writing his monumental *History of England*, Macaulay drew widely on ballads from the Pepys and Roxburghe collections among others, as well as on printed satires and political songs and manuscript libels and lampoons. He quoted from them freely in order to show popular feeling on social, political, and economic issues, and used them not only to illustrate the people's attitudes, but also to formulate his own judgements. The edition of his *History* prepared by C. H. Firth reproduces in facsimile thirty-six of the ballads to which it refers, including 'The Clothiers' Delight' (published between 1674 and 1679), of which he remarked: 'One of the most remarkable of the popular lays chanted about the streets of Norwich and Leeds in the time of Charles the Second may still be read on the original broadside. It is the vehement and bitter cry of labour against capital. It describes the good old times when every artisan employed in the woollen manufacture lived as well as a farmer.'[14]

The word 'lays' recalls Macaulay's own *Lays of Ancient Rome* (1842), an attempt to supply the historical ballads (albeit in English) which the Romans had neglected to preserve for themselves. The book proved highly popular, and was still in print in 1946, when I purchased a new copy, priced fourpence, published in Stead's Bairn's Library. The ballads of Rome followed an earlier venture of Macaulay's, when he was still at Eton, to supply similar material for the English Civil War.[15] Both these offerings were literary, rather than vernacular, in style, but as early as 1826 Macaulay appears to have written an election squib, which was issued as a street ballad in Leicester when he was acting as clerk to the radical candidate, a Derbyshire cotton-manufacturer called William Evans. 'A New Song', to the tune of 'Derry Down', begins:

> So you doubt whom to choose of our Candidates three;
> Come hither, good Weavers, and listen to me;
> And tho' not an Æsop, yet if I am able,
> I will tell you my mind in the guise of a fable.
> *Derry Down, &c.*[16]

A copy of the sheet, annotated by Macaulay and initialled 'TBM', is one of some eighty ballads which he pasted into the scrap-book now preserved at his old college, Trinity, Cambridge. He was a keen collector, and at one stage in his life, between the 1820s and the 1840s, 'bought every halfpenny song on which he could lay his hands, if only it was a decent, and a genuine, undoubted poem of the people'. So wrote his nephew, G. O. Trevelyan, adding: 'It is hardly too much to say that Macaulay knew the locality, and, at this period of his life, the stock in trade, of every bookstall in London.' On one occasion he was 'followed from the bookstall, where he had bought a parcel of ballads, by a crowd of children whom he overheard discussing among themselves whether or not the gentleman was going to sing'.[17] Other copies were sent by friends. Of a batch from T. F. Ellis, Macaulay wrote in 1841: 'I like that on Ips, Gips and Johnson best. "Napoleon" is excellent, but hardly equal to the "Donkey wot wouldn't go".'[18]

His fascination with ballads was partly due to the feel of history in them.

In 1850, at the time of 'No Popery' agitation occasioned by the re-establishment of a Catholic hierarchy in England, he wrote to his sister Fanny: 'Yesterday the ballad-singers were entertaining a great crowd under my windows with bawling: "Now all the old women are crying for fear, The Pope is a-coming: oh dear!"'[19] Unfortunately, he does not seem to have obtained a copy of this sheet.

W. W. Wilkins, writing in 1860, described Macaulay as 'the only native historian' to have considered 'ephemeral productions' (by which he meant ballads and the like) 'worthy of his particular study and use'.[20] Since then there have been others, though the list is not long. C. H. Firth, strongly influenced by Macaulay, wrote: 'Ballads are useful as a supplement to graver historical authorities, and throw a light upon the history of the past which we could not derive from other sources.'[21] This comes from one of a series of articles on what he calls 'the ballad history' of different periods. Firth also edited the monumental and invaluable volume *Naval Songs and Ballads* (1908), and amassed his own formidable collection of original sheets, now shared between the Bodleian and Sheffield University libraries.[22]

The Hammonds made effective use of literary evidence, especially novels and poetry; but, perhaps surprisingly, they seemed ignorant of popular balladry. The exception which proves the rule is the fine manuscript piece 'General Ludd', culled from the Home Office papers, which they printed in *The Skilled Labourer* (1919). Their contemporary Dorothy George cites several ballads in *London Life in the Eighteenth Century* (1925); and in *England in Transition* (1931), she comments on 'The Clothiers' Delight', quotes from 'The Roast Beef of Old England', and refers to 'Hang care, the parish is bound to save us'.[23]

It was left to E. P. Thompson to make a post-war breakthrough in *The Making of the English Working Class* (1963), in which ballads and their singers are mentioned frequently.[24] Texts are not only cited; they are woven into the narrative. They are accepted as historical material, a matter of fact, which is refreshing by comparison with the attitude of many others, before and since. The problem is not purely British, however. Robert Brécy complains in his *Florilège de la Chanson Révolutionnaire de 1789 au Front Populaire* (Paris, 1978): 'How many serious historical works do not even cite the title of songs connected with the facts analysed: scorn for the "minor genre"? Refusal to consider the song as a historical document? Or simply ignorance of their existence?'[25] Roberto Leydi, in *Canti Sociali Italiani* (Milan, 1963), pointing out that songs are the voice of the participants in historical events, regrets that it is 'a voice which too often historical methodology, even on the progressive side, forgets to hear

JACK THE CHIMNEY SWEEP.

MY name it is Jack All chimney sweep chim-
　　ney sweep,
O my name it is Jack All chimney sweep ;
My name it is Jack All, and rob both great and
　　small,　　　　　　　　　[I die,
And my life must pay for all when I die, when
And my life must pay for all when I die.

I furnish'd all my rooms every one, every one,
I furnish'd all my rooms every one ;
I furnish'd all my rooms with black brushes and
　　black brooms,
Besides the chimney pot which I stole which I
　　stole.

I sold candles short of weight, that's no joke,
　　that's no joke,
I sold candles short of weight that's no joke ;
I sold candles short of weight and they nap'd
　　me by the sly,
All rogues must have their right so must I , so
　　must I,
All rogues must have their right so must I.

O they told me in the jail where I lay where I
　　lay,
O they told me in the jail where I lay,
They told me in the jail that I should drink no
　　more brown ale,
But I swore I'd never fail 'till I die 'till I die.

O they told me in the hole where I lay where I
　　lay,
They told me in the hole where I lay,
They told me in the hole, that the candles that
　　I stole,
Was to light me to the hole where I lay where
　　I lay,
Was to light me to the hole where I lay.

A going up Holborn hill in a cart, in a cart,
Going up Holborn hill in a cart ;
Going up Holborn hill, at St. Giles' had my fill,
And at Tyburn made my will that went hard,
　　that went hard,
And at Tyburn made my will that went hard.

Now I must leave the cart toll the bell, toll the
　　bell,
Now I must leave the cart toll the bell ;
Now I must leave the cart sorrowful broken
　　heart,
And the best of friends must part so farewell,
　　so farewell,
And the best of friends must part so farewell.

*Pitts, Printer, wholesale Toy and Marble warehouse,
6, Gt. St. Andrew Street, Seven Dials.*

'Jack the Chimney Sweep'. Street
ballad from Macaulay's scrap-
book.

Lord Macaulay is taken for a ballad vendor.

A ballad singer, in Thomas Rowlandson's *Street Scene*.

Song-writer Tommy Armstrong: one of only two known photographs.

One of the few ballads by Joseph Mather which found its way into print for sale in the streets.

and to fix on as an irreplaceable parallel to reliance on official
documentation'.[26]

It would be tiresome to list, let alone attempt to examine, the many
histories which neglect ballad evidence; but one might single out N. A. M.
Rodger's *The Wooden World: An Anatomy of the Georgian Navy* (1986). The
book is admirably written, and based on a masterly study of primary
sources, particularly the Admiralty Papers. It is in effect a sustained
critique of 'the common opinion, derived from Masefield's *Sea Life in
Nelson's Time*, that naval discipline was harsh and oppressive, officers
frequently cruel and tyrannical, ratings drawn from the dregs of society,
ill-treated and starved'. Rodger's purpose in writing the book was 'to test
the traditional view of the internal life of the Navy by studying the evidence
in detail for a limited period'. He concentrates on the period of the Seven
Years War, though he has drawn evidence from, and would apply his
conclusions to 'the whole period from 1740 to 1775'.[27] In the course of a
book of well over four hundred pages, he quotes three lines of one ballad
from a secondary source and two verses of another from a primary
source.[28] Yet recruiting and the press-gang, shipboard life and conditions,
are perennial topics in the balladry of the time, and this bears crucially on
'the traditional view of the internal life of the Navy'. If Professor Rodger
had viewed this evidence and found it wanting, one would feel differently;
but to all intents and purposes he ignores it.

Dating

In considering street literature, there are of course problems to be faced.
Its sheer size is daunting—one of the many collections extant in Britain,
that of Sir Frederic Madden at Cambridge, runs to 17,500 items. Ballads
were printed both on broadsides, sheets of various sizes, printed on one
side only, and in garlands, booklets usually about eight pages long. Dating
is sometimes difficult, since imprints are often lacking, even after 1797,
when, as a consequence of naval mutinies, they were first required by law.
The period when a particular printer was at work can sometimes be
determined precisely from street and trade directories, with changes of
address sometimes allowing fine tuning. The dating of others, especially in
the seventeenth and early eighteenth centuries, has entailed careful
research into wills and the like, by such commentators as Cyprian Blagden
and R. S. Thomson.[29] Internal evidence is available in some cases, from
subject-matter, datable allusions and references, and even the mention of
dates themselves. Some printers gave their sheets cumulative stock
numbers, which help with dating. For example, John Harkness of Preston
issued 'A New Song on the Birth of the Prince of Wales' as his number 71.

It was not dated, but must have appeared on or soon after 9 November 1841. Harkness's number 85 was 'A New Song on the Preston Guild 1842'. It follows that numbers 72 to 84 were issued in between, though this may not necessarily have been their first publication.[30] Between 1557 and 1709 some three thousand ballads were entered in the registers of the Stationers' Company of London.[31]

The Ballad Trade

The printing of ballad sheets was usually a commercial enterprise, and those involved set out to appeal to popular taste in order to sell as many copies as possible. As an anonymous writer pointed out in the *National Review* for 1861:

They are almost always written by persons of the class to which they are addressed; and the very sameness of them, the family likeness which runs through each separate branch of them, shows that they are adapted to and meet the wants and views of that class. . . . Ballads still form an important, perhaps the chief part of the reading of a large class of our population. One London firm alone, the successors of Catnach the Great, have on stock half a million of ballads, more than 900 reams of them; and even in these degenerate days, when a ballad makes a real hit, from 20,000 to 30,000 copies of it will go off in a very short time.[32]

With sales of this order, some printers made fat profits, though others made only a marginal living. To set up in a small way required only modest capital. In 1835, for example, a new, hand-operated Albion press was delivered by sea from London to Hull for John Forth of Bridlington at an inclusive cost of £14. 10s., subject to a discount of 10 per cent for prompt payment.[33] James Catnach (1792–1841), who was printing in London from 1813 to 1838, made £10,000 from street literature. The income was mainly in 'coppers' (pennies and halfpennies) which, in order to kill germs, were boiled 'in a strong decoction of potash and vinegar before exchanging them, which used to make them look as bright as when they were first coined'.[34] In Birmingham, Joseph Russell, who was in business from 1815 to 1839, at almost exactly the same time as Catnach, made £12,000. G. J. Holyoake commented that the 'little fortune' came from 'printing and selling Catnach songs', the term being used generically, and added: 'Had Macaulay visited Birmingham he would have gone over Mr Russell's copious ballad store with delight. He had the finest collection in all the Midlands.'[35]

Russell combined business acumen with political radicalism, and his 'little fortune' was bequeathed to set up a secular school. In 1819 he was imprisoned for six months for printing, publishing, and selling an edition of William Hone's *Political Litany*, a copy of which an informer had purchased from his shop. Various other ballad-printers were politically active. Two other Birmingham ballad-printers, James Guest and Thomas Watts, were gaoled in 1834 for selling unstamped periodicals.[36] William Stephenson, who printed at Bridge Street, Gateshead, between 1821 and 1838, was described as 'An ardent reformer, nay a staunch republican in politics, an active townsman who delighted to probe and expose all town abuses'.[37] In Manchester both James Wheeler (printing 1838–45) and his son-in-law John Livsey (printing 1833–50) were staunch Chartists.[38] Thomas Willey of Cheltenham was involved in the Chartist Land Plan of 1847,[39] and in the following year published 'A Song for the Times; illustrative of Passing Events. Liberty or Bondage! or, A Voice from the Oppressed'.[40] This is a highly literary and declamatory poem of twenty-six stanzas, which survives in the Home Office papers, thanks to its having been sent to an MP by an alarmed Tewkesbury resident, with the comment: 'They [sic] were found in the cottage of a labourer and I understand they have been extensively circulated, which fact taking in conjunction with frequent meetings of Chartists from all quarters in this neighbourhood is making politicians of the agricultural labourers.'[41] Willey's usual publications were street ballads, though he was also a jobbing printer. About 150 of his sheets have survived, bearing some 275 different titles.[42] If, as seems likely, he was in business from the early 1830s to the early 1850s, this is an output of fewer than 10 sheets a year, though he may well have issued others which have not survived. The bulk of the titles (and this underlines the commercial nature of the enterprise), of which there are more than 180, involve sentimental, popular, or comic items, including several Jim Crow songs, 'Flora, the Lily of the West' and Sheridan's 'Here's to the maiden'. Over 40 titles, including 'The Golden Glove', 'Bold Robin Hood', 'Joan's Ale was New', 'The Golden Vanity', and 'The Female Drummer', are from oral tradition. Fairs, races, and hunting feature in a handful of pieces, and there are nine or ten patriotic songs, like 'Albion my Country' and 'The British True Blue'. Half a dozen items are concerned with crime, and of these, two deal with executions: 'An Affecting Copy of Verses Written on the Body of Harriet Tarver, Who was Executed April 9th, 1836, at Gloucester, for Poisoning her Husband in the town of [Chipping] Camden' and 'An affecting Copy of Verses, written on James Greenacre, Who was Executed May 2nd, 1837, for the Horrid Murder of Hannah Brown'. In fact, Willey probably published far more such sheets. W. E. Adams, who was born in Cheltenham in 1832, and at the age of 14 apprenticed as a printer on the *Cheltenham Journal*, wrote that Thomas Willey, whom he described as 'our local Catnach', was always ready with a 'last dying speech' for every criminal who was executed at Gloucester. It was generally the same speech, altered to suit the name and circumstances of the new culprit; and it was invariably adorned with a ghastly woodcut, showing the figure of a man or a woman, as the case might be, dangling from a gallows. The passage leading to Willey's printing office was crowded on the morning of an execution with an astonishing collection of ragamuffins and tatterdemalions, greasy, grimy, and verminous. Soon they were bawling their doleful wares all over town.[43]

Yet one of Willey's ballads on criminals has a markedly different orientation. It is a wry piece about prison conditions entitled 'The County Livery':

> There is a place in Horsley, I know it very well
> There's such a place upon the earth, some call it little hell;
> And to the place where I was sent for three long months 'tis true
> To wear the County livery, the yellow and the blue.

The prisoners' work on the treadmill features strongly:

> 'Twas early the next morning, just by the break of day,
> The turnkey he came up to me, and this to me did say—
> Arise my hearty fellow, to the mill you now must go,
> And you shall wear the county livery, the yellow and the blue.

Twenty of Willey's titles, just under 10 per cent, involve social comment of this kind or political material of some sort. Sir Andrew Agnew's abortive Sunday observance measure of 1833 is ridiculed in 'The Agony Bill', while the Poor Law Amendment Act of the following year is bitterly attacked in 'The New Gruel Shops' and 'The Fatal English Poor Law Bill'. The complaint is widened in 'Past, Present, and Future. Or, the Poor Man's Consolation':

> In former days the labourers were all call'd happy men,
> And well they might, a labourer could keep a grunter then.
> But in these times a grunter to a poor man is but lent,
> 'Tis hard that he must kill and sell the pig to pay his rent.
> *So now my bold companions, the world seems upside down,*
> *They scorn the poor man as a thief, in country and town.*
>
> In older times the poor could on a common turn a cow,
> The commons are all taken in the rich have claimed them now.
> If a poor man turns a goose thereon, the rogues will it surround,
> The rich will have the kindness just to pop it in the pound.
>
> Now if a man is out of work, his parish pay is small,
> Enough to starve himself his wife and little children all.

> They'll make him work for a crown a week to keep his family.
> And the devil he will shake the rich for all their cruelty.
>
> They build up large workhouses now, to part the man and wife,
> That they may no more children get, 'tis true upon my life,
> They take their children from their arms and send them different ways,
> And fifteen pence allow to keep a man for seven days.

The golden age also seems to be in the past in 'My Grandfather's Days', 'Conversation of the Rose, Shamrock and Thistle', and 'Forced to be Contented', the last of which deals with the disappointment felt after the hopes raised by the Reform Act of 1832:

> They said reform would do us good
> It has not yet I wish it would,
> For thousands they're wanting food
> Must starve and wait contented.
> *Oh! dear Oh! dear what times are these,*
> *The rich will do just as they please,*
> *The poor are starving by degrees*
> *And forced to be contented.*

However, a technical innovation is given an enthusiastic reception in 'The Great Western Rail Road. Or the Pleasures of travelling by Steam', which was probably published in 1839. If many sheets complain at the lot of the labourer and even the farmer, at least two express pride in the miners of the Forest of Dean: 'The Gloucestershire Colliers' and 'The Jovial Foresters'.

It was not only printers with radical sympathies who produced ballads with pointed political and social comment. News and comment, together with entertainment, were among the main functions of ballads from the earliest days of the trade until the time (between the late nineteenth and the mid-twentieth century, depending on the area) when they were overtaken by cheap, popular newspapers. The medium was freely employed not only by commercial printers, but also by a wide range of political and social pressure groups. Ballads on behalf of candidates in municipal and parliamentary elections were legion. Bodies anxious to influence the views or reform the manners of the working classes were quick to see the value of the medium. In the 1790s, for example, the Association for Preserving Liberty and Property Against Republicans and Levellers was anxious to counter what it regarded as seditious propaganda. One 'friend to Church & State' wrote to John Reeves, the secretary, to send some pieces of his own composition:

It occured [sic] to me, that any thing written in voice [?verse] & especially to an

Old English tune . . . made a more fixed Impression on the Minds of the Younger
and Lower Class of People, than any written in Prose, which was often forgotten as
soon as Read. . . . By printing copies of the inclosed, as Common Ballads, and
putting them in the hands of individuals; or by twenties into the hands of Ballad
Singers who might sing them for the sake of selling them. I own I shall not be
displeased to hear Re-echoed by Every Little Boy in the Streets during the
Christ.^mas Holidays.—

> Long May Old England, Possess Good Cheer and Jollity
> Liberty, and Property, and No Equality.[44]

At about the same time, a similar thought occurred to two other corre-
spondents. 'Britannicus' sent his own pieces in the hope that the association would 'employ some fellow creatures to recommend at Viva Voce in
the Streets', and commented: 'It was the Ancient as well as modern
Custom to excite Men to Good or Bad actions by songs & they never failed
producing their effect on the Multitude as Verses have many advantages
over Prose.'[45] 'Fidelia' also expressed her views:

I have had many Opportunities of observing the influence of the new seditious
doctrines upon the lower Class of People, that class that the wicked and designing
principally intend to use as their Engine, they are incapable of reading or
understanding any good or serious address to set them right, but through the
medium of *vulgar ballads* surely much instruction might be convey'd and much
patriotic spirit awakened; witness *Ça Ira*. Every serving Man and Maid, every
Country Girl, and her Sweetheart, in Towns and Villages will buy a halfpenny
ballad to a popular tune, upon this idea I have written one calculated entirely for
the medium of their understandings.[46]

Resistance to such material is evident in a report of a scene at Covent
Garden theatre in 1792, when a woman attempting to sing a loyal ballad to
the tune 'Hearts of Oak' was shouted down.[47] At the same time, T.
Harpley of the Phoenix Printing Office in Liverpool used the content of
songs and handbills dropped in the streets as a barometer of disaffection.[48]
Such dropping, rather than selling, is unusual. Perhaps it was in response
to the actions of John Reeves and other vigilantes regarding both 'gross
publications' and those that were politically suspect. According to Francis
Place, 'The association printed a large number of what they called loyal
songs, and gave them to ballad singers; if anyone was found singing any but
loyal songs, he or she was carried before a magistrate.'[49]

The doctrines of the French Revolution were countered by the Cheap
Repository Tracts, of which up to two million copies per year were sold at a
penny each for a period in the 1790s. They were written by Hannah More
(1745–1833) and her associates, who borrowed the street ballad form they
despised to advise the poor to work hard and trust in God and the gentry.

The customary format and woodcuts of the broadside were used, and street-ballad printers and their distribution networks were utilized. Other printers, seeing a market, cashed in by issuing their own edifying sheets. There was a pious strain in street balladry, from early songs like 'A godlie newe songe declaringe the lovinge kindnes of the Lorde towarde them that feare him' of 1577[50] to 'The Spiritual Railway' of the nineteenth century:[51]

> God's word the fire, his truth the steam,
> Which drives the engine and the train;
> Now all who would to glory ride,
> Must come to Christ, and there abide.

Campaigners against the evils of drinking also used ballads to put over their message. The teetotal movement, launched in Preston in 1832, was assisted by the sheets of the local printer, John Harkness, though this piety did not prevent his supporting militant textile-workers during the great strike of 1853–4. Groups of unemployed or striking workers frequently had sheets printed, and sold them to raise money. The practice has links both with traditional songs of seasonal *quête* and with the rhymed sheets with a request for a gratuity which the bellman distributed at Christmas to the people whose houses he watched over.[52] Bellmen survived only until the early nineteenth century, but rag-and-bone men continued to leave appeals for goods in verse form until at least the mid-twentieth. As recently as 1974, one S. Lee, appealing to Birmingham householders for waste woollen material, left on their doorsteps a message beginning:

> The above, with most respectful feeling,
> Begs to inform you what he deals in,
> He's not come your purse to try,
> Yourself to sell and he to buy.[53]

This could be paralleled almost exactly by nineteenth-century examples.

By selling ballads, strikers not only raised money, but publicized their case, aroused sympathy, and kept up morale. Hewitson, historian of Preston, wrote: 'Ballad-like verses, depicting the grievances of the operatives, and soliciting charity on their behalf, were dolefully sung, from town to town, by squalid-looking bands of men, women, and children.'[54] Charles Dickens was more sympathetic: 'We . . . reach a locked-up and smokeless factory, at the gates of which a knot of young girls are singing and offering for sale some of the Ten Per Cent. Songs, taking their name from the origin of the strike. . . . The songs are not remarkable for much elegance and polish, but they possess some earnestness and fire, and are undoubtedly composed by the operatives themselves.'[55] The 'earnestness and fire' must have concerned the mill-owners, for action was taken to suppress the singing of such ballads in the streets of Preston, as a speaker complained to a meeting of 'operatives' in 1853:

Not content with prohibiting the convention of their open air meetings, in the face of our boasted freedom of utterance, the magistrates had given orders to the policemen to prevent the turn-outs from singing a harmless ballad in the streets. While be it remembered, other parties were allowed to sing songs relating to all manner of things, some of the most immoral and licentious character without interference or hindrance.[56]

Proceedings against ballad-sellers under local by-laws or for breach of the peace seem to have been favoured methods of suppressing their wares. Even under the Commonwealth, when penalties against authors, printers, and sellers of unauthorized ballads were instituted, the laws weighed most heavily on the humblest of the three, the sellers. The ballad-singer was assumed to be, if not merely a nuisance, a rogue, like Shakespeare's Autolycus, or a thief, like Jonson's Nightingale. Hogarth and Rowlandson frequently show wretched men and women peddling ballads in miry streets or in the midst of close-packed crowds at executions. John Masefield wrote of Ledbury, where he was born in 1878:

> I never crossed the town without the sight
> Of withered children suffering from blight,
> Of women's heads, like skull-bones, under shawls,
> Of drunkards staggering with caterwauls,
> Of starving groups in rags, with boots unsoled,
> Blear-eyed, and singing ballads in the cold.[57]

It is paradoxical that street-ballad singers were also held in affection, and their passing was regretted. For Wordsworth in 1805, 'single and alone, / An English Ballad-singer' was an essential part of the London street scene, as were 'files of ballads [which] dangle from dead walls'.[58] In 1840, Douglas Jerrold looked back to the same time:

During the war it was his [the ballad-singer's] peculiar province to vend half-penny historical abridgements to his country's glory; recommending the short poetic chronicle by some familiar household air, that fixed it in the memory of the purchaser. . . . No battle was fought, no vessel taken or sunken, that the triumph was not published, proclaimed in the national gazette of our Ballad-singer. . . . It was he who bellowed music into news, which, made to jingle, was thus, even to the weakest understanding, rendered portable. It was his narrow strips of history that adorned the garrets of the poor; it was he who made them yearn towards their country, albeit to them so rough and niggard a mother.[59]

Jerrold laments, prematurely perhaps, the disappearance of such singers, while remarking: 'Still, however, we have the Political Ballad-singer; still the street minstrel celebrates the downfall of a ministry; still he has at times something to sing about the royal household. Now and then, too, he fearlessly attacks a growing vice.' Twenty years later the political ballad still flourished: 'We must own that the ballad-singer handles the names and doings of those who sit in high places with a familiarity scarcely equalled by old Punch himself.' The same anonymous writer adds, 'on the whole, the ballad-singer is a Liberal, though of an old-fashioned kind, and loses no opportunity of telling the Tories that he, for his part, does not look upon them as the men whom he desires for his rulers'.[60]

Political songs were only part of the ballad-singer's repertoire, which also included battles, executions, disasters, domestic life, local events, sex and scandal, adventure and fantasy. Thomas Middleton summarized it in 1620 as 'fashions, fictions, felonies, follies',[61] but that is to ignore the core of social comment which was often present.

The many references in the plays of Elizabethan dramatists to ballads demonstrates that these were widely known in most sections of society. Many themes were common to plays and ballads, as is shown by the 'Ballads that Illustrate Shakespeare' in Percy's *Reliques of Ancient English Poetry*. The same collection includes a piece by William Elderton, the leading ballad-writer of Shakespeare's time, who died in 1592 after a career which included both the law and the stage. Some twenty of his pieces have survived, including 'The panges of love and lovers fittes' (1559),[62] which was extraordinarily popular in its day, and 'A new ballad ... Treason ... against the young King of Scots' (1581), which was loosely based on an incident of 1578.[63] Edward White was fined twelve pence for printing another Elderton item, 'A newe Ballade, declaryng the daungerous shootyng of the Gunne at the Courte' (1579),[64] and Elderton himself was imprisoned for a time.[65]

He was succeeded as the best-known ballad-journalist of the day by Thomas Deloney (?1543–1600), eight of whose ballads are still extant.[66] Deloney also ran foul of the law, in 1596, with 'a certain Ballad, containing a Complaint of great Want and Scarcity of Corn within the Realm', in which the queen was shown 'speaking with her People / Dialogue wise in very fond and undecent sort'. Deloney, who came from a Norwich family of Huguenot silk-weavers, also wrote fiercely patriotic pieces on the Spanish Armada of 1588 and the victorious expedition to Cadiz in 1596. 'The Spanish Ladies Love to an English Gentleman', which was often reprinted, was also inspired by the Cadiz adventure, in which Deloney may have been personally involved. He was also moved by the earlier history and legends of Britain to write ballads on such events as the Peasants' Revolt of 1381 and such figures as Lady Godiva and Sir Guy of Warwick. Deloney also wrote several extremely successful novels. He nevertheless died 'poorly'.

Martin Parker (died ?1656) was an alehouse-keeper who turned ballad-writer in the 1620s.[67] He was attacked, along with a score of others of his trade, in *The Downfall of Temporising Poets, unlicenst Printers, upstart Booksellers, trotting Mercuries, and bawling Hawkers* (1641): 'Rather than lose half-a-crown, you will write against your own fathers. You will make men's wills before they be sicke, hang them before they are in prison, and cut off heads before you know why or wherefore.' In the same year a writer of Puritan sympathies wrote of 'one Parker, the Prelates' Poet, who made many base ballads against the Scots'.[68] Parker's most famous piece, written in 1643, was 'When the King enjoys his own again', which predicted the ultimate victory of Charles I and the cavalier cause. The refrain was originally 'When the King comes home in peace again', and one verse refers to three astrologers of the time:

> What Booker can prognosticate
> Concerning kings' or kingdoms' fate?
> I think myself to be as wise
> As he that gazeth on the skies,
> My skill goes beyond the depths of a Pond,
> Or Rivers in the greatest rain,
> Whereby I can tell
> All things will be well,
> When the king enjoys his own again.

The ballad's tune was used for a great variety of songs, a sure sign of its immense popularity, and its words inspired all kinds of royalists: Stuarts, Hanoverians, and Jacobites. As late as 1820 a ballad in defence of Queen Caroline was entitled 'The Queen shall enjoy her own again'. Even more long-lived was Parker's 'Sailors for my Money' (1635), which lasted in various metamorphoses for a good three centuries.

Writers such as these were despised, none the less. Parker himself was said to 'bathe his beak' in nut-brown ale to find inspiration. Deloney was dismissed by Thomas Nash as 'the Balletting Silke Weaver of Norwich'. A character in Dryden's play *Sir Martin Mar-all* (1668), when offered five shillings, replies: 'Hang your white pelf: sure, Sir, by your largess, you mistake me for Martin Parker, the Ballad-maker'. Yet Dryden had his own collection of street ballads, and thought Parker the best ballad-maker of his day. All the same, such writers, and many others of lesser fame, had a secure and lasting place in the affections of the people.

More literary figures were sometimes represented (if seldom credited) on ballad sheets. An anthology of popular verse could be built up from such sheets and would include pieces by Jonson, Fielding, Garrick, Gay, Goldsmith, Byron, Dickens, and a host of lesser writers like Charles Mackay, Charles Wolfe, and Eliza Cooke. Songs from the opera-house, pleasure garden, parlour (even boudoir), and music-hall include the work of Charles Dibdin, William Shields, Henry Russell, Henry Clay Work, and many more.

Ordinary people also contributed. Dickens noted that the Preston Ten Per Cent songs were written 'by the operatives themselves', and the anonymous author of an article on street ballads in the *National Review* of 1861 commented that street ballads were 'almost all written by persons of the class to which they are addressed'. Charlotte Burne remarked that in Shropshire as late as the 1880s it was still common practice 'to "make a ballet on" any passing event of interest', and 'what a common and easy feat ballad-making was considered'.[69] She refers, I think, to oral and manuscript, rather than printed, ballads. At the end of the nineteenth century, G. M. Trevelyan wrote: 'As late as fifty years ago humble folk occasionally wrote ballads on events of the day according to the old tradition. I have seen a genuine ballad about a fire, the last verse of which begins "O London County Council".'[70] This may have been the fire of 1890 at Forest Gate Industrial School, Poplar. A fragment of one ballad on the subject was remembered until 1971 by a local man, Samuel Webber:

> Oh hark what dreadful tidings is this we have to hear
> Before the bells cease ringing to end a dreary year?
> A fatal fire was raging which spread dismay around;
> Twenty-four poor children lost their lives in a fire at Forest Gate School.[71]

What Michael MacDonagh wrote of music-hall songs must also have been true of most of the street songs which they superseded:

the vast bulk of these ballads of the people are produced by 'free-lances'—that is to say, men who are not professional song-writers, but labourers, artisans, tradesmen, literary amateurs, journalists, actors, music-hall artistes—some of whom write these songs with a view to supplement their incomes, while others spin them out more as a hobby than for a profit.[72]

Nevertheless, there were professional writers in both fields. The standard rate ranged from a shilling a ballad to twopence a line, and there is a story that James Catnach kept a fiddler to play over a proposed ballad to various well-known tunes to determine whether it would be acceptable.

Of course, the form had its own canons and traditions, which had both strengths and weaknesses. Harland and Wilkinson wrote in 1870:

The ballad-singers of the present day are not much in advance of their prede-cessors, who followed the same trade three centuries ago. They are never at a loss for a melody suited to some doleful tale; nor do a few deficient or redundant syllables impede the course of the minstrel's drone. The frame-work of the old ballad is preserved almost entire; but the skeleton is re-clothed with the muscle and sinew of some similar event of modern date. . . . It is . . . much easier for those whose 'business is sheets' to imitate a given model, than to invent an entirely new framework for a popular Song or Ballad.[73]

Few of the ballad-writers, singers, and sellers are identifiable. John Morgan, who was born in about 1800, wrote (and, unusually, signed) ballads which were issued by James Catnach and other Seven Dials printers and also on his own account. One sheet 'Printed for the Author, John Morgan, Anne Street, Westminster' must have appeared in 1846 (see below, page 290).[74] Another, 'Little Lord John out of Service', concerns events of 1855. 'All readers', writes the *National Review* con-tributor, 'will remember Earl Russell's mission to Vienna, and his seces-sion from the Aberdeen Cabinet. About the same time happened the disgraceful demonstrations as to the Sunday question, when Lord Ebury was threatened, and the mob of boys broke some windows in Belgravia. Upon which events the ballad-writer, meditating, produces the following:

> You lads of this nation, in every station,
> I pray give attention, and listen to me,
> I'm little Jack Russell, a man of great bustle,
> Who served Queen Victoria by land and by sea:
> They call me a Proosian, an Austrian, a Roosian,
> And off to Vienna they sent me afar;
> They'd not me believe then, they vowed I'd deceived them,
> And called me Friend of the great Russian Czar.
> *I'm little Jack Russell, a man of great bustle,*
> *I'm full of vexation, grief, sorrow, and care,*
> *I have got in disgrace, and am now out of place;*
> *But I never broke windows around Bel-ge-rave Square.'*[75]

Upon enquiring about the authorship of street ballads, the *Review* contributor was told, 'Oh, any body writes them'. He was delighted, therefore, to find one signed by Morgan, and to be told that he was still alive and living in Westminster: 'Mr Morgan followed no particular visible calling as far as our informant knew, except writing ballads, by which he could not earn much of a livelihood, as the price of an original ballad, in these buying-cheap days, has been screwed down to somewhere about a shilling sterling.'[76]

Another poor street author was Reuben Holder, who sold verses of his own composition in Bradford in the late 1830s and early 1840s.[77] He was born at Hunslet in 1797, and was brought up as a collier, starting work driving a gin-horse at the pit-mouth at the age of 5, and going underground three years later. Subsequently he became a brick-maker, then made a living from the sale of fish and verses. The number of his hawker's licence, 5405A, was printed on some of the sheets. His first piece accepted for publication was 'On the Death of a Girl who was Drowned in the Bradford Beck'; but he is best known for his coverage of social and political issues, such as the introduction of the new Poor Law to Bradford and the riot it occasioned (1837), and the Chartist movement and the flight of Peter Bussey to America (1839). Holder was sympathetic to ordinary people, if not to Chartism or Socialism, and he fervently campaigned as a reformed drinker on behalf of teetotalism. He was renowned for parading with a long rod fastened to a barrel with both the ends knocked out, while delivering in a rasping voice his 'Lines on the Teetotal Barrel' (1840), beginning:

> You drunken, fond fuddlers, give ear to my story;
> Of drinking it's time you began to be weary;
> The way to be sober, I'd have you to know it,
> Don't drink from a barrel till you can see through it.

Holder stood in the market on Saturdays, and on other days meandered through the old thoroughfares, Kirkgate, Ivegate, and Westgate. He often varied his itinerary by taking his stand at the gates of such mills as Wood & Walker's, Rand's, or Marshall's, where he recited his verses on 'The Depressed State of the Times', 'A Cry for Bread', 'The Evils of the Nation', or, perhaps, his 'Verses on the New Starvation Poor Law'. These somewhat depressing themes he varied by others of a livelier sort, such as his 'Song on the Otley Statutes', 'On the Christening of the Prince of Wales' (in fact a complaint at the cost to the nation of the royal children), or 'The Florentine Venus'.

George Davis (1768–1819) of Birmingham also campaigned against the evils of drink, though before the days of teetotalism. He was born of 'miserably poor' parents, but was able, thanks to a benefactor, to attend the local grammar school for four years, before serving his time as a printer on the *Birmingham and Staffordshire Chronicle*. Some of his poems were published in the newspaper, and in 1790 *Saint Monday; or Scenes from Low-Life*, a mock-Augustan piece running to twenty pages of verse, was printed at his own expense.[78] It is an attack on Saint Monday rather than a celebration:

Doubtless you know the *Fox* in *Castle-street;*—
There all the scum of the creation meet;
For days together at the liquor stick,
And keep ST. MONDAY up for the whole week.
Hawkers and *Ballad-singers* here repair,
Sworn foes to dull sobriety and care;
And, yielding to tumultuous noise the sway,
Guzzle an hundred gallons in a day.

The deaths of his mother, father, and fiancée in rapid succession caused Davis to fall into despair and start drinking. He was soon reduced to hawking his poems and ballads round public houses, and later entered the workhouse, where he died at the age of 51. Some of his pieces were issued over his initials by street-ballad printers, including Joseph Russell; others, without imprint, he probably commissioned on his own account. Some are personal and moralistic, such as 'On Going into the Workhouse' and 'The Spiritual Bankrupt'. National events inspired 'The Battle of Waterloo' and 'Meditations at St Helena by N. Buonaparte', but local happenings were the focus of 'Hampden Song', 'The Union Mill', and 'Whitsun Fair in Birmingham'.

Singer/Song-writers

If it was a natural thing for writers from the lower depths both to seek to express themselves and to eke out a living by means of street ballads, not all chose to do so, especially from the second half of the eighteenth century onwards. Joseph Mather (1737–1804) of Sheffield was a journeyman file-maker who for a time may have been an independent small master.[79] To help support his wife and three children, he turned to performing songs of his own composition in taverns in the evenings, in the streets late on Saturdays after the payment of wages, and at seasonal festivals, fairs, and races (sometimes seated on a donkey or even a bull, facing the tail). He could not write, though he was able to read (the Bible was a deep and lasting influence on his work), so he had to memorize his songs. Their subject-matter included local events and characters, and the pleasures of artisan life in Sheffield, from horse-racing, bull-baiting, and cock-fighting to singing, dancing, and drinking.[80] The tone and content changed dramatically when, in a period of hardship occasioned by loss of markets as a result of the American War of Independence, the large manufacturers strove to do away with the protection once offered to small masters and journeymen, and to impose a free-market economy. In these struggles, which lasted from 1784 to 1791, Mather's songs played an important part. In 1787, for example, Jonathan Wilkinson, the master cutler of the day, widely held to be responsible for lowering piece-rates by demanding thirteen to the dozen, was forced to leave the theatre when the audience in the 'gods' serenaded him with Mather's song 'Watkinson and his Thirteens' (see illustration).[81] This, one of only two of Mather's songs to have been issued as a broadside, was still in oral circulation some eighty years later. Mather himself frequently sang outside the cutlers' hall, and often spent the night in the town gaol for his pains. Once, probably after what has been called Sheffield's rehearsal for Peterloo, in 1795, when the local Volunteer Corps fired on a crowd and Mather wrote and sang 'Norfolk-Street Riots', he was found guilty of abusing the magistrates, the constables, and the clergy in song, and was bound over to keep the peace for a year. Although he was silenced, his forceful songs continued to be sung. 'God save Great Thomas Paine' was originally written in 1794 for a meeting to protest the prosecution of reformers like Hardy, Muir, Skirving, and Palmer (see Chapter 7). One of the counts against Muir, who was sentenced in 1793 to fourteen years' transportation, was that he had lent a copy of Thomas Paine's works to a relative.

> God save great Thomas Paine,
> His *Rights of Man* to explain
> To ev'ry soul.
> He makes the blind to see
> What dupes and slaves they be,
> And points out liberty
> From pole to pole.[82]

After his enforced silence, Mather returned not to radicalism, but to religion. One of his last pieces, 'Repentance', remained in the Methodist repertoire for many years. He died in poverty, but he had retained the affection of the working class of Sheffield, and thousands thronged to his funeral. His songs were gathered together and printed in 1811 by John Crome (1757–1832), a Scotsman who settled in Sheffield and became a lifelong radical. A further edition, enlarged by items recovered from oral tradition, appeared in 1862.

There were many other song-writers of working class or lower middle-class origin. Not all were as politically inclined as the mature Mather, of course. Many had radical sympathies, including Robert Burns (1759–96), who is the exception to the rule that their reputation was mainly local. Susanna Blamire (1747–94), a Cumberland-dialect writer, is similarly exceptional in being a woman song-writer.[83] Robert Anderson (1770–1833) of Carlisle, a great admirer of Burns, was known as 'The Cumberland Bard', but a few of his pieces were reworked in standard English and travelled further afield.[84]

In Birmingham, John Freeth (1731–1808) was the best known of several ballad writers.[85] For forty years, starting in 1763 with a piece in praise of the local beer, he poured out a stream of songs on subjects as diverse as canals, cock-fighting, prize-fighting, bull-baiting, the game laws, land and sea battles, the proposed enclosure of Sutton Coldfield, miners' demonstrations, the Gordon riots, the impeachment of Warren Hastings, and the turning of a theatre into a Methodist chapel. Freeth started his working life as an apprentice brass-founder, but from 1768 until his death, he kept a tavern and coffee-house, where he entertained the customers with songs which were later printed in *Aris's Birmingham Gazette* and subsequently issued in sixpenny volumes with titles like *The Political Songster* (seven editions, 1766–98), *A Touch on the Times* (1783 and 1803), and *New Ballads to Old Familiar Tunes* (1805). He was known as 'the Bard of Freedom', and 'one of the best political ballad writers and election poets in the Kingdom'.[86]

Among the many Lancashire song-writers were the remarkable Wilsons. Michael Wilson (1763–1840) was the son of a hand-loom weaver who had moved to Manchester from Edinburgh. He himself worked as a calico printer, then a furniture broker. His songs include light-hearted pieces like 'Jone's Ramble fro' Owdam to Karsy-Moor [Kersal Moor] Races'; but he was 'at heart a Jacobin', and excelled at political ballads, one of which (only partly recovered) was set to the tune of 'Gee-up, Neddy' ('Gee ho dobbin'), which is printed below on page 228.

THE PETERLOO MASSACRE

Come, Robin, sit deawn, an' aw'll tell thee a tale,
Boh first, — prithee, fill me a dobbin*a* o' ale;
Aw'm as drey, mon, as soot, an' aw'm hurt i' mi crop,
Havin' laft Sam o' Dick's wheer aw fear he mun stop.
For the gentlemen cavalry,
Cut 'em down cleverly;
Real Royal yeomanry!
Cavalry brave!

Mr Hunt neaw coom forrard an' spoke a few words,
When the Peterloo cut-my-throats shaken'd ther swords,
Aw thowt sure enoof they wur runnin' ther rigs,
Till aw seed moor nor twenty lay bleedin' like pigs.

Boh lets ta'e a peep o' these Peterloo chaps,
'At ma'es sich a neyse abeawt cullers an' caps,
See what they'n composed on, an' then we may judge,
For it runs i' mi moind 'ot ther loyalty's fudge.

a gill

Theer's the taxman, exciseman, the lawyer, an' bum,
The pensioner, placeman, an' preycher, that hum:
The fat-gutted landlord, o' licence in fear,
Cuts the throats o' his neybours who buy his bad beer.[87]

Two of Michael Wilson's seven sons, Thomas (?1780s–1840) and Alexander (1804–46), were also song-writers. Thomas was the most prolific of all, with some thirty-five pieces to his credit. His subjects included war ('Young Edward slain at Waterloo') and local events ('Rough Joe in search of a Wife' and 'The Meddling Parson'). Among Alexander's songs are several on the adventures of an invented character named Johnny Green, including his trips from Oldham to see a balloon ascent and the Liverpool railway. Many of the Wilsons' songs are lost; but a few were printed on broadsides, and John Harland gathered together as many as he could find into a little book, *The Songs of the Wilsons*, which ran to four editions between 1842 and 1866.

The tradition of such writing was particularly long-lived in the northeast of England, where it was linked with the music-hall. 'Culture for the people, not of the people . . . socially conservative, aggressively patriotic and politically disabling' is a recent critic's summation of the music-hall.[88] Another complains that music-hall songs, unlike the broadside ballads which they helped to supplant, are 'not a genuine expression of the discontent or opinion or policy of an oppressed stratum of society, but . . . a true-blue and ultra-conservative declaration of loyalty or a knowing bit of sarcasm'.[89] These remarks are generally valid; nevertheless, in some respects the entertainers of Tyneside remained close to their working-class audience. Ned Corvan (1829–65), while sharing the jovial imperialism of many music-hall writers, celebrated popular sports such as horse-racing, prize-fighting, and rowing, and in 'The Toon Improvement Bill' lamented the loss of playing space which resulted from the building of Newcastle's central station. He felt a deep sympathy for keelmen and miners, and one of his best songs, 'The Queen has sent a Letter', deals with the New Hartley pit disaster of 1862.[90]

Ballads of this kind, like those on calamities of any nature, have a long pedigree. They continued in Scotland at least until 1959, when the fire at Auchengeich colliery and the resulting deaths of forty-seven men inspired a traditional-style piece,[91] and in England until 1973, when the Lofthouse pit disaster gave rise to a considerable body of verse and song.

Among the songs by collier Tommy Armstrong (1848–1919) of Tanfield, County Durham, was 'The Trimdon Grange Explosion'. Armstrong's work covered a wide range of subjects: a murder, a ghost, a flood, the birth of a child, and the local market. His approach is often light-hearted, and he has a marvellous sense of the ludicrous, as in 'Durham Gaol', which is about his own imprisonment. The heart of his work, not surprisingly, concerns mining, and he was known as 'the pitman's poet'. One of several pieces on strikes, 'The Oakey Evictions', was written in 1885 at the Red Roe public house in Tanfield, during a song contest between Armstrong and a fellow miner, William McGuire of Gateshead. The subject, chosen by the audience, was the eviction of strikers from their company houses at Oakey colliery. The weapon used was ridicule, directed against the 'candymen' (rag-and-bone men) who were hired to carry out the strikers' furniture. Elsewhere, Armstrong approaches the vehemence of Joseph Mather. 'Durham Strike' refers to the three-month strike and lock-out of 1892, and its chorus runs:

> May every Durham colliery owner that is in the fault,
> Receive nine lashes with the rod, and then be rubbed with salt;
> May his back end be thick with boils, so that he cannot sit,
> And never burst until the wheels go round at every pit.

Armstrong's songs were sung in pubs, working men's clubs, and local music-halls. They were published in a small book,[92] and can still be heard not only in the north-east but further afield.

Many singer/song-writers of recent years, consciously or otherwise, have chosen to follow in the footsteps of Mather and Armstrong, though they have endeavoured, by using modern media, to reach a national audience. Like the ballad-writers of the past, they cover 'the whole surface of man's life, political and social'. Unemployment, the environment, women's rights, Scots, Welsh, and Irish nationalism, nuclear weapons, war and peace: most of the great issues of the day, as well as the ordinary details of everyday life, have been treated by contemporary song-writers ranging from the obscure to the famous. The song-writing career of veteran Ewan MacColl (born 1915) spanned half a century, from 'The Manchester Rambler' (oddly enough, to a tune from Haydn's 94th symphony), associated with the campaign for access to the countryside and the mass trespass on Kinder Scout in 1933, to songs of the miners' strike of 1984–5, including 'Daddy, what did you do in the strike?' and 'Only doing their job'. These songs are unashamedly partisan. They reflect history, but also seek to affect it; they chart human society, but also hope to change it for the better.[93]

1

THE COUNTRY

ARCADIA, Eden: an earthly paradise is among the perennial dreams of mankind. Traditional songs reflect it, but use the delights of nature more as a backcloth against which action takes place than as a matter for centre-stage. The scene is set with stock phrases. The Robin Hood ballads, many of which were already well known by the fourteenth century, often have openings like 'In summer time, when leaves grow green', and one has this magnificent first stanza:

> When shaws be sheene, and shraddes full fayre
> And leaves both long and large,
> It's merrye walkyng in the fayre forrèst
> To heare the small birdes songe.[1]

Phrases like 'Abroad as I was walking', 'As I walked (roved) out', and 'As I was a-walking (rambling)' are among the classic openings of folk-songs. The time is usually a morning in spring, May, June, or midsummer. The place is a highway, a meadow, a field, 'near a spring', 'through the woods', 'by a riverside', 'down by a shady grove', or 'amongst the new mown hay'. The journey is 'for my recreation', 'to view the fields so green', or 'to hear the birds whistle and the nightingales sing', but a lovers' meeting often ensues. The occasion may give rise to a lament at death, infidelity, or separation, or an outburst of joy at lovers' union or reunion. Frequently a walker meets a worker who is shepherding, ploughing, looking for a lost cow, mowing, or sowing, and the encounter is amorous. The landscape is luxuriant, with green bushes, convenient cocks of hay, banks of sweet primroses, dewy grass, or small birds singing.

Such conventions were familiar and well loved, as were Homer's wine-dark sea and rosy-fingered dawn, which Goethe thought 'utterly natural', to his listeners.[2] They were a convenient way of launching a song and attracting the immediate attention of an audience; yet they were more than empty formulae. For many centuries, walking was the habitual means of travel of the poor, which explains why it was so common in songs. The countryside provided opportunities for private encounters, sexual and otherwise, which were lacking in the crowded dwellings of the past. The advent of spring and early summer put new heart into people, and provided a brief period of respite between the rigours of winter and the onset of the hard, continuous work of haymaking, sheep-shearing, and harvesting.

Country Work

Country work was itself the subject of a huge number of songs. The approach was often idyllic. 'A proper new Ballad, Intituled The Mery Life of the Countriman, etc. wherin is Shewed his contented minde, and laboursome toyle mixed with pleasure: most pleasante and delightfull: to be songe to the tune of *Lacaranto*', published between 1585 and 1616, begins:

> A Prince dothe sit a slippery seate,
> and beares a carefull minde:
> the Nobles, which in silkes doe jet,
> do litle pleasure finde.
> Our safegard and safetie, with many great matters, they scan;
> and non lives merrier, in my mynde,
> than dothe the plaine countryman.
>
> Although with patchèd clothes he go,
> and stockinge out at heele,
> he little knowes the greife and wo
> that mightie men do feele;
> But merrely whistles, and plowes up the thistles a pace.
> When sunne goes downe so rounde as a crowne,
> his oxen he doth unbrace.[3]

'The Happy Husbandman; or, Country Innocence', which appeared in the late seventeenth century, has a similarly positive view of men and women's work:

> My young Mary do's mind the Dairy,
> While I go a Howing and Mowing each Morn;
> Then hey the little spinning-wheel
> Merrily round do's reel,
> While I am singing amidst the corn.[4]

Although such pieces often originated in towns, they found favour with country singers. 'A Sweet Country Life', which dates from the eighteenth century, remained in oral circulation until the twentieth:

5838

A sweet country life is to me both dear and charming,
For to walk abroad in a fine summer's morning.
Your houses, your cities, your lofty gay towers
In nothing can compare with the sweet shady bowers.

.   .   .   .

As Johnny the ploughboy was walking alone,
To fetch home his cattle[a], so early in the morn;
There he spied pretty Nancy all among the green bushes,
She was singing more sweetly than blackbirds or thrushes.

'Twas down in the meadows, beneath the high mountain,
Where she sat a milking by the side of a fountain;
The flocks they were grazing in the dew of the morning,
Bright Phoebus did shine, and the hills was adorning.[5]

Some of the songs coming from country people themselves express a similarly rosy view. One, dating from the late nineteenth century reflects satisfaction in the singularly monotonous, back-breaking task of hoeing turnips.[6] 'I have done some hoeing', A. G. Street wryly commented in *Farmer's Glory* (1935), 'and it cured me of any desire to sing about it.'[7] Yet sing the farm-workers did, and with relish. 'The songs the labourer most delights in', according to a writer of 1898, 'are those that are typical of the employment in which he happens to be engaged.'[8] This may explain the appeal of the turnip-hoeing song, and of others on haymaking, harvesting, and even, as George Orwell testifies, hop-picking.[9] However, shepherds and ploughmen were the aristocrats of land labour, and enjoyed the lion's share of the songs.

Shepherds

Shepherds were renowned for playing instruments and singing, to relieve the solitude of their occupation. W. H. Hudson recalled one man whose voice could be heard a mile away as he followed his flock on the Wiltshire downs.[10] The choice of songs was wide. Caleb Bawcombe, a shepherd described at some length by Hudson, learned songs from his father, also a shepherd, born in 1800:

Though not soft nor tender with his children he was very fond of them, and when he came home early in the evening he would get them round and talk to them, and sing old songs and ballads he had learnt in his young years—'Down in the Village', 'The Days of Queen Elizabeth', 'The Blacksmith', 'The Gown of Green', 'The Dawning of the Day', and many others, which Caleb in the end got by heart and used to sing, too, when he was grown up.[11]

[a] horses

Many of the shepherds' songs celebrated their own calling. In some, the shepherd has a sexual or sentimental role; in others, he is seen at work. Many were home-made. Willie Scott, who was born in 1897 and worked for over fifty years as a shepherd in the border country between England and Scotland, has a big repertoire, which includes what is an occupational song *par excellence*:

> I'm a shepherd and I rise ere the sun is in the skies;
> I can lamb the yowes wi ony o them a'.
> I like my flock to feed, to look fresh and fair indeed,
> But I wish the cauld east winds would never blaw.
> *I can smear my sheep and dip, I can udderlock and clip,*
> *I can lamb the yowes wi ony o them a'.*
> *I can parrock, I can twin, aye, and cheat them wi a skin*
> *But I wish these cauld east winds would never blaw.*

The song deals at some length with the craft and skills of the shepherd, as is clear from the chorus, in which 'smearing' means applying the mixture of tar and butter used before sheep-dip became available; 'udderlocking' is pulling wool away from the udder to give access to the lamb; and 'parrocking' and 'twinning' are ways of persuading a ewe to accept another's lamb by confining it with her in a small enclosure, or parrock, or by tying her dead lamb's skin around it. At the end, the piece exhorts 'neebor herds' to quench their thirst not with 'the fiery liquor', but with water from 'the bonny bubbling streams'. It was written in about 1880 by a shepherd from Ettrick valley called Amos, and was first heard by Willie Scott in 1906.[12]

The same pride and the same preoccupation with wind and weather, but with rather less technical detail and a completely different attitude towards strong drink, occur in another home-made song which Thomas Hughes printed in *The Scouring of the White Horse* (1858). It derives ultimately from Martin Parker's 'Sailors for my Money'; but the process of adaptation and remaking was a time-honoured feature of traditional-style composition.

SHEPHERDS' SONG

> Come, all you shepherds as minds for to be,
> You must have a gallant heart,
> You must not be down-hearted,
> You must a-bear the smart;
> You must a-bear the smart, my boys,
> Let it hail or rain or snow,
> For there is no ale to be had on the Hill
> Where the wintry wind doth blow.

When I kept sheep on White Horse Hill
My heart began to ache,
My old ewes all hung their heads,
And my lambs began to bleat.
Then I cheered up with courage bold,
And over the Hill did go,
For there is no ale to be had on the Hill
When the wintry wind doth blow.

I drive my sheep into the fold,
To keep them safe all night,
For drinking of good ale, my boys,
It is my heart's delight.
I drove my sheep into the fold,
And homeward I did go,
For there is no ale to be had on the Hill
When the wintry wind doth blow.

We shepherds are the liveliest lads
As ever trod English ground,
If we drops into an ale-house
We values not a crownd.
We values not a crownd, my boys,
We'll pay before we go,
For there is no ale to be had on the Hill
When the wintry wind doth blow.[13]

Such songs reinforced shepherds' self-esteem, and bolstered their standing in the eyes of others. Nevertheless, an expression of disenchantment is heard from time to time. 'Poor Shepherds'[14] attacks enclosures, low wages, and unemployment. Another home-made song sung in 1909 by 'Shepherd' Haden of Bampton, Oxfordshire, after giving details of the hard life, firmly rejects it: 'I'll never keep sheep on the downs any more, / For there's neither a limb nor a tree.'[15]

Ploughmen

Like shepherds, ploughmen also sang, both at work and at leisure. Flora Thompson refers to coarse tales told during lunch-breaks in the fields, and adds: 'Songs and snatches on the same lines were bawled at the plough-tail and under hedges and never heard elsewhere.'[16] John Clare mentions 'the ballad in the ploughman's pocket'. 'They were always singing or whistling,' said Arthur Lane (1884–1975) of Corve Dale, Shropshire. 'When we were ploughing with horses, go out and 'ld sing all day, happy as could be, and the horses liked it.' Lane also remembered, as a live-in farm-worker, spending evenings in the barn lying in the straw and singing such songs as 'Jolly Fellows that Follow the Plough':

One'ld sing a song, then another'ld sing a song, and then we used to have our eyes shut, singing, passing the time away. Well, it'ld come on eleven o'clock, twelve o'clock, one o'clock; we used to go on singing, then perhaps we'd go to sleep—some would. When you wakened it'ld be two o'clock, perhaps. Then we'ld get up to go to bed.[17]

Fred Kitchen (1891–1969) tells a similar story in his book *Brother to the Ox* (1940), which Raymond Williams has described as 'one of the few very direct and unmediated accounts of a rural labourer's life'.[18] Kitchen became a hireling, as he calls it, in 1904, at a wage of 2s. 6d. a week, plus board. He spent his evenings in the stable with the other farm lads, seated on the great corn bin or a truss of hay: 'He was considered a poor gawk who couldn't knock a tune out of a mouth-organ or give a song to pass away the evening.' Other diversions were playing dominoes, draughts, fox-and-geese, tip-cat, or telling tales: 'At least, the other men did—folklore tales—whilst I sat with my ears open, and probably my mouth, taking it all in.'[19] The same thing was happening in the bothies of north-east Scotland (see below).

A combination of pride and protest can be found in the songs of ploughmen, as of shepherds; not usually within a single piece, but certainly within the corpus. Like the shepherd, the ploughman (or waggoner, horseman, or carter, as he was alternatively called in different areas) is often depicted as being extremely attractive to women. In 'The Pretty Ploughboy',[20] he is the social inferior of the lady who falls in love with him; her parents have him press-ganged to sea, but she buys his discharge and triumphantly marries him. A later version[21] features a factory boy instead of a ploughman, but the outcome is the same. A 'pretty wench' vows, 'If a carter I can't have I'll go single to my grave',[22] and another declares 'With my saucy ploughboy I mean to live and die.'[23] A third comes across a ploughman while she is gathering nuts, and the outcome seems inevitable:

She then came to young Johnny as he sit on his plough.
She said, 'Young man, I really feel I cannot tell you how'.
He took her to some shady broom and there he laid her down;
Said she, 'Young man, I think I feel the world go round and round'.[24]

By contrast, the eponymous hero of 'Roving Ploughboy'[25] sets out to seek—and find—his sexual fortune in a dozen towns, from Oxford to Rochdale. In so doing, he emulates the amorous odysseys of sailors, soldiers, miners, and journeymen which were a source of perennial delight for singers and listeners.

The ploughman's dedication to his work was a byword, and he would spend Sunday mornings walking round the fields to appraise the skill of others. Such pride and dedication are often tempered by dissatisfaction with the rewards. Deference turns to defiance in what is perhaps the most widely known of all farm-workers' songs. The version given here came from Maurice Ogg (1946–80), a Lincolnshire carpenter who was always keen to pick up a song as he travelled round in the course of his work. He reported that it could still be heard in local pubs in the 1970s.

THE PLOUGHMAN'S SONG

It was early one morn at the break of the day;
The cocks were a-crowing. The farmer did say:
'Come arise, my good fellows, arise with goodwill,
For you 'osses are waiting their bellies to fill'.

When four o'clock comes round we hastily rise
And into the stable we merrily fly;
A-brushing and a-rubbing away we do go,
For we're all jolly fellows that follow the plough.

When six o'clock comes round at breakfast we meet;
We sit round the table and heartily eat.
A bit in our pocket and away we do go,
For we're all jolly fellows that follow the plough.

The farmer comes round; as he does he will say:
'Wheer 'ast tha bin all on this fine day?
You 'aven't ploughed one acre, I'll swear and I'll vow.
You're all idle fellows that follow the plough'.

The wag'ner stepped out and he made this reply:
'What you have said is a jolly big lie.
We've all ploughed one acre, I'll swear and I'll vow.
We're all jolly fellows that follow the plough'.

The farmer turned round and he laughed at the joke.
He said: ' 'S gone two o'clock, lads, it's time to unyoke.
Unharness them 'osses and rub them down well,
And I'll bring you a pint of my very best ale'.[26]

The song's lasting appeal derives from its realistic depiction of the ploughman's routine, combined with its perhaps more idealized representation of the spirited stand taken against an unfair employer. This account of a day's work in the 1860s and 1870s is typical of the era of horse-power on the land:

These hired farm hands, both boys and young men, had to rise at 4 o'clock to feed and water their horses, etc.; at some farms a bell was rung at that hour, and the horse-keeper boys have told me that if they were not quickly down the farmer would soon be after them. After tending to the horses, etc., came breakfast, the head ploughman came along at 5 o'clock, and at 6 o'clock the men and their teams started off to the fields; they continued to plough until 2 o'clock with a break of half an hour at 10 o'clock for 'beaver' [food]. By 2 o'clock each team was supposed to have ploughed an acre (ploughing an acre being deemed a day's work). The horses would then be shut out from the plough, and they and the men get back to the farm, when the horses would be watered, etc. Then came dinner, after which the horses would be cleaned and combed, stable littered, and the animals fed and made comfortable (or 'racked up' was the term used) for the night and the men's day's work ended; this was an ordinary day.[27]

Deference and Protest

The deep satisfaction which could derive from farm work sometimes obscured other considerations, and songs emphasizing the harmony between master and man in their joint endeavours frequently surfaced at celebrations such as sheep-shearing feasts and harvest homes. In other pieces, bountiful patrons ensured the well-being of workers. A grateful nobleman in 'The Jolly Thresherman'[28] presents a small farm to an industrious, sober, deserving, deferential labourer. The song was in print as early as about 1700 under the title of 'The Nobleman's Generous Kindness; or, The Country Man's Unexpected Happiness',[29] and turned up in oral tradition a good two hundred years later, until its pipe-dreaming was replaced by the football pools. Another transition to land-owning status by a worthy worker is found in 'The Farmer's Boy',[36] also a country favourite, in which a penniless orphan, in good Victorian style, marries a farmer's daughter and inherits his farm.

When criticism is levelled at farmers, it is often occasioned by a falling away from former bounty. 'When this Old Hat was New' has its gaze firmly

directed towards better times gone by. This text was issued in the 1820s,
and the tune was noted in 1907.

WHEN THIS OLD HAT WAS NEW

* Last few words repeated from this point

I am a poor old man in years, come listen to my song,
Provisions now are twice as dear as when that I was young.
It was when this old hat was new and stood upon my brow,
Oh, what a happy youth was I when this old hat was new.

It is but four score years ago the truth I will declare,
When men they took each other's words, they thought it very fair,
No oaths or bonds they did require, men's words were so true,
This was in my youthful days, when this old hat was new.

When the time of harvest came and we went out to shear,
H[ow o]ften we were merry made with brandy, ale and beer.
[And when] the corn it was brought home and put upon the [mow]
[Laboure]rs' paunches were well filled when this old hat was new.

[The farmer] at the board head stood the table for to grace,
[And gree]ts all as they came in all took their proper place.
[The wife] she at the table stood to give each man his due,
[And O] wha[t] plenty did abound when this old hat was new.

But now the times are altered, the poor are quite done o'er,
They give to them their wages like beggars at the door.
Into the house we must not go although we are but few,
It was not so when Bess did reign and this old hat was new.

The commons they are taken in and the cottages pulled down,
Moll has got no wool to spin her linsey-wolsey gown.
The weather's cold and clothing thin and blankets are but few,
But we were clothed both back and skin when this old hat was new.

When Romans in this land did reign the commons they did give
Unto the poor in charity to help them for to live,
But now the poor is quite done o'er, we know it to be true.
It was not so when Bess did reign and this old hat was new.[31]

The song was 'very popular among the Lincolnshire peasantry during the last twenty years of the eighteenth century'.[32] One of its variants included a further reference to enclosure: 'The lawyer he up to London is gone / To get the act passed before he return.'[33] However, it derives from 'Time's Alteration', written in about 1624 by Martin Parker, which looks back to still earlier times, 'when this old cap was new'. Parker complains of a variety of abuses, but chiefly castigates luxurious life-styles and a lack of care for the poor:

> Good Hospitalitie was cherisht then of many,
> Now poore men starve and die, and are not helpt by any:
> For Charitie waxeth cold, and Love is found in few:
> This was not in time of old, when this old Cap was new.[34]

William Cobbett levelled against farmers the same accusations of high living and indifference to the needs of workers. Describing the sale of a Surrey farm in 1825 he wrote that 'the system' transformed the farmers 'into a species of mock gentlefolks', 'while it has ground the labourers down into real slaves'. He continued: 'Why do not farmers *feed* and *lodge* their workpeople, as they did formerly? Because they cannot keep them *upon so little* as they give them in wages. This is the real cause of the change.'[35]

Writing at about the same time, John Clare made much the same point in very similar words. Like Cobbett, he loved the humble objects of everyday life, and used their supersession to epitomize social change:

> That good old fame the farmers earned of yore
> That made as equals not as slaves the poor
> That good old fame did in two spearks expire
> A shooting coxcomb and a hunting squire

> And their old mansions that was dignified
> With things far better than the pomp of pride
> At whose oak table that was plainly spread
> Each guest was welcomd and the poor was fed
> W[h]ere master son and serving man and clown
> Without distinction daily sat them down
> W[h]ere the bright rows of pewter by the wall
> Served all the pomp of kitchen or of all
> These all have vanished like a dream of good.[36]

The message of Cobbett and Clare was echoed in street ballads which poured from the presses with such titles as 'Advice to Farmers'[37] and 'Swaggering Farmers'.[38] 'The New-fashioned Farmer' once more regrets times past and complains of current pretension:

> In former times, both plain and neat, they'd go to church on Sunday,
> Then to harrow, plough and sow they'd go upon a Monday.
> But now, instead of the plough tail, o'er hedges they are jumping;
> Instead of sowing of their corn their delight is in fox-hunting.[39]

Yet, in the early years of the twentieth century, country people were singing about how much better things had been in the days of Queen Victoria. One song, from George Fradley (1910–85) of Sudbury, Derbyshire, was adapted from a piece written by Harry Clifton for the music-hall in the 1860s:

> The farmer's sons went after stock as soon as they could walk,
> But now they go to grammar school to teach them how to talk.
> They weren't afraid of work those days but what a difference now:
> They want a machine to milk the cow and a tractor before they can plough.[40]

Another, 'Hoo happy we liv'd then', looks back with regret to 'former days', but reaches a surprisingly firm conclusion:

> May Providence befriend us an' raise an honest heart,
> When the poorest had his burden an' too lang had felt the smart;
> But tak' the largest farms an' divide 'em into ten,
> And the poor may live as happy noo as ivver they did then![41]

Enclosure

There were plenty of straightforward attacks on farmers and the agricultural system. Enclosure, which had gone on sporadically since about 1450, greatly increased in the eighteenth and nineteenth centuries. Between 1700 and 1760 there were more than two hundred Acts of Parliament ('The lawyer he is up to London gone . . .') for this purpose;

between 1761 and 1844 there were some four thousand.[42] Cobbett was against enclosing the commons, and wrote: 'Nothing that man could devise would be more injurious to the country than this.'[43] Popular opposition manifested itself in anonymous letters[44] and rhymes, such as the famous epigram of 1821:

> The fault is great in man or woman
> Who steals a goose from off a common,
> But what can plead that man's excuse
> Who steals a common from a goose.[45]

A less well-known verse was posted on the fence of newly enclosed fields at Winderton, Warwickshire:

> There's hedges and ditches quick to be found,
> Posts and rails cut out and put down,
> And when you have finished and hung up your gates,
> Some of you'll be glad to sell your estates.[46]

The veiled threat in the last line was not altogether idle. Surveyors were harassed, and fences destroyed. At West Haddon in Northamptonshire 'a great Number of Persons assembled' on 1 August 1765 'for the purpose of a pretended FOOT-BALL MATCH', but instead 'tore up and destroyed great Part of the INCLOSURES of the Common Field of the said Parish (which had been made in pursuance of an Act of Parliament obtained for that Purpose) and burnt and destroyed large Quantities of Posts and Rails'.[47] There was a riot as late as 1870 at Fakenham in Norfolk, when a schoolmaster named Flaxman, who lived on the heath, organized the Association for the Defence of the Rights of the Poor (which later became the first of the Norfolk labourers' unions). After being imprisoned for a time in Norwich Castle, Flaxman was welcomed back to Fakenham by an enthusiastic crowd who sang 'Don't be fidgety, we shall get our common back again.'[48] The rest of the words do not seem to have been recorded, which is a pity, because ballads opposing country enclosures are extremely rare. Indeed, I know of only one, from the manuscript 'Charnwood Opera' of 1753.[49] Several ballads opposing town enclosures have survived, however, including 'A New Song, entitled No Inclosure' (see illustration),[50] from Nottingham. References to enclosure crop up in other ballads of general complaint, such as 'When This Old Hat Was New'. 'Past, Present and Future' (quoted in the Introduction) tells us: 'In olden times the poor could on a common turn a cow, / The commons are all taken in, the rich have claim'd them now.' 'Medley's Remarks on the Times' (see Chapter 2), issued in 1809, speaks for the small farmer.

In the year of this ballad's publication, Helpstone was enclosed, together with many other Northamptonshire villages. John Clare poured out his regret at the extinction of ancient customs and the deterioration in the quality of life in entry after entry in his journals, and in poem after poem. His anguish and keen sense of personal loss anticipate reactions in recent years to the despoliation of the countryside by agribusiness. Clare wrote: 'Enclosure came, and trampled on the grave / Of labour's rights, and left the poor a slave'; 'Inclosure, thou'rt a curse upon the land, / And tasteless was the wretch who thy existence plann'd'; and, in a significant reference to footpaths which recalls the theme of roving out: 'Inclosure came, and every path was stopt; / Each tyrant fix'd his sign where paths were found / To hint a trespass now who cross'd the ground.' Among the most moving, not merely of his poems on enclosure, but of all his poems, is 'Remembrances', which includes this memorable verse with its masterly change of rhythm in the fourth line:

> By Langley Bush I roam, but the bush hath left its hill,
> On Cowper Green I stray, 'tis a desert strange and chill,
> And the spreading Lea Close Oak, ere decay had penned its will,
> To the axe of the spoiler and self-interest fell a prey,
> And Crosberry Way and old Round Oak's narrow lane
> With its hollow trees like pulpits I shall never see again,
> Enclosure like a Buonaparte let not a thing remain,
> It levelled every bush and tree and levelled every hill
> And hung the moles for traitors—though the brook is running still
> It runs a naked stream, cold and chill.[51]

The Swing Disturbances

Some early nineteenth-century causes lacked poets and balladeers. For all the sympathy and passion their case inspired, the Tolpuddle martyrs apparently received only a passing reference in a single ballad.[52] The Swing disturbances of a few years earlier affected thirty-six counties (albeit sixteen of them marginally). Some 1,500 incidents were recorded between January 1830 and September 1832, and just under 2,000 people were brought to trial, of whom 19 were hanged, 644 gaoled, and about 500 transported.[53] Such events left indelible memories (some of which later found their way into print), but no ballad came to light until 1896, when a Hampshire clergyman, Thomas Roach, published a text which he 'took down from the lips of an old man, now bedridden, who, as a lad of 17, was present on the occasion referred to in the first lines'. The informant, who wished to be known only as M.H., claimed that he had received 'many a pot of beer' for singing the song. It had been written by his brother, who was later transported to Van Diemen's Land, presumably for his part in

A NEW SONG,

ENTITLED

No Inclosure!

Or, the Twelfth of August,

TUNE,—" Come all you Scamping Blades."

YOU Freemen all of Nottingham come listen to my
    Song,
I trust it now will please you it is not very long;
It's of a Great Inclosure that now is laying out,
o now my Lads of Nottingham mind what you are about.

         To my fal de ral de ra.

Your Rights and your Liberties I would have you to
    revere,
And look unto Posterity I think them always dear;
To us and to our Children by the Charter that prevails,
So now my Boys united be and have no Posts or Rails.

         To my fal de ral de ra.

Men Traps and Spring Guns set on every Piece of
    Land,
With threaten'd Prosecutions if on the Ground you stand;
But since my Boys we've Liberty now let it far prevail,
And spurn at those that do propose a Fence of Post and
    Rail.

         To my fal de ral de ra.

Let's suffer no Encroachments upon our Land to be,
But to repel such Tyranny let's ever now agree;
Let neither House nor Stable upon it for to stand,
But let ev'ry brave Freeman enjoy his Right of Land.

         To my fal de ral de ra.

See Reynald's now unkennel'd he strides along the
    Field,
We'll chase him 'till he's tir'd then force him for to yield;
For when our Blood is rous'd our Spirits never fail,
We'll close pursue the sordid Crew and have no Posts or
    Rails.

         To my fal de ral de ra.

There's Dimond Brave and Captain Flash don't join
    us in the Pack,
They'll skip and fawn and jump about when once the
    whip doth crack ;
When once the Chase is over let Harmony prevail,
And we'll drink to those that doth oppose the Plan of
    Post and Rail.

         To my fal de ral de ra.

Tupman, Printer, High-Street.

'A New Song, entitled No Inclosure!' Street ballad.

MY MASTER & I,

Says the master to me, is it true ? I am told,
Your name on the books of the Union's enroll'd,
I can never allow that a workman of mine,
With wicked disturbers of peace should combine.

CHORUS.
You stingy old farmers,
The men you have scorned,
And you wish that Ben Taylor
Had never been born.

I give you fair warning, mind what you're about,
I shall put my foot on it and trample it out ;
On which side your bread's buttered, now sure you
can see,
So decide now at once for the union or me.

Says I to the master, it's perfectly true,
That I am in the union, and I'll stick to it too,
And if between union and you I must choose,
I have plenty to win, and little to lose.

For twenty years mostly my bread has been dry,
And to butter it now I shall certainly try ;
And tho' I respect you, remember I'm free,
No master in England shall trample on me.

Says the master to me, a word or two more,
We never have quarrelled on matters before,
If you stick to the union, ere long I'll be bound,
You will come and ask me for more wages all round.

Now I cannot afford more than two bob a day
When I look at the taxes and rent that I pay,
And the crops are so injured by game as you see
If it is hard for you it's hard also for me.

Says I to the master, I do not see how,
Any need has arisen for quarreling now,
And though likely enough we shall ask for more
wage,
I can promise you we shall not get first in a rage.

There is Mr. Darlow I vow and declare,
A draper and grocer in Huntingdonshire,
He sticks up for the labouring men, they all say
He has caused the farmers to rise the men's pay.

There is Mr. Taylor so stout and so bold,
The head of the labourer's union I'm told,
He persuaded all the men to stick up for their
rights,
And they say he's been giving the farmers the
gripes.

H. P. Such, Printer & Publisher,
Union St, Boro'

'My Master & I'. Street ballad.

Bothy musicians

A Westmorland shepherd, the late Isaac Cookson of Gillhead, Bampton (now Cumbria).

. An engraving of 1874 from G. Mitchell's *The Skeleton at Plough*.

Four oxen at wheel-plough, from W. H. Pyne's *Microcosm*, 1808.

the Labourers' Revolt. At least one other person must have known the
song, for it was noted from him in 1906. His version was slightly different
from M.H.'s text, which begins:

> On the thirtieth of November, last 1830,
> Our Owlesbury lads they did prepare,
> All for the machinery,
> And when they did get there,
> My eye! How they let fly;
> The machinery fell to pieces
> In the twinkling of an eye.
> *Oh! Mob, such a mob*
> *Never was seen before,*
> *And if we live this hundred years*
> *We never shall no more.*[54]

The rest of the song deals with the imprisonment and trial at Winchester
of 'the Owlesbury lads', of whom 'Some they transported for life / And
some they cast to die'. No doubt other items of this kind failed to survive
for want of an interested or sympathetic pen.

Poaching

No such lack seems to have affected poaching songs and ballads, which
survive in very large numbers.[55] The taking of deer, sheep (though these
were strictly speaking in a different category, since they were not wild), and
fish were celebrated in song, as was the poaching of rabbits, hares,
partridges, and pheasants. For some poachers, the activity was simply
sport; but for others, sometimes in organized gangs from the towns, it was
merely a source of quick money. Many were driven by necessity. James
Hawker (1836–1920) wrote: 'Poverty made me Poach,' but added: 'I have
poached more for Revenge than Gain.' He had a long memory: 'The mid-
1840's were wretched times. Sheep Stealing, Highway Robbery and
Burglary were common. It was not Safe to go out after Dark. If a Man stole
a Sheep he had 14 years Transportation. If hunger made a man go into the
woods to get a pheasant, he too would get fourteen years.'[56]

Although, as G. M. Trevelyan wrote, 'there was never a truce to the
poaching war in old England',[57] in some periods it raged with particular
intensity. During the reign of George III alone (1760–1820) in what the
Hammonds called 'a crescendo of fierceness',[58] thirty-two game laws were
passed, and this was by no means the last legislation of its kind. There
ensued what Harry Hopkins has termed 'the long affray'.[59] On one side
were ranged, with the full backing of the law, landowners, gamekeepers,
and (until 1827) spring-guns and man-traps; on the other, poachers, poor,

desperate men who at least had the advantage of popular sympathy. I do not know of a single song which supports landowners and gamekeepers. All are on the side of the poachers. Some are light-hearted. The well-known 'Lincolnshire Poacher'[60] was even reputed to be a favourite of George IV's. More often, they were deeply serious, especially when chronicling skirmishes and battles in the poaching war. One of the earliest is 'Bill Brown'.[61] Its eponymous hero went out poaching with two companions near Sheffield in 1769. Although he was unarmed and carried only snares, he was shot by a gamekeeper called John Shirteliff (Shirtley in the ballad), and was left to die. Despite the evidence of Brown's companions, Shirteliff was acquitted at his trial. The same ballad was adapted in 1837 to commemorate a pitched battle in Deene Thorpe Wood, Northamptonshire, between twenty-five poachers from Sudborough and a party of Lord Cardigan's keepers. One poacher, William Mays, was killed, and several were afterwards imprisoned. The title of the sheet, 'Sudborough Heroes',[62] leaves no doubt as to the sympathies of its author. It was one of a steady stream of such publications. 'Claughton Wood Poachers' describes a battle in 1827 between a group of farmers and keepers and six poachers from Preston. It concludes with these defiant words:

> So now my lads keep up your hearts and do not let them fail
> For if ever we get our liberty we will range the woods again.[63]

By contrast, 'The Blackburn Poachers' commiserates over the killing of a keeper and issues a conventional warning:

> Ye will young men from this sad tale a solemn lesson learn
> If e'er enticed by wicked men, from their allurements turn.[64]

The well-known 'Van Diemen's Land' and its sequel, 'Young Henry the Poacher' (for which, see below), conclude with similar exhortations.

The poaching war continued unabated, none the less. Committals in England under the game laws reached 4,500 a year by the mid-1840s (the time Hawker recalled) and 'the gamekeeper's trade was now becoming more dangerous than the soldier's'.[65] Four 'gallant' poachers (a standard epithet in ballads) were sentenced to death in Liverpool in 1843 for killing one of Lord Derby's keepers in another pitched battle, but as a result of powerful pressure from public opinion, three were reprieved. Part of the persuasion was provided by a ballad entitled 'The Fate of the Liverpool Poachers'.[66] The death of another keeper in 1851 led to the transportation of four Nottinghamshire poachers for manslaughter. No street ballad on the case has survived, but in 1906, a fragment of a song with a magnificent tune was noted by Percy Grainger from Joseph Taylor (born 1833) of Saxby-All-Saints, Lincolnshire, under the title 'Rufford Park Poachers'.[67]

The story of poaching and its reverberations in song still had a long way to run. As recently as 1984, 'Who Owns the Game?' was recorded from Fred Whiting (born 1906) of Kenton, Suffolk:

WHO OWNS THE GAME?

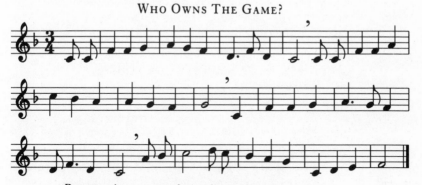

Pay attention you poachers wherever you be,
Can you answer my question and tell unto me
Who owns the wild hare that runs over the lea?
With a fal-the-ral, deedle dal, fal-the-ral dee.

Now a hare it may feed on a field for a day
And tomorrow quite likely be four fields away;
Yet the landowner tells you, 'She's my property',
And sings fal, etc.

And a pheasant may feed on a stubble nearby;
He'll fill up his crop and away he will fly,
Then he'll roost for the night in another man's tree,
With a fal, etc.

Now I say they're wild but the law don't agree,
And if I got caught poaching then fined I should be;
But I'll just take my chance for a dinner that's free,
And sing fal, etc.

My grandfather killed a pheasant in some parson's fir tree,
And was transported to some country far over the sea;
And he never came back, so my father told me,
With a fal, etc.

Now my father picked oakum for months two or three.
They were hard, hungry times for my mother and me;
We lived on pea soup, and 'taters and dumplings for tea,
And sang fal, etc.

'Never you be a poacher', my mother told me,
'Or locked up like your father you surely will be'.
Her tune changed when I snared a big hare for our tea:
She sang fal, etc.

Now the squire calls a shoot and hoes off with his gun,
And the pheasants he shoots he just kills them for fun.
He's got no empty pantry just like you and me,
And sings fal, etc.

I snared my first rabbit before I was nine,
And if ever I'm caught, well, I'll pay up the fine;
And I'll still use my gun for as long as I see,
And sing fal, etc.[68]

Like smugglers, poachers usually enjoyed the support of the communities from which they came. Hawker has some revealing anecdotes about receiving help even from strangers. Once when he was running away, keepers shouted to some men in his path to stop him, but they allowed him to pass unhindered when he hurriedly told them, 'Killed two Hare to feed Hungry Kids.' On another occasion he avoided the police simply by opening a house door at random and walking in. He found a surprised family at table, but was allowed to stay until the danger had passed.[69]

Hiring Fairs

If attitudes like this were deeply ingrained, so was participation in seasonal observances like Plough Mondaying, Maying, and mumming. These were part of a whole web of customary practices; and, as Bob Bushaway has shown, rites and rights were closely connected.[70] The seasonal pattern included fairs of all kinds, which, except for hiring fairs, are discussed in Chapter 5. Hiring fairs were alternatively known in different localities as 'statutes', 'mops', or 'feeings'. Some were annual, some six-monthly. They took place, again according to local custom, on May Day or at Whitsun, Michaelmas (possibly the most common), Martinmas, or even Christmas. Farm-workers, male or female, who wished to find an employer presented themselves at the due time and place, armed with some small token of their trade. A waggoner would have a piece of whipcord pinned to his lapel, and a servant girl would sport a few strands from a mop. They would tell farmers what skills they had to offer, and bargain over wages and conditions. 'I can sowe, I can mowe, / And I can stacke, / And I can doe, / My master toe, / When my master turns his backe':[71] this traditional rhyme, dating from 1641 or earlier, recalls the 'reap and mow, plough and sow' of the Victorian 'Farmer's Boy'. The equivalent for a housemaid, according to a ballad opera of 1762 in which there was a hiring scene, was:

> Of all your house the charge I take,
> I wash, I scrub, I brew, I bake;
> And more can do than here I'll speak,
> Depending on your bounty.[72]

In return, the farmer would make his offer:

> Here's five pounds of standing wages.
> Daily, well thou shalt be fed
> With good cabbage, beef, and bacon,
> Butter-milk, and oaten bread.[73]

If agreement were reached, the farmer would give a small advance of wages, variously called an 'earnest', 'arles', a 'feeing' or 'fastening penny', or 'hence-money'. After the business of the day came socializing and merry-making: 'It was the great rendezvous of the year, and high jubilation and happiness everywhere prevailed.'[74] The ritual went on in many areas until the First World War, and in the Lake District and parts of Ireland until the Second, and even later. It has been described many times by writers, from John Clare to Thomas Hardy to Melvyn Bragg;[75] but, in addition, farm-workers have given their own accounts, either in interviews or in their own writings.[76] Jack Beeforth (born 1891) of Wragby in North Yorkshire reported this (probably apocryphal) dialogue:

A lad goes to t'hirings and he meets a farmer who says: 'Ista for hiring?' 'Aye', says t'lad. 'What can you deea?' says t'farmer. 'Oh, ommost onnything on a farm', says t'lad. 'Well, thoo looks a likely lad', says t' farmer. 'Wheer were you last?' 'Wi' 'im ovver theer', says t'lad. 'Can you get youself a character?' says t'farmer, 'and then I'll hire you'. So the lad goes ovver to t'feller he wer wi', and asks 'im for a character. 'Nay, lad, you doan't want to go wi' 'im. He'll hunger yer and work yer, and you'll have a right bad time'. So the lad goes back to t'farmer. 'Well, have you got a character?' says he. 'Why', says t'lad, 'I haven't got one for me, but he's just given me a right one for thee'.[77]

Warnings of this kind feature in traditional rhymes. One, dealing with farms in eastern Fife, implies that it is summer there before the crop can be sown, and winter before it can be harvested: 'Ladeddie, Radernie, Lathockar, and Lathone, / Ye may saw wi' gloves off, and shear wi' gloves on.'[78]

Songs like 'The Weary Farmers' are along similar lines:

On cauld kail and tawties
They'll feed ye up like pigs,
While they sit at their tea and toast,
Or ride into their gigs.
The mistress must get 'Mem'—and ye
Maun lift your cap to her;
And ere ye find an entrance
The master must get 'Sir'.[79]

'Mutton Pie',[80] which is still widely sung, portrays a farmer whose idea of generosity is to arrange for the carcass of a dead sheep to be cooked as a meal for his men. Such songs were sung after work in Scots bothies and English stables, and also in public houses during the hiring fairs themselves. Gathered together would be 'a good many itinerant singers and sellers of ballads, many of which are of the most obscene character', according to an observer of 1843.[81] The ballad-sheets were carefully calculated to appeal to farm-workers. 'You servant lads and lasses gay come listen for a while', says 'Kendal Fair' (1850).[82] 'A New Statute Song, in praise of the Country Lads and Lasses, England's Pride',[83] dating from the late 1870s, is relaxed and genial, but nevertheless encourages workers to 'have jolly good p[l]ay / And stick up for your wages too'. 'Hiring Day', which leaves a blank in the text so that the singer can insert the name of his own town, also exhorts 'farmer lads' (a piece of townie's confusion) to 'Stand up like Britons for your wage', while also dwelling on the sexual opportunities provided at the fair:

When Polly is hired, oh dear! oh
Off to a dancing room she'll go,
And on the light fantastic toe,
She'll dance at —— Hirings;
Then with her lover fine and gay,
O'er fields and meadows they will stray
And with each other they will play,
Going home from —— Hirings.[84]

This is the mirror image of the anxieties of those who campaigned against what they regarded as the immorality of the hirings. The curate of Driffield, the Revd J. Skinner, published a dossier of such complaints in 1861. This was sent to him by an inspector of schools in Herefordshire:

When the *business* of the day has drawn to a close, the *pleasures* of the evening commence. The inexperienced lad and lass, with the fruits of their last year's labours in their pockets, are naturally led for refreshment to the neighbouring public-house. The place is filled to suffocation with visitors—all in the hey-day of youth—most without moral control, and all without the control of masters, or betters, or parents, or elders in life. To the stupefying effects of tobacco are added the intoxicating consequences of deleterious beer and spirits, and the maddening results of dancing and music. Each female selects her male companion for the evening, whose duty it is to see her to her distant home at the close of the amusements in the darkness of the night. Decency forbids me from entering into further details, and I cannot picture to you the proceedings of the night to its close. The very devils in hell would delight and be satisfied with the orgies and revels that follow.[85]

The attitude of the participants, as expressed in song at least, was lighter-hearted. Even so, some street ballads were highly critical of farmers. Both 'We Will not Stop Again'[86] and 'Country Hirings' date from the early 1840s. The latter, which remained in oral circulation until the twentieth century, recalls some of the complaints made by Clare and Cobbett:

> The farmer and the servant together they used for to dine,
> But now they are in the parlour with their pudding, beef and wine,
> The master and the mistress, their sons and daughters all alone,
> And they will eat the beef, and you may pick the bone.[87]

In England, criticism of farmers is on the whole sharper in street ballads than in songs circulating orally, which is surprising, since farm-workers are quite capable of expressing themselves with considerable vehemence. To give just one example, I happened to speak in 1971 to John McCarthy, a herdsman and general worker of Tile Hill, Warwickshire. At the age of 45, after working for a particular employer for fifteen years, he had been dismissed without a stated reason, and been required to vacate his tied house within a month. 'One minute they're treating you like the family', he said, 'and the next minute they're treating you like an old workhorse that they've had the best years out of. They'd just shoot you, I think, if they had their way.'[88]

Bothy Ballads

In Scotland, songs with this kind of emotional charge abounded in oral tradition. They are known as 'bothy ballads' or 'cornkisters'.[89] In north-east Scotland, especially Aberdeenshire, unmarried farm-workers, hired for six-monthly terms at Whitsun and Martinmas, were lodged in the chaumer (loft above the stable) or bothy (outhouse) on the farm. Their main form of entertainment was instrumental music and singing. The term 'bothy ballad' covers anything which they sang, whereas 'cornkisters' (from the great 'kist', or chest, of corn for the horses on which the men sat, kicking the heels of their boots in time to the music) refers to pieces dealing specifically with farm life. A wide range of Scots songs thus received an airing; but, in an extraordinary explosion of creativity, a repertoire of new songs came into existence to express 'the whole life of the farm servant—the ecstasies of love, the miseries of marriage, the meanness of masters, the greed of mistresses, and above all the pride in the plough'.[90] Among the best known is 'Drumdelgie'. The farm of this name is near Huntly, on the Banff–Aberdeenshire border, and the same name is also used for the farmer. As David Kerr Cameron points out in *The Ballad and the Plough* (1978), the song

authentically catalogues the hurry of the farm winter morning, the feeding and grooming of the horses in the stable, the snatched breakfast with pints (laces) still untied, the sweat that can be wrung from the ploughmen's shirts after an hour or so of manning the barn-mill or corn-dresser as they wait for daylight to let them out to the plough or the carting home of turnips for the feeders' byre.[91]

DRUMDELGIE

There's a fairmer up in Cairnie,
Wha's kent baith far and wide
To be the great Drumdelgie,
Upon sweet Deveronside.

The fairmer o' yon muckle^b toon
He is baith hard and sair,
And the cauldest day that ever blaws
His servants get their share.

At five o'clock we quickly rise
And hurry down the stair;
It's there to corn our horses,
Likewise to straik their hair.
Syne, after working half-an-hour
Each to the kitchen goes,
It's there to get our breakfast,
Which generally is brose.^{c}

We've scarcely got our brose weel supt,
And gi'en our pints^d a tie,
When the forman cries, 'Hallo, my lads!
The hour is drawing nigh'.
At sax o'clock the mull's put on,
To gie us a strait wark;
It tak's four o' us to mak' to her,
Till ye could wring our sark.^{e}

And when the water is put aff,
We hurry doon the stair,
To get some quarters through the fan
Till daylicht does appear.
When daylicht does begin to peep,
And the sky begins to clear,
The forman he cries out, 'My lads,
Ye'll stay nae langer here!
There's sax o' you'll gae to the ploo,
And twa will drive the neeps,^{f}
And the owson^g they'll be after you
Wi' strae raips^h roun' their queets'.^{i}

But when that we wer gyaun furth,
And turnin' out to yoke,
The snaw dank^j on sae thick and fast
That we were like to choke.
The frost had been sea very hard,
The ploo she wadna go;
And sae our cairting days commenced
Amang the frost and snow.

^{b} big farm ^{c} oatmeal and water ^{d} laces ^{e} shirt ^{f} turnips ^{g} oxen
^{h} straw ropes ^{i} ankles ^{j} came down

Our horses being but young and sma'
The shafts they didna fill,
And they aft required the saiddler[k]
To pull them up the hill.
But we will sing our horses' praise,
Though they be young and sma',
They far outshine the Broadland's anes
That gang sae full and draw.

Sae fare ye weel, Drumdelgie,
Far I maun gang awa';
Sae fare ye weel, Drumdelgie,
Your weety weather and a'.
Sae fareweel, Drumdelgie,
I bid ye a' adieu;
I leave ye as I got ye—
A maist unceevil crew.[92]

Trade Unions

The farm-workers of the north-east of Scotland, like their fellows in East
Anglia, had a secret society known as the 'Horseman's Word', which
Hamish Henderson has described as 'a kind of cross between a farm
servant freemasonry, a working class Hellfire Club, and a "primitive
rebel" trade union'.[93] They also made various attempts to form trade
unions proper. As early as 1872 in Scotland, there were demands for
improved conditions, shorter hours, increased pay, and the replacement of
hiring fairs by a system of regular monthly wages. In the same year,
150,000 of the 650,000 farm-workers in England flocked to join the new
National Agricultural Labourers' Union. At the inaugural conference one
delegate remarked: 'Sir, this be a blessed day: this 'ere Union be the
Moses to lead us poor men up out of Egypt.'[94] The biblical imagery was
familiar to men inspired by the oratory of Joseph Arch (1826–1919), the
Methodist lay preacher who was one of the prime movers in the formation
of the union in Warwickshire. He was the son of a shepherd, and
remembered as a 'little chap' his father's wages of between eight and ten
shillings a week in the 1830s. At the time poaching was 'so prevalent that it
is hardly an exaggeration to say that every man you met was a poacher'.[95]
(Arch was still taking issue with the game laws forty years later, when he
testified before a select committee of the House of Commons in 1873.)
His first employment, like that of Cobbett and Jude the Obscure, was bird-
scaring. He was 9 years old, and the pay was 4*d.* for a twelve-hour day. At

[k] whip.

13 he was ploughing; then he was a stable-lad at 8s. a week, and by the age of 16 he was working as a mower, at 1s. 6d. a day. When he was 21, he was a sort of contractor for mowing, hedging, and hurdle-making, and employed up to twenty-five men.

The steady improvement in Arch's fortunes might have led him to side with other employers, but he remembered his origins too well for that. The measure of independence he had achieved enabled him to champion the labourers, and when a group of them approached him for help in forming a union, he readily agreed. A campaign song quickly emerged, written by 'E.R.' of Harbury, to the tune (now apparently lost) of 'Winkey Wam':

> The Farm Labourers of South Warwickshire
> Have not had a rise for many a year,
> Although bread has often been dear,
> But now they've formed a Union.
> *The Union, the Union,*
> *There's nothing like the Union;*
> *So if you want to have your rights,*
> *Then come and join the Union.*[96]

The union, in what came to be called 'the revolt of the field', achieved marked success, and average wages rose by 20 per cent, to 14 shillings a week. However, in 1874, the prices of farm produce began to fall, and wages with them. Strikes ensued. Shepherds and waggoners declined to join them, since they were paid a shilling a week more than other farm-workers. After the great lock-out of 1874, the union was broken. Five years later it was down to 20,000 members; and after a steady decline, it ceased to exist in 1896. In the meantime, although Arch had been triumphantly elected to Parliament (in 1885), the labourers had 'returned to their age-old submissiveness'.[97] The phrase is strange, especially coming from such writers as Cole and Postgate, and fresh attempts to organize farm-workers were only a few years away.

Both Arch's union and its successor sustained the struggle by songs, which featured prominently at meetings. There were a few pieces, such as 'The Farmer's Boy', from the traditional repertoire. Some new songs were cast in traditional form: 'Come all you bold fellows that follow the plough' is the opening of a Somerset union song which ends: 'May God bless our hero, the brave Joseph Arch.'[98] Most were written to hymn tunes like the Old Hundredth ('The Labourer's Prayer', by one Benjamin Britten) or to the tunes of popular songs like 'Sammy Slap, the Bill Sticker' ('The Great Unpaid') and 'Old Uncle Ned' ('The Lock-out').[99] Many of these appeared in a booklet of eighteen *Songs for Singing at Agricultural Labourers'*

Meetings published by Arch's union, and were reissued in revised form in 1909 as the *National Agricultural and Rural Workers' Union Song Book*. At least one of the items from the first edition, 'My Master and I' (see illustration),[100] was issued as a ballad-sheet.

As agricultural trade unionism declined after the defeat of 1874, farm-workers emigrated in their thousands, or moved to the towns. The process had begun long before 1874, but accelerated thereafter. In 1851 agriculture employed a quarter of males over 20, but by the end of the century the proportion of males aged 14 and over in agriculture had sunk to less than a tenth. Joseph Arch declined into old age and dependence on the bottle. Ironically, the public house in his native village of Barford now bears his name. The little house in which he lived, inherited from his father, of which Arch was so proud, still stands opposite the church, where as a boy he peeped through the keyhole to see what happened at a communion service:

First, up walked the squire to the communion rails; the farmers went up next; then up went the tradesmen, the shopkeepers, the wheelwright, and the blacksmith; and then, the very last of all, went the poor agricultural labourers in their smock frocks. They walked up by themselves; nobody else knelt with them; it was as if they were unclean—and at that sight the iron entered straight into my poor little heart and remained fast embedded there.[101]

Arch, his peccadilloes forgotten, is now held in loyal affection in his village, and is regarded beyond it as one of the pioneers of the trade union movement. The farming slump in the 1930s was as bad as anything Arch had known. He would probably have considered 'Misery Farm' flippant, but the song summed up the feelings of many:

> We're miserable, oh so miserable,
> Down on Misery Farm.
> So are the animals, so are the vegetables,
> Down on Misery Farm.
> The hens won't lay, we can't make hay,
> We work all day and get no pay.
> We're miserable, so miserable,
> Down on Misery Farm.[102]

Recent Developments

George Orwell heard this in Kent in the 1930s, sung by hop-pickers.[103] Orwell had a close knowledge of the hardships of working on the land, but in *1984* he nevertheless used the countryside as a symbol of quintessential England. During the twenty years leading up to Orwell's fatidic date,

farming enjoyed unprecedented success in England, combined with
equally unprecedented criticism of its massive transformation of the
landscape, which has been characterized as 'the theft of the
countryside'.[104] Paradoxically, more and more people are wishing to live in
the countryside; in the past decade the process of counter-urbanization
has reduced the population of every British city with more than a quarter
of a million inhabitants except Plymouth. Some cities have declined
dramatically: Glasgow by 15 per cent, Manchester by 17 per cent, and
London by 10 per cent. At the same time, the populations of Cornwall,
Somerset, Norfolk, Powys, and the highlands and islands of Scotland have
all grown by 10 per cent.

Another paradox is that country work, now heavily mechanized and
highly productive (too productive in some respects, as the grain mountain
testifies), is still among the lowest paid. Anton Lagzdins, a Lincolnshire
farm-worker, wrote to me in 1986:

I was brought up on my father's smallholding, learning all agricultural skills as I
grew up, progressing to part-time work on local farms during school holidays and
eventually going to work the land full time. My early years of employment on farms
were enjoyable but the older I get the more I realise that I have to get out of the
industry if I am ever to achieve a decent standard of living. My wife and I have
recently bought a derelict cottage and have nearly completed renovation after two
years' hard slog. We hope to leave our tied cottage home of twelve years as soon as
I can find regular alternative work.

He also expresses himself in the song 'Shiny Dew':

People think my life is clean and easy,
All's provided and the rest is free.
If every picture turned out just as painted
Everything would be all right with me.
Give me green, give me blue,
Starlit skies, and moonlight too.
Give me trees, and give me water,
Every morning shiny dew.

But cold winds blow the fields of love and labour;
Diesel fumes and dust are all I breathe.
My just reward is merely an existence,
Although the mouths are countless that I feed.

I don't envy all the fruits that people savour:
Just one or two would fill the need in me.
The simple things in life are all I ask for:
That doesn't mean to say that I receive.[105]

2

THE TOWN

OLD NED'S A RARE STRONG CHAP

[Like a fine old Eng - lish
gen - tle - man, One of ___ the ol - den time.]

When I liv'd at whoam wi' feyther and mother I ne'er had any fun,
They made me negur*a* from morn to neet so I thowt fro' them I'd run;
Then my brass I sav'd for a spree, Manchester came deawn to see,
And don'd mysel' in my Sunday duds, and set off reet full of glee.

a labour?

To th'Piccadilly first I went and then into the teawm I coom,
And there I seed fine things and look'd at the Infirmary moon[b];
And there I seed such dandies, by gum they made me mad,
They made such game o' my country talk 'cause I wur a country lad.

A rosy cheek'd lady then I met, eh! such a dashing blade;
Hoo[c] ask'd me if I'd walk wi' her, and hold 'n my arm she laid.
Thinks I, hoo's fawn in love wi' me, it s'll be a decent job,
But we had not walk'd aboon twenty yards ere I catched her fist i' my fob.

To a factory next I went, I ne'er had been i' one before;
There were twisting thrums and reels and strops, I'm sure were mony a
　　score.
They said owd Ned turn'd every wheel, and every wheel a strop;
By gum, thowt I to myself, owd Ned's a rare strong chap.

To the owd church then one Monday morn to see folks wed I went,
And tho' I did no gawm beawt wur,[d] to learn it I wur bent;
What creawds o' folk wur there, a mon hit me with a stick,
And said, 'Young man, doff your hat, I'd have you do it quick'.

Then I stood up among the ruck.[e] Thinks I, What comes on next?
So throng they wur and jumbled so, and they wur aw perplex'd;
For whither a mon geet hold o' the reet lass I think he could na tell,
I wur shov'd and jamm'd among 'em so, I'd near been wed mysen.

Then after this to the play I went, where a mon come eawt to sing,
And he squeek'd and squall'd and quaver'd so, he made aw the place to ring.
Some said that he sung weel, and some did grunt and groan;
Says I, I'll beat such singing as this, so I sung Bob and Joan.

When aw wur o'er and done, and aw the folk come eawt,
Away I went to the Blackymoor's Yead and geet a gill[f] o' stout;
And there I seed such game, by gum I'd like to ha'e stay'd,
But my brass aw being done I whistled whoam again.[1]

Despite its northern origin, the earliest printed version of this ballad
seems to be that issued by William Wright of Birmingham in the 1820s or
1830s. It must date from after 1825, when a gas-lit clock—'the Infirmary
moon'—was installed at the hospital in Manchester's Piccadilly. By the
same year, 20,000 power-looms were working in the town, which explains
the episode of the steam-driven factory. 'Owd Ned' was the affectionate
name given to the steam-engine. Oral versions circulating in Lancashire
and Yorkshire use the tune of 'The Fine Old English Gentleman', and
move the action to Oldham and Leeds respectively. Although the factory is
still mentioned, the chief event is now the church visit, no longer for a

　　　　　[b] clock　　[c] She　　[d] know what it was　　[e] crowd　　[f] half-pint

wedding but for an ordinary service; and the opportunity is taken to satirize High Anglican ritual from a Nonconformist standpoint.

Countrymen in Town

A common element in all versions is the canny countryman's look at the town through fresh eyes. This theme has a long history, and it became increasingly popular during the nineteenth century, as urbanization progressed. In 1801 only 20 per cent of the English lived in towns; in 1901, 70 per cent. The country bumpkin and the outlandish sailor were regarded as fair game by the sharp people of the big towns. The conflicts which ensued seem to have sold ballads to both parties. One side might enjoy its triumph, while the other took its defeat as a salutary lesson; but next time the positions might be reversed.

In one piece a quick-witted London urchin hears John Hodge, who is from the country (with a name like that, he could hardly be from anywhere else), musing aloud that he will hide his money, a guinea, in his mouth for fear of pickpockets. The boy immediately calls out that Hodge has robbed him. A crowd gathers, judges that the boy is telling the truth, and awards him the guinea.[2] A Yorkshireman in London takes better precautions than Hodge: he sews a fish-hook into his pocket, and a woman who attempts to rob him leaves behind her diamond ring.[3] This may not be so fanciful as it appears. An epidemic of pickpocketing in Birmingham rag market in the 1930s was countered by people lining their pockets with fish-hooks, albeit with the purpose of enabling police to arrest anyone with bloody fingers. According to another ballad-sheet, a Birmingham boy in London goes to the theatre and sees the king, but finds 'two bad shillings' in his change. He recoups his loss by giving the coins to a woman in payment for her favours. In a public house he then scornfully rejects the offer of a gold ring for ten shillings, 'For a Birmingham lad knows brass from gold'.[4]

The enticements offered were frequently sexual. In a piece by Thomas Wilson, Rough Joe comes from the country to seek a wife in Manchester. He finds 'a girl with a sweet loving smile', but soon loses her, along with his watch and his money, and departs, resolving to marry a country girl.[5] A Scots counterpart, a farm-labourer called Jock Hawk, picks up a woman in Glasgow, and quickly finds himself bereft not only of money, but also of his clothes:

> They've ta'en frae me my watch and chain,
> My spleuchan[g] and my knife;
> I wonder that they didn't tak'
> My little spunk o' life.[6]

[g] tobacco pouch

Songs relating similar misfortunes are common. In 'Bumpkin's Journey to London' a countryman is befriended by a woman acting, he thinks, 'out of good nature':

> She pull'd off my cloaths from my foot to my head,
> And begod while they dried I laid down in bed,
> But alas what she did while I took my repose
> The baggage hopp'd off with my money and cloaths.
>
> In distress and reduced to a start so forlorn,
> Was naked and cold as a baby just born;
> I roar'd out for help but no help to be had,
> They seeing me naked they swore I was mad.[7]

For much of the nineteenth century, prostitution and robbery went hand in hand. In 1817 a parish constable said that in one of the brothels of St Giles's, London, 'there was a gentleman robbed about a week or a fortnight since of all his clothes and his watch; they left him stark naked, and the girl was stopped with his clothes, and brought down to the watch-house'.[8] Ballads give warnings of such things, and also show how to turn the tables. 'The Rigs of London Town', widely diffused on broadsides and in oral tradition, describes how a countryman gains the advantage:

> Her lips they were so sweet and red,
> I cuddled and kissed her there in bed;
> And while she lay there fast asleep
> Out of the bed then I did creep.
>
> I stole her watch, her silken gown,
> Her silver snuff-box and five pound;
> Away I crept into the night,
> Taking the lot for my delight.[9]

For a visitor, the unfamiliarity of towns was compounded by the hostility of their inhabitants. On arriving in London from County Clare, Pat Molloy is confronted by a cockney 'with a donkey selling delph' who refuses to let him pass, and insultingly invites him, 'pointing over to the ass', to speak to his brother. Pat pretends to whisper in the animal's ear and drops in a quid of tobacco, which makes it jump about so much that the cart is upset and all the earthenware broken. The cockney has Pat taken in charge, and the magistrate demands to know what he said to the donkey. His answer causes the case to be dismissed:

> I told the ass, says Paddy, he had got the wrong address.
> Noble Ireland was no longer in distress;
> We got rid of all the landlords and the country to ourselves we had;
> And when the animal heard the news, bejeepers, he went mad.[10]

On this occasion, not only does the countryman come out best, but he triumphantly scores a political point.

Ian Macdonald is more conformist. He is one of the many thousands driven out of the highlands and islands of Scotland by land clearances, and he finds Glasgow all the more disorientating because his grasp of the English language is shaky. A fittingly macaronic song, with English and Gaelic alternating, tells his story. It was written by 'an island man', probably from Skye.

> When I came to Glasgow first,
> Am mach gu tir nan gall,[h]
> I was like a man adrift,
> Air iomrall's dol air chall;[i]
> The noise it seemed like thunder,
> Chuir e tuaineallaich 'nam cheann,[j]
> And oftentimes I wished I was,
> Air ais an tir nam beann.[k]

Some people make fun of the newcomer's outlandish ways, and try to steal his money. In the ensuing fight, Macdonald gives a good account of himself. The policeman who stops the fight turns out to be from Portree in the Isle of Skye himself. He mildly reprimands Macdonald, and gives him advice on adjusting to city life. The outcome is happy:

> Thug mi taing gu cridheil dha,[l]
> And went on my way,
> Tha iomadh bliadhn' o'n latha sin,[m]
> I'm in Glasgow till this day:
> 'S aithne dhomh gach cuil a th'ann,[n]
> I know my Glasgow well,
> 'S ann an coibhneas mor ri m' choimhearsnaich,[o]
> I ever more shall dwell.[11]

Town Sights

Despite their disadvantages, towns exerted a powerful attraction. A ballad entitled 'The Praise of London'[12] appeared as early as 1632, but the capital's fascination is perennial. In the 1830s 'a poor country lad' up to see 'The London Sights' marvels at the fashions: ladies with skirts to the ground, huge bonnets like 'a coal-scuttle stuck on the head of a poker', and large bags carried over the shoulder like a cabbage-net; men sporting monocles, high collars, high-waisted frock-coats, and wide trousers, 'For.

[h] Out to a foreign land   [i] Losing my way   [j] It made my head dizzy   [k] Back in the land of the hills   [l] I thanked him heartily   [m] There is many a year since then   [n] I know every corner of it   [o] In amity with my neighbours

the gentlemen's waists are a-top of their backs, / And their large cossac trowsers fit just like to sacks'.[13] 'The Treats of London', written in 1815, sets out at some length the entertainments available, from Bartholomew Fair to Vauxhall Gardens, and from cricket (mentioning 'Lord's Cricket Ground that is new': it was opened in 1814) to prize-fighting and cock-fighting.[14] The Tower of London is often featured. Lincolns Inn Fields elicits from one visitor the remark: 'Do you call these fields? Indeed, says I, They ain't like the fields in Somersetshire.'[15] 'The Sights of London', issued in the 1840s, mentions 'little Vic's big palace ... the wholesale manufactory for little kings and queens'. This sheet, with its references to the new Nelson's column, a panorama of the Chinese War, and the rebuilding of the Houses of Parliament, presents a lively evocation of the capital. It concludes with a sly allusion, comprehensible only to an insider, to one of the haunts of the most lowly, sordid prostitutes, who could be bought for a few pence:

> You can see our Halls of Science, you can see our Fancy Fairs,
> You can see our Panorama if you go to Leicester Square.
> For that's the spot for fashion, for bustle, noise and gally,[P]
> You'll see a lot of foreign puppys, but you won't see Cranbourn Alley.[16]

People were drawn to the towns by fairs and sporting events (for which, see Chapter 5), but even the everyday bustle of town life proved exciting. The teeming life of the streets features over and over again in street ballads. 'The Humours of London', which probably dates from the 1790s, deals with itinerant vendors:

> When I to London first came in,
> How I began to gape and stare!
> The cries they kick'd up such a din,
> Fresh lobsters, dust, and wooden ware;
> A damsel lovely and black ey'd,
> Tript thro' the streets and sweetly cry'd,
> Buy my live sprats! buy my live sprats!
> A youth on t'other side the way,
> With coarser lungs did echoing say,
> Buy my live sprats![17]

There are sheets from the 1820s with self-explanatory titles like 'The Comical Streets of London'[18] and 'Shop Windows, or, Amusements of London'.[19] Catnach's 'How to get a Living; or, The Rigs of London' emphasizes the cash nexus:

[P] bad language

So to conclude and end my ditty,
These are the rigs of town, and city,
Every thing is very funny
Any thing can be bought for money,
Money will banish care and strife, sir,
Money will buy a blooming wife, sir,
For money you can purchase plenty,
But money won't find a maid of twenty.
So now good folks my song is quite done,
These are the rigs, and sprees of London.[20]

Half a century later, the vogue continued, with 'Life in the Streets of London'. Sprats were still on sale, at a penny a plateful. There was a quack doctor and a man selling 'One hundred and fifty songs . . . For a farthing'. Other street folk included cabmen, busmen, policemen, and 'unfortunate girls'.[21] Mention of the latter reminds one that there were 80,000 professional prostitutes in the streets of London in the 1860s, a figure which excludes many thousands of amateurs known as 'dolly mops' and of those kept in luxury in private apartments. Prostitution was not confined to London, of course. Provincial ballads such as 'Sunday Night', which was issued in several towns in the mid-nineteenth century, frequently mention it. The Leeds version runs:

Above the barracks there you will meet,
With naughty girls from Regent Street.
Who up to your elbows close will steer,
And whisper softly, 'Good night my dear'.
And if with them you dare to stop,
They'll gammon[q] you to stand a drop,
And they'll diddle you out of your cash all right,
In —— Lane on a Sunday Night.[22]

Less venial love features in 'Saturday Night', which appeared, suitably adapted, in both Sheffield and Birmingham. Crowds of people buying and selling, street entertainers, working people enjoying a precious moment of leisure: everything contributes to the bustle and excitement.

Then maids with their baskets are to and fro walking
In Shambles to bargain with butchers for meat;
While some ballad singers so slowly are walking,
And warbling so sweetly their lays to the street.

q persuade

> There's calendars crying, and people 'come buying'
> Around this old fellow in crowds such a sight;
> For as suits your palates, confessions and ballads,
> Are all at your service on Saturday night.
>
> Of hammers and files no more of their din is,
> Round the door of the workhouse the workmen are ranged,
> While the masters their banknotes and snug little guineas
> Are counting and strutting about to get changed.
> Having reckon'd they ne'er stop, but jog to the beer-shop,
> Where the fumes of tobacco and stingo invite;
> And the oven inhabits a store of Welsh rabbits
> To feast jovial fellows on Saturday night.[23]

Equivalent scenes in Manchester are celebrated in 'Victoria Bridge on a Saturday Night',[24] and its neighbour has a different piece, 'Oldham on a Saturday Night'. 'Owdham Streets at Dinner Time', dating from about 1830, shows the factory-workers coming out for their midday break:

> In Owdham streets at dinner time
> The workfolk how they flock,
> Just as you hear the church clock chime
> Each day at half-past twelve o'clock.
> In such a hurry crowds you meet
> At the turn of every street;
> You'd think all t'world, as I'm a sinner,
> Wur come to Owdham o' getting their dinner.[25]

Town Work

In a later ballad, 'Oldham Workshops' (1857), the archetypal countryman wanders round the town, remarking on the various sights. Like his counterpart in 'Old Ned's a Rare Strong Chap', he sees and marvels at the steam-engine: 'But then owd Neddy engine I think he beats the whole, / He's fond o summut warm sure, for they feed him up a coal.'[26] Of all the attractions which towns afforded, the greatest were the prospects for employment. At one time each town had its dominant trade, and song-writers were well aware of it. 'The English Rover' (1800–2), for example, provides a catalogue of towns, trades, and sexual adventures. There is button-making in Birmingham, weaving at Coventry, shoe-making at Nottingham, lace at Aylesbury, stay-making at Cambridge, stocking-weaving at Leicester, and many more.[27] In other ballads, usually entitled 'Jack of All Trades', the emphasis shifts from different towns to trades within a particular town—Bristol, Birmingham, Liverpool, Dublin and others, no doubt. The theme of wandering is retained in first lines like 'I am a jolly roving blade', and the verbal dexterity of the verses seems to have made them very popular.[28] 'Dublin Jack of All Trades' remained in oral circulation until the twentieth century:

> In College Green a banker was—and in Smithfield a drover,
> In Britain Street a waiter and in George's Street a glover;
> On Ormond Quay I sold old books—in King Street a nailer,
> In Townsend Street a carpenter and in Ringsend a sailor.
>
> In Cole's Lane a jobbing butcher—in Dame Street a tailor,
> In Moore Street a chandler and on the Coombe a weaver.
> In Church Street I sold old ropes—on Redmond's Hill a draper,
> In Mary Street sold 'bacco pipes—in Bishop Street a Quaker.[29]

Innovations in transport also brought people into the towns, both as workers in the construction and operation of new systems and as users when they were in place. The opening first of canals then of railways was saluted in celebratory songs. John Freeth, himself a shareholder, greeted the opening of Birmingham's first canal in 1769 with:

> This day for our new navigation
> We banish all care and vexation.
> The sight of the barges each honest heart glads
> And the merriest of mortals are Birmingham lads.[30]

'The Croydon Canal' (1809) was 'written by a Gentleman', 'most zealously and ably sung by one of the Proprietors', and published in *The Times*.[31] Such pieces were not aimed at ordinary people, who would be digging canals, not investing in them. 'Paddy on the Canal' (1847) is concerned with 'the art of navigation' only in the sense of handling 'the pick and the shovel, / Likewise the wheelbarrow and spade', but 'Paddy on the Railway', of about the same time, deals with an Irishman's adventures, or misadventures, as a passenger.[32]

Railways were enormously successful. As early as 1851 they were carrying 80 million passengers a year. Thirty years later the figure was 600 million, and by 1901, 1,100 million. Initially, though, attitudes were ambivalent. There was concern over loss of jobs in the coaching trade, and the potential of the new system was not always recognized, owing to the unpopularity of its supporters. When the line from Liverpool to Manchester was opened in 1830, people took the opportunity to demonstrate. M. Sturge Gretton wrote:

My grandfather who was . . . one of the guests of the Liverpool and Manchester Railway on the occasion of the running of their first passenger train, used to recount how the Duke of Wellington, who was also a guest, became plastered in mud in his efforts to shield the ladies from the filth that the populace, ranged along the line, was flinging at the travellers.[33]

At Manchester, Fanny Kemble related how tricolour flags were displayed, and how there was hissing and booing:

The vast concourse of people who had assembled to witness the arrival of the successful travellers, was of the lowest order of mechanics and artisans, among whom great distress and a dangerous spirit of discontent with the Government at that time prevailed. Groans and hisses greeted the carriageful of influential personages in which the Duke of Wellington sat. . . . High above the grim and grimy crowd of smiling faces a loom had been erected at which sat a tattered, starved-looking weaver, evidently set there as a representative man, to protest against the triumph of machinery, and the gain and glory which the wealthy Liverpool and Manchester men were likely to derive from it.[34]

Nevertheless, from its inception, the Manchester and Liverpool railway carried twice as many passengers as had the old coaches. The eponymous hero of a series of ballads by Alexander Wilson (1803–46), including 'Johnny Green's Trip fro' Owdam to see the Liverpool Railway', recognized at least one advantage for working people:

> For weavers then to th'wareheause soon,
> Will ta'e their cuts[r] by twelve at noon,
> Besoide th'saveation o' their shoon,
> They'll noan so oft get bated[s].

Johnny and his wife, Nan, are so keen to see the railway—this is in 1831 or 1832–that they sell a sucking pig to raise 'ready brass' for the expedition. After walking to Manchester, they see the train arrive from Liverpool, and are amazed at its speed, which seems 'next to floyink'. They are shown the coach in which Wellington travelled, which prompts this comment:

> Eawt Nan said tey'd ha' sarv't him reet
> To ha' dragg'd him on through dry and weet,
> For hoo'd a ridden him day an' neight,
> If he'd naw teyn off some taxes.

By this time their money has run low, so they are unable to ride on the train as they had intended. They pass an inn, the Star in Deansgate, and notice the coachmen looking blue: 'Aw'm sure their jaws han nowt to do, / Sin th'Liverpoo Railway gaited' [began]. After viewing the infirmary clock, they return home. The political situation, together with their fear of

---

[r] lengths of cloth   [s] fined (for late delivery)

cholera and the resurrection men, give them cause for concern, but Nan suggests that they can use the railway to try their luck elsewhere:

> There's weary wark, aw understand,
> They're burkink deaud folk all o'er th'lond,
> What's wur, th' Reform Bill's at a stond,
> An' th'cholera's coom by th'mail road.
> They'n feort eawr Nan to deoth these chaps,
> Hoo says, 'Eh! John, aw'll wesh meh caps;
> Do thee lay deawn thea looms an' traps,
> We'n cut eawr stick by th'railroad'.[35]

Changes in Towns

The growth, transformation, and industrialization of towns which went hand in hand with the development of canals and railways gave rise to mixed feelings. In a song of 1828, a Birmingham man returning home after a twenty-year absence finds his town so altered that he declares: 'I can't find Brummagem.' Among the changes he notices is an increase in the number of factories:

> I remember one John Growse,
> A buckle-maker in Brummagen.
> He built himself a country house
> To be out of the smoke of Brummagem,
> But though John's country house stands still
> The town itself has walked uphill;
> Now he lives beside a smoky mill
> In the middle of the streets of Brummagem.[36]

'Manchester's Improving Daily', another song of about the same time, is far more positive in its attitude to change, on the other hand.

> This Manchester's a rare fine place,
> For trade and other such like movements;
> What town can keep up such a race,
> As ours has done for prime improvements
> For of late what sights of alterations,
> Both streets and buildings changing stations,
> That country folks, as they observe us,
> Cry out, 'Laws! pickle and presarve us!'
> *Sing hey, sing ho, sing hey down, gaily,*
> *Manchester's improving daily.*

Reference is made yet again to the infirmary clock, and also to the widening of thoroughfares and the macadamizing of their surfaces, to steam-power and spinning-jennies, and to the impending introduction of 'steam coaches' to Liverpool and elsewhere. The final verse mentions the ship canal, the first parliamentary bill for which was defeated in 1825:

> Thus at improvements on we go,
> We're ever trying at invention;
> Now objects starting up to view,
> And catching all our spare attention;
> Then the ship canal, and all such scenes, sir,
> Tho' some may call them fancy's dreams, sir,
> They'll all succeed, you need not fret, sir,
> As soon as John Bull's out of debt, sir.[37]

A note of bitterness comes into a later version, published under the title 'The Scenes of Manchester I Sing' after the opening of the railway and the death of Huskisson during the proceedings:

> The scenes of Manchester I sing,
> Where the arts and sciences are flourishing;
> Where smoke from factory chimneys bring
> The air so black, so thick, and nourishing;
> Where factories that by steam are gated[t],
> And children work half suffocated,
> It makes me mad to hear folk, really,
> Cry Manchester's improving daily.
>
> There's steam loom weavers, and cotton spinners
> Have sixty minutes to get their dinners,
> And then to make the people thrive, O,
> They're rung up in a morning at four and five, O.
> Then if you get a drop on Sunday
> To get yourselves in 'tiff for Monday,
> The raw lobster[u] pops you in the Bailey[v],
> Since Manchester's improving daily.[38]

There is a strong feeling of nostalgia in 'Manchester's an Altered Town', of which John Harkness of Preston issued two separate editions in the 1840s, and also an adaptation covering Liverpool.

> Once on a time this good old town was nothing but a village,
> Of husbandry, and farmers too, whose time was spent in tillage;
> But things are altered very much, such building now allotted is,
> It rivals far, and soon will leave behind the great Metropolis.
> *O dear O, Manchester's an altered town, O dear O.*[39]

　　　　　　[t] driven　　　[u] policeman　　　[v] prison

Town Life

Many of the changes mentioned in later verses—the opening of the Garden of Zoology, the replacement of the old bridge by Victoria Bridge, the reorganization of the police, the institution of a borough council—took place in 1838 or 1839. There is a hint of John Clare's desolation at the transformation of the countryside by enclosure, but the mood is long-suffering, almost resigned. It is in contrast with the anger at squalid living standards in Manchester and other towns expressed by Engels in *The Condition of the Working Class in England* (1845) at the time when such ballads were circulating. Housing features in few songs, although the enormous popularity of the sentimental 'Home, Sweet Home' shows the deep longing for a secure, stable home which pervaded Victorian times. Rents are mentioned among items of household expenditure in a series of sheets dealing with family finances. The sums involved in the weekly budget increase in successive editions: twelve shillings, fifteen, sixteen, eighteen, one pound one, one pound two, and finally, twenty-five shillings. The last version was the most popular, and over a dozen editions of 'How Five and Twenty Shillings was Expended in a Week' were issued, with minor variations, in Birmingham, Bristol, Leeds, London, Nottingham, Preston, and no doubt elsewhere.[40] According to John Burnett, the wage of a semi-skilled urban worker in the mid-nineteenth century was between fifteen shillings and a pound per week, while the 'comfort line' was reached at 'something over £1 a week, depending on the size of the family'.[41] The ballad's budget of twenty-five shillings thus represents the aspirations of its readers and singers, more than the reality of their situation, but its minutely detailed references to everyday matters nevertheless provides a vivid picture of town life.

Not only the cost, but the quantity and quality, of food were constant preoccupations. Both the giving of short measure and the adulteration of food, especially bread, are castigated in a series of ballads like 'A New Touch of the Times' (see illustration),[42] which can be dated 1774 from its reference to the lord-mayorship of John Wilkes. During the French and Napoleonic wars, complaints about swindling, profiteering, and the imposition of high prices intensified. Those buying up food so as to bring about an increase in prices were especially hated. 'The Badger's Downfall' (1800) protests:

> There's a gang called hucksters that ride up and down
> Forestalling the markets in capital towns,
> They buy all the butter, potatoes, and greens,
> And the greatest of villains is call'd the best man.

There's another curs'd tribe called badgers of corn,
Much better for us had they never been born;
They buy up the grain with their ill-gotten gold,
When they sell it again, they receive double fold.[43]

A similar piece entitled 'Forestalling done over' was published in Newcastle between 1811 and 1815:

Come, all you poor people, I pray lend an ear,
And of the roguish Badgers you quickly shall hear;
It's their daily study, and long they've contriv'd
To raise our provisions, and starve us alive.
So you Farmers, and Badgers, and Millers, I'm sure
You all deserve hanging for starving the poor.

There's the farmers and badgers and forestalling crew
They all stand considering to know what to do.
In raising the grain they will all play their part,
But the D——l will take them in his packet-cart.[44]

'British Spectator' (1801), with its chorus of 'Since knavery is now all in
fashion, / And roguery is just in its prime', proposes an even more drastic
solution:

Forestallers in each market town do increase,
Of cattle and corn, of butter and cheese,
The poor to relieve, and the land to redress,
Send one half o'er to Botany, and hang up the rest.[45]

Many sheets castigated those felt to be responsible for the plight of the
poor. They were not specifically directed to an urban audience, of course,
and 'brother thrasher' is addressed in

MEDLEY'S REMARKS ON THE TIMES

Ye Gentlemen of England, I pray you all draw near,
The distress of our country you quickly shall hear,
'Tis concerning the year eighteen hundred and nine,
The people complain of being such hard times.
The world's as full of roguery as a poet's full of rhymes,
'Tis lords and other great men make such hard times.

They still keep continually to enclose the land,
So that the poor farmer cannot it withstand;
The wine drinking gentlemen have got all our right,
And the poor farmers is ruined quite.

There's many a poor man that did keep a cow,
Flock of geese, two or three pigs, and an old sow;
His rights are ta'en from him, he's nothing at all
So now on the Parish his family must fall.

Poor tradesmen in Yorkshire, their case it is bad,
They're out of employment, no work to be had,
By the stoppage of trade, they're in poverty too,
Many hundreds and thousands for soldiers do go.

They say 'tis the war that makes things so dear,
Provisions, tea, sugar, soap, tobacco, and beer,
I believe it is a trade all the world o'er,
But the heaviest burden is laid on the poor.

We have nothing but roguery I vow and protest,
Bakers, Butchers, and millers, as well as the rest,
They will cheat you with flour and blow up your meat
And if it stinks a little, they say it's quite sweet.

O how the shop-keepers palaver and cant,
Saying ladies and gentlemen what do you want?
We have fine congou*w* tea, sugar white and brown,
They'll cheat you with weight tho' the scales bump down.

There's Swill the landlord he'll cheat you with froth,
And the linen draper will cheat you in cloth,
The shoemaker will clap on an infamous sole,
And the tailor a patch will sew into a hole.

Another gang of vilians ride up and down,
Cornfactors, hucksters and stokers*x* in every town,
Who buy up provisions and all kinds of grain,
And they gain double fold when they sell them again.

By all such rogues as these in our own county,
Our flourishing islands is kept in poverty,
There's nothing but roguery, all cheat that can,
And the greatest of vilians is thought the best man.

So now brother thrasher my song is at an end,
When all rogues are hang'd the times they will mend.
A cart load of halters will scarce be enough,
There's no better doing till Jack Ketch*y* has his due.*46*

---

w cheap   *x* stockpilers   *y* the hangman

Health

According to John Burnett, the adulteration of food 'prevailed in the first half of the nineteenth century to an unprecedented and unsupposed extent, and had far-reaching social, economic and medical consequences'.[47] The first Adulteration of Foods Act was passed only in 1860, and further legislation was needed before the problem was contained. Ballad-writers were well aware of the subject. 'London Adulterations, or, Rogues in Grain, Tea, Coffee, Milk, Beer, Bread, Snuff, Mutton, Pork, Gin, Butter, etc.', which dates from about 1825, is set with delightful irony to the tune of 'The Roast Beef of Old England'.[48] The more simply titled 'Adulterations' of the mid-century anticipates the campaign of our own times against additives:

> Now they say in these go-ahead days I think sirs,
> We scarcely know what we eat or drink sirs,
> Every thing we are obliged to run for,
> But now we are daily taken in and done for;
> For they get up such fine imitations
> By chemical poisons and alterations,
> It would puzzle the deuce to discover a partaker
> Of the right down wholly genuine article.
> *Oh! what swindling imitations*
> *These are, the days of adulterations.*
>
> Now they rarely seemed to have formed a junction,
> To bilk poor people without compulsion[z];
> From a round of beef to a Yarmouth herring,
> Things are anything but what they're appearing,
> For they sell us a pound of sugar so bland, oh,
> And an ounce of that stunning four bob hyson[a],
> It's three parts birch broom, the other part's poison.
>
> .   .   .   .
>
> Leg of Beef soup, do you know what that is?
> Cat's meat's the lean, and candle the far is;
> With salt and pepper, to give it a spice in,
> And just to thicken it they drop a lump of size in.
> The rich plum duff boys love to taste, sirs,
> It's smashed black beetles in coblers' paste, sirs.
> And sausages, oh! you had better eat floor-dust,
> They make them out of red flannel and saw-dust.[49]

---

[z] compunction   [a] four-shilling green tea

A NEW
TOUCH of the TIMES
OR
SUCCESS to TRUE-BLEW.

GOOD People of England I'd have you be wife
Your corn keep at home for yo'r own families
And not let the Farmers fo over us reign,
But pull down the prices of alforts of grain.
CHORUS.
For Wilkes is Lord mayor, & he is head & chief,
Long time youv'e carefs'd him, he'll give us relief
For he and the City are mafter of all,
And he vows that thefe villians they fhall have a fall
  The corn factors they are contriving each day,
To buy up our corn and fend it away;
But they in their Rog—y now are found out, [rout
For Wilkes is Lord Mayor, he'll put them to the
  The miller you know is as bad as the reft,
He does his endeavour the Poor to diftrefs;
His confcience is large, & for Rog—y don't lack,
For out of each bufhel he will fteal a Peck.
  Next in comes the Baker with his Rog-fh tricks,
With his allum & Whiting his flower to mix;
He fays I've borrow'd money, the fum it is great,
But I'll make it up quick by a fhort Weight.
The fhopkeepers are contriving by day & by night,
To cheat the poor it is all their delight; [is big,
And their Weight run fhort till their confcience is
To buy a fkimming difh hat, & a large bufhy Wig
  The butcher drunk home from the alehoufe does
With his fteel by his fide to blow up his Veai; (reel,
But they are all Ro—s, & We will them condemn
For thy'll kill an old EWE and fell it for Lamb.
  The Landlady too in the bar fhe does fit,
With tea & cream, and china compleat;
Such a fpunging old ba—d fure never Was known
If they fee you in liquor they'll fcore two for one.
Then in comes the farmer with his hands full of chink
And he fays brother Rog—s, together let's drink;
Come fill up the bottle each man boldly call
If the poor We can mafter they fhall pay for all.
  So to conclude and make an end
We drink a good health to both King and Queen
Likewife to brave Wilkes our Worthy Lord mayr
He'll pull down the prices of bread meat & beer.

'A New Touch of the Times'.
Street Ballad.

Manchester Royal Infirmary in 1899, showing the celebrated clock.

Victoria Bridge, Manchester, in 1859, seen from Blackfriars Bridge.

Manchester Royal Infirmary in about 1853.

The tone is light-hearted, as befits 'A new Comic Song', but the message is clear enough. Wider questions of public health were often treated in a similar manner.

Problems of health, as of housing, attracted a great deal of attention from radicals and reformers, but made relatively few appearances in balladry. Doctors were regarded with great hostility because of their connection with body-snatching (see Chapter 4), and it took many generations to disperse the opprobrium after the Anatomy Act of 1832 legitimized the acquisition of cadavers. In any case, poor people were more likely to go to a herbalist or a quack doctor. Quack remedies were widely sold, and are mentioned in several of the ballads already mentioned, including 'Victoria Bridge on a Saturday Night':

> If troubled with pthisic, there are doctors with physic,
> With lozenges, boluses, poppies and pills,
> With ointment for drawing, with baccy for chawing,
> Would blister your chops, till you're red in the gills.

Another Manchester sheet, 'Morrison's Wonderful Vegetable Pills', is entirely devoted to what appears to have been a panacea:

> These pills are very wonderful below and up above sir,
> They'll cure a damsel in the sulks or a maiden that's in love sir,
> They will the Cholera Morbus cure and that is very feasible
> They'll cure a dog of the whooping cough or a pig that's got the measles.[50]

The reference to cholera appears flippant, though people sometimes laugh about things in order to avoid crying. Alternatively, it may be a piece of black humour, like today's jokes about Aids. Like the anger evoked by the use of pauper bodies for dissection, the fear of cholera worked at a subpolitical level; but it seems to have contributed to some of the turbulence in towns during epidemics. There were four major outbreaks, some at periods of great social tension. The worst, in 1846–9, killed more than 50,000 people. An earlier epidemic, in 1831–2, inspired 'The Cholera's Coming', to the tune of 'The Campbells are Coming':

> The cholera's coming, oh dear, oh dear,
> The cholera's coming, oh dear!
> To prevent hunger's call
> A kind pest from Bengal
> Has come to feed all
> With the cholera, dear.[51]

'Cholera Humbug, the Arrival and Departure of the Cholera Morbus' contained this speculation:

> Some people say it was a puff,
> It was done to raise the Doctor's stuff,
> And there has now been near enough,
> About the Cholera Morbus.[52]

There is a story that a street vendor who was hawking this, or possibly another similar ballad, in the streets of Bilston 'dropped down in mortal agony' from the disease 'while still giving vocal effect to his wares'.[53] Yet much of the piece deals with the slump then current and with the tension over the Reform Bill between its rejection by the House of Lords in October 1831 and its passage in June 1832 after William IV's famous threat to create more Whig peers. Its treatment of cholera itself is not serious.

The same might be said of a ballad on vaccination issued some forty years later. There were serious epidemics of smallpox, as of cholera, resulting in 35,000 deaths between 1837 and 1840 and 44,000 between 1870 and 1873. Attempts to stem the progress of the disease by a programme of vaccination were greeted by a good deal of opposition. Those against included Joseph Arch. The programme was ridiculed in a ballad entitled 'Are You Vaccinated?', published in 1871. It can be dated precisely because of its reference to the impending marriage of the Marquis of Lorne and Princess Louise, one of Victoria's daughters.

> They'll vaccinate the tories,
> And they'll vaccinate the whigs,
> They'll vaccinate all little boys,
> That associate with prigs[b].
> They'll vaccinate the snobs you know,
> Oh, won't that be a sight,
> They'll vaccinate Johnny of Lorne,
> Upon his wedding night.[54]

Slum Clearance

Despite problems of health and housing, towns continued to grow. Their population, having doubled between 1780 and 1830, doubled again between 1841 and 1901. The slums of the 1920s and 1930s were among the great social problems of their time, and they produced a fierce desire for amelioration. Ewan MacColl, brought up in Salford only a few years after the era described by Robert Roberts in *The Classic Slum* (Manchester, 1971), sang of his affection for it, but also of his anger, in 'Dirty Old Town':

[b] thieves

I'm going to take a good sharp axe,
Shining steel, tempered in the fire,
Going to cut you down, like an old dead tree,
Dirty old town, dirty old town.[55]

Yet the bleak blocks of monolithic high-rise flats which replaced the old
slum houses after the Second World War swept away communities too.
Almost 150 years on, 'They're changing dear old Brummagem' provides a
curious echo to 'I can't find Brummagen':

They're changing dear old Brummagen before our very eyes;
Places that we knew so well are hard to recognise:
In Balsall Heath and Ladywood, in Aston and Newtown,
The blocks of flats are going up, the homes are coming down.

Oh, the old folks miss their neighbours, the friendly doorstep chat;
Life is very different in a fourteenth storey flat.
They've planned a bright new city without a single slum;
They call it redevelopment, but will it still be Brum?

Oh, the Bull Ring is so altered now you've really got to search
To find the only landmark left, St Martin's Parish Church.
They've cleared whole streets of tunnelbacks, destroyed a neighbour-
     hood,
And shifted half the families right out to Chelmsley Wood.[56]

Similar sentiments are expressed in 'The Owl of Oldham'[57] and also,
with reference to the East End of London, in 'See it come down', written
in 1974. In the latter, though, prophetically as it turns out, the author looks
forward to the demise in their turn of the tower blocks:

We was all one like where we lived, wish we was now.
We 'ad debts and dole and kids but we did have neighbours.
Where our street was they wanna build some tombstone tower,
A monster concrete moneybox for strangers,
Every last square foot of it worth a hundred pound.
Some day we'll see it come tumbling down, see it come down.[58]

In 'The Jeelie Piece Song' the plight of those living in multi-storey
blocks is put in terms of mothers' difficulty in throwing down sandwiches
to their children. In the four-storey tenements of Glasgow this had always
been the practice, but in the new estates like Castlemilk it was not so easy.

The Jeelie Piece[c] Song

I'm a skyscraper wean[d]; I live on the nineteenth flair;
But I'm no' gaun oot tae play ony mair,
'Cause since we moved tae Castlemilk, I'm wastin' away
'Cause I'm gettin' wan meal less every day.
Oh ye cannae fling pieces oot a twenty storey flat,
Seven hundred hungry weans'll testify to that.
If it's butter, cheese or jeely, if the breid is plain or pan,
The odds against it reaching earth are ninety-nine tae wan.

On the first day ma maw flung oot a daud o' Hovis broon;
It came skytin' oot the windae and went up insteid o' doon.
Noo every twenty-seven hoors it comes back intae sight
'Cause ma piece went intae orbit and became a satellite.

On the second day ma maw flung me a piece oot wance again.
It went and hut the pilot in a fast low-flying plane.
He scraped it aff his goggles, shouting through the intercom,
'The Clydeside Reds huv giat me wi' a breid-an-jeely bomb'.

On the third day ma maw thought she would try another throw.
The Salvation Army band was staundin' doon below.
'Onward, Christian Soldiers' was they piece they should've played,
But the oompah man was playing a piece an' marmalade.

We're wrote away to Oxfam to try an' get some aid,
An' a' the weans in Castlemilk have formed a 'piece brigade'.
We're gonnae march to George's Square demanding civil rights
Like nae mair hooses over piece-flinging height.[59]

[c] jam sandwich   [d] child

3

INDUSTRY

To protest at the planned closure of their rolling mill, a group of steelworkers from Gartcosh, near Glasgow, trekked to London in January 1986 through snow, strong winds, and freezing rain. On arriving at the Houses of Parliament, they defiantly sang 'The Braes of Killiecrankie',[1] a traditional ballad about the undoing of the English in battle. To keep up their spirits on the journey, they had sung a song of their own composition, 'The Gartcosh Commandos', which refers to a shop steward, Tommy Brennan:

> On the third day of Jan'ry nineteen eighty-six
> We went off to London to put Maggie in a fix.
> We didn't take a jet-plane, we didn't take a car,
> We walked it all the bloomin' way with the lads of Castlecarr.
> *We're the Gartcosh commandos, we're doon from old Gartcosh,*
> *We haven't got a gaffer, wee Tommy is the boss;*
> *And we'll cause the biggest rally you've ever come across;*
> *Just remember we're the Gartcosh commandos.*[2]

The effort proved unsuccessful, for the Gartcosh works closed a few months later, but the song served to put across the workers' case, and it was heard by a wide audience in radio news bulletins.

Work and Song

Manufacture, both in its original meaning of production by hand and in its later extension to mechanized industry, has a long connection with song. Many songs take work as their subject, but are not sung during labour; others, while often not dealing with work, are sung to accompany it. The requirements of communal tasks gave rise to songs which served both to stimulate and to co-ordinate the efforts of those involved. Rhythms were designed or adapted to particular tasks, and group work-songs of this kind still exist in primitive societies, and existed until recently even in developed countries. One thinks of waulking songs[3] from the Hebrides and sea-shanties from England and elsewhere. Chain-gang chants were sung in the penitentiaries of the United States until well within living memory. As recently as the 1950s, men quarrying Portland stone in Dorset had a whole repertoire of cries, chants, and songs, including 'Mademoiselle from Armentières' and 'Roll, Chariot' (a spiritual turned sea-shanty), to synchronize their precise and skilful hammer blows.[4]

Individual tasks might also be accompanied by song, sometimes to provide a general background (as in the BBC's *Music While You Work* of the Second World War), sometimes to give a specific rhythm. Lulling a child to sleep (or dandling, for the reverse effect), milking a cow, churning butter, spinning, knitting, weaving: almost any sort of manual labour could be lightened with a song to lift the spirit and pass the hours. When a priest in eighteenth-century France congratulated some poor people on their singing, he was told 'that they sang at work not because they were happy, but in order to diminish their sorrows and to forget the pain of their labour'.[5] The same would have been true of many others, including Cornish miners: a visitor in 1784 was amazed to see that, during the eighty-fathom descent by ladder, they 'run up and down these slippery places like lamp-lighters, singing and whistling all the way'; in addition he 'saw two figures that hardly wore the appearance of human beings, *singing at their work*', nearly half a mile below ground.[6]

Songs sung at work were frequently escapist as regards subject-matter, dealing for preference with anything other than the work itself. The women who fulled cloth previously steeped in urine by waulking it (wringing and beating it by hand) sang of sweethearts and castles, swift horses and epic combats. Sailors' shanties did at times comment on their work and the conditions in which they lived, but the main topics were sex and drink.

By applying chemical and mechanical techniques to fulling cloth and using steam to power ships, the industrial revolution did away with the need for waulking songs and sea-shanties and, indeed, for work-songs of most kinds. Nevertheless, they lingered for a very long time. By a quirk of cultural history, both are still with us, sung now for their own sake, and for the pleasure of communal music-making.

Bedlams and Beggars

A genre established long before the industrial revolution was that of songs in praise of particular trades. Work which involved mobility seems to have been particularly favoured. Before they were replaced by machines, itinerant flax-hecklers and wool-combers each had their songs. The predilection for a footloose, unfettered existence recalls, if not the reality, at least the songs of the bedlam boys and mad maudlins, the former inmates of the Bethlehem Hospital for the Insane in London, who wandered around the country eking out a living as best they could:

> To find my Tom of Bedlam, ten thousand years I'll travel;
> Mad Maudlin goes with dirty toes to save her shoes from gravel.
> *Yet will I sing, Bonny boys, bonny mad boys, Bedlam boys are bonny;*
> *They still go bare, and live by the air, and want no drink or money.*[7]

A. L. Beier has stated that 'vagrancy was one of the most pressing social problems of the age' of the Tudors and early Stuarts, and that 'the crime was taken so seriously because to the dominant classes vagabonds appeared to threaten the established order'.[8] Nevertheless, songs celebrating beggars enjoyed a considerable vogue. Richard Brome's play *Jovial Crew; or, The Merry Beggars* of 1641 had several such pieces. A later edition (of 1684) introduced what is perhaps the most famous of all beggar songs, which also appeared as a street ballad:

THE BEGGARS' CHORUS IN THE JOVIAL CREW

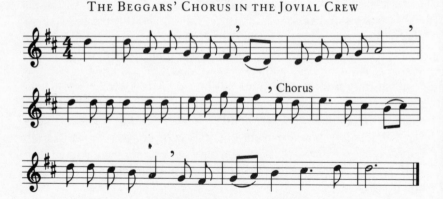

There was a jovial Beggar, he had a wooden Leg;
Lame from his Cradle, and forced for to Beg:
And a Begging we will go, we'll go, we'll go,
And a Begging we will go.

A Bag for my Oatmeal, another for my Salt,
A little pair of Crutches, to see how I can Halt[a]:

A Bag for my Bread, another for my Cheese,
A little dog to follow me to gather what I leese[b]:

A Bag for my Wheat, another for my Rye,
A little Bottle by my side, to drink when I am dry:

[a] limp   [b] lose

To Pimlico we'll go, where merry we shall be,
With ev'ry Man a Can in's Hand, and a Wench upon his Knee:

And when that we're disposed, we ramble on the Grass,
With long patch'd Coats for to hide a pretty Lass:

Seven years I served, my old Master Wild;
Seven years I begged whilst I was but a Child:

I had the pretty knack, for to wheedle and to cry;
By young and by old, much pitied e'er was I.

Fatherless and Motherless still was my complaint,
And none that ever saw me, but took me for a Saint:

I begg'd for my Master and got him store of Pelf;
But Jove now be praised, I now beg for myself;

Within a hollow Tree, I live, and pay no Rent;
Providence provides for me, and I am well content,

Of all Occupations, a Beggar lives the best,
For when he is weary, he'll lie him down and rest:

I fear no Plots against me, but live in open Cell:
Why who would be a King, when a Beggar lives so well?[9]

The tune and metre were taken up and used widely in other songs, and versions of 'The Beggars' Chorus' remained in oral tradition until at least 1952. One of them specifically rejects factory routine, and it is clear that as the regulation and industrialization of society progressed, the longing for freedom has intensified:

> There's a bed for me where e'er I lie and I don't pay no rent;
> I've got no noisy looms to mind and I am reet content.
>
> I can rest when I'm tired, I need no master's bell,
> A man'd be daft to be a king when beggars live so well.[10]

Itinerant Workers

Such sentiments would have been readily embraced by the members of the so-called hippy convoys of 1986, though Beier argues that the 'masterless men' of his book had less in common with modern drop-outs than with 'the unemployed of the Great Depression of the 1930s, or the jobless millions of today's inner cities'.[11] I am not entirely convinced. People who are unemployed wish to work, whereas beggars have a trade of a kind, which is sometimes envied by those in conventional occupations because of what they fancy to be its untrammelled nature. This is why itinerant tradesmen were envied, especially since they were thought to take advantage of their travels for amorous adventures, as did the eponymous heroes of 'The Rambling Miner'[12] and 'The Roving Journeyman'.[13] The latter is not unlike the tramping journeymen—travelling brothers—of the past. Among other mobile workers of the nineteenth century were the navvies, who prided themselves on their prowess both at work and at play.

THE NAV[V]Y BOYS

It's first when I set out on tramp I was but very young,
My mind was bent on merriment, on joy, and on fun:
My mind was bent on merriment, and ne'er could give it o'er,
For still my mind was quite content on Paddy's green Shamrock shore.
With my laddy fal de de, with my laddy fal de do,
With my laddy fal de de, we are nav[v]y boys, you know.

When I became a nav[v]y I own I was dismayed,
To see our noble hacksmen[c] on them a while I gazed,
Likewise our noble barrow-men, who ne'er could give it o'er,
In hopes that they would meet again on Paddy's green Shamrock shore.

On Monday morn when we go out our work to begin,
The noise of our tools, brave boys, does make the valleys ring;
We will drive our piles and bore our holes, by one, by two, by four—
The best of our navigators come from Paddy's green Shamrock shore.

When the rain it does come on we are happy then as kings,
We are off into the ale-house, and the bell then loudly rings,
We call for liquor of the best, and our bumpers they run o'er,
The very first toast that we drink is Paddy's green Shamrock shore.

[c] sub-contractors

When we meet a bad landlady, the truth to you I tell,
We do our whole endeavours it's for to please her well:
But at the pay we slope her*d*, as we've oft done before,
And with her money drink a health to Paddy's green Shamrock shore.

When we meet a bonny lass we give to her a kiss,
We take her in our arms, my boys, I own it is no miss;
We take her in our arms, and kiss her o'er and o'er,
But still the one that we like best is on Paddy's green Shamrock shore.

Come all you roving nav[v]ys that listen to my song,
I hope you'll not be angry if I've said anything wrong;
I own I am a nav[v]y bold, the truth I will deplore,
Many a happy day I spent on Paddy's green Shamrock shore.[14]

The romantic outlook of such a piece seems out of place in the context
of the painful reality described in such books as *The Railway Navvies*
(1965) by Terry Coleman or *Navvyman* (1983) by Dick Sullivan. At least
one recent song, however, gives sanguine advice. It is 'MacAlpine's
Fusiliers' by Dominic Behan:

I've worked till sweat has had me bet with Russian, Czech and Pole,
On the shuttering jams upon the hydro dams or down below the Thames in a hole.
I've grafted hard and I've got my cards, and many a ganger's fist across my ears.
If you pride your life, don't join, by Christ, with MacAlpine's Fusiliers.[15]

Iron and Steel

To ballads exalting the trade of beggar or navvy, one could add a mountain
more, on the trades of sailor, fisherman, keelman, lace-maker, housewife, dustman, servant, lock-maker, potter, chimney-sweep, and even
newspaper-seller, not to mention the farm-workers of chapter 1. The iron
and steel trades, mining and textiles, were particularly prolific.

'Here's a health to the jolly blacksmith, the best of all fellows',[16] begins
one; and another gives him primacy over a wide range of tradesmen:

Of all the brave trades of ancient renown,
The blacksmith's the foremost and shall wear the crown,
For he is a bonny laddie and I love him weel,
He works for his living in iron and steel.[17]

The cutlers of Sheffield claimed pre-eminence through pieces such as
'The Jovial Cutlers', 'The Cutler's Song', and 'The Cutlin' Heroes'; but
they also complained bitterly in 'The Grinders' Hardships',[18] and Joseph
Mather (1737–1804) (see Introduction) wrote songs about his trade which

d leave her without paying

are among the most searing in the English language. 'The File Hewer's Lamentation', which is probably autobiographical, likens the cutter of files successively to a beggar, a debtor, and a slave, and its last verse seethes with the desire for vengeance against those responsible. Unfortunately, the tune prescribed, 'A Pilgrim Blithe and Jolly', has not come to light.

> Ordained I was a beggar, and have no cause to swagger;
> It pierces like a dagger—to think I'm thus forlorn.
> My trade or occupation was ground for lamentation,
> Which makes me curse my station, and wish I'd ne'er been born.
>
> Of slaving I am weary, from June to January.
> To nature it's contrary—this, I presume, is fact.
> Although, without a stammer, our Nell exclaims I clam^e her,
> I wield my six-pound hammer, till I am grown round-back'd.
>
> I'm debtor to a many, but cannot pay one penny;
> Sure I've worse luck than any; my traps^f are marked for sale.
> My creditors may sue me, the bailiffs may pursue me,
> And lock me up in gaol.
>
> As negroes in Virginia, in Maryland or Guinea,
> Like them I must continue—to be both bought and sold.
> While negro ships are filling I ne'er can save one shilling,
> And must, which is more killing, a pauper die when old.
>
> My troubles never ceased, while Nell's bairn time increased;
> While hundreds I've rehearsed, ten thousand more remain;
> My income for me, Nelly, Bob, Tom, Poll, Bet, and Sally,
> Could hardly fill each belly, should we eat salt and grains.
>
> At every week's conclusion new wants bring fresh confusion,
> It is but mere delusion to hope for better days,
> While knaves with power invested, until by death arrested,
> Oppress us unmolested by their infernal ways.
>
> A hanging day is wanted; was it by justice granted,
> Poor men distress'd and daunted would then have cause to sing—
> To see in active motion rich knaves in full proportion,
> For their unjust extortion and vile offences swing.[19]

Like cutlery-making in Sheffield, nail- and chain-making in the Black Country were carried on in small workshops and outhouses attached to dwellings. Outworkers, often women, had to collect rods; and from a hundredweight (112 lbs), they were expected to return 104 lbs of chain. For each pound short, they were fined a penny; for each pound over, they

^e starve ^f belongings

received a bonus of a halfpenny. 'That was the meanness of the masters' was the recollection of George Dunn (1887–1975), speaking of the lowest grade of chain, known as 'slap'.[20] He himself worked as a chain-maker for well over fifty years at Noah Bloomer's in Quarry Bank, which continued in production until the 1970s. One of the local ironworks, Corngreaves, held religious services on the shop-floor which included prayers like this:

> Let shinglers, puddlers feel thy power
> When here, the sacred praying hour,
> At morning dawn, O spirit, strive,
> And let thy work great God revive.
>
> May rollers and roll turners, too,
> And furnacemen the path pursue.
> The path of love the saviour trod
> To lead our souls safe back to God.
>
> Smiths, fitters, engineers, unite,
> And come well armed into the fight;
> Let faith and prayer your weapons be,
> Fight till poor sinners are set free.[21]

If religion was here part of the official routine, it was also invoked by workers in disputes.

> Our masters must stand at God's bar
> A just account to give
> For keeping back the labourer's hire,
> Which he ought to receive'.

This is from 'The Nail Maker's Lamentation', written during the great strike of 1862 by J. Knowles (1821–1903) of Lye, near Stourbridge, whose daughter dictated the text in 1932. The growing production of nails by machine from about 1830 onwards caused a progressive fall in the rates paid to hand-workers. The reductions, or 'discounts', as they were called, led in turn to a series of bitter strikes:

> Oh the discount, oh the discount,
> With it we can't agree.
> For twenty shillings we will have
> Before at work we'll be.[22]

By the late 1860s those employed in nail-making had declined from 50,000 to 20,000, and in the 1890s a former secretary of the defunct Nailmakers' Union said: 'Nailmaking is one of the worst trades in the kingdom. There are scores of men in this parish [Bromsgrove] who are not

earning nine shillings a week for seventy, eighty, or ninety hours work, and
out of these earnings have to pay from one shilling to eighteen pence a
week for firing, and about sixpence for keeping their tools in order.'[23]

As iron- and steel-making became the large-scale, highly mechanized
industry of the late nineteenth and early twentieth centuries, songs
lingered in small workshops, but did not move to the big factories.
Curiously, though, the contraction of the industry in the 1970s and 1980s
met with resistance from the workers, who had recourse to the well-
springs of song. 'The Ballad of the Q4', by Matt McGinn (1928–77), used
during the campaign in 1971 against the closure of the Upper Clyde
shipbuilding yard, when a work-in set a new pattern for action, expresses
the old craft pride:

> The *Mary* and the *Lizzie* they were made right here,
> But ye'll never see the likes of them, I fear.
> They were the finest ever sailed the sea,
> They were built by the hands o' men like me.[24]

Songs featured, too, in the ultimately unsuccessful attempts to keep open
the steelworks at Shelton Bar, Staffordshire (1973); Shotton (1973),—
where, instead of the street ballad of the past, an EP record of songs was
produced[25]—and, as we have seen, Gartcosh (1986).

Mining

Among mining songs, 'The Bonnie Pit Laddie', dating back to 1655 or
earlier, is perhaps the oldest:

THE BONNIE PIT LADDIE

The bonnie pit laddie, the canny pit laddie,
The bonnie pit laddie for me, O.
He sits in his hole as black as the coal,
And brings the white siller to me, O.

The bonnie pit laddie, the canny pit laddie,
The bonnie pit laddie for me, O.
He sits on his cracket[g] and hews in his jacket,
And brings the white siller to me, O.[26]

The Scottish 'Collier Laddie' (later adapted as 'The Ploughman Laddie')[27] may well be contemporary with the English song, but we cannot be
sure of its existence until 1792, when Robert Burns published his version.
However, the lady's preference for a collier might possibly derive from the
famous earlier sequence in which allegiance is pledged in a song of that
name to a gypsy laddie.

O see ye not yon hills and dales
The sun shines on saw brawlie?
They a' are mine and shall be thine,
Gin ye leave your collier laddie.

If you had a' the sun shines on
And the earth conceals sae lowly,
I would turn my back on you and it a',
And embrace my collier laddie.[28]

The collier at work is emphasized in 'A new Song, in Praise of the Coal-
miners', which probably dates from the early 1770s:

You Coal miners of *England* your Skill is so pure,
You excel all other Callings, that is to be sure:
For those that despise you are highly to blame,
For the Good of the Country there's many one slain.

[g] stool

Our Coals they are hacked and digged, I say,
And those are our Barrow-men that barrow them away
They convey them to the Banks all under the Ground,
Where thousands of Years they have laid unfound,

They pull the Corves[h] to 'em, saying, Boys come again
With the Master's consent they lay them on the Plain;
Our Coals they are hacked and digged, I say,
And these are our Carters that cart them away,

With Carts and Waggons each Man plays his Part,
They load them to the River with a most joyful Heart;
Our Country Gentlemen as we understand,
They at the Wine Tavern doth mortgage the Land.

But us poor Coal-miners we stand to their Test,
With Fendings[i] and Bargains we still do make Shift,
We go to our Labour with joy and Content
We live on the portion that Haev'n hath us sent.

There's Meat Drink and Cloathing for Lad and Man
And the overplus money goes to the Ale can:
There's the Hatters and Dyers they're all on a Row,
There's the Brewers and Bakers do make a fine show.

There's *Dolly* in the Kitchen, and *Betty* in the Hall,
And straight to the Scullion for more Coals they call,
There's the Ale house and Gin-shop, doth help to vend
The more Coals they burn, the more money we spend.

Some go to *Flanders*, and some go to *Spain*,
And some to *Virginia*, quite o'er the Main:
Some go to *London* as we understand,
And so they convey the Coals out of the Land.[29]

The other side of the coin was the danger—the flood, fire, explosion, and collapse of workings—to which miners were exposed. As the industry expanded throughout the nineteenth century and into the twentieth, casualties multiplied. It has been estimated that some 250,000 men, women, and children have been maimed in British pits.[30] Individuals incapacitated by an accident would have sheets of verses printed to hawk round. To counter suspicions of imposture, efforts were made to include some form of authentication, as in 'The Submissive Petition of the Distressed Hugh Boyd' (1777) of Yorkshire.[31] Substantially the same sheet turns up in 1784 as from 'Hugh Boyd, Late a Collier, at Parton, near Whitehaven, Cumberland'.[32]

[h] baskets   [i] provisions

Major loss of life in the pits inspired sheet after sheet. These were often without imprint, and were probably run off by jobbing printers for sale by colliers who wished to raise money for the families of their dead comrades. 'The Oaks Pit Explosion'[33] (Barnsley, 1866) and 'A Copy of Verses'[34] (Cymmer colliery, Glamorgan, 1856) are without imprint. Others bear the name and address of a local printer, such as J. Ford of Sheffield on the 'Poor Colliers' Widows' Weeping Lamentation'[35] (Rawmarsh, 1851) and D. Thomas of Wallcroft, Lancashire, on 'The Late Colliery Explosion' (Wigan, 1854).[36]

Such productions normally begin with an invocation such as 'You feeling Christians' or 'Each feeling heart'. They give brief details of the catastrophe, inserting reflections such as 'One moment we're in health and bloom, / Next in eternity'. The piece normally concludes with references to the plight of the victims' dependants, calculated to inspire the generosity of others. A given text was readily adapted to different disasters by changes in place-name and date. 'Lines on the Dreadful Explosion at Bunkers Hill Mine'[37] (Staffordshire, 1875) easily became 'Lines on the Terrible Explosion near Barnsley'[38] (1875). Both have the same woodcut of a funeral cortège near a church, and the same concluding exhortation:

> Oh, God help the widows and fatherless babes
> Who are now left in grief to lament,
> For kind loving fathers, and husbands so dear
> That were killed by this sad accident.
> May God in his mercy now pardon the sins
> Of those who so suddenly fell,
> And receive them above in the mansions of love
> With heavenly angels to dwell.

A similarly resigned conclusion is reached in a ballad on the disaster at Starlaw in Scotland, which was printed and sold at a halfpenny, and was probably the work of a miner. Rab Morrison of Woolmet colliery, Midlothian, sang it as late as the 1950s, to a variant of the tune, 'Still growing'.

THE STARLAW DISASTER

It was eighteen and seventy, April the ninth day;
Nintey-six men and boys for their work took their way.
In health and in strength down the shaft they did go,
Never dreaming of how many would lie low.

For about twelve o'clock on that same fatal day,
'The pit-shaft's on fire', the roadsman did say.
And quick through the workin's the alarum he gave,
All praying to their maker their sweet lives for to save.

All eagerly ran to get on to the cage,
But the fire in the shaft like a furnace did rage.
All praise to young John Steel who at the engine did stand,
And forty-eight safe on the bank he did land.

William Ralston, William Rushford and young David Muir,
By that terrible disaster you will see them no more.
Patrick and Peter M'Comiskie, aye, and Swanson likewise,
By that terrible disaster in their cold grave now lies.

Now widows and orphans who are now left to mourn,
By that awful disaster they will never return.
But God is so merciful, as all mankind knows,
He will share in their sorrow and soften their woes.[39]

The facts of the event are closely followed in the ballad: there were fifty-six men in the pit, of whom some forty-eight were saved, largely through the courage and presence of mind of the engine-man, John Steel. As Hamish Henderson says, 'it is both chronicle and elegy', but the fierce anger which miners felt is passed over. The same song, with its strengths and weaknesses, was pressed into service, among several others, to commemorate the Blantyre disaster seven years later.[40] Indignation and even questioning seldom surface in such pieces.

Even Tommy Armstrong (1848–1920), 'the pitman poet' (see Introduction), who is perfectly capable of incisive writing—on strikes, for example—sticks very much to the normal pattern in dealing with the Trimdon Grange explosion (County Durham, 1882). He has some memorable and deeply moving lines, such as these:

> Let us think of Mrs Burnett,
> Once had sons but now has none,
> By the Trimdon Grange explosion,
> Joseph, George and James are gone.

Yet his conclusion is conventional enough:

> God protect the lonely widow,
> Help to raise each drooping head;
> Be a father to the orphans,
> Never let them cry for bread.
> Death will pay us all a visit,
> They have only gone before;
> We may meet the Trimdon victims
> Where explosions are no more.[41]

This was the tradition, and it continued at least until 1973, when the deaths of seven men at Lofthouse colliery in Yorkshire inspired ten poems and songs, some of them printed or duplicated for sale in the streets. Only one of these contained even a hint of bitterness, the piece by Walter Greaves (born 1907), a blacksmith of Crosshills, near Keighley:

> It's no disaster the Coal Board said
> Only seven were not spared
> At least ten miners must be dead
> Before disaster can be declared
> So when these miners are picketing again
> Let us hope it will not be soon
> Remember heroes do not change
> The newspapers change their tune.[42]

Greaves was partly influenced by 'The Gresford Disaster' (Denbighshire, 1934), one of the few songs to express similar disenchantment,[43] but it has been suggested that he was at variance with local opinion, perhaps because of his departure from traditional practice. Miners also had a tradition of powerful songs of protest, however, as can be seen in A. L. Lloyd's classic anthology *Come All Ye Bold Miners* (1952).

Worsted

The worsted industry traced its roots back to Jason and the Golden Fleece, and its patron was Bishop Blaise, whose flesh was scored with iron combs before he was beheaded in AD 316. Processions held on the saint's day, 3 February, may date from medieval times, but records are abundant only in the late eighteenth and early nineteenth centuries. At Bradford there were septennial pageants, which ended in 1825 when class conflict—there was a strike of combers—put an end to it. Broadsides give the itinerary, order of march, and celebratory verses (by Thomas Rawnsley, a wool-broker from Bourne, Lincolnshire):

> By this our Trade, are thousands daily fed,
> By *Us* supplied with Means to earn their bread,
> In various Forms our Trade its Work imparts,
> In different Methods, and by different Arts
> Preserves from Starving Indigents distress'd:
> As Combers, Spinners, Weavers and the rest.[44]

The trade in general was on show, the parade being led in person by 'The Masters on Horseback', wool-staplers, worsted-spinners, manufacturers, and merchants. Next came people dressed as the king, queen, and various members of the royal family, Jason, Bishop Blaise, a shepherd, and a shepherdess. Finally, *in propria persona*, came foremen, wool-sorters, and the wool-combers themselves. The 1811 sheet states that 'A Public Dinner will be provided at the Talbot Inn, for those Gentlemen who wish to celebrate the day', and in 1804 the toasts are listed as:

1st. The King.—2d. The Queen and Princesses. 3d. The Prince of Wales. 4th. The Memory of Bishop Blaze.—5th. Town and Trade of Bradford. 6th. The Worsted Manufactory, and may it long be the Pride of Britons, and the Envy of their Enemies.—7th. Our Fleets and Armies, and may their Success procure a speedy and honourable Peace.—8th. The People of England, and may they never forget the Value of Order and good Government, &c. &c.

Similarly worthy sentiments were expressed in many weavers' songs. 'The Joley Weaver' dates from 1719:

> Fram whear cam all the bravery as all our gentils wear,
> Do not the skilfull weaver fine cloatches for them prepar;
> Or whear should we have garmentes to hid our nakednes,
> If that thear was no wevers to weave them wel for us.
> The painfull prudunt housewif that taks such care to spin,
> In thes old ingless nasion much praise and glore win
> If it was not fur the wevers they would not spin nur card,
> Then 1000 must li idel then, that would be labring hard.
> The cumbers and the diers, huksturs and shearmen to,
> Likwis the pricklous taylor would nothing have to do.
> Then all must lose their callinges in sitey and in town
> If ear thes trad of weaving, if ear this trad of weving,
> Shoud be by all laid doune.[45]

Alongside such expressions of craft pride, there were complaints about wages, conditions, and unemployment. 'The Clothiers' Delight', by which

Macaulay set so much store (see Introduction), was written by the West Country balladeer Thomas Lanfiere, and printed between 1674 and 1679.[46] Its bitter irony is somewhat unusual, for many such pieces, like the miners' disaster ballads, were designed to inspire not the indignation, but the charity, of the purchaser or hearer. 'A doleful tale, sung to a doleful tune, often imposes upon the kind-hearted,' wrote the Leicester manufacturer William Gardiner (1770–1853). 'During a bad trade', he added,

some of my workmen formed the project of going into the south of England in the character of beggars. One was a comber, who had travelled all over the country with his blank in search of work, and who led the party. Though all young men, and unmarried, they wrote a ditty describing their wives and children in want of bread. When they returned I questioned them upon their proceedings, and learnt that in the city of Exeter they collected 2*l.* 17*s.* 6*d.* in one day. The chief delinquent could scarcely keep his countenance when poor women ran across the street to give them a pittance: they had a good hot supper every night, to which their wallet supplied plenty of bread. In their defence they said they took it up as a trade, and as in all trades there was deception, they did not consider themselves worse than their masters.[47]

More genuine, perhaps, were those 'weavers from the North, singing about the town ballads of Distress' whom William Cobbett encountered in Wiltshire in 1826.[48] Plenty of such ballads have survived, including the 'Lament of Two Stocking Makers, from Nottingham', issued in the early 1840s:

> Pardon our visit to this place,
> And wait while we explain our case,
> And then we think you'll pity take,
> Nor us in our distress forsake.[49]

Some complaints have a far sharper tone, harking back to the spirit of 'The Clothiers' Delight'. 'Jone o' Grinfield', of about 1815, ends more or less in despair, relieved only by sombre humour on the part of John and fierce rage on the part of his wife. Their house is stripped of its contents by bailiffs, save for an old stool, but this, too, is removed by more bailiffs. John takes his last length of cloth to the master, and says he can work no more:

> Then aw coom out and left him to chew that,
> When aw thought again aw wur vext till aw sweat,
> To think that we mun work to keep him and awth set
> All the days o' my life and still be in their debt;
> So I'll give o'er trade an work with a spade,
> Or go and break stones upoth road.

Our Margit declared if hoo'd cloas to put on,
Hoo'd go up to Lundun an see the big mon
An if things didn't alter when hoo had been
Hoo swears hoo'll feight blood up toth e'en,
Hoo's nought again th' Queen but likes a fair thing
An hoo says hoo can tell when hoo's hurt.[50]

The ballad was frequently reprinted, and earlier versions mention the king rather than the queen. John, from Greenfield, near Oldham, was a fictional character who appeared in a large number of pieces, some of which were written by Joseph Lees of Glodwick, a schoolmaster and a weaver. The first of the series, 'Jone o' Grinfilt's Ramble', written in 1803 or 1804, deals with the eponymous hero's visit to Oldham to enlist.[57] The sequel dates from the beginning of a period of great difficulty for hand-loom weavers, when average weekly wages fell from between eighteen and twenty-four shillings (in 1814) to five or six shillings (in 1832). It is quoted in part, under the title of 'The Oldham Weaver', in Mrs Gaskell's novel of Manchester working-class life, *Mary Barton* (1848).

'The Hand-loom Weavers' Lament', which is roughly contemporary with 'Jone o' Grinfield', opens in uncompromising vein:

You gentlemen and tradesmen, that ride about at will,
Look down on these poor people; it's enough to make you crill;
Look down on these poor people, as you ride up and down,
I think there is a God above will bring your pride quite down.
You tyrants of England, your race may soon be run,
You may be brought unto account for what you've sorely done.

However, the ballad concludes merely with the hope of a return to the *status quo ante*:

And now, my lads, for to conclude, it's time to make an end;
Let's see if we can form a plan that these bad times may mend;
Then give us our old prices, as we have had before,
And we can live in happiness, and rub off the old score.[52]

The 'old prices' may well be those pertaining immediately before the reduction in rates, and many of the struggles of nineteenth-century workers involved resistance to the imposition of reductions. The more remote era of the late eighteenth century also had something of the glow of a golden age, for cotton weavers' earnings averaged twenty-five shillings a week at that time. Subsequently, because of the trade's becoming over-subscribed, and later, because of the introduction of steam-power, especially in the 1820s, wages declined. The weekly earnings of Bolton weavers fell successively from 25s. in 1800 to 14s. in 1811 to 9s. in the early 1820s and 5s. 6d. in 1829. Weavers were obliged to give up their independence and seek employment, if they could find it, in factories.

Factories

Employers preferred youths and women, since they could pay them less than men, and they tended to be more malleable.

> Where are the girls? I'll tell you plain,
> The girls have gone to weave by steam;
> And if you'd find one you must rise at dawn
> And trudge to the mill in the early dawn.[53]

Older men adapted less well to factory work, and were more resentful of the discipline involved. Previously they had been able to combine weaving with other occupations, such as schoolmastering in the case of Joseph Lees or, more commonly, working on their own or others' land. They had been able to determine their own hours, working as much or as little as they needed or wished. They could keep up Saint Monday (take Monday or other days off) if they so desired, and choose to work harder or longer during the rest of the week to compensate. 'It would be wrong', wrote T. S. Ashton, 'to imagine that what the ordinary man sought above all was continuity of work. . . . It is true that workers resented the imposition of unemployment . . . But leisure, at times of their own choice, stood high on their scale of preferences.'[54]

The long, fixed hours in factories and their rigid rules were found especially irksome, and E. P. Thompson has described the workers' sentiments in a seminal paper entitled, 'Time, Work-Discipline and Industrial Capitalism' (1967). The tyranny of the clock was particularly resented, and wry, epigrammatic songs like this still circulate:

> A pal of mine once said to me,
> 'Will you knock me up half past three?'
> And so, promptly at half past one
> I knocked him up and I said, 'Oh, John,
> I've just come round to tell you,
> You've got two more hours to sleep'.[55]

People without clocks and watches—and these were once the majority—were wakened at the right time for work either by a friend—someone returning from the night-shift, perhaps—or by a professional knocker-up. Such a person, for a small fee, went round at the appointed time and tapped on bedroom windows with a long stick to waken those within. The practice continued in northern England until well within living memory. A woman born in Batley in 1933 learned this song from her mother:

Four o'clock at Sullivan's door and I knocks, knocks, knocks,
I go down to McGilligan's door and I knocks, knocks, knocks,
My work is very tiring but still I never stop
Till it strikes half past seven by the old church clock.[56]

After arriving on time at the factory, the worker was committed to long
hours at a relentless machine and subjected to a system of discipline which
included fines and peremptory dismissal. In a song entitled 'Hand-loom v.
Power-loom' the weaver is told to dismantle his loom and go to work in a
factory:

So come all you cotton-weavers, you must rise up very soon,
For you must work in factories from morning until noon;
You mustn't walk in your garden for two or three hours a day,
And you must stand at their command and keep your shuttles in play.[57]

Like 'The Hand-loom Weavers' Lament', this was sung by John
Grimshaw of Gorton, near Manchester. He was known as 'Common'
Grimshaw, presumably to distinguish him from a fellow townsman,
Robert Grimshaw, whose factory with its thirty power-looms at Knott
Mill, Manchester, was destroyed in 1790 within a few weeks of opening.
The action, which had been threatened in a series of anonymous letters, is
said to have delayed the introduction of power-looms to Manchester by
sixteen years. A derisive ballad entitled 'Grimshaw's Factory Fire' by yet
another Gorton man, a hand-loom weaver and bleacher called Lucas,
revealed 'the feelings of the working-classes of that day on the introduction of machinery and steam-power':

For coal to work his factory
He sent unto the Duke[j], sir;
He thought that all the town
Should be stifled with the smoke, sir;
But the Duke sent him an answer,
Which came so speedily,
That the poor should have the coal,
If the Devil took th' machinery.[58]

Luddism

Reaction to becoming slaves to a machine at best or being rendered
unemployed at worst frequently led to wrecking of innovatory devices.
John Kay's home was attacked in 1753 by workers protesting his flying
shuttle, and a few years later Blackburn spinners smashed Hargreaves'
spinning-jennies. At Leicester in 1773, stockingers broke up a frame

[j] [of Bridgewater]

capable of weaving twelve pairs of hose at once, and six years later their fellows in Nottingham destroyed hundreds of Arkwright's frames. At Leicester again, Joseph Brookhouse's worsted-spinning frame was wrecked in 1787, and in the mêlée the mayor was fatally injured by a blow to the head from a stone.

Leicestershire is the reputed home of Edward Ludlam, or Ned Lud. The word 'Luddite', which first appeared in print in 1811, is said to derive from the name of 'an ignorant youth . . . of the name of Ludlam, who, when ordered by his father, a framework knitter, to square his needles, took a hammer and beat them into a heap'. Another version of the story has it that Lud was 'a person of weak intellect who lived in a Leicester village about 1779, and who in a fit of insane rage rushed into a stockinger's house and destroyed two frames so completely that the saying "Lud must have been here" came to be used throughout the hosiery districts when a stocking-frame had undergone extraordinary damage'.[59] Oral tradition identifies the village as Anstey, and until recently its inhabitants were known as 'Neddoes'. After the death of his mother in 1763, Ned Lud is said to have been apprenticed there to a stocking-weaver by the parish. He was thrashed for laziness, and retaliated by hammering a frame to pieces. Or, as another version of the story says, he smashed a frame to vent his anger at being mercilessly taunted for being stupid. There was a local saying: 'As daft as Ned Lud, who ran ten miles to see a dead donkey'.[60]

Luddites were far from being mere blind wreckers. They opposed machinery for the very good reason that it jeopardized their livelihood. The stockingers also felt that it lowered standards of workmanship, thus compounding its adverse effects. Lord Byron agreed:

By the adoption of one species of Frame in particular, one man performed the work of many, and the superfluous labourers were thrown out of employment. Yet it is to be observed that the work thus executed was inferior in quality; not marketable at home, and merely hurried over with a view to exportation. It was called, in the cant of the trade, by the name of 'Spider work'. The rejected workmen, in the blindness of their ignorance, instead of rejoicing at these improvements in arts so beneficial to mankind, conceived themselves to be sacrificed to improvements in mechanism. In the foolishness of their hearts they imagined that the maintenance and well doing of the industrious poor were objects of greater consequence than the enrichment of a few individuals by any improvement, in the implements of trade, which threw the workmen out of employment and rendered the labourer unworthy of his hire.[61]

His bitter and passionate address to the House of Lords on 27 February 1812 failed to prevent the ultimate passage into law of a bill to make frame-breaking a capital offence.

The new act did not entirely deter frame-breakers. One ballad, 'General Ludd's Triumph',[62] found its way in 1812 to the Home Office, probably having been sent by an informer as evidence of sedition. The manuscript copy cheekily uses the tune 'Poor Jack', by the ultra-patriotic Charles Dibdin. Another piece, 'Hunting a Loaf', appeared in print, albeit without details of its origin. Because of a reference to the assassination of the Prime Minister, Percival (which was originally thought to be the work of the Luddites), it must date from 1812. It comments:

> For Derby it's true, and Nottingham too,
> Poor men to the jail they've been taking,
> They said that Ned Lud as I understood,
> A thousand wide frames has been breaking.
>
> Now is it not bad there's no work to be had,
> The poor to be starv'd in their station;
> And if they do steal they're strait sent to the jail,
> And they're hanged by the laws of the nation.[63]

The croppers of the West Riding of Yorkshire were highly skilled workmen who trimmed the nap on woollen cloth with huge hand-shears. In 1806, some 3,000 of them were at work, together with 2,000 apprentices. When trade was good, they could earn thirty shillings a week, at a time when an agricultural labourer was paid only eight shillings. The introduction of shear-frames partially mechanized the process, and the output with a frame equalled in eighteen hours what took eighty-eight hours by hand. Potentially, at least half the croppers would be put out of work if the frames were widely used. Under the Combination Acts of 1799 and 1800, strikes and trade union organization were illegal (though by no means unknown), so the croppers secretly banded together to resist by smashing the offending frames or even by burning down the workshops in which they were housed. To carry out their work of destruction, they carried great hammers, known as Enochs, from the name of one of the partners of the firm that made them, Enoch and James Taylor of Marsden. Ironically, the same firm also made the shear-frames, which gave rise to the saying 'Enoch has made them and Enoch shall break them'. The Government deployed special constables and also soldiers. It is said that a greater military force was arrayed against the Luddites in England in 1812 than against the French armies in Spain, and Byron made fun of the 'marchings and counter-marchings' of the soldiery.

Despite the strong military presence, there were several attacks, including that on Foster's Mill, between Horbury and Ossett (near Wakefield), which took place on 9 April 1812 and was triumphantly commemorated in

song (see Introduction). Three days later the croppers were less successful: their famous assault on Rawfolds Mill in the Spen valley was
successfully repulsed by the owner, William Cartwright, and some workers and soldiers. Eight men later stood trial at York for their part in the
attack, three others involved having already been hanged (and their bodies
delivered to the surgeons to be dissected and anatomized) for the murder
of the owner of another mill, William Horsfall. Five of the eight were
found guilty, and hanged. They included John Walker, who had enlisted in
the Royal Artillery at Woolwich to try to escape detection. He was
remembered for many years afterwards at the Shears Inn (not far from
Rawfolds, and still standing) for his singing of 'The Croppers' Song':
'Long before Walker had come to the end of his song the rollicking chorus
was eagerly caught up by his delighted audience, and when the end was
reached the refrain was twice repeated with extraordinary vigour, many of
the men beating time on the long table with their sticks and pewter mugs.'
The piece itself is clearly home-made, and is closely related to a song that
tells of a conflict between keepers and poachers. On the other hand, the
reverse might possibly be true, for I have come across no version of the
poaching song dating from as early as 1812.

THE CROPPERS' SONG

Come cropper lads of high renown,
Who love to drink good ale that's brown
And strike each haughty tyrant down
With hatchet, pike and gun.
Oh, the cropper lads for me,
The gallant lads for me,
Who with lusty stroke the shear frames broke,
The cropper lads for me.

> Who though the specials still advance
> And soldiers nightly round us prance,
> The cropper lads still lead the dance
> With hatchet, pike and gun.
>
> And night be night when all is still
> And the moon is hid behind the hill,
> We forward march to do our will
> With hatchet, pike and gun.
>
> Great Enoch still shall lead the van,
> Stop him who dare, stop him who can.
> Press forward every gallant man
> With hatchet, pike and gun.[64]

By 1817, out of 3,625 croppers, only 860 had full employment.[65] From the second quarter of the nineteenth century the factory system was dominant, and a new subculture was generated, albeit drawing on traditions inherited from the workshop system (which continued to exist in some areas and trades). The harsh and demanding regime of the great factory bastilles was humanized by close camaraderie among the workers, by their sense of humour, and even by their rivalries.

Factory Songs

In the grim linen mills of Belfast, the routine until within living memory was from six in the morning until six at night, with meal breaks of one and a half hours, on weekdays, and from six till noon, with a break of half an hour, on Saturdays. In the spinning rooms the work of removing full bobbins of yarn from the frames and replacing them with empty ones was the work of the doffers, sometimes girls, sometimes young women, often barefoot, wearing aprons (called rubbers), and wielding pickers to dig out yarn which wrapped itself round the roller when the thread broke. The bobbins were large and heavy. The work was hard, noisy, and dirty, and the wages low, but the doffers still found the energy to sing:

> You'll easy tell a doffer when she comes in the town,
> With her long yellow hair and her ringlets hanging down;
> With her rubber round her waist and her pickers in her hand,
> You'll easy tell a doffer for she'll always get her man.
> She'll always get her man, she'll always get her man,
> You'll easy tell a doffer for she'll always get her man.
>
> And you'll easy tell a weaver when she comes in the town,
> With her long dirty hair and her stockings hanging down;
> With her ol' ugly pick and her fingers up her nose,
> You'll easy tell a weaver anywhere she goes,

For she never gets a man, she never gets a man,
You'll easy tell a weaver for she never gets a man.[66]

The weavers would retaliate by singing the same song adapted to favour themselves, or others like this:

The yellow belly doffers,
Dirty wipers down;
The nasty, stinking spinning room,
The stink will knock you down.[67]

There is a Dundee joke about the weavers' dislike of spinners. It tells of a weaver who goes to see the registrar to make arrangements for her wedding: 'So he says to her, "Now you're a spinster?" And she says, "No, look, I'm a weaver". And he says, "Now, look, lassie, doon on this form, put you're a spinster". She says, "Dinna ca' me a spinster, because I'm a weaver". So he says to her, "Look, lassie, are you ignorant?" She says, "Aye, fower month".'[68]

The Belfast spinners, for their part, sang (to the tune of 'The Girl I Left Behind Me') the 'Snuff Box Song', of which one version runs:

I give me curse to any girl
Who learns to be a spinner,
That has a discontented mind
From breakfast time to dinner.

When the mill it goes on
The belts is all a-crakin'[k];
The frames go like the railway train
And the ends is always breakin'.

When the gaffer he goes by
His tongue goes clitter clatter;
He rares and tears and he curses and swears
And says, What is the matter?

My frames are workin' very bad
And I can't take no dinner.
I take out my box and take a pinch,
And perhaps I'll spin the better.[69]

Not only were these songs sung in the mill, they were probably improvised there, too.

Strikes

The complaints about working conditions expressed here are cogent and direct, but there is a kind of resignation, albeit tempered with wry humour.

[k] creaking

Other pieces, regarding trade union organization, for example, are, not surprisingly, much more combative. It is ironic that many songs dealing with the world of work have as their subject-matter people who are not working, either because they have been locked out by their employers or because they have withdrawn their labour. Under such circumstances, songs served to raise workers' morale, to promote solidarity, to project their views, and to raise funds. The earliest strike songs extant, as far as I know, stem from the Tyneside keelmen's 'stick' of 1822[70] and the north-eastern miners' dispute of the same year[71] over their 'bond', or contract; but there may have been earlier ones which are now lost. From then on, though, time after time, in industry after industry, disputes gave rise to a solitary verse, a single song, or perhaps even a whole crop of ballads. Some of these have survived in oral tradition, some in manuscript, and some in printed form.

As they marched through the East End of London in 1888, striking match-girls from Bryant and May's factory sang to the tune of 'John Brown's Body':

> We'll hang old Bryant on a sour apple tree (*ter*)
> As we go marchin' in.
> Glory, glory, hallelujah (*ter*)
> As we go marchin' in.[72]

A strike of women chain-makers at Cradley Heath, Staffordshire, in 1910, left its mark in a local song:

> The lady chainmakers have all gone on strike.
> The gaffers they think they can pay what they like;
> They work 'em so hard both by night and by day,
> And for it they all get such terrible pay.[73]

Mary Brooksbank (1897–1980) worked in the jute mills of Dundee. She wrote several fine songs about her experiences, including one with the immortal couplet: 'Oh, dear me, the world's ill divided, / Them that work the hardest are the least provided.' She first went on strike in 1912, and remembered these lines sung on that occasion, which went to the tune of 'Tramp, Tramp, Tramp', from the American Civil War (also used for election chants):

> We are out for higher wages as we have a right to do,
> An' we'll never be content till we get oor ten per cent,
> For we have a right tae live as well as you.[75]

The vehemence of the match-girls was equalled, still in the East End but almost exactly a century later, by men and women picketing Rupert

Murdoch's fortified printing works at Wapping in 1986–7. Among their songs was one to the tune of a sea-shanty which they had probably learned at school; another put new words to a First World War song:

> What shall we do with Rupert Murdoch (*ter*),
> Early in the morning.
> Burn, burn, burn the bastard (*ter*),
> Early in the morning.
>
> If you want to find Rupert Murdoch ⎫
> We know where he is   ⎬ *bis*
> He's hiding behind the old barbed wire.
> We've seen him (*bis*),
> Hiding behind the old barbed wire.[76]

All sorts of disputes inspired a ballad or two, but for the most part, these had only local circulation. London dockers struck in August 1889 for their famous 'tanner': a rate of sixpence an hour. Inspired leadership was provided by Bill Tillett, Tom Mann, and John Burns. There were mass meetings and spectacular demonstrations. On 25 August a great march of thousands of dockers left Poplar town hall for the City. With its bands, banners, slogans, and floats, the scene in some ways resembled craft processions like those in honour of Bishop Blaise. Men in costume depicted scenes from dock life. Britannia in a Union Jack skirt was partnered by Father Neptune. One scene contrasted a director's dinner (a huge plate piled high with meat and vegetables) with a docker's meal (a crust of bread and a tiny herring). Thanks to substantial monetary support from Australian trade unionists and a good deal of public sympathy at home, the strike ended in September with the 'full round orb' of the dockers' tanner granted from November. Songs also featured in the campaign. Like Mary Brooksbank's strike piece, this, too, went to the tune of 'Tramp, Tramp, Tramp':

THE DOCKERS' STRIKE

At the docks there is a strike that the company don't like.
A tanner on the hour they'll have to pay.
Like slaves they'd have us work, far more than any Turk,
And make us sweat our lives out every day.
Strike, boys, strike for better wages.
Strike, boys, strike for better pay.
Go on fighting at the docks,
Stick it out like fighting cocks,
Go on fighting till the bosses they give way.

Every morning there are flocks for employment at the docks,
Hard working men who scarce can get a meal;
With wives and children dear, it would make you shed a tear
If only you knew the hardship that they feel.

If it's slavery that you seek, for about a quid a week,
They'll take you on as soon as you come near.
Sweat your guts out with a will or they'll try your job to fill,
But that won't wash with working men, that's clear.

We'll stand up for our rights, and the company we will fight,
Supported by our brothers everywhere,
For we have friends galore—the good old stevedores,
And the seamen and the firemen they are there.

Starvation, 'tis they bids to a man with seven kids,
When he brings home only fifteen pence a day,
For what can you get to eat on seven-and-six a week,
When it often takes it all the rent to pay?

Here's a health to Mr Burns, he's done us all a turn,
Ben Tillett, Mann and Mr Toomey, too;
We won't give in a bit, for we've got 'em in a fit,
And we've put the old dock company in a stew.[77]

George Dunn revisiting Noah Bloomer's chainshop at Quarry Bank, near Dudley, 1974.

Leicestershire stocking weaver of the 1850s.

(Above) A cropper at work in 1814.

Brian Deacon of Leicester on the eve of his wedding in 1984.

The Submiffive PETITON of the Diftreffed.

HUGH BOYD,

Late COLLIER in Darnel, near Sheffield, in the Weft-Riding of Yorkfhire.

Who was confined fix Days and fourteen Hours under Ground, with fix more, by reafon of the Roof falling upon them, by which Accident he loft two of his Fingers, which renders him incapable or gaining his Family Bread, which confifts of four Mother-lefs Orphans, fhe dying foon after he was delivered from the Pit, which happened the fecond of September. 1777.

GOOD Chriftians who my diftrefs do fee,
Look with an eye of pitty upon me,
My great diftrefs is vifible to all,
Which makes me for relief to call.

In feventy feven at Darnal where I wrought
In a coal Pit this trouble on me brought,
A ftone fell from the roof upon my arm and breaft,
And ever fince I have been much diftreft.

I for my family am oblig'd to afk
To me a proper but unwilling tafk,
I'm left a widower my duty's to provide
Them bread and all I can befide.

Three of them ftand by me as you fee
A heart of ftone muft furely pitty me
Their tender mother in the grave is laid
And I their Father left to afk them bread.

I was brought up a collier, I pretend
In hopes that colliers now will prove my Friend
When I adifmal catastrophe relate
The which makes my misfortune ftill more great.

In September laft alas the fatal Day
One morning then, alas the roof gave way,
Six of us there were confin'd under ground,
Nor none expected e'er we could be found.

We were reliev'd as providence would have
Yet ftill I wifh that mine had been my grave
Not that I had furvived thus to fee;
My helplefs infants fad extremity.

Into an hofpital I was receiv'd,
And ftayed there until I was relived.
But to my loft as you fhall underftand
I loft two fingers off my right hand.

This keepeth me from following any trade,
To help to get my tender Infants bread,
I'm here an object great, O pity me,
Give fuch relief as you feem meet to be.

I for your welfare from my heart will pray,
For what you're pleas'd to grant to me to day
Who afks it here, whole heart's with grief o'er come,
To feek relief, obliged thus to roam.

My mournful cafe unto you I have told,
My helplefs cafe I freely do unfould,
I'm no impoftor you may underftand
It's only truth or look at my right hand.

May heaven above reward them for their good
Who to my tender Infants give their food,
Whofe helplefs cafe fure fympathy doth crave
Their poor Innocent Infants live to fave.

The above is a True Cafe, as Witnefs our Hands,

William Johnfton, Efq. James Howard. Stewards to the above Colliery.

'The Submissive Petition of the Distressed Hugh Boyd'. Broadside.

Striking women chainmakers after a distribution of bread at Cradley Heath in 1910.

THE Civil Authorities regret to find the deluded Keelmen still continue to insult His Majesty's Boats, by throwing Stones when protecting those that are willing to work ; and finding Forbearance any longer will endanger the Lives of those so employed,—This is to caution the peaceable Inhabitants, and Women, and Children, to keep within their Houses during the Time the Keels are passing from the Staiths to Shields, as the Marines have Orders *to fire on the first Man that shall dare to throw a Stone at them.*

November 23rd. 1822.   G. Angus, Printer, Newcastle.

Notice from the Civil Authorities to the Keelmen and Inhabitants of Newcastle, 1822. Handbill.

THE STRIKE
ALPHABET.

A stands for Alphabet, I've turned it into rhyme,
And it's written on the people striking at the present
time.

B stands for Butchers, the people they have shocked
For the people say they'll buy no more, until the price
is dropped.

C stands for Carpenters. they all want better pay,
They want ninepence an hour, and work nine hours
a-day.

D stands for Demonstrations, they are making every
day,
They want a fair day's work, also a fair day's pay.

E stands for Engineers, who acted like noble fellows,
For they freely sent two hundred pounds, to help the
Warwickshire labourers.

F stands for Foreigners, who to England they did come
To work while men were on the strike, but they
quickly drove them home.

G stands for Gold, in which this country does abound
But still there are plenty of starving people to be found

H stands for Homes, of our labouring men you know
Which they scarcely can provide for, the wages are
so low.

I stands for Interest, and the labourers they can see,
Their only way to gain it is by staunch unity.

J stands for John Bull, who brags of his noted fame
The working men create the wealth, and the masters
pocket the same.

K stands for kindred, which we all hold very dear,
But many friends are parted, and are labouring elsewhere.

L stands for Labouring men, who work all hours you
know,
And when they are old and feeble to the workhouse
they can go.

M stands for Masters, they are not all alike,
Some gave way to the men, before they would have
a strike.

N stands for Newcastle, where the strikes they first
began,
They showed an example to every working man.

O stands for Offices, which our Lords and Dukes they
fill,
They little care for the working man, when he's going
down the hill.

P stands for Parliament, where whigs and tories shout
But the interest of the working man they always do
leave out.

Q stands for Quarter day, it always comes too soon,
And the working man if he don't pay, he soon must
quit his home.

R stands for Railway men, who work all hours a day
And are exposed to many dangers for very little pay

S stands for strikes, the men want shorter time,
Instead of working ten hours, they are determined to
work nine.

T stands for Tallymen, they are going to strike, it's true
Where they used to take a shilling a-week, they swear
they will have two

U stands for Unity, may the men join hand-in-hand,
And a victory all win right throughout the land.

V stands for Victoria, head of this nation,
She wants better pay, or she'll throw up her station,

W stands for Washerwomen, O crikey, here's a go,
They want better wages, soap. soda, starch and blue.

X stands for Ten, the hours men used to toil,
But nine they think is quite enough throughout the
English soil.

Y stands for Brigham Young, for more wives he's
going to strike,
He wants five for every week day, and ten for Sunday
night.

Z stands for Zoological Gardens, where wild beasts
you can see,
And if they all turn out on strike, won't it be a jolly
spree.

Disley, Printer, High Street, St. Giles, London.

'The Strike Alphabet'. Street Ballad.

Some strikes, like those of the Kidderminster carpet-weavers in 1828[78] and the northern miners in 1844, inspired a whole series of verses, handbills, proclamations, and printed ballads. A national wave of strikes in 1852–3, the subject of the ballad, 'Striking Times',[80] included a dispute in the cotton trade at Preston. The workers there started a rolling strike for the restoration of a 10 per cent decrease in rates which they had agreed to accept on a temporary basis in 1847. The employers responded by closing all the mills and locking out some 25,000 workers. A prolonged struggle ensued. The newspapers and periodicals descended, including *Household Words*, represented by Charles Dickens, who opposed the strike but sympathized with the strikers, and later put his experience of both into *Hard Times* (1854) (see Introduction). Between thirty and forty of the sheets from this strike, many with more than one song, are still extant. They were produced mainly by the local printer, John Harkness, though in many cases he prudently, if illegally, omitted his imprint. Without naming the author Dickens reprints 'Ten Per Cent! A New Song on the Preston Strike', by William Abbott of Bamber Bridge, which exhorts:

> So now, my boys, don't daunted be,
> But stand out to the fray;
> We ne'er shall yield, nor quit the field,
> Until we've won the day.[81]

Dickens remarks that 'These ballads vary constantly to meet the exigencies of passing events.' Their circulation was clearly an important feature of the workers' campaign. Another, to the sprightly tune of 'The King of the Cannibal Islands', begins:

> Have you not heard the news of late
> About some mighty men so great?
> I mean the swells of Fisher Gate,
> The Cotton Lords of Preston.
> They are a set of stingy blades,
> They've locked up all their mills and shades,
> So now we've nothing else to do
> But come a-singing songs to you.
> So with our ballads we've come out
> To tramp the country round about,
> And try if we cannot live without
> The Cotton Lords of Preston.[82]

It is perhaps a measure of the ballads' success in rallying support and raising funds that the Preston magistrates prohibited their performance by giving 'orders to the policemen to prevent the turn-outs from singing

[them] . . . in the streets'.[83] Despite sympathetic press coverage and over £100,000 subscribed by supporters, after eight months the operatives were obliged to accept defeat and go back to work on the cotton lords' terms.

A further wave of strikes in 1872 again drew a wide variety of workers in many different parts of the country. (The farm-labourers' part in it, together with some of their songs, has been mentioned in Chapter 1.) Disley's 'Strike Alphabet' (see illustration)[84] can be dated closely, for it refers to the donation made to Warwickshire labourers in April 1872 by the Amalgamated Society of Engineers. The piece is remarkable for its combination of militancy and good humour.

Unemployment

If strikes and trade union struggles have remained a feature of British industrial life to the present day, so has unemployment. 'O, why don't you work / Like the other men do?' asked a song of 1908, and then answered with another question: 'How in hell can I work / When there's no work to do?' This song, 'Hallelujah, I'm a Bum', which was printed by the 'Wobblies' (Industrial Workers of the World), became popular on both sides of the Atlantic.[85] (The tune was subsequently used for a song opposing the First World War, for which, see Chapter 8.) Demonstrators in the 1930s sang, to the tune of 'The Policeman's Holiday':

> Who starves kiddies in the U.A.B./?
> Who puts twopence on the workers' tea?
> Who wants war because they'd like to see
> Swollen profits sweated out of you and me?
> Who's laid plans upon conscription bent,
> No one but the National Government!
> That is why the ranks of Labour all united shout:
> Take your cards and beat it, Neville,
> Clear out![86]

In Scotland they sang 'We're the lads fae the tap o' the hill, / We never worked, we're never will, / We're on the Bureau', to the tune of 'Bye, Bye, Blackbird'.[87] In Northern Ireland they showed a bitter humour which would surely be appreciated as much now as it was then.

> Last night I had a dream—bad 'cess to my dreaming,
> I thought I was standing at the labour borue;
> But when I got inside the clerk he said he was sorry
> For keeping me standing so long in the queue.

/ Unemployed Assistance Board

'Just take a seat, for I'm sure you're tired.
Sit down and rest and I'll sign up for you,
And if you're feeling hungry just call the attendant'.
I shouted, 'Good heavens, is this the borue?'[88]

Indeed, workers' attempts in the 1980s to resist the spread of unemployment and the decline in the industries in which they are employed seem to have rekindled the fires of popular creativity. The miners' strike of 1984–5 was defensive rather than offensive, conservative rather than revolutionary. Coal had powered the industrial revolution and the development of modern Britain. Miners took great pride in their long history of struggle, and were fiercely determined. They faced the full might of the state machine, and the surprising thing is not that they were defeated, but that they resisted for so long. The sustained, active support of the women of mining areas was vital; so were the meetings, demonstrations, collections, and concerts. As in the miners' strike of 1844, a profusion of poems and songs sprang from those involved and from their supporters. They were performed in pubs and clubs and on the streets, published in pamphlets and on flimsy sheets, and circulated on videos and cassettes. The material, which would repay detailed study, was uniform in commitment, but diverse in quality. The veteran singer/song-writer Ewan MacColl contributed what are probably the two outstanding songs: 'Daddy, What Did You Do in the Strike?' and 'Only doing their Job'.[89] The tune for the latter is based on 'The Chapter of Kings', which was used for both 'Jone o'Grinfilt' and 'The Keelman's Stick'. The text, reflecting views widely held by the strikers and their families, deals with police partiality. The song is unashamedly partisan, as well as acerbic and pugnacious. It takes in fascism in the 1930s and the wider issues of the 1980s:

If you're black or just brown, if you're jobless and down,
If you speak for a world which is saner,
If you stand up and fight for what's yours by right,
If you're an anti-nuclear campaigner:
Remember the chap in the comical hat
Is one of humanity's crosses—
Wherever there's trouble, whatever the struggle,
He'll be on the side of the bosses.

During the same strike, Peter Coe's song on unemployment also developed into a general critique of social ills. Both his inspiration and his title came from a graffitto which he saw on a bridge in Bradford: 'It's a Mean Old Scene'.

IT'S A MEAN OLD SCENE

Chorus

Monday morning, stand in line; four million forms for you to sign.
You're unemployed, so take your time. It's a mean old scene.
Land of hope and tarnished glory, my old man once voted Tory,
But now he tells a different story. It's a mean old scene.
'It's a mean old scene' was written on the wall;
'It's a mean old scene', don't you hear me when I call?
It's a mean old scene.

Plaster's cracking on my ceiling, windows leak and paper's peeling;
Rent arrears, but I'm appealing. It's a mean old scene.
And the landlord's knocking at my door; lost my job, can't pay no more,
And now I'm one of the idle poor. It's a mean old scene.

Oh relatives 'phone, no use lying; husband's left and the kids are crying,
Solicitors write but you keep replying. It's a mean old scene.
And I've taught kids from Pakistan, Bangladesh and Vietnam,
For strangers in a foreign land. It's a mean old scene.

Oh unemployment cures inflation; fanatics breed assassination;
Indifference leading to starvation. It's a mean old scene.
It's the same in many a northern town, mills and shipyards run aground;
We built them up, you knock them down. It's a mean old scene.

Now a mining man is worth his hire but the National Coal Board still conspire.
Come on, MacGregor, and light my fire. It's a mean old scene.
Civil servant's indignation, leaking secret information;
Got six months from a grateful nation. It's a mean old scene.

Greenham women form a chain, dancing with the sons of Cain;
Don't want no cruise or no hard rain. It's a mean old scene.
I'm stuck in bed on a Sunday morning, aching head, still tired and yawning.
Headlines carry an early warning. It's a mean old scene.[90]

4

CRIME

DURING the last few hundred years, the chief punishments have successively been (albeit with overlaps) execution, transportation, and imprisonment. Until they were brought to an end in 1868, public executions provided perennial fascination, and even entertainment. Indeed, they were often more of a popular celebration than the awesome ritual intended. Foreign visitors marvelled at the proceedings. 'Those who go gaily to be hanged, or at least show no fear', wrote a Swiss traveller in 1694, 'cause people to say that they died as *Gentlemen*; and it is to deserve this praise that most die like beasts, showing no feeling, or like madmen, thinking only of entertaining the spectators.'[1] In the eighteenth century the great Tyburn fairs, near the present Marble Arch, attracted thousands, and Edward Thompson has described the hangings there as 'a central ceremonial'[2] of London life at the time. Swift evoked the spectacle in his poem on Tom Clinch (1726).[3]

A very similar scene is depicted in Hogarth's celebrated engraving of 1747 of the idle apprentice's execution. The dense press of spectators is partly accommodated in stands. A pigeon is being released to fly back to Newgate Gaol with news of the prisoner's safe arrival. The man himself is making slow progress through the throng in a cart which also carries his coffin and a chaplain who exhorts him to repent. The triple tree of the gallows awaits. Although executions were meant to deter crime, pickpockets are at work in the crowd. The holiday atmosphere is underlined by the presence of sellers of cakes, apples, oranges, and drink. A woman of substantial proportions holds a child, and at the same time, with hand cupped to her ear, sings or shouts the apprentice's 'Last Dying Speech & Confession'. The words can be read on the sheet she proffers for sale.

Gallows literature of this kind flourished for centuries. Its origins seem to lie in the privilege sometimes accorded those about to die of making a valedictory statement. James Hopkinson (born 1819) was often taken to

Gallows Hill in Nottingham, and remembered that 'Sometimes from the cart in which a criminal was drawn to the place of execution he would address the assembled thousands either to attest his innocence to the last, or caution his hearers about keeping bad company and coming like him to an untimely end.'[4] Such speeches were reported in newspapers and printed on broadsheets. It was a short step to versification, whereupon the sufferer was said to be twice executed, 'At the Gallowes first, and after in a Ballad Sung to some villanous tune'.[5] Some early examples include 'Of the endes and deathes of two Prisoners, lately pressed to death in Newgate' (1569),[6] 'A woefull ballade made by master George Mannyngton an houre before he suffered at Cambridge castell' (1576),[7] 'The Lamentable lyfe and death of Robert Sturman who suffered at Tyburne the 24th of Januarie' (1594),[8] and 'Luke Huttons lamentation: which he wrote the day before his death, being condemned to be hanged at Yorke this last assizes for the robberies and trespasses committed'.[9] (Hutton, a Cambridge undergraduate who took to housebreaking, was executed in 1598.)

Some even managed to sing their own farewells. James McPherson was hanged at Banff in 1700, after a long career as a robber. A week elapsed between sentence and execution, which was a long time by later English standards. (An Act of 1752 provided that a condemned criminal be hanged two days after sentence, or three, if the second fell on a Sunday.) A reprieve was known to be on its way for McPherson, but its timely arrival was circumvented by the simple expedient of putting the town clock forward. In view of such unseemly haste, it seems most improbable that the prisoner would have been allowed to delay proceedings by singing; but tradition holds that he did precisely this, accompanying himself on a fiddle, which he defiantly broke across his knee before going to his death:

> Fareweel ye dungeons dark an' strang,
> And all beneath the skies.
> McPherson's time will no be lang:
> Below thon gallows tree I'll hing.[10]

McPherson's 'rant', as it was called, was later admired by Burns, who included a reworking of it in his own poems, and by Carlyle, who found it 'wild and stormful', 'dwelling in ear and mind with strange tenacity'.

Another spirited farewell which circulated for many years, apparently without benefit of print, is ascribed to a contemporary of McPherson's, Jack or John Hall. Hall was born of poor parents who lived in a court off Grays Inn Road, London, and who sold him for a guinea at the age of 7 to be a climbing boy. Readers of Charles Kingsley's *Water Babies* (1863) will know how such boys (and girls) swept chimneys by scrambling up inside them. The young Hall soon ran away from this disagreeable occupation, and made a living as a pickpocket. Later he turned to housebreaking, for which he was whipped in 1692 and sentenced to death in 1700. He was reprieved, then released, but returned to crime and was rearrested in 1702 for stealing luggage from a stage-coach. This time, he was branded on the cheek and imprisoned for two years. Finally, having been taken in the act of burgling a house in Stepney, he was hanged at Tyburn on 17 December 1707.

JACK HALL

O my name it is Jack Hall, chimney sweep, chimney sweep,
O my name it is Jack Hall, chimney sweep.
O my name it is Jack Hall and I've robbed both great and small,
And my neck shall pay for all when I die, when I die,
And my neck shall pay for all when I die.

I have twenty pounds in store, that's no joke, that's no joke,
I have twenty pounds in store, that's no joke.
I have twenty pounds in store, and I'll rob for twenty more,
And my neck shall pay for all, when I die, when I die,
And my neck shall pay for all when I die.

O they tell me that in gaol I shall die, I shall die,
O they tell me that in gaol I shall die.
O they tell me that in gaol I shall drink no more brown ale,
But be dashed if ever I fail till I die, till I die,
But be dashed if ever I fail till I die.

O I rode up Tyburn Hill in a cart, in a cart,
O I rode up Tyburn Hill in a cart.
O I rode up Tyburn Hill, and 'twas there I made my will,
Saying, The best of friends must part, so farewell, so farewell,
Saying, The best of friends must part, so farewell.

Up the ladder I did grope, that's no joke, that's no joke,
Up the ladder I did grope, that's no joke.
Up the ladder I did grope, and the hangman spread the rope,
O but never a word said I coming down, coming down,
O but never a word said I coming down.[11]

The characteristic metre of Hall's goodnight is used widely for other
songs, from those of the Diggers of 1649 (see Chapter 7) to the songs of
the Irish famine of some three hundreds years later. In between came
ballads of villains and heroes, including Kidd, Benbow, Byng, Paul Jones,
and Nelson. No early copy of the Hall piece survives, and the text given
here was put together by Cecil Sharp from fragments sung by Devon and
Somerset singers in the early twentieth century. The tune, 'Chimney
Sweep', was mentioned in 1719 and (probably) printed the following
year.[12] The earliest text of the song is this fragment which Francis Place
recollected from the 1780s:

I furnish'd all my rooms, ev'ry one, ev'ry one,
I furnish'd all my rooms, ev'ry one.
I furnish'd all my rooms with mops, brushes, and hair brooms,
Wash balls and sweet perfumes, them I stole, them I stole.

I sail'd up Holborn Hill in a cart, in a cart,
I sail'd up Holborn Hill in a cart.
I sail'd up Holborn Hill, at St Giles's drunk my fill,
And at Tyburn made my will in a cart, in a cart.[13]

A full version (see Introduction) was printed by John Pitts, sometime
between 1820 and 1844, and by 1849 G. W. Ross, a music-hall performer,
had produced his ribald derivative, 'The Ballad of Sam Hall'. A *Punch*
cartoon of that year (see illustration) shows him singing it at the Cyder
Cellar, Chelsea.[14] Ross's version in turn gave rise to many others, some of
them obscene, which are still current in Britain and the United States.
Meanwhile, the original Jack Hall continued to circulate orally both in
England and Ireland.[15]

Implicit in the song of Jack Hall are sympathy and even admiration for
him, which are at variance with at least one near-contemporary view.
Captain Alexander Smith wrote of Hall in his *Complete History of the Lives*

and Robberies of the Most Notorious Highwaymen, Footpads, Shoplifts and Cheats of Both Sexes, published in 1719:

This most notorious villain was bred a thief from his mother's womb, and there is no sort of theft but what he was expert in, as housebreaking, going on the footpad, shoplifting, . . . pilfering, . . . picking pockets of watches, money, books or wipes, that's to say, handkerchiefs. . . . This most notorious malefactor thought it no injustice to rob everybody; and all his vices, whatever deformity the eye of the world apprehended to be in them, his unaccountable wickedness looked upon as no less than absolute in all his virtues.

A similar gulf between sentiment and reality occurs with Dick Turpin, who in popular balladry achieved 'popularity such as no *Plutarch's Lives* ever attained among the cultured classes'.[16] He is perhaps the only highwayman whose name is nationally known to this day. He was an Essex man who quickly graduated from butcher's apprentice to cattle-thief, then smuggler, housebreaker, and murderer, as well as highwayman. When his own area grew too hot for him, he moved north, and for a time made a living out of dealing in horses in the Yorkshire village of Welton, using the name Palmer (the maiden name of his wife or mother, depending on the account followed). He was arrested after a quarrel over his shooting of a neighbour's cockerel while drunk, and his identity came to light when his former schoolmaster, James Smith, happened to see a letter from Turpin to his brother-in-law in Essex, and recognized the handwriting. John Palmer, now revealed as Richard Turpin, was promptly tried at York on a charge of horse-stealing, and hanged. This was in April 1739, when Turpin was 34 years old.

> Now Turpin he's condemned to die,
> To hang upon yon gallows high;
> Whose legacy is a strong rope,
> For stealing of a dung-hill cock.
> O poor Turpin, hero,
> O poor Turpin, O.[17]

He went to his death in the 'undaunted manner' which was *de rigueur*. *The Gentleman's Magazine* reported that 'as he mounted the Ladder, feeling his right leg tremble, he stamp'd it down, and looking about him with an unconcerned Air, he spoke a few words to the Topsman, then threw himself off, and expir'd in five Minutes'.[18] He had earlier spent the large sum of £3. 10s. to pay five men to follow his corpse as mourners, and to supply them with white hatbands and gloves (white being one of the colours of mourning). His grave was dug very deep to discourage body-snatchers, but the next morning it was found empty. An angry crowd searched York for the body, and found it laid out in a doctor's house, awaiting dissection. After venting their wrath on the doctor's equipment and materials, the people triumphantly returned the body to its resting-place, adding a considerable quantity of quicklime to ensure that it would be disturbed no more. How much the action was due to the widespread popular detestation of body-snatchers and how much to admiration for Turpin is impossible to say; perhaps something of both.

For much of the seventeenth and eighteenth centuries highwaymen were commonplace, and their numbers increased dramatically after every war and during every period of distress. As late as 1802, confronted with the prospect of peace with France, a sailor resolved:

> I will take to the road for,
> I'd better do that than worse;
> And everyone that comes by I'll cry:
> 'Damn you, deliver your purse'.[19]

Many highwaymen, such as Nevison, Maclaine, and Turpin, not to speak of the fictional MacHeath of *The Beggar's Opera* (1727), were celebrities, and there were scores of lesser note. 'The vulgar', wrote Macaulay, 'eagerly drank in tales of their ferocity and audacity, of their occasional acts of generosity and good nature, of their amours, of their miraculous escapes, of their desperate struggles, and of their manly bearing at the bar and in the cart.'[20] There were also female highwaymen. One, Mary Pile,[21] was sentenced to seven years transportation in 1785, at the age of 20, and sailed in the first convict fleet to Botany Bay. Another was celebrated in a ballad, albeit one dealing with love rather than crime. Its heroine, Sylvia, robs her true love in the guise of a highwayman, to test whether he will surrender the ring she has given him as a token of love. He makes no bones about losing 'his watch and store', but says: 'This diamond ring's a token dear, / I'll lose my life ere it I'll spare,' thereby passing the test.[22] In some versions Sylvia later restores his property and reveals the imposture, but tells him that if he had given up the ring she would have shot him dead.

Macaulay's comment on highwaymen refers to the seventeenth century, but it is applicable to a wide range of places and periods, from the time of Robin Hood and his merry men[23] to the Great Train Robbers of 1963,[24] and from American outlaws[25] to Australian bush-rangers.[26] Many such people were celebrated in ballads, though their heroic status was in fact often dubious. Turpin himself was a callous, somewhat incompetent ruffian, but dash and daring seem to have been conferred upon him. A ballad entitled 'The Dunghill Cock; or Turpin's Valiant Exploits'[27] was

printed in about 1796, though it probably dates from much earlier. In it
Turpin successively robs a lawyer, an exciseman, a judge and a usurer, and
also outwits them, in a manner that recalls Robin Hood's encounters with
unpopular monks and sheriffs. The song circulated orally until the
twentieth century, and stories of Turpin's deeds continued to be told long
after the age of highwaymen was past. Elements from elsewhere gravitated
to the Turpin canon. The ride from London to York, for example, was
transferred to Turpin from 'Swift John' Nevison, who accomplished the
feat in 1676. Black Bess, the wonder horse, seems to have been invented
by W. H. Ainsworth, in whose novel *Rookwood* (1834) Turpin is shown in a
very favourable light. Forty years after the publication of the book, Richard
Jefferies reported that the favourite set of prints on the walls of the most
humble cottage showed Turpin with Black Bess on the famous ride to
York.[28] In the twentieth century, films and television have perpetuated the
glamour of Turpin in particular, and highwaymen in general.

Crime against property was (and is) often regarded sympathetically by
those who had (and have) few possessions of their own. It seems that when
violence against people occurs in the course of such crime, it is often
overlooked. Turpin's daring and success obscured his crudeness of
method, just as the brutality shown by the Great Train Robbers in their
theft was overshadowed by the magnitude of their haul (two million
pounds). On the other hand, crimes specifically directed against the
person, while exciting intense interest, also arouse deep repugnance,
albeit mingled with fascination. Nor do crimes against the dead escape
condemnation; on the contrary, they arouse particular detestation.

Body-snatching

In the early eighteenth century there was a considerable increase in the
numbers of doctors and students undergoing training in anatomy. During
their study, they were no longer expected merely to observe dissections of
human bodies, but to perform them. However, the number of corpses
available was limited. In London, for example, surgeons were allowed the
bodies of six executed felons per year from Elizabethan times until 1723,
when the figure was increased to ten. In Edinburgh, only one malefactor's
body was allowed yearly from 1505 until 1694, when the provision was
extended to include

those bodies that dye in the correction-house; the bodies of fundlings who dye
betwixt the tyme that they are weaned and their being put to schools or trades; also
the dead bodies of such as are stiflet at birth, which are exposed, and have none to
owne them; as also the dead bodies of such as are *felo de se*; likewayes the bodies of
such as are put to death by sentence of the magistrat.[29]

This was still entirely inadequate to meet the demand, and the deficiency was made up by illegally exhuming freshly buried corpses or carrying off the bodies of those hanged. Defending the corpse would be relatives, friends, or workmates, who were keen to ensure a decent burial. Sailors were particularly active in this regard. They needed to be, for a quarter of those hanged at Tyburn in the first half of the eighteenth century had been to sea.[30]

It was not only body-snatchers who were hated and feared, the obloquy spread to their paymasters, the doctors. Sailors had a particular dislike for doctors, partly because of the cavalier medical treatment some of them had received at sea—there were cases of surgeons stealing and selling medicines—and partly because they saw hospitals ashore, with the connivance of those in charge, as providing prey for the press-gangs.

Unseemly struggles took place over bodies after executions. Samuel Richardson, writing to his brother in 1741 after a visit to Tyburn, remarked on the 'Tumult' between 'the Friends of the [five] Persons executed' and people 'sent by private Surgeons to obtain Bodies for Dissection'. 'The Contests between these', he went on, 'were fierce and bloody, and frightful to look at.' One of the bodies was rescued and 'carried to the Lodging of his Wife, who not being in the way to receive it, they immediately hawked it about to every Surgeon they could think of; and when none would buy it, they rubb'd Tar all over it, and left it in a Field hardly cover'd with earth'.[31]

In order to make the death sentence more awesome, the Murder Act of 1752 added to the death penalty the compulsory delivery of all bodies for dissection after execution (as we have seen in the case of some of the Luddites), and instituted seven years' transportation for anyone attempting to recover such corpses. The provision for dissection was by no means universally observed; nevertheless, the supply of cadavers greatly increased. Even so, it was not sufficient to keep pace with the demand. The theft of bodies therefore continued, and those engaged in it were given the macabre name of 'resurrection men'. No corpse was immune. Even the body of Laurence Sterne, who died in London in 1768, was stolen. When it turned up for dissection, a friend of Sterne's was present at the demonstration, and was horrified to recognize it. He seems to have recovered at least the skull, which is now preserved at Coxwold, Sterne's former home, near York.

The distress about such happenings was widespread. In a poem by Robert Southey, a surgeon who has dissected many bodies fears the same fate for his own corpse, and takes elaborate precautions to avoid it:

And all night long let three stout men
The vestry watch within;
To each man give a gallon of beer,
And a keg of Hollands gin;

Powder and ball and blunderbuss,
To save me if he can,
And eke five guineas if he shoot
A Resurrection Man.

And let them watch me for three weeks,
My wretched corpse to save;
For then I think that I may stink
Enough to rest in my grave.[32]

Thomas Hood put this macabre speech into the mouth of a newly departed wife who comes as a ghost to her husband's bedside:

O William dear! O William dear!
My rest eternal ceases;
Alas! my everlasting peace
Is broken into pieces.

I thought the last of all my cares
Would end with my last minute;
But tho' I went to my long home,
I didn't stay long in it.

The body-snatchers they have come,
And made a snatch at me;
It's very hard them kind of men
Won't let a body be.

You thought that I was buried deep,
Quite decent like and chary,
But from her grave in Mary-bone,
They've come and boned your Mary.

The arm that used to take your arm
Is took to Dr Vyse;
And both my legs are gone to walk
The hospital at Guy's.[33]

Like William, relatives tried to protect bodies by burying them deep. In one case, snatchers found a new grave with apparently neither coffin nor body; but when they looked more carefully, they found 'a sort of cave along one side of the grave',[34] with the coffin concealed in it. Another expedient was to place huge stones over graves or to erect formidable iron cages, called 'mortsafes'. Many of these still exist in cemeteries, but they were available only to the well-off. Ultimately, the only sure way of protecting a body was to keep vigil over the grave for as long as necessary, as Southey's surgeon knew. Even this might be circumvented by the snatchers: 'We got the watchers into the public-house, and so entertained them with our songs and stories that our object was accomplished quietly, and we left the watchers boasting what they would have done if the body-snatchers had dared to come.' The speaker here is a doctor who as a student took part in expeditions to the country villages around Sheffield to procure bodies for the medical school. It was dangerous work, 'for not only were the feelings of families grievously wounded, by fears or realities, but there existed an ever-smouldering popular indignation, which the slightest incident might any day have caused to break out in riot and outrage'.[35]

What made matters worse was the propensity of body-snatchers to select victims from the ranks of the living. As a Gateshead ballad put it:

> Good people all attention give,
> And mind well what I say,
> The resurrection men that's now about,
> Will take both the living and the dead away;
> All the church yards the country round,
> By these villains are surveyed,
> And all that's buried through the day,
> At night they steal away.
>
> They've got instruments will draw them from the grave,
> And leave the coffin there still,
> Besides they've plasters for the use,
> To take the living off as well;
> The resurrection trade was ne'er so good,
> As they the story tell,
> That four pounds was once the price of a corpse,
> But now the price is twelve.[36]

The instruments mentioned were probably iron hooks. A hole was dug where the head lay, and the hooks were used first to tear open the coffin, then to pull out the body. 'Plasters' were perhaps pads used to suffocate the living.

A series of scandals, including the murder of a child in 1752 by two women body-snatchers who sold the corpse for 2s. 6d. and were later hanged in Edinburgh, eventually led to the appointment of a select committee of the House of Commons. The evidence received was devastating, and the committee's report (1828) was strongly in favour of reform. Four years later a new Anatomy Act empowered the Home Secretary to issue licences permitting the lawful acquisition of cadavers for dissection, but not without the powerful impetus given by a fresh series of murders. In 1827 an Irishman, William Burke, was living in Edinburgh, where he met a fellow countryman, William Hare. They stole the body of an old soldier from its coffin before burial, substituting for it a quantity of bark from a tan-yard. They received the sum of £7 10s., which so delighted them that over a period of nine months they murdered at least sixteen people. They chose victims, mainly women and children, from the margins of society. The bodies (one of them allegedly still warm) were accepted by the medical school with no questions asked. The method of killing was smothering, for which 'burking' later became a synonym. The body of the last to die, an old woman, was discovered before Burke and Hare could take it away, and they were arrested. Hare, who was probably the worse of the two, promptly turned king's evidence, thereby saving his own skin and ensuring that Burke would be convicted and sentenced to hanging. The execution, in January 1829, was attended by a hostile crowd of some 40,000 people, including Sir Walter Scott, a keen follower of murder trials and a collector of ballads and broadsides relating to them. He noted in his journal:

Burke the murderer hanged this morning. The mob, which was immense, demanded Knox [the surgeon who had bought the bodies] and Hare, but, though greedy for more victims, received with shouts the solitary wretch who found his way to the gallows out of five or six who seem not less guilty than he. But the story begins to be stale, although I believe a doggerel ballad upon it would be popular, however brutal the wit.[37]

In fact, there were over twenty ballads on the subject (for example, 'William Burk's Execution'; see illustration) one of them to the tune of 'McPherson's Rant' not to speak of a score of books and pamphlets and twenty-three prose broadsides.[38]

After the execution, Burke's body was dissected before a class of medical students, and was then put on public exhibition. There were 30,000 visitors. It was then salted down for future use, and the skeleton is still preserved in the Anatomical Museum at Edinburgh University. No action was taken against Dr Knox, but his career suffered, and he died an obscure general practitioner in Hackney. A quatrain which did not neglect to ascribe a share of the blame to Knox survived in oral tradition until recent years. It was used as the chorus for a song written in 1970 by Angus Russell of Kilwinning, Ayrshire.

CRIME

Burke and Hare

To help the folk at medical school
Word is spread around.
A body nae mair than ten days' auld
Will bring in fourteen pund.
It's a terrible thing, but true to say
In this age o' grace,
A man's worth puckle[a] when alive
But plenty when he's deid.
An it's doon the close an up the stair,
An but and ben[b] with Burke and Hare.
Burke's the butcher an Hare's the thief
And Knox is the man that buys the beef.

[a] *little*   [b] backwards and forwards

An in the dark o' mony a nicht
When a' guid folk are sleepin',
By the dyke an' in the kirkyaird
Come two shadows creepin'.
An many a man that's cauld richt throu'
An safely laid away,
He never thocht it was nae the last
He'd seen the licht o' day.

But no content wi howkin'*c* deid—
A ploy that aye gets harder—
They started pickin' healthy folk
And then committin' murder
And in the dark to the countryside
Creeps a fearsome pair:
Be ye man or wife or wean*d*
Ye're no safe frae Burke an' Hare.

But noo Auld Reekie*e* can sleep at last
These twa will trade nae mair:
It's the gallows-tree for William Burke
And a pauper's grave for Hare.[39]

In fact, Burke and Hare were not grave-robbers; nor did they operate in the country. Hare would undoubtedly have been lynched had he remained in Edinburgh, so he made his way south and found work as a labourer. It is said that he ended his days as a blind beggar in London, his eyes having been destroyed when fellow workmen discovered his identity and threw him into a lime-pit.

Murder

Ballads expressing popular revulsion against murderers continued to appear throughout the nineteenth century. 'Then along would come the ballad singer', wrote Edwin Grey of his childhood in Harpenden:

He would pass slowly along the roadway by the front of the houses, singing some harrowing verses made up specially for the occasion, the singer fitting some sort of drawling tune to the words, the more harrowing and bloodcurdling he could make the sordid theme appear the better in all probability would be the sale of his papers, for many of the people would buy whether they could read it or not; the verses would be there for anybody to read who wished. These verses were printed on single sheets of cheap paper, and sold at one penny or halfpenny per sheet.[40]

The last such singer heard by Grey was a man with verses on the murder of

c digging up   *d* child   *e* Edinburgh

Harriet Lane by Henry Wainwright, in 1875. In 1890 George Sturt recorded in his journal a man 'hawking (Autolycus-like) from door to door in the villages': 'He had with him topical songs etc: including something . . . about the woman lately hanged at Newgate. He regretted his small stock of this particular sheet: had sold so many—they did *take* so. This sort of thing circulates amongst the healthiest class of people,—the rural working class namely.'[41]

In 1896 a booklet[42] with no fewer than five songs to traditional or popular tunes was devoted to the multiple murders of Mrs Dyer, the baby farmer, and as late as 1903 the case of Samuel Dougal gave rise to a street ballad. Dougal had seduced a woman for her money, then killed her so that he might freely pursue his hobby of seducing young women, which he did apparently by persuading them to take off all their clothes, so that he could, among other things, give them lessons in bicycle riding. The murderer himself mentioned the sheet in a letter he wrote from Chelmsford gaol:

I see there were at the show at Bishops Stortford two men, one playing a banjo and singing a ballad on the Moat House, etc. [Dougal's farm, and the scene of the crime], and the other was dispensing of the copies of the song at 1*d.* each, and doing a good business. I saw one verse of the song in the local paper, and no doubt you may see a copy of it in your neighbourhood. If you do, make a note of it for me, please.

Richard Altick, who quotes the letter, wryly comments: 'He did not make it clear whether he wanted to order a quantity or sue the printer.'[43] Dougal was hanged. The sheet, unfortunately, does not seem to have survived.

During the nineteenth century, and especially during the Victorian era, public preoccupation with crime was intense. A whole book has been written solely on the part played by crime and criminals in the works of Charles Dickens.[44] It has been suggested that 'the Victorian psyche may have found murder to be a kind of immoral equivalent to war',[45] yet there were plenty of real wars to attract people's attention. The Victorian era was one of sexual prudery, and it might be contended that murder (which often had a sexual element) was a kind of moral equivalent to sex. Certainly, there was an immense gallows literature of the streets. Like that of Burke and Hare, a single case might inspire a whole series of sheets on the circumstances of a murder and its discovery, later developments during enquiries, the trial, possibly the confession, and finally the execution of the criminal. Verisimilitude was taken to its furthest extent perhaps in one of the many ballads dealing with the rape and murder of Mary Ashford near Birmingham in 1817, in which a firsthand account of the events is given through the persona of the victim's ghost.[46] Some sheets provided comprehensive coverage: 'They included a prose résumé of the murder itself, a confession (if such had been vouchsafed by the condemned man, or in some circumstances even if he had not), perhaps a lugubrious ballad allegedly composed by him in the death cell, and finally a description of the execution itself, including the sufferer's last dying spech.'[47] Stock wood-cuts were used, often with a space which permitted the printer to adjust the hanging bodies shown in accordance with the number of people executed on a particular occasion. For an important murder, a new cut might be commissioned, which would itself be re-used subsequently on other occasions.[48]

Sheets on the most sensational murders sold in enormous numbers. It has been suggested, for example, that as many as two and half a million copies respectively of the sheets on Rush and the Mannings were sold in 1849. Maria and Frederick Manning were hanged at Horsemonger Lane gaol in London for the murder of Maria's lover. James Rush was executed six months earlier at Norwich for murdering the recorder, Isaac Jermy, and his son. The case shows that even provincial murders could arouse metropolitan, and even national, interest. The figures are probably exaggerated, but sales were undoubtedly very high, as is confirmed by various street vendors interviewed by Henry Mayhew. One 'running patterer', who had started his career in 1828 at the age of 16 with 'The Last Dying Speech and Full Confession of William Corder' (see illustration),[49] stated:

There's nothing beats a stunning good murder. Why there was Rush—I lived on him for a month or more. When I commenced with Rush, I was 14s. in debt for rent, and in less than fourteen days I astonished the wise men in the east by paying my landlord all I owed him. Since Dan'el Good [1842] there had been little or nothing doing in the murder line—no one could cap him—till Rush turned up a regular trump for us. Why I went down to Norwich expressly to work the execution. I worked my way down there with 'a sorrowful lamentation' of his own composing, which I'd got written by the blind man expressly for the occasion. On the morning of the execution we beat all the regular newspapers out of the field; for we had the full, true and particular account down, you see, by our own express, and that can beat anything they can ever publish; for we gets it printed several days afore it comes off, and goes and stands with it right under the drop.

Another of Mayhew's informants, a ballad-singer (otherwise known as a 'street screamer'), told how he had been paid a shilling, the standard fee, to write a piece on Rush. He explained:

I write most of the Newgate ballads for the printers in the [Seven] Dials, and, indeed, anything that turns up. I get a shilling for a 'copy of verses written by the wretched culprit the night previous to his execution'. I wrote Courvoisier's sorrowful lamentation [1840]. I called it 'A Voice from The Gaol'. . . . I did the helegy, too, on Rush's execution. It was supposed, like the rest, to be written by the culprit himself, and was particularly penitent. I didn't write that to order—I knew they would want a copy of verses from the culprit. The publisher read it over, and said, 'That's the thing for the street public'. I only got a shilling for Rush. Indeed, they are all the same price, no matter how popular they may be. I wrote the life of Manning in verse.[50]

Not surprisingly, such productions are often of poor quality. They exude unrelieved gloom, and are as dark and melodramatic as the plays they often inspired. Victims, predominantly female, clasp their hands, lift their eyes to the unresponsive heavens, and plead in vain for mercy. Revolting detail is not spared, as in the 'Verses on Daniel Good':

> And when she was dead this sad deed to hide,
> The limbs from her body he straight did divide,
> Her bowels ript open and dripping with gore,
> The child from the womb this black monster tore.[51]

Nevertheless, the message is usually moralistic: 'Oh, pray, young men, by me take warning' or 'Oh, drink, thou cursed beverage, what acts thou prompts us to do.' The writing frequently falls into bathos or incongruity: 'Then with a sharp hatchet her head he did cleave. / She begged for mercy. . .' or:

> Oh listen to this railway wonder
> Poor Briggs received the fatal wound
> Between Old Ford Bridge and Hackney Wick
> And very near great London town.[52]

Or again:

> Eliza Chestney to her Mistress ran,
> Saying, 'Dearest mistress, who is this man?'
> And, while she pressed her mistress to her heart,
> A bullet pierced in a dangerous part.[53]

Such carelessness, such clumsiness, such insensitivity arouse hilarity instead of pity in a reader today, though not apparently, in his counterpart of the last century. On the contary, Altick says, referring to a whole range of matter, not merely street ballads: 'It is not an exaggeration to say that the spread of the reading habit through the Victorian populace, with all its profound political, social and cultural consequences, was signally assisted by the presence of murder as a topic of perennial interest.'[54]

An execution ballad of 1690.

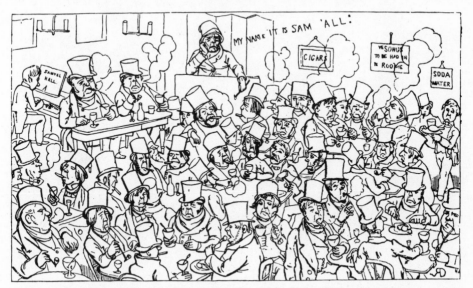

G. W. Ross singing 'Sam Hall' at the Cyder Cellar, Chelsea. *Punch cartoon*, 1849.

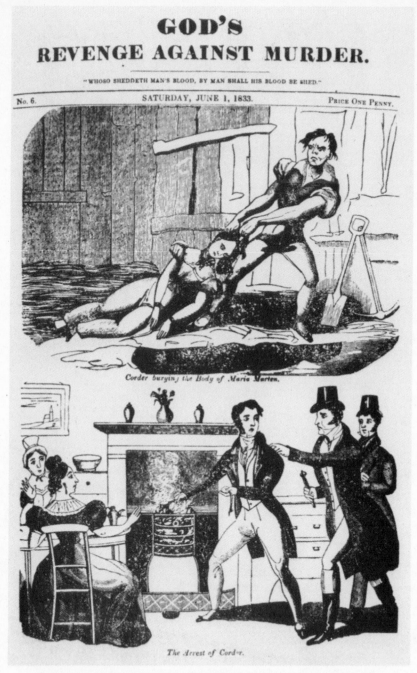

GOD'S
REVENGE AGAINST MURDER.

"WHOSO SHEDDETH MAN'S BLOOD, BY MAN SHALL HIS BLOOD BE SHED."

No. 6.   SATURDAY, JUNE 1, 1833.   PRICE ONE PENNY.

Corder burying the Body of Maria Marten.

The Arrest of Corder.

Sensational news sheet of 1 June 1833 showing Corder burying the body of his victim, and his subsequent arrest.

CONFESSION AND EXECUTION OF
WILLIAM CORDER,
THE MURDERER OF MARIA MARTEN.

Since the tragical affair between Thurtell and Weare, no event has occurred connected with the criminal annals of our country which has excited so much interest as the trial of Corder, who was justly convicted of the murder of Maria Marten on Friday last.

THE CONFESSION.

"Bury Gaol, August 10th, 1828.—Condemned cell. "Sunday evening, half-past Eleven.

"I acknowledge being guilty of the death of poor Maria Marten, by shooting her with a pistol. The particulars are as follows :—When we left her father's house, we began quarrelling about the burial of the child: she apprehended the place wherein it was deposited would be found out. The quarrel continued about three quarters of an hour upon this sad and about other subjects. A scuffle ensued, and during the scuffle, and at the time I think she had hold of me, I took the pistol from the side pocket of my velveteen jacket and fired. She fell, and died in an instant. I never saw her even struggle. I was overwhelmed with agitation and dismay :—the body fell near the front doors on the floor of the barn. A vast quantity of blood issued from the wound, and ran on to the floor and through the crevices. Having determined to bury the body in the barn (about two hours after she was dead. I went and borrowed a spade of Mrs Stow, but before I went there I dragged the body from the barn into the chaff-house, and locked the barn. I returned again to the barn, and began to dig a hole, but the spade being a bad one, and the earth firm and hard, I was obliged to go home for a pickaxe and a better spade, with which I dug the hole, and then buried the body. I think I dragged the body by the handkerchief that was tied round her neck. It was dark when I finished covering up the body. I went the next day, and washed the blood from off the barn-floor. I declare to Almighty God I had no sharp instrument about me, and no other wound but the one made by the pistol was inflicted by me. I have been guilty of great idleness, and at times led a dissolute life, but I hope through the mercy of God to be forgiven. WILLIAM CORDER."

Witness to the signing by the said William Corder, JOHN ORRIDGE.

Condemned cell, Eleven o'clock, Monday morning, August 11th, 1828.

The above confession was read over carefully to the prisoner in our presence, who stated most solemnly it was true, and that he had nothing to add to or retract from it.—W. STOCKING, chaplain ; TIMOTHY R. HOLMES, Under-Shertff.

THE EXECUTION.

At ten minutes before twelve o'clock the prisoner was brought from his cell and pinioned by the hangman, who was brought from London for the purpose. He appeared resigned, but was so weak as to be unable to stand without support; when his cravat was removed he groaned heavily, and appeared to be labouring under great mental agony. When his wrists and arms were made fast, he was led round twards the scaffold, and as he passed the different yards in which the prisoners were confined, he shook hands with them, and speaking to two of them by name, he said, "Good bye, God bless you." They appeared considerably affected by the wretched appearance which he made, and "God bless you !" "May God receive your soul !" were frequently uttered as he passed along. The chaplain walked before the prisoner, reading the usual Burial Service, and the Governor and Officers walking immediately after him. The prisoner was supported to the steps which led to the scaffold; he looked somewhat wildly around, and a constable was obliged to support him while the hangman was adjusting the fatal cord. There was a barrier to keep off the crowd, amounting to upwards of 7,000 persons, who at this time had stationed themselves in the adjoining fields, on the hedges, the tops of houses, and at every point from which a view of the execution could be best obtained. The prisoner, a few moments before the drop fell, groaned heavily, and would have fallen, had not a second constable caught hold of him. Everything having been made ready, the signal was given, the fatal drop fell, and the unfortunate man was launched into eternity. Just before he was turned off, he said in a feeble tone, "I am justly sentenced, and may God forgive me "

The Murder of Maria Marten.
BY W. CORDER.

COME all you thoughtless young men, a warning take by me,
And think upon my unhappy fate to be hanged upon a tree ;
My name is William Corder, to you I do declare,
I courted Maria Marten, most beautiful and fair.

I promised I would marry her upon a certain day,
Instead of that, I was resolved to take her life away.
I went into her father's house the 18th day of May,
Saying, my dear Maria, we will fix the wedding day.

If you will meet me at the Red-barn, as sure as I have life,
I will take you to Ipswich town, and there make you my wife ;
I then went home and fetched my gun, my pickaxe and my spade,
I went into the Red-barn, and there I dug her grave.

With heart so light, she thought no harm, to meet him she did go
He murdered her all in the barn, and laid her body low :
After the horrible deed was done, she lay weltering in her gore,
Her bleeding mangled body he buried beneath the Red-barn floor.

Now all things being silent, her spirit could not rest,
She appeared unto her mother, who suckled her at her breast ;
For many a long month or more, her mind being sore oppress'd,
Neither night or day she could not take any rest.

Her mother's mind being so disturbed, she dreamt three nights o'er,
Her daughter she lay murdered beneath the Red-barn floor ;
She sent the father to the barn, when he the ground did thrust,
And there he found his daughter mingling with the dust.

My trial is hard, I could not stand, most woeful was the sight,
When her jaw-bone was brought to prove, which pierced my heart quite ;
Her aged father standing by, likewise his loving wife,
And in her grief her hair she tore, she scarcely could keep life.

Adieu, adieu, my loving friends, my glass is almost run,
On Monday next will be my last, when I am to be hang'd ;
So you, young men, who do pass by, with pity look on me,
For murdering Maria Marten, I was haug'd upon the tree.

Printed by J. Catnach, 2 and 3, Monmouth Court.—Cards, &c., Printed Cheap.

189

'Confession and Execution of William Corder'. Broadside.

WILLIAM BURK'S

Execution.

Let old and young unto my song a while attention pay,
The news I'll tell will please you well, the monster Burke's away.
At the head of Libberton Wynd he finished his career,
There's few, I'm sure, rich or poor, for him would shed a tear.

Chorus.

Now Burke, the murderer, is dead, his troubles here are o'er,
We can't tell where his spirit's fled, he'll Burke the folk no more.

Eighteen hundred and twenty-nine, let it recorded be,
Twenty-eight day of January he suffer'd on a tree.
To Edinbro', numbers did go, that day before 'twas noon,
For to see Burke, that cruel Turk, receive his awful doom.

They brought him from the Calton Jail, some time in the night,
They thought the crowd would do the job had they waited till
daylight,
From the Lock-up they brought Burk out about the hour of eight,
Where about forty-thousand folk impatiently did wait.

The injur'd crowd, they groan'd aloud, this monster to behold,
Who in his time had thought no crime to murder young and old.
When the scaffold he did ascend, the people all did cry,
Bring out Will Hare, we think it fair, that he also should die.

As round his neck the rope it went, the shouts did rend the sky,
Its " Burk him, Burk him," the blood-hound, the people all
did cry.
The shouts they did continue on, until he was cut down,
The like was never heard before in Edinbro' town.

His bloody den, it does remain, for strangers to behold,
Where him and Hare, they did not spare the lives of young or
old.
In memory his bones will be preserv'd for years to come,
Ye Burkites! now beware, lest you do meet with the same
doom.

One of the many sheets dealing with the body-snatchers Burke and Hare.

The Lads of Virginia

Printed and Sold by J. Pitts, 14, Great
St. Andrew Street, Seven Dials.

COME all you young fellows wherever you be
Come listen awhile and I'll tell ye,
Concerning the hardships that we undergo,
When we get lag'd to Virginia.

Such clever young fellows myself I have seen,
That is more fitting to serve George our king,
Those hard hearted judges so cruel have been,
To lag us poor lads to Virginia.

When I was an apprentice in fair London town
Many hours serv'd duly and truly,
Till those buxom young lasses led me astray,
My work I neglected more and more every day
And for to maintain it went on the highway,
By that I got lagh'd to Virginia.

When we came to Virginia that old ancient town,
The place that is so much admir'd
Where the captain he stands with the cane in his hand
With our aching hearts before him done stand,
With the tears in our eyes in a foreign land,
Was sold for a slave in Virginia.

When I was in England I could live at my ease,
Rest my bones down on soft feathers,
With a jug in my hand and a lass on my knee,
I thought myself fit for all weathers :
But now in Virginia I lay like a dog,
Our pillows at night is a brick or a log,
We dress and undress like some other sea hog,
How hard is our fate in virginia.

Old England Old England I shall ne'er see more
If I do it's ten thousand to twenty,
My bones are quite rotten my feet is quite sore,
I'm pinioned with the fever and am at death's door,
But if ever I live to see seven years more,
Then I'll bid adieu to Virginia.

'The Lads of Virginia.'
Street Ballad.

The Treadmill in the Borough Gaol at Leicester in 1823.

The Execution of Mary Evans at York, 10 August 1799, by Thomas Rowlandson.

Some of the murder ballads went into oral tradition, which is not surprising, since they had a number of traditional elements. The opening appeal to the listener has an ancient pedigree: 'Good people I pray draw near' or 'Come all you wild and wicked youths.' Nouns or adjectives are often used in complementary pairs: troubles and trials, grief and pain, sad and wretched, beautiful and fair. Certain nouns seem to require more or less automatic qualification by particular adjectives. Murderers are base, cruel, wicked, inhuman, and wretched. Their deeds are sad, foul, dreadful, horrid, and brutal; and their victims are innocent, as is the blood which is spilled. Breasts are milk-white, unless they are guilty. Prisons, cells, and gaols are dreary, dismal, and gloomy. Justice is stern, and sentences are awful. Graves are silent. A key word is 'fatal', which is applied to day, night, spot, and tree (of the gallows). One might add to the list 'deluding tongue', 'wedded wife', 'silver streams', and 'rattling chains'. Such devices are part of the common currency of balladry; it is merely their abusive, tasteless, or disproportionate use which becomes irksome.

The street-ballad writers were well acquainted with traditional patterns of phraseology and structure, and in some cases what they wrote was easily assimilated into oral currency. For example, the murder of Maria Marten by William Corder came to light in 1828. A ballad (see illustration) tells us that Maria's grave was seen in a dream by her mother. In fact it was her stepmother who claimed to have had the dream, and there have been suggestions that her knowledge of the site of the grave derived in reality from some sort of complicity with Corder. Sympathy for the victim, the powerful motifs of both the murdered sweetheart and revelation in a persistent dream and the traditional cast of the original text helped it to circulate orally for a century, almost unchanged. Here is one verse from the printed sheet, followed by the equivalent passage from a version noted in 1907, which, if anything, is an improvement:

> Her mother's mind being so disturbed, she dreamt three nights o'er,
> Her daughter she lay murdered beneath the Red-barn floor;
> She sent the father to the barn, where he the ground did thrust,
> And there he found his daughter mingling with the dust.

> Her mother had a dreadful dream, she dreamed it three nights o'er,
> She dreamed that her dear daughter lay beneath the Red Barn floor.
> They sent her father to the barn and in the ground he thrust,
> And there he found his daughter dear lay mingling with the dust.[55]

In the early nineteenth century there were more than two hundred capital offences in England and Wales, ranging from treason, murder, and forgery to shop-lifting goods worth more than five shillings and picking pockets of items worth over one shilling. Sir Samuel Romilly told the House of Commons in 1810 that he believed 'there was no country on the face of the earth in which there had been so many different offences according to law to be punished with death as in England'.[56] Some two hundred people were hanged every year, and thousands more had their death sentences commuted to transportation, often for life. Other offenders received initial sentences of transportation, usually fourteen or seven years (popularly known as fourteen or seven penn'orth).

Transportation

This punishment was started in a rather desultory fashion in Elizabethan days, but had become fairly regular practice by the time of Charles II. A century later, in 1775, transportation had evolved into 'a major ingredient of English criminal law'.[57] Some 30,000 people a year were transported to America from England alone. 'The Poor Unhappy Transported Felon's Sorrowful Account of his Fourteen Years Transportation at Virginia, in America' is a seventy-two-verse narrative to the tune of 'Death and the Lady'. The transportation in question must date from 1671. It is possible that the piece is fictional, but it was deemed of sufficient interest to be published at least five times in London during the eighteenth century and once in Dublin.[58] The sombre, moralizing tone recalls many of the execution ballads. James Revel, the felon in question, is the son of poor but honest parents who endeavour to provide him with some education. He is bound apprentice, but falls into bad company, runs away, and takes to a life of crime. He is caught and, at the age of 17, sentenced to fourteen years' transportation. After a seven-week passage to Virginia, he is put on sale with others: 'Some view'd our limbs, and others turn'd us round / Examening like Horses, if we're sound.' Revel's purchaser kits him out for work:

> A canvas shirt and trowsers then they gave,
> With a hop-sack frock in which I was to slave:
> No shoes nor stockings had I for to wear,
> Nor hat, nor cap, both head and feet were bare.

The treatment is harsh:

> Much hardships then in deed I did endure,
> No dog was ever nursed so I'm sure,
> More pity the poor Negroe slaves bestowed
> Than my inhuman brutal master showed.

After twelve years the master dies, and Revel is bought by another owner, who is much more humane. On the expiry of his sentence, Revel returns home, and is reunited with his parents. He concludes with the customary warning:

> My country men take warning e'er too late,
> Lest you should share my hard unhappy fate;
> Altho' but little crimes you have done,
> Consider seven or fourteen years to come.
>
> .   .   .   .
>
> Now young men with speed your lives amend,
> Take my advice as one that is your friend:
> For tho' so slight you make of it while here,
> Hard is your lot when once they get you there.

With the secession of the American colonies, prisoners could no longer be sent there, and a serious problem arose as those sentenced to terms of transportation began to accumulate in the inadequate prison accommodation. Starting in 1776 the hulks of two old warships, *Justitia* and *Censor*, were moored in the Thames off Woolwich, and convicts were quartered on board. Each day they went ashore in parties to work on the banks of the river, raising gravel or sand and cleaning the foreshore. Further hulks were subsequently provided at Sheerness and Portsmouth, and what began as a temporary expedient lasted until 1857. Many of those sentenced to transportation served their whole time on the hulks, but most remained there only while waiting for a ship to 'the Bay'; for the authorities had hit upon the idea of sending convicts to Botany Bay in Australia. The first convict fleet, consisting of six transports, three supply ships, and two escorting men-of-war, left England in May 1787 and arrived in Botany Bay in January 1788. Some 759 convicts were on board, 568 men and 191 women. Of these, 23 died *en route*, a number regarded at the time as small. Over the next eighty years some 160,000 men and women from the British Isles were sent out to various parts of Australia, as transportation came to be the principal means of punishment. Later, it was replaced by imprisonment at home. Transportation to New South Wales ceased after 1846. The last convicts sailed for Van Diemen's Land in November 1852, and the island changed its name to 'Tasmania' at the beginning of the following year. From then on, prisoners were sent only to Western Australia. The Penal Servitude Acts of 1853 (partly) and 1857 (almost completely) abandoned transportation as a penalty, and the last transports sailed in 1868. Theoretically, smugglers of counterfeit coins remained liable to transportation for life until the Coinage (Colonial Offences) Act of 1853 was repealed in 1975.

Transportation ended only after a long debate, with reformers arguing that a carefully regulated prison system was preferable. As early as 1838 a parliamentary enquiry stated: 'Your Committee need hardly repeat that the well-proven effect of transportation is to demoralise, not to reform an offender.' The contrary view, expressed by a barrister in 1833, was that 'The only punishment they [criminals] dread is transportation.' A third opinion was that transportation was in principle a good thing, but in practice not harsh enough. A magistrate in 1828 referred to 'letters which we are frequently in the habit of seeing written by persons under transportation to Botany Bay to their friends here, in which they speak of their very comfortable situation, and express their desire that their friends should some how or other find means of following them'.[59] At about the same time officials of Newgate gaol considered that transportation was seen by prisoners as more of a reward than a punishment. A woman called Charlotte Newman committed a crime simply in order to follow her husband to Botany Bay; it was felt that an example needed to be made of such temerity, and she was hanged instead. Other wives petitioned to be allowed to follow their husbands, and a few were successful; details can be found in Robert Hughes's book *The Fatal Shore* (1987). The discussion continued in many books and pamphlets. Returned convicts, including the Chartist John Frost, published accounts of their experiences,[60] and more or less fictionalized narratives such as Clarke's *His Natural Life* and Derricourt's *Old Convict Days* appeared long after the end of transportation.[61] These incline towards the pessimistic side of the argument, as does the street literature. Indeed, the dread of transportation survived in song and balladry until recent years.

The change of destination from America to Australia was easily managed, simply by reissuing old sheets with the names changed. Thus, James Revel's adventures were transferred from Virginia to Botany Bay, and to add verisimilitude, firm dates of 1806–21 were added to the title.[62] The same process was at work in oral tradition. A broadside entitled 'The Lads of Virginia' (see illustration), which must date from before 1776, was reissued several times in the nineteenth century, and also circulated orally until at least 1907.[63] It gave rise to 'Australia', an adaptation differing only in name, which, although it does not seem to have been printed, remained in oral tradition until at least the 1970s.[64] Such remaking of songs, often with minimal changes, was common. It ensured that an attitude, or complex of attitudes, once established, would persist for some time. In this way ballads not only reflected social history, but also affected it.

New songs were also written. Indeed, a favourite title was 'A New Song on . . .' (though the novelty was sometimes more in the assertion than the content). The change in destination for those being transported was soon reflected in the substance of ballads, however. Not surprisingly, a major preoccupation was the state of mind of those about to make a hazardous sea journey of 13,000 miles, with the unknown at the end. 'The Jolly Lad's Trip to Botany Bay', which was probably issued in the early 1790s, attempts to make light of things:

> Now many a bonny lass in Botany may be seen,
> Who knows but she might be an Indian queen?
> Deck'd out with diamonds see the British fair.
> A fig for transportation, little do we care.[65]

The writer is clearly ignorant of conditions in Australia, and seems to be whistling in the dark. 'A New Song, Made upon the Lads sent to Botany Bay' is in fact concerned with life in the hulks and preparations for departure. The convicts promise to send news:

> And when to Botany Bay we come some letters we do write,
> And to our favourite blowings⟋ we do them indite,
> The usage of this place all the lads they did say,
> And the orders they receiv'd when they came to Botany Bay.[66]

Other ballads express the heart-break of parting. 'Farewell to Your Judges and Juries', issued several times in the early nineteenth century, consists of a dialogue between a man transported for seven years and his true love, Polly. It concludes:

> How hard is the place of confinement
> That keeps me from my heart's delight.
> Cold chains and cold irons surround me,
> And a plank for a pillow at night.
>
> How often I wish that the eagle
> Would lend me her wing, I would fly,
> Then I'd fly to the arms of my Polly,
> And in her soft bosom I'd lie.[67]

The elegiac quality was completely lost when the piece was rewritten for a musical play called *Little Jack Sheppard*, which was first produced in London in 1885. A rollicking 'toora lie oora lie addity' chorus was added, and a lively tune was adopted, both of which were completely at variance with the mood of the earlier song.[68] There was nothing jolly about transportation, and the predominant feeling in many contemporary ballads was one of despair. 'The Transport', otherwise known as 'Botany Bay', was widely published as a street ballad in the early nineteenth

⟋ women

century, and for the next hundred years was frequently found in oral
tradition, usually to magnificent, soaring tunes.

> Come all young men of learning, a warning take by me,
> I'd have you quit night walking and shun bad company;
> I'd have you quit night walking, or else you'll rue the day,
> When you are transported and going to Bot'ny Bay.[69]

In other ballads, the perspective changes. Instead of bidding farewell to
people leaving the British Isles, we travel with them to the antipodes and
instead of looking forward with apprehension, we look back with longing.
Possibly the most widely known of such pieces was 'Van Dieman's Land'
(as it was usually spelled on ballad sheets), which tells of the apprehension
and transportation of three poachers. It may have been written in response
to an Act of 1828 specifying transportation only for a third offence of
poaching except when violence was offered to a gamekeeper or if three
men, one of whom carried a gun or bludgeon, were found in a wood. More
than 250 men were convicted under the new Act in the first year, but it is
not known how many of these were actually transported. Professor Shaw
estimates that only about 300 poachers in all were transported to
Australia,[70] an average of only about fourteen per year; but no poacher
could be sure that he would escape.

VAN DIEMAN'S LAND

> Come all you gallant poachers, that ramble void of care,
> That walk out on a moonlight night with dog, gun, & snare,
> The lofty hare and pheasant you have at your command,
> Not thinking of your last career upon Van Dieman's Land.

Poor Tom Brown from Nottingham, Jack Williams & poor Joe,
They were three daring poachers, the country well does know,
At night they were trepann'd[g] by the keepers hid in sand
Who for fourteen years transported us unto Van Dieman's Land.

The first day that we landed upon that fatal shore,
The planters they came round us, full twenty score or more,
They rank'd us up like horses, and sold us out of hand
Then yok'd us to the plough, my boys, to plough Van Dieman's Land.

Our cottages that we live in are built of clods and clay,
And rotten straw for bedding, and we dare not say nay,
Our cots we did surround with fire, we slumber when we can,
To drive away wolves and tigers, upon Van Dieman's Land.

It's often when I slumber, I have a pleasant dream,
With my sweet girl a sitting down by a purling stream,
Through England I've been roaming with her at my command,
But I awaken broken hearted, upon Van Dieman's Land.

God bless our wives and families, likewise that happy shore,
That isle of great contentment which we shall see no more,
As for our wretched females see them we seldom can,
There's twenty to one woman upon Van Dieman's Land.

There was a girl from Birmingham, Susan Summers was her name,
For fourteen years transported, we all well know the same,
Our planter bought her freedom and married her out of hand,
She gave to us good usage upon Van Dieman's Land.

But fourteen years is a long time, that is our fatal doom,
For nothing else but poaching, God knows that's all we've done,
You should leave off night walking and poaching every man,
If you did but know the hardships upon Van Dieman's Land.

Now if I had ten thousand pounds, laid down all in my hand,
I would give it all freely, my freedom would command,
I'd come back again to England, live and die a free man,
Bid adieu to all poaching, likewise Van Dieman's Land.

So all you gallant poachers, give ear unto my song,
It's a bit of good advice, although it is not long,
Throw by your dog, gun & snares, unto you I speak plain,
For if you knew our hardships you'd never poach again.[71]

Even a new ballad like this makes use of themes and even phraseology
from earlier pieces, for the producers of such material were working

---

[g] trapped

within a tradition. The text given here was issued by William Wright in Birmingham between 1831 and 1835. Editions in other towns as far apart as Portsmouth and Newcastle retain the references to Nottingham and Birmingham, which seems to confirm the Midlands origin of the piece. As it travelled further afield, though, new localities were inserted. An Irish version has Nenagh town,[72] and a Scots version, Glasgow. The latter has a much sharper edge than the Birmingham text, and includes this bitter verse:

> Although the poor of Scotland do labour and toil,
> They're robbed of every blessing and produce of the soil;
> Your proud, imperious landlords, if we break their command,
> They'll send you to the British hulks, or to Van Dieman's Land.[73]

Back in the Midlands, an apparent sequel, 'Young Henry the Poacher',[74] may stem from an incident in 1829 on the Warwickshire estate of D. S. Dugdale, MP, after which eleven poachers were sentenced to death for shooting at keepers. The sentences were commuted to transportation for life in five cases and for fourteen years in the remaining six (thus providing eleven of Shaw's average of fourteen poachers for the year in a single batch). Warwickshire place-names such as Southam and nearby Harbury (usually rendered as 'Harbourn') predominate in the earlier printings, and a new consoling female usually hails from Wolverhampton.

At least one other ballad seems to have been inspired by 'Van Dieman's Land'. It is 'The Female Transport', otherwise known as 'The Female Convict' or 'The Female Sailor'. The central figure and narrator, Sarah Collins or O'Brien, is reared by a tender father after her mother's death, but falls into bad company and is sentenced to fourteen years' transportation for an unspecified crime, which may well be prostitution. After a brief mention of the voyage ('The seas was rough, ran mountains high, with us poor girls was hard'), she gives details of convict life:

> They chain'd us two by two and whip'd and lash'd along,
> They cut off our provisions if we did the least thing wrong,
> They march us in the burning sun until our feet are sore,
> So hard's our lot now we are got upon Van Dieman's shore.

She mentions the 'dreadful beasts' roaming at night, which recall the 'wolves and tigers' of 'Van Dieman's Land'—in all probability the now extinct Tasmanian devil and wolf, the latter also known as a tiger. A coda makes the conventional appeal:

Come all young men and maidens do bad company forsake,
If tongue can tell our overthrow, it would make your hearts to ache.
You girls I pray be ruled by me, your wicked ways give o'er,
For fear like us you spend your days upon Van Dieman's shore.[75]

The mood in most of these ballads is similar. The transports are shocked, resentful, deeply unhappy, but seldom indignant; they speak more in sorrow than anger, and their gloom is relieved only by flashes of spirit or humour. For an expression of fierce resistance to the penal system, we must look to 'Jack Donohue'[76] or 'Moreton Bay',[77] which were produced not in England but in Ireland and Australia respectively. These lead on to the vivid sagas of the bush-rangers; but that is another story.

Yet a defiant attitude is sometimes adopted, even in Britain, and conventional expressions of penitence and warnings to others give way to bold affirmations, and indignation succeeds commiseration. One Newcastle sheet was issued immediately after five men had been sentenced, mainly for stealing, either to fourteen or fifteen years' transportation. Without condoning crime, it makes a strong attack on the conditions which help to produce it. The printer is T. Dodds, a man of radical sympathies.

Farewell Address To their Countrymen and Friends, Of all these unfortunate
    Men who received their several Sentences, of Transportation, at the Summer
    Assizes for the year 1842, by the Judges of the Northern Circuit

The assizes they are over now, the Judge is gone away,
But many aching hearts are left within the town today;
Tho' crime is bad, yet poverty's made many one to be
A transport from his native land, and across the raging sea.

Oh! 'tis a cruel sentence for a man to leave his wife,
His children, and his dearest friends, all dearer than his life;
To leave the land that gave him birth, to see it p'rhaps no more,
And drag a wretched life in chains, upon a distant shore.

The rich have no temptations, they have all things at command,
And 'tis for pleasure and for health, they leave their native land;
But a starving wife and family, makes a poor man's heart to break,
And makes him do what brings a blush of shame upon his cheek.

Their sentence some deserve to get, and laws were made to be
Preservers of the public peace, and of society;
But great distress and want of work, starvation, and disease,
Makes inmates for the prison-house, and transports for the seas.

Oh! think a sentence of one's life, for fifteen years or less,
What tears they cost a family, what anguish and distress;
What heart but mourns the transport's fate, what eye but sheds a tear,
For tho' we hate the crime we hold man's liberty more dear.

Oh would our Rulers make a law for man to earn his bread,
And make sufficient wage to keep his wife and children fed,
The Judges would have less to do, and half their pay might be
Devoted to the public good, and bless society.

The Prisons would be empty soon, and transport ships would then
Bring o'er the seas a load of corn, and not a load of men;
Act after act our rulers make, but one they will not do,
To do to others as they would themselves to be done unto.

Would they but pass an act for man to work and earn his bread,
Crime would soon dwindle from the land, and transportation fled;
Would providence direct their hearts to make such laws, and then
Instead of outlawed slaves we might have free and honest men.[78]

Prisons

In the eighteenth century, prisons and houses of correction were used only for those awaiting trial or the infliction of penalties (except for debtors, who were detained until their debts were paid). The prisons were often squalid, overcrowded, and disease-ridden. Prisoners were herded together and left mainly to their own devices. Some regulation was imposed from within, as a new inmate would quickly find out:

> Welcome, welcome, brother debtor,
> To this poor but merry place,
> Where no bailiff, bum or setter
> Dare to show his frightful face.
>
> But, kind sir, as you're a stranger,
> Down your garnish you must lay,
> Or your coat will be in danger,
> You must either strip or pay.

This is from 'The Humours of the Fleet',[79] written in 1749 or earlier. The hardships of confinement might well inspire a jocular response of this kind, and resilience was needed even more when, under the influence of innovators who wished to see the penal system act as more of a deterrent and do more to reform the prisoners, the regime became more formal and much more severe.

Treadmills of one kind or another had existed from Roman times. Their use in English prisons was authorized by the Penitentiary Act of 1779, and a huge wheel was developed which prisoners walked on both the outside and the inside. A visitor at Leicester county gaol saw 'a poor man walking the treadmill, like a squirrel in a cage. He could not leave off, however tired he was—he would have been hit by it.'[80] The large wheel at Leicester, shown in a water-colour of 1823 (see illustration), was not used very widely but a smaller version later became quite common. It was developed by William Cubitt, who was knighted for this and other achievements. His name lives on in that of a construction firm, but the treadmill was abolished by the Prisons Act of 1898. The only extant example is in the county gaol (now a museum) at Beaumaris, Anglesey.

The first of Cubitt's machines was set up at Brixton prison in 1817. 'It was used,' wrote Mayhew and Binny,

merely to employ the prisoners, and keep them from louting about the gaol. . . . The prisoners style the occupation 'grinding the wind', and that is really the only denomination applicable to it—the sole object of the labour of some 150 men, employed for eight hours a day, being simply to put in motion a big fan or regulator, as it is called, which, impinging on the air as it revolves, serves to add to the severity of the work by increasing its resistance.[81]

'A New Song on the Times', issued probably in 1819, complains that:

> Cubit has planned out a wheel
> That every man should have his fill
> So if you do the least thing
> They bundle you off to the Treading Mill.[82]

Many other responses to the device exist in ballad form, including 'The Tread Mill', which expresses the wish that various bad characters, such as informers, liars, wife-beaters, givers of short weight, and 'All rich folks that grind the poor' be consigned to the treadmill.[83] (This parallels a broadside of about 1790 which suggests that various unpopular people, including 'monopolisers who add to their store / By cruel oppression and squeezing the poor', be sent to Botany Bay.)[84]

The installation of the machine at Manchester in 1824 gave rise to a lively piece to the tune of 'Nae luck about the house':

> In Manchester New Bayley
> We've got a new corn mill,
> And those whose actions send them here,
> Of it will have their fill:
> Prisoners let this a caution be,
> Obey me in a crack,
> Or I will take my whip and flog
> You right well o'er your back.

So work, work, mind, mind,
And work with free good will,
In Manchester New Bayley
We've got a treading mill.

The narrator works his way through a prisoner's day, starting with the rising bell at six o'clock. There is a kind of rough humour, combined with menace: 'Mind your work or you will get / The lash across your hide.' Prison routine is described, including the technique of treading the mill:

When these treadles you come to tread,
Mind how you take your steps,
For if your foot should chance to slip,
You'd get a smack i'th'chops.[85]

The only hope for the prisoner is to look forward to the end of his sentence. The 'shinscraper', as it was called, was described in a parliamentary report of 1835 as 'the most tiresome, distressing, exemplary punishment that has ever been contrived by human ingenuity',[86] and it left its mark on traditional song, as well as on street balladry:

At six o'clock our turnkey comes in,
With a bunch of keys all in his hand.
'Come, come, my lads, step up and grind,
Tread the wheel till breakfast time'.

. . . .

At nine o'clock the jangle rings.
All on the trap, boys, we must spring.
'Come, come, my lads, step up in time,
The wheel to tread and the corn to grind'.[87]

The insistent rhythm in this 'Gaol Song' leads one to wonder whether it was sung to accompany the stepping at the tread-wheel, just as songs were used to lighten the hard labour in the chain-gangs of American penitentiaries. However, the regime of strict silence imposed in British gaols makes this unlikely.

Songs dealing with prison life had a wide appeal, judging by the frequency of their appearance as street ballads. One, recalling the use of thieves' argot in eighteenth-century songs, uses such expressions as 'faking' (thieving), 'skilly and whack' (gruel and bread), and 'bone the tout' (hit the policeman). It evokes life in the new Victorian prisons opened in the middle decades of the nineteenth century, and copies are largely identical save for names: Belle Vue[88] (which succeeded the New Bailey in

Manchester), Kirkdale[89] (now Walton, Liverpool), Wakefield[90] or Warwick gaol,[91] or even simply County Gaol.[92]

'Wakefield Jail, or, Face the Wall' is quite different, though its subject is still the oppressive discipline and grim labour. Apart from the tread-wheel, it mentions oakum-picking (unravelling ropes and separating the fibres) and shot drill (picking up and putting down cannon-balls, by numbers). The resilience of the piece is far removed from the fatalism and despondency of many of the transportation and murder ballads.

> Kind friends if you will listen unto my little rhyme,
> A verse or two I'll try and sing to pass away the time.
> It's about the Wakefield Prison I'm going to relate,
> The treatment that the prisoners get up to this present date.
> And when they get you there they drive you to despair,
> They put you in a suit of plaid and cut off all your hair,
> And give you oakum for to pick, and put you through your drill,
> And send you for a week on what they call the mill.
> *It makes you feel so sad, when you wear a suit of plaid,*
> *And a pair of buckle shoes upon your feet.*
> *They feed you on the best, clap a number of your chest,*
> *And don't they tog you up so blooming neat, face the wall.*
>
> Now, every morning at half-past five the bell begins to toll,
> And every prisoner has to rise his bed to fold.
> There's another one rings soon after that, but for that you need not care,
> There['s] another one rings at six o'clock and for work you must prepare.
> That bell is for the treadmill, they'll have you out in time,
> Along with a lot more prisoners they place you in a line,
> They call your names out one by one as you stand in a row,
> And shout get out, to the left about, and the mill you have to go.
>
> The diets they are different, and they all stand in a line,
> There is number one and number two according to your time.
> There's a pint of skilly night and morn, as sure as I'm a sinner,
> And a pint of soup three times a week, you cop that for your dinner.
> You do not get so fat there on what you get to eat,
> With half a pound of potatoes and a little Australian meat.
> And mind that you do cop that, for they often stop your bread,
> And you're sure to be reported if you chance to turn your head.[93]

The prison at Wakefield is incongruously situated in Love Lane. It was opened in the 1840s, and the ballad probably dates from soon after that time. It seems to have gone into oral tradition, for Fred Kitchen (1891–1969) recalled singing it in the carrier's cart on the way to Doncaster Martlemas fair. In both content and attitude it is similar to the even more jaunty 'Durham Gaol', which was written by the local song-smith, Tommy Armstrong (1848–1919), after serving a sentence for stealing a pair of stockings from the co-operative shop at West Stanley.

> Yil get yor meat en clais for nowt,
> Yor hoose en firin' free;
> Awl yor meet's browt te th' dor—
> Hoo happy ye shud be!
> Thor's soap en too'l, en wooden speun,
> En e little bairne's pot;
> Thae fetch your papers ivory week
> For ye te clean your bot.[94]

This is one of the few songs known to have been written by an ex-prisoner. However, as recently as 1975, convicts at Peterhead in Scotland circulated 'Paddy's Song', which they had written about one of their number, Patrick Mehan. Mehan had been sentenced to life imprisonment for murder, though he vehemently protested his innocence. The forensic evidence against him was later discredited, and he received a pardon.

> In Peterhead Prison locked up in the hole
> There's a man well known for his pranks.
> No shining halo encircles his head
> 'Cause he's blasted too many banks.
> Five long weary years alone in the hole
> Protesting that justice went wrong,
> And the convicts sing loud when they reach the refrain,
> Why don't they let Paddy go home?
> *Free Paddy Mehan, free him today,*
> *Don't leave him to rot down the hole.*
> *Free Paddy Mehan, free him today,*
> *Why don't they let Paddy go home?*[95]

At Long Lartin prison in the early 1980s (as a lecturer, not an inmate) I found that prisoners took a keen interest in songs about crime and punishment, but did not contribute any of their own. They were particularly intrigued by 'Gaol Song', for they saw its treadmill routine as a metaphor for their own circumstances. They no longer had the ironic conception of gaol as a home from home, as in Armstrong's 'Durham Gaol', and their lack of songs squares with the experience of a prisoner in Wormwood Scrubs, who wrote in 1985:

I'm afraid to have to tell you that song in prison seems now to be a very rare thing. . . . The only singing that I have heard in the course of everyday activities is the odd snatch of 'Please release me, let me go' or 'I talk to the trees, that's why they put me away', and in all my time inside I have only heard one parody of a song, sung by a cleaner in Wandsworth. It was at a time when the Prime Minister had made some ill-advised remarks about 'Maggie May' [a song about a prostitute] and had had operations to remove an eye and straighten varicose veins (or vice versa). The verse, as I recall, went thus:

> Oh Maggie, Maggie May,
> They have took an eye away,
> And with luck next week they'll be wiring up her jaw.
> Soon she'll have a wooden leg and a Worzel Gummidge head,
> And she won't be wrecking Britain any more.

He concludes: 'I think a life sentence may well knock the song out of a fellow.'[96]

A song like 'Derry Gaol' might inspire a prisoner to sing if he (or she) had a release date which was not too distant. It seems to be descended from 'Gaol Song' of the nineteenth century, and its details of prison life are long out of date. None the less, it is still sung, and its caustic, laconic wit seems freshly minted.

DERRY GAOL

> When Derry Gaol I first did see
> A suit of clothes they gave to me,
> And the fleas came out and did me hail:
> 'Here's more fresh meat for Derry Gaol'.
> *Musha rorum da, fal the diddle da,* } *bis*
> *Way down in Derry Gaol.*

At six o'clock the mugs are laid,
At seven o'clock the grace is said,
With a pint of milk as thick as lead
Would scourge your belly like salt petre bread.

At half past eight the bell does ring,
Then on parade we all fall in,
And the turnkey bawls for smarter gear.
Well, if we was smart we wouldn't be here.

In Derry Gaol the work is hard,
Breaking stones out of the yard;
We're breaking the stones till half past ten,
Then it's out there breaking stones again.

On Sunday morn the bell does ring,
And then for chapel we all fall in;
Down on our knees we thank the Lord,
But we can't think what to thank him for.

At eight o'clock we are locked up
For the bugs and fleas to bite us up,
And our poor body can get no rest
For it is which bug can bite the best.

Now if I was the gaoler and he was me
I'd get up one morning and set me free;
And I'd leave for me pals the bunch of keys,
And I'd leave for the gaoler the bugs and fleas.[97]

5

PASTIME

Bartholomew Fair

FOR seven and a half centuries from 1133, interrupted only by outbreaks of plague, Bartholomew Fair was held annually at Smithfield in London. In Elizabethan times it was the chief cloth fair in England, but by 1641 it had become devoted largely to entertainment. Under Charles II it was extended from three to fourteen days. The theatres closed for the duration, and the actors went to Smithfield to perform in booths. It became fashionable to go there. Evelyn, John Locke, and Pepys, the last-named repeatedly and often in aristocratic company, all record their visits. As late as 1778 the fair was patronized by royalty, in the persons of the duke and duchess of Gloucester, but in 1805 Wordsworth was exclaiming: 'what a hell / For eyes and ears! what anarchy and din / Barbarian and infernal!'[1]

Ben Jonson's *Bartholomew Fair*, first produced in 1614 and revived during the Restoration, portrays the swarming life of the fair, including a rascally ballad-singer named Nightingale: 'Ballads, ballads! fine new ballads: Hear for your love and buy for your money.' His wares include 'The Ferret and the Coney', 'A Preservative against the Punks' Evil', 'Goose-green Starch and the Devil', 'A dozen of Divine Points', 'The Godly Garters', 'A Fairing of Good Counsel', 'The Windmill blown down by the Witch's Fart', and 'Saint George, that O! did break the dragon's heart'. His *pièce de résistance* is 'A Caveat for Cutpurses' (specially written by Jonson, and later sold as a street ballad), which, with pointed irony, serves in one scene of the play to distract a man while he is being relieved of his purse.[2]

In the same year as the play, a ballad specifically about the fair appeared under the title of 'Roome for Companie'.[3] It was followed, over the years, by many others which set out to extol the delights, and sometimes to chronicle the pitfalls, of the occasion.

In House of Boards, Men walk upon Cords,
As easie as Squirrels crack Filberds;
But the Cut-purses they do bite and run away,
But those we suppose to be Ill-Birds.

For a Penny you may zee a fine Puppet-play,
And for Two-pence a rare piece of Art;
And a Penny a Cann, I dear swear a Man,
May put zix of 'em into a Quart.

This 'Ancient Song of Bartholomew-Fair', published in 1719–20, continues:

At every Door lies a Hag, or a Whore,
And in Hosier-Lane, if I a'n't mistaken;
Zuch plenty there are of Whores, you'll have a pair,
To a single Gamon of Bacon.[4]

The misadventures of country people at fairs, as in towns generally, had unfailing appeal, especially if robbery or sexual discomfiture (or both) were involved. The eponymous hero of 'Roger in Amaze; or The Countryman's Ramble through Bartholomew Fair' of about 1682, who also uses 'z' in place of an initial 's', finds his money gone when he comes to pay for beer, so 'They doft my hat for a groat, then turned me out of doors'.[5] Similar themes turn up in ballads of the early nineteenth century celebrating the pleasures of food and fairings; monsters, animal and human; menageries and multitudes:

There's crowding by days and by nights,
And Music on every side pleasing ye;
Here's a mob's round the Fiddles and Fights,
And Pickpockets of your cash easing ye.
Then buy you up the ballads I've here,
For I want to be taking the pelf, sir,
If you won't you may go to the Fair,
And sing of its Wonders yourself, sir.[6]

'Countryman's Visit to Bartholomew Fair' probably dates from 1809. Its metre was later employed for a sea-shanty, which has given us the tune:

COUNTRYMAN'S VISIT TO BARTHOLOMEW FAIR

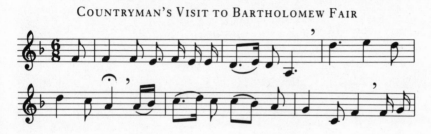

I came to London on the other day,
High randy dandy O,
All for to sell my load of hay,
And my galloping randy dandy O.
My cousin said when I came there,
High randy dandy O,
Cousin, stop to see the fair,
And my galloping randy dandy O.

I took my cousin Poll's advice,
I sold my hay and got my price,
I saw the man they call the mayor,
He came for to proclaim the fair.

And when I saw the man approach,
I wished Apollo had his coach,
After he was gone away,
The fools they all began to play.

With salt box and with rolling pin,
They rattle for to call them in,
I lost my cousin in the fair,
Then I was shov'd I know not where.

I got into a sausage stall,
All nice and hct they loud did bawl,
I being both hungry and dry,
I feasted of their stinking fry.

I met a lady fine and gay,
She took me for to see the play,
The play indeed was very fine,
The lady she was very kind.

A coach was called from the rank,
And drove us down to Salt-Petre Bank,
Although the lady was dress'd so nice,
The bed was swarming with bugs and lice.

Of all the money of my hay,
I had but sixpence the next day,
Then I did stamp, curse, and swear,
I'll go no more to Bartholomew Fair.[7]

The question of suppressing Bartholomew Fair was first raised as early as 1678, by the London Corporation. Objection was made to the prolonged interruption of normal trading which it caused, as well as to the concomitant crime, hooliganism, drunkenness, and immorality. A lengthy war of attrition ensued, which eventually led to the fair's decline and ultimate suppression in 1855.

Other Fairs

During the nineteenth century many other fairs were attacked, and between 1792 and 1888 the numbers in England and Wales fell by a third (from 1,545 to 946).[8] The trend, however, was not as clear-cut as the figures suggest. While some counties showed dramatic losses (the number in Kent falling from 127 to 31), others remained steady, and six even increased (the number in Lancashire, for example, rose by 10, to 51). Moreover, some of the counties where there were reductions nevertheless saw the introduction of new fairs.

In some cases, fairs declined because of demographic and commercial changes. In others, they were neutralized or suppressed only after long resistance. In Birmingham, civic approval was withdrawn in 1851, but the popularity of fairs was on the increase, the numbers attending them being swelled from surrounding areas, including the Black Country, whose miners were particularly keen attenders. The rip-roaring atmosphere of the Birmingham fairs is evoked in Marjorie Hessell Tiltman's novel *Quality Chase* (1939). Vendors, small tradesmen, and showmen supported the fairs, but their opponents, industrialists and moralists, eventually won the day when, in 1875, the council decided to banish the fairs from the centre of the town to beyond its boundary. There was an even longer struggle in Leicester, where the Humberstone Gate fairs also grew in popularity during the nineteenth century. Some 30,000 people patronized the October fair in 1888; and in the following year on the Saturday alone between 12,000 and 13,000 visitors came by special train from virtually every town within a hundred miles. After protracted negotiations, the corporation managed to buy out the fairground rights of all claimants for £20,000, and the last fair was held in May 1904.

It has been said that fairs were 'an intrinsic part of English popular culture',[9] and this is certainly borne out by the profusion of songs and ballads on the subject. Some deal not so much with the fair itself as with happenings on the way there or back: a trial of wits ('Scarborough Fair'[10]), the mock-serious death of a horse ('Widdicombe Fair'[11]) or an amorous encounter ('Strawberry Fair'[12]). 'Brigg Fair'[13] is a fine love lyric, suffused with melancholy. 'Darlington Fair'[14] tells of a meeting which ends in marriage, and a similar expectation features in 'The Plowman's Glory', one of *Four Excellent New Songs* published in Edinburgh in 1778 which remained in oral tradition until this century.[15] Such hopes of marriage were perhaps naïve, for statistics often showed, as at Bromley in Kent, 'a bulge of bastard births each year in December–January, about nine months after the spring fair'.[16] Some ballads frankly revelled in the sexual opportunities available at fairs and wakes; others ostensibly warned of them, though their sub-text is probably the same. Nelly, a milkmaid, frolics in the hay on the way home from a wake with the appropriately named Roger, and 'When eight months were over and nine coming on' gives birth to a boy whom she proposes to call 'Young-Roger-coming-home-from-the-wake'.[17] At Birmingham fair, pretty Nancy meets a man called 'Young Rambleaway' (she should have guessed the worst from his name), and the outcome is predictable:

> When twenty-four weeks were over and past,
> This pretty fair maid she fell sick at last;
> Her gown wouldn't meet nor her apron string tie,
> And she longed for the sight of young Rambleaway.[18]

The traditional function of fairs as occasions for trade still lingers in a few places. John R. Allan gives a remarkable description, written in 1935, of Aulton market, which was held at the beginning of November on the glebe of St Machar in Old Aberdeen:

The fair was of very great antiquity and even when I was a child it was one of the leading events of the social year. The war [of 1914–18] killed it as it killed many other ancient institutions. The last time I saw the Aulton Market there were no more than a dozen horses on the field, and no gingerbread and no whisky tents. How different thirty, forty years ago. Maybe five hundred, maybe a thousand horses changed hands that day. The whisky tents seethed with roaring, drunken crowds. Great piles of gingerbread and chipped apples (a handful for a penny) melted off the stalls like snow wreaths in thaw; roistering farmers staked their shillings in hopeless attempts to find the lady or spot the pea; fiddlers played reels, pipers piped laments, boxers took on all comers for a guinea, and ballad singers made the afternoon hideous with the songs of Scotland. As the evening came on, gas flares lit up the lanes between the booths, making the shadows yet more drunken as the wind troubled the flames. The town people now came in for their evening's fun—engineers from the shipyards, papermakers up from the Don and hundreds of redoubtable ladies from the Broadford mill. Though the twin spires of St Machar stood raised like pious hands in horror, and though the tower of King's College maintained her aloof communion with the stars, the saturnalia roared and swirled unheeded on the glebe.[19]

Allan gives no details of the songs he heard, but other horse-fairs had their own ballads. Weyhill fair in Hampshire, which still exists, had a ballad describing the different kinds of horses on sale, and also the tricks of the sellers:

> Now some upon the road were shewn,
> An' other found upon soft ground;
> An' up the hill their heads were turned,
> Ah' that's the way to shew 'em.
> They can gain or lose an inch or two,
> Oh yes, they this, an' more can do,
> To find the sort that will suit you,
> All at the fair at Weyhill.[20]

By a simple change of name, the piece was transferred to Howden in Lincolnshire.[21] Perhaps the oldest song of horse-selling is 'Warrikin [Warrington] Fair',[22] which contains a reference to a bailiff who was in office in 1548. It deals less with the fair itself, though, than with a termagant wife's recovery of the cash her husband omits to collect for his horse. Other fairs, originally for livestock, are now held purely for pleasure, which is reflected in ballads like 'The Rigs and Fun of Not-tingham Goose Fair.[23] The same fair provided a scene for Alan Sillitoe's novel *Saturday Night and Sunday Morning* (1958).

The ancient civic involvement with fairs occasionally features in ballads. Coventry Great Fair, which dates from a charter of 1218, opened from at least the fifteenth century with a grand procession which included the mayor and the corporation. In 1678 a woman representing Lady Godiva joined for the first time, and eventually she became the chief attraction. St George, Jason, Bishop Blaise, shepherds and shepherdesses, weavers, wool-combers, and people of other trades were also represented. The proceedings became more and more boisterous and ribald, and official participation ceased in 1829. In 1845 the bishop of Worcester protested against 'a Birmingham whore being paraded through the streets as Lady Godiva', and four years later the main fair was moved from the town centre to the outskirts. 'Coventry Fair' probably dates from the 1850s:

Fill up a bumper and rejoice and let the toast go round,
Fill and drink to every lass in Coventry town,
And to the noble minded lass who in her skin tite dress,
Who's followed by all trades likewise the pretty shepherdess.[24]

The diversions, entertainments, and sports afforded by fairs and wakes provided staple themes for ballad-writers for several centuries. The London frost or blanket fairs (the latter name deriving from the practice of using blankets to make booths) were set up on the frozen Thames during particularly hard winters. Activities held on the ice included bull-baiting, horse and coach races, puppet plays, throwing at tethered cocks, ox roasts, skittles, football, sliding and skating, drinking and eating. During the exceptionally severe frost which lasted from early December 1683 until February 1684, John Evelyn observed that a printing press was set up on the ice 'where the people and ladyes took a fancy to have their names printed, and the day and yeare set down when printed on the Thames: this humour took so universally, that 'twas estimated the printer gain'd £5 a day, for printing a line onely, at sixpence a name, besides what he got by ballads, &c.'[25] A dozen ballads describe the same fair, and the tradition continued until the last frost fair of 1814–15: 'The Humours of Frost Fair' concludes:

Now to conclude my icy song,
I'm glad to see the frost is gone,
And ships and barges all afloat,
And watermen towing of their boats;
Black diamond barges do appear,
That coals they may not be so dear,
So toss a bumper off with cheer,
And bid adieu to frosty fair.[26]

Those frequenting fairs, according to an eighteenth-century garland, included not only 'tag, rag, and bobtail', but farmers' wives (and presumably farmers) and also 'Gentry in their Coaches'.[27] A similar social spread is implied in an early nineteenth-century sheet entitled 'A True Description of a Trip to the Fair', which mentions lads, lasses, men, wives, and children, and adds that 'Some on horses and some on foot, some in chaise will repair, / Some loading in waggons to ride to the fair'.[28] As the century progressed, fairs, especially in or near urban and industrial areas declined in the favour of both the middle classes and the genteel. The attendance of a young barrister at Salisbury fair in Hardy's story *On the Western Circuit* (1891) is very unusual, and it leads directly to a personal disaster, his marriage to a servant girl. Mill girls are mentioned specifically in 'The

Humours of the Feast',[29] plough-boys and 'counter jumpers' (shop assistants) in 'The New Rigs and Humours, Scenes, Sights and Sprees of the Fair'.[30]

In 'Eccles Wakes' there is ill feeling between the local people and 'fine dress[y] work folk from Manchester', including putters-out (those who gave out work to be done at home), warpers (who laid down the warp threads for weavers), and cutters (who cut completed cloth from the loom). The ballad was written, probably in the late 1820s, possibly to the tune of 'Jone o' Grinfilt', by the unknown author of 'Manchester's Improving Daily'.

ECCLES WAKES

In August last, it being holiday time,
And being myself a young lad in my prime,
To see Eccles wakes it was my intent,
So I dressed in my best and away then I went,
With Nell & a few men, & Robert the ploughman,
And Sally, and Ally, and Moll.

Each lad hugged his lass as we passed along,
And when we came there it was wonderful throng.
There were some buying Eccles, some Banbury cakes,
For the lasses and lads that attend at the wakes,
For Ned treated Sally, and Bob treated Ally,
And I bought a Banbury for Moll.

Your fine dress work folk from Manchester town,
They strutted as if all the wake was their own;
Putters-out and warpers, yes cutters and all,
Dressed like master & dame, jeered both me & Moll,
I ne'er saw their fellows in spreading their umbrellas
Ere rain from the elements fall.

There were filberts as large as the eggs of our poot*a*,
And gingerbread, jannock*b*, as big as my foot,
We eat and we crack'd, and did both stuff and eat,
Till I thought we should burst 'twas so good and so sweet,
Thus me and my love ranged all the wake over,
Partaking of all in the street.

The bellart*c* ere long tied the bull to the stake,
The dogs were set on, some pastime to make,
He jostled about gave a terrible roar,
Tossed the dogs in the air, and the folks tumbled o'er.
Such shouting and bawling, such pushing and hauling,
I ne'er in my days saw before.

Mrs Rice in the dirt spoiled her muslin gown,
Mrs Warpingmill had her new petticoat torn,
Their spouses (poor creatures) in quitting the mob,
Had their coats torn to spencers*d*, robbed Stitch of a job,
Rent aprons and shawls which they got in their falls,
Made many poor wretches to sob.

But too my good folks the fun ended not here,
A Banbury merchant attended the fair,
Crying buy now or toss—the bull chanced him to spy,
Gave his basket a toss, but chose not to buy,
I thought to the wakes they were coming with cakes
Confectioners down from the sky.

Next followed the race for the leathern prize,
Tits*e* entered the field amidst bustle and noise,
Now Dobbin, now Short, now Ball was the cry,
Though Dobbin beat Short, Ball passed both by,
Disputing who won, to fighting they ran,
And the winner came off with black eyes.

When racing and betting were both at an end,
To a house each went, with his sweetheart or friend,

a pullet   *b* honestly   *c* bull-baiter   *d* short jackets   *e* nags

Some went to Shaw's, others Philip's chose,
But me and my Moll to the hare and hounds goes,
With music and cakes to finish the wakes,
Among wenches and country beaux.

When morning approached, quite willing and glad,
I went with my Moll to her mammy and dad,
Unwilling to part with my joy and delight.
I gave her a ball*f* and then bade her goodnight,
What before we'd been doing, you're not to be knowing,
But time will bring all things to light.[31]

The fair, despite—or probably because of—its popularity, was suppressed
in 1877 after sustained pressure from the Eccles clergy.

The polarization in attitudes to fairs was caused partly by the rowdiness,
robbery, drinking, and sexual licence which were frequently (and favour-
ably) mentioned in ballads, but disliked by the respectable. Women's
running for prizes, stripped to their smocks, was regarded as indecent; still
more so the nude races by men and boys which took place in several parts
of the country, and lingered in Lancashire until at least the 1870s. Finally,
the baiting and fighting of animals aroused humanitarian disgust. Nevertheless, fairs remained firmly fixed in popular esteem, and songs about
them continued to be written and sung until well into the twentieth
century. 'Tavistock Goosie Fair'[32] (1912) and 'Rawtenstall Annual Fair'
(1932) are two examples.[33] The opposition expressed itself in other
forums and by other means. One piece, current in the 1870s, guys two of
the objectors at Bloxwich, the parson and the schoolmaster:

Then the Methody Parson is heard tu complain
'Them horrid Wake Fokes bin a comin' again.
No rest con I get nayther night nor by day,
If it goes on much longer I'll run right away.

'For my residence is in the midst ov the fun,
An' the din is soo deffnin' I'm ommust undun,
I mun goo tu the Doctor an' ty him complain,
For I raly bin suffrin' from Wake on the Brain'.

Then theer's the Skulemeaster who lives on the Green,
He's welly druv mad with the horrible din,
An' he wishes the Shows an' the Stalls, an' Steam 'osses,
In a much warmer place—bekos he so cross is.[34]

The closure of fairs, for whatever reason, was regarded by many with
deep regret. A case in point, Greenwich fair, held at Easter and Whitsun-

f drink

tide, had no charter, but merely grew, possibly from something as simple as the custom of rolling down the hill, for which people, both children and adults, singly or in pairs, assembled at Easter. Voltaire, arriving in London in 1726, felt himself 'transported to the Olympic games' when watching horse- and foot-races there, and took the maidservants and country girls there for ladies, so attracted was he by their calico dresses, their 'neatness, vivacity, and pleased contentedness'.[35] By the 1760s the proceedings were attracting up to 15,000 people; and in the first half of the nineteenth century the fair was even more of a draw, with visitors travelling from London by steamboat (after 1815) and railway (1836). Yet, at the same time, Francis Place, who had been there as a child and returned in 1824 and for the next fifteen years, rejoiced that respectable people no longer allowed their children to attend: 'They have learned how to enjoy more rational amusements than could be found at Tea-Gardens and Fairs, filled with all sorts of person.'[36] On Easter Sunday evening in 1838 the attendance is said to have been 200,000 (presumably of the unrespectable). The following year Dickens wrote in *Sketches by Boz* that Greenwich fair was 'a periodical breaking out, we suppose, a sort of spring-rash: a three days' fever, which cools the blood for six months afterwards, and at the expiration of which London is restored to its old habits of plodding industry, as suddenly and as completely as if nothing had ever happened to disturb them'.[37] In 1850 the spring fever was unduly high, for there was 'a very serious riot, with much demolition of property'. This proved to be 'a prelude to the discouragement of the Fair and to its extinction'. Its parting is lamented in 'Poor Old Greenwich Fair' (see illustration).[38]

In 'Happy Land. Comic Version', which dates from the mid-1850s, 'putting down the fairs' in general, and the suppression of Fairlop (1853) and Bartholomew (1855) fairs in particular, are linked with a wide range of working-class complaints about social and political developments (see Chapter 7).

The place of fairs was taken in part by exhibitions and agricultural shows, which were celebrated very much after the style of the classic fairs. A single Birmingham printer, William Pratt, issued four ballads on the 1851 exhibition: 'The Crystal Palace', 'Exhibition of All Nations', 'The National Exhibition', and 'Uncle Ned's Visit to the Exhibition';[39] and there are parallels from other printers. 'The Ramble through the Agricultural Show'[40] or 'The Great Agricultural Show'[41] also continue the tradition of fair-ballads. Pleasure gardens such as Tinker's in Manchester and Trentham Park in Staffordshire received similar treatment,[42] as did visits to the races and steamboat excursions such as the fair-time sea trip from Glasgow to the popular resort of Rothesay on the Isle of Bute:

> Last Hogmanay at Glesca Fair,
> There was me masel' an' sev'ral mair,
> An' we a' resolved tae hae a tear
> An' spend the nicht in Rothesay, O.
> We wandered throught the Broomielaw,
> Through wind an' rain, an' sleet an' snaw,
> An' at forty meenits efter twa,
> We got the length o' Rothesay, O.[43]

This was popularized in the music-halls of the late nineteenth and early twentieth centuries, though it is based on a country song, 'The Tinkler's Waddin', written in 1792 by a weaver called William Watt.[44] 'Rothesay, O' treats with high good humour the squalid accommodation which the holiday-makers find for the night, while other excursion pieces deal with shipboard conditions.

Along with fairs, various other recreations were under attack. In 1803 sabbath-breaking, intemperance, and cruelty to animals were all castigated in the Vice Society's 'Address to the Public'. In due course the three issues each gave rise to its own pressure group, in the shape of the Lord's Day Observance Society (1831), temperance bodies of various persuasions, from moderationist to prohibitionist (from 1829), and the Society for the Prevention of Cruelty to Animals (1824), which was later given the 'Royal' prefix (1840). All were initiated by the well-to-do, but received some support from working-class people and organizations. Yet there was a strong counter-impulse to use Sundays for sport and recreation, to see drinking as pleasurable, and to take passionate delight in blood sports.

Drink

Drinking is firmly entrenched in traditional culture, with songs like 'John Barleycorn', of which the earliest printed version dates from 1624,[45] and pieces in praise both of particular brews and of beer in general. 'Bring us in good Ale'[46] dates from the fifteenth or early sixteenth century, 'The Man that Waters the Workers' Beer'[47] from the 1930s. The 1830 passage of the Beerhouse Act, known as Billy's Beer Bill, removed many of the restrictions on the sale of beer, and was saluted in a street ballad:

> Come one and all, both great and small,
> With voices loud and clear,
> And let us sing 'Bless Billy the King
> Who bated the tax upon beer'.[48]

The temperance movement responded with ballads of its own, hoping, as evangelizers like Hannah More did with theirs, to reach the public of the popular sheets. Preston was one of the strongholds of teetotalism, and in the 1840s and early 1850s the local printer, James Harkness, issued a whole series of sheets with titles like 'Teetotal Boy', 'A Warning to Drunkards', 'The Drunkard's Farewell', 'The Doings of Drink and Teetotalism', and 'The Reformed Drunkard's Children's Song'.[49] Other temperance ballads, such as 'A Word of Advice',[50] issued in Bristol, were less melodramatic in tone, more concerned to argue a case. Some advocates of temperance would accept beer, though not spirits. Others were against all alcohol. 'The Temperance Alphabet', by John Embleton, appeared in London in the 1860s or 1870s:

> A stands for Alcohol, a demon-like name,
> Invented by devils men's minds to inflame;
> Like the mark set on Cain, its bare name is a curse,
> It steals health and reason, and beggars your purse.
>
> B stands for Beer, with its white frothy head,
> Bids you drink deep, your spirits to cheer,
> Till, like the treacherous foam, of the ocean's deep bed,
> You are driven headlong to despair.[51]

Despite such efforts, the consumption of beer increased steadily to the record level in 1876 of 34.4 gallons per head of the population per year. After this, as a result of regulation, rather than persuasion, it fell. Drinking songs have continued in oral tradition to the present day, but one would be hard put to it to find a song of the teetotal variety.

Cock-fighting

Campaigns against cruelty to animals ran counter to a number of long-standing entertainments, such as cock-fighting. Not that opposition dates only from the nineteenth century; as early as 1583 Philip Stubbes wrote in his usual scathing manner of those who 'flock thicke and three folde to the Cock-fightes', adding that 'They have houses erected for that purpose, flags and ensignes hanged out, to give notice of it to others, and proclamation goes out, to proclaim the same, to the ende that many may come to the dedication of this solemne feast of mischiefe.'[52] Some of the 'houses' have survived to this day, either re-erected (the Denbigh and Bridgnorth cockpits are now respectively at the Welsh Folk Museum, St Fagan's, and the Avoncroft Museum, Bromsgrove) or restored on their original sites (as at Welshpool, behind the National Westminster Bank, and at Eton, behind the Cockpit Restaurant). Others are shown on early maps, such as Speed's of Leicester (1610). Samuel Pepys, recording a visit to a new pit, remarks on the social cross-section of those attending, and also on the gambling:

1663, December 21.—To Shoe Lane to see a cock-fighting at a new pit there, a spot I was never at in my life; but, Lord! to see the strange variety of people, from Parliament man, by name Wildes, that was Deputy Governor of the Tower when Robinson was Lord Mayor, to the poorest 'prentices, bakers, brewers, butchers, draymen, and what not; and all these fellows one with another cursing and betting. I soon had enough of it. It is strange to see how people of this poor rank, that look as if they had not bread to put into their mouths, shall bet three or four pounds at a time and lose it, and yet bet as much the best battle; so that one of them will lose 10 or 20 pounds at a meeting.

In the eighteenth century the main promoters of the sport were the gentry of the shires, according to William Gardiner (1770–1853) of Leicester, at least:

Wakes and fairs were continually occurring, in which the lower orders indulged all sorts of sports, as cock-throwing, football, and single-stick. The work-people had their clubs, foot-ales, and candle-blocks. The farmers had their sheep-shearing, Maypoles, and harvest-cart. In the upper classes, dancing and cards prevailed; but the grand amusement among the gentry was cock-fighting. The mains to be fought were advertised in every paper, and were as common as the cricket matches of the time. Sometimes, one hundred cocks were slaughtered in a day.[53]

Matches and individual contests were celebrated in ballads, though these, curiously enough, seem seldom to have been printed. 'A New Song, called The Bird Fancier' deals with cock-fighting at the Black Dog public house in Bethnal Green, probably in the late eighteenth century:

> Come you bird fanciers that in pigeons delight,
> For to hear the birds sing and to see the cocks fight,
> If you go to the house where the sports to be seen,
> At the black dog, upon Bethnell-green.[54]

'The Lee Bridge Cocking' describes a main between Shropshire and Cheshire which took place in 1779, but it was not published until over a century later.[55] 'The Hathersage Cocking'[56] is said to date from 1715, but was not printed before the nineteenth century. It then circulated widely, partly in print, but mainly in oral tradition, with changing details of local rivalries, people, and places, including Holbeck, Liverpool, Oldham, and Walney. The Walney version begins:

> It's a ye cockers far and near
> I'll tell of a cock match when an' whear

At Tumblers Hill they all did say
The charcoal black and the bonnie gray.
Wi' a hip and a ha and a loud hourra
The charcoal black and the bonnie gray.[57]

The longevity and wide distribution of the 'Bonny Grey' family of songs shows the tenacious appeal of cock-fighting, but opposition was also expressed in verse and ballad. George Crabbe wrote memorably in *The Parish Register* (1809) of 'th'inhuman cocker' who 'damns the craven fool that lost his stake, / And only bled and perished for his sake'. A few years earlier a Birmingham gun-maker, James Probin, unflatteringly portrayed the cockers of a particular town in 'The Wednesbury Cocking'.[58] Probin was in the habit of going to Darlaston for gun-locks, and on one occasion stopped to watch a main of cocks at Wednesbury, and was inspired to write about it. This may not be 'the most famous of English provincial ballads', as Matthew Hodgart has claimed,[59] but it was known to Robert Graves[60] and to Samuel Butler, whose father, having heard it sung 'in my nursery by poor old Mrs Bromfield, my nurse', repeated it at Shrewsbury school, where it was done into Greek hexameters.[61] The ballad was also greatly appreciated in less literary circles. Joshua Vernal wrote in 1859:

Although its wit is ribald and gross, yet its delineations of character are correct. Those who knew the 'black country' forty years ago, can bear testimony to its truth. How often has it been sung with a roaring chorus. How frequently did some of us old ones join in that chorus, and think it the best of songs, as we drained the foaming tankard again and again. ... It was once as popular and effective as 'Lillibulero', or as 'Shall Trelawney Die?'[62]

It was not appreciated at Wednesbury, however. On the contrary, as a local historian records, it 'greatly infuriated the cockers, and the guard of the mail coach *Nimrod* venturing on one occasion to give a few bars of the melody on his bugle while passing through the town, was attacked and savagely stoned for his pains'.[63] The tune was known well enough to be prescribed for other texts, not only the local 'Bloxwich Wake Bull-baiting' (see below), but also 'Windsor Election';[64] however, the sole version which has survived in oral tradition has verses only half the length of the original.[65]

A whole series of laws—of 1895 in Scotland and of 1835, 1849, 1911, and 1952 in England and Wales—has failed to stop cock-fighting altogether. In recent years, cases have been reported from Fermanagh (1970s), London (1976), Hitchen (1983), and Bridgnorth (1985).[66] Bull-baiting has long since disappeared, however, though street names remain as witnesses to it, as well as the bulldogs and Staffordshire bull-terriers which are the descendants of those bred for it.

Bull-baiting and Running

For centuries, bulls (and also bears) were chained up so that dogs might be set on them for the amusement of spectators, who included 'persons of the most exalted rank, without exception of the fair sex'. So wrote Joseph Strutt in 1801, adding, specifically on bull-baiting, that 'this cruel pastime was ... universally practised on various occasions, in almost every town and village throughout the kingdom, and especially in market towns'. By Strutt's time, though, it was 'attended only by the lowest and most despicable part of the people'.[67] The last public bull-baiting seems to have been at Bunbury in Cheshire in 1848, but others may have been held privately after that date. However, there does not appear to have been a prolonged, clandestine pursuit of the sport, as in the case of cock-fighting. Nor is there evidence that bull-baiting ballads found favour in oral tradition. Indeed, the existence of such ballads at all seems to have been confined largely to the Midlands. Of these, one deals with an occasion in 1743 when the baited bull escaped and ran through the town of Bloxwich in Staffordshire,[68] another, in the same town in 1779, with the disappearance beforehand of the animal assigned for baiting.[69] Two early nineteenth-century pieces, 'A New Song called Bloxwich Wake Bull-baiting'[70] and 'Darlaston Wake Bull-baiting'[71] are more concerned, after the style of 'The Wednesbury Cocking', with dissension among the baiters than with the baiting itself.

Even in the Midlands there was opposition to the sport, and in 1798 the Birmingham Loyal Association, a volunteer militia made up of shop-keepers and tradespeople, marched to a baiting with colours flying and drums beating, took possession of the bull, and placed it in the town gaol for safe keeping. The event was recorded in the 'ballad chronicles' of a local writer, William Mackay. In one of them the bull has a soliloquy, to the tune of 'Cease rude Boreas':

> Fellow creatures! (so I count ye),
> Pity now my dreadful fate,
> While fields afford you nature's bounty,
> Think what horrors me await.
> My tongue, I'm sure, ne'er spoke sedition,
> Yet savage foes do me assail,
> In Peck Lane lock'd, Oh! hard admission;
> Perhaps tomorrow sent to gaol.[72]

A clergyman, Abraham Smith, tells in *A Scriptural and Moral Catechism*

(?1834) how, while cholera was prevalent, bull-baiting was more or less suspended in the Black Country, but afterwards enjoyed a revival. He gives instances from Sedgley, Darlaston, and Rowley Regis (where at the wake 'a Bull's tongue was torn out of his mouth, both his horns were broken off, and iron horns riveted on the bleeding stumps'), and provides a cautionary tale:

A few years ago a Bull was baited at Toll End, Tipton, when a monster, in a human form, undertook to pin (a term used by the Bull baiters) or seize the animal by the mouth with his own teeth! Accordingly a way or path was instantly made for him to do so. But his end was come; death was in waiting to pierce him with his lance! The moment the wretch attempted to seize the nose of the bull, the animal caught him with his horn in the neck, directly under his ear, the blood immediately gushed out in a torrent, and in attempting to run home he fell down on the road and expired.[73]

If bull-baiting had few defenders after the early nineteenth century, the case was different with bull-running. The practice of pitting one's own courage, endurance, and agility against a bull allowed to run freely through the streets is still followed in parts of France and Spain. It was once customary in several English towns, including London, Tutbury, and Stamford. There were also occasions on which bulls escaped from a market such as Smithfield in London, and provided impromptu entertainment. 'The Lads of St Catharine's' tells how sailors seized on a stray bullock and drove him through the streets out of sheer mischief:

> We drove him into Moorfields, among the Brokers Row,
> Where the bullock he began to cut a noble shew,
> Their chairs and their tables they all went to wrack,
> Likewise their pots and saucepans, and glasses they went smack.[74]

Another sheet, 'The Bullock Hanker's Medley', dating probably from the 1820s, tells of much the same kind of exercise, organized deliberately:

> Come listen awhile you bullock hunters,
> Unto what I now shall sing,
> Concerning of a bull the other morning,
> Out of Smithfield we did bring;
> He did bellow we did follow,
> While the lads in crowds did hollow,
> Mad bullock through the streets did ring.

The chaotic and boisterous progress includes incidents like these:

> Then up alleys and streets we drove him,
> The people all shut their doors.
> And the lads they all laughed at the fun,
> For to see how he toss'd the whores;

Poor Old Greenwich Fair

Come all you lads and lasses to my ditty lend a ear
Do you know the rogues have done away with poor
    old Greenwich fair,
When at Easter and at Witsuntide we used to go so gay
By wind and steam so merrily to pass dull care away.

Now at Easter and at Witsuntide no more we shall repair,
Oh cruel was the rogues who done away with Greenwich
    fair,

We used to go to Greenwich fair and there have such a lark
to see the pretty maidens rolling down through Greenwich
    park,
then into the swings they hasten and go flying in the air,
there was never such a pretty place as poor old Greenwich
    fair.

there was roasted pigs and nanny-goats in Greenwich fair
    was sold,   (gold
where was hats and ladies' bustles trim'd with California
there was lovely cooks & breeches saveloys & hot pea soup
three sticks a penny in the hole and pricking in the loop,

What lots of fun and humour used to be at Greenwich fair
there was Billy Punch and Judy too in all their glory
    there
there was firing at the target and lollypops to sell,
And private rooms for ladies to play at Bagatelle.

I never shall forget the time and I'm sure will never you
When old Brown upon his salt box used to play the rat too
Last Friday night the Baker's wife did solemnly declare,
She saw the ghost of Billy Richardson dancing round the
    fair

She saw the ghost of Algiers too, which made old doughy
    jump
He had eleven gas lamps hanging to his rump
She saw old Woombell's elephant dancing in the dark
And then upon the fair ground met the ghost of Billy Clark

Nine pretty maids in Greenwich Park one easter I did see
Who wished to look and see a cock climb up a chestnut tree
But what a lark the bough it broke and they could not
    hold fast
When down they came upon their bums a rolling on the
    grass.

Oh cruel was the naughty rogues how could they ever
    dare
to sign a long petition to kill old Greenwich fair
May they never see a comfort may they never taste a nut
May they die upon the river with a scratcher in their guts

Old Greenwich was delightful when the shop boys were
    let loose
the Barber sold his lather box the tailor sold his goose,
The cobler sold his lapstone to banish grief and care,
And sally pawned her linen smock to go to Greenwich far

then weep you lads and lasses lie down and shed a tear.
And cry oh dear we never more shall see old Greenwich fair

W. Dwyer, 18, Gt. St. Andrew Street, Seven Dals.

'Poor Old Greenwich Fair'. Street ballad.

THE FOX CHASE;

OR,

The Huntsman's Harmony,

BY

The Duke of BUCKINGHAM's Hounds.

To an excellent new Tune much in Request.

ALL in a Morning fair,
Within to take the Air,
I heard some hollow moft clearly;
Then drew myſelf near,
To ſhun who they were,
That hollow'd and harmed ſo early.

Near they were Gentlemen,
From the Duke of *Buckingham*,
They were going to make a Chaſe;
Of cry Joue did I think,
Beſet of this Tune was full,
And ſo I drew near to the Place.

Then in *Wreckldate* Scroggs,
We caſt about our Dogs,
In the Place where the Game was likely;
But the like ne'er was ſeen,
Since a Huntſman I've been,
For our Hounds found a Fox muſt quietly.

There's *Dido* and *Spenter*,
And the Sam of Round *Dowlm*,
Who hollow'd and yet looks behind him;
With *Jowler* and *Rockwood*,
And who was the Game full,
Then at worth the Covers which find him.

Sly *Tabal*, cries, away,
Hark *Jowler*, hark away,
Our Huntſmen ſoon them did hear him,
Tom *Migher* cries, Ti *Loon*,
Uncouple all now *Ronall*,
Or off we jog ne'er come nigh him.

Then *Copper* and *Cauteffe*,
Were thrown off in the Caſe,
With the famous *Thumper* and *Cryer*;
Several good Hounds beſide,
Whole Strength there was fully try'd,
Not one in the whole Pack did tire.

Our Hounds came in a Pace,
And fall into the Chaſe,
Away they purfu'd this poor Creature;
The *Engliſh* and *French* Horn,
Encourag'd our Hounds that Morn,
Our Cry became greater and greater.

It could not be expreſt,
Which Hound did run the beſt,
For they all run a Breaſt together;
As you have not heard of late,
When they ran the Valleys together.

To the Moor then we twin'd,
With full Speed againſt the Wind,
Thinking we might have croſs'd it over;
But our Hounds ran ſo hard,
They made the Fox afraid,
And fore'd him to return to his Cover.

Upon the Hills he ran along,
His Cover was full ſtrong,
But I think he had no great Eaſe o't;
They run with ſuch a Cry,
That Echhoes made them fly,
I'll aſſure you our Sport it was pleaſant.

Homewards then he did hie,
And in *Wreckldate* did try,
Thinking that the Wind might ſave him;
But our Hounds ran ſo cloſe,
That they fet him by the noſe,
Our Hortimen alſo did deceive him.

Elydre *Flamgs* rode amain,
And with what ſpeed the Plain,
Mr *Flemgs*, his Hortes did met Favour;
And ſoon up the high Hills,
And down to the low Dale,
Eſpecting his Death for their Favour.

Mr *Tadal* rode his Part,
Although the Chaſe was ſtout,
A Default was ſeldom or never;
But ever by and by,
To the Hoſanſt lao wou'd cry,
Milam, *Milam*, hark away again.

Tom *Hoſanna*, he rode ſtout,
Yet help'd us in our Sport,
Who came in both circling and ſweating;
But when in his Poſt,
He wou'd cry, *Lilly Flora*,
Hark to *Jowk*, near *Traveler* ſtout ſtum line.

To *Sephim's* Woods he goes,
Being purſu'd by his Foes,
Our Company after him did follow;
An I neurpiece we lou'd,
Made our Huntſman's Heart full gla,
For we gave him many a Hollow.

The Chaſe was almoſt run,
So the Sport was juſt done,
He thought to have roul'd the River,
But our Hounds being in,
They after him did ſpin,
And ſo they d'ſtroy'd him for ever.

Then *Lepping* toot the Horn,
As round us e'er the blown,
Tom *Milam* lift him with his Deſtruction,
The Country Peope al,
Came fiockling to his Fa,
That's Honour enough for a Foxleaus.

So Whooping we proclaim'l,
God puſh the Noble Duke,
For our Hounds had run ſo much Glory;
That we all'd might tale Roots,
Plac we had Sport we know,
And ſhere is an End of the whole Story.

Newcaſtle upon Tyne: Printed and Sold by *JOHN WHITE*.

'The Fox Chase', Street ballad.

A ballad to commemorate

THE GREAT NORTH RUN

FROM

NEWCASTLE TO SHIELDS

which took place on June 28th 1981
in memory of and 'eftor the stile' of the

old Tyneside songwriters

(who surely would have written a song about it)

CHORUS

They closed Newcastle - you couldn't ride a bike through it
The folks from Fellin' flocked to see the fun
Hebburn and Jarrow had never seen the like of it
And 'canny sheels' was crowded for the Great North Run.

The Tyne bridge creaked and groaned beneath the weight of it
The new bridge gasped and gaped at what it saw
The railway bridge which claims its been about a bit
Said, 'I've never seen a race like this before.'

Brendan of Gateshead was the man who thought of it
Mike of Elswick the first to cross the line
Old folks, young folks, waitresses and coonsillors
It took them twenty minutes just to cross the Tyne.

Kevin from England who likes to kick the ball a bit
Put down his money and then ran with all his might
The local 'journal' even sent its editor
To see that the writers got the story right.

There was Neil from work and Trev from university
A lad on crutches, (cheered from the start)
And wheelchair heroes fighting all adversity
Winning doesn't matter - its the taking part

Geordie Ridley would have made a song of it
The Blaydon Races never looked so fine
And those who came must be glad they came along with it
To write another chapter in the history of the Tyne

To the author's tune
Written by K. Gregson
Calligraphy R. Murphy
Illustration P. Murphy

'The Great North Run'. Street ballad.

Rowlandson's etching records the scene at Balls Pond, Newington, during a three-day cricket match between women's sides from Hampshire and Surrey which began on 3 October 1811. The Hampshire team was victorious.

Heenan (on the left) *v*. Sayers at Farnborough, 17 April 1860.

Bull Baiting,
COCK FIGHTING,
AND
DOG FIGHTING,

AT AN END
BY ACT OF PARLIAMENT.

In an Act of Parliament, passed on the 9th of September, 1835, is the following Clause:

" *Whereas*, Cruelties are greatly promoted and encouraged by Persons keeping Houses, Rooms, Pits, Grounds, or other Places, for the FIGHTING OR BAITING OF DOGS, BULLS, BEARS, or *other Animals*—and for FIGHTING COCKS—and by Persons *aiding or assisting therein*; and the same are great Nuisances and Annoyances to the Neighbourhood in which they are situate, and tend to demoralize those who frequent such places. Be it, therefore, enacted—that, from and after the passing of this Act, if any Person shall *keep or use any House, Room, Pit, Ground, or other Place*, for the purpose of *running, baiting, or fighting any Bull, Bear, Badger, Dog, or other Animal*, whether of domestic or wild nature or kind—or *for Cock Fighting*—or *in which any Bull, Bear, Badger, Dog, or other such Animal, shall be baited, run, or fought*;—every such Person shall be liable to a Penalty not exceeding FIVE POUNDS, nor less than TEN SHILLINGS, for every Day in which he shall so keep and use such House, Room, Pit, Ground, or Place, for any of the purposes aforesaid. —Provided always, that the Person who shall *act as the Manager* of any such House, Room, Pit, Ground, or other Place—or who shall *receive any Money* for the admission of any Person thereto—or who shall *assist in any such baiting, or fighting, or Bull-running*, shall be deemed and taken to be the Keeper of the same for the purposes of this Act, and be liable to all such Penalties as are by this Act imposed upon the Person who shall actually keep any such House, Room, Pit, Ground, or other Place, for the purposes aforesaid."

We, the undersigned Constables of Wolverhampton, beg to draw the attention of the Public to the above Act of Parliament.

WILLIAM SAVAGE,
HENRY CRUTCHLEY, } Constables.

Wolverhampton, October 12, 1835.

Printed by WILLIAM PARKE, Wolverhampton.

A handbill of 1835.

> Some up alleys they were running,
> And some down streets were a flocking
> Where he tossed an old Birmingham Turk
> Who was singing about Wedgbury Cocking.[75]

The bull-running at Bethnal Green replaced bull-baiting in 1816. It attracted up to a thousand Spitalfields weavers for three days each year, together with journeymen from other parts of London. Francis Place took part, but later expressed his disapprobation:

This hunting of bullocks used to collect the greatest of blackguards, thieves and miscreants of all kinds together. Its cruelty was atrocious, it led to every species of vice and crime, and proves how very low were peoples notions of morality, and how barbarous their dispositions since they could permit such a vile and mischievous pastime to be pursued without interruption for a long series of years.[76]

The runnings at Bethnal Green were stopped in 1826. At Tutbury in Staffordshire they lasted only until 1778, having been established four hundred years earlier by John of Gaunt. The story goes that Robin Hood after fighting eight men nearby (killing five and pardoning three) went towards the town, but

> Before we came to it, we heard a strange shouting,
> And all that were in it look'd madly,
> For some were a Bull-back, some Dancing a Morris,
> And some singing *Arthur a Bradly*.

He goes on to celebrate his wedding there, as is told in 'A New Ballad of Robin Hood: shewing His Birth, Breeding, Valour and Marriage, at *Titbury* Bull-running'.[77]

At Stamford in Lincolnshire the running, held on 13 November each year, persisted until 1839. Local belief had it that Earl Warren had initiated the running during the reign of King John. The procedure was as follows:

On the morning of the eventful day the bell of St Mary's tolled for the thoroughfares to be cleared of children and the infirm . . ., spectators crowded the windows and housetops, bold athletes stood below on the tip-toe of expectation, and then out bounced the bull. Teased into fury to afford prime sport, the beast would test to the utmost the watchfulness and agility of the bullards, and many an unfortunate 'runner', caught ere he gained a cask round which those hard pressed might manoeuvre, would be shot in the air to descend to the music of the multitude. One great object was to 'bridge' the bull, *i.e.*, pitch him over the parapet into the Welland, and if this feat were accomplished by noon the butchers had to provide another bull. Sometimes to goad it to frenzy men would gash the flesh of a tame, inoffensive animal, and apply vitriol to the gaping wounds. At one time it was

THE
NORTHERN COLLEGE
LIBRARY

BARNSLEY

customary after the running to chain the poor beast to a peg and bait it with dogs. In the evening the friendly axe would come to the rescue, and the tormentors would end their orgies with a supper of 'bull beef'.[78]

As early as 1785 the local newspaper commented: 'What a pity it is so barbarous a custom is permitted to be continued, that has no one good purpose to recommend it, but is kept as an orgy of drunkenness and idleness to the manifest injury of many poor families, even tho' the men escape bodily hurt.'[79] Three years later the mayor issued a curious proclamation stating that bull-running would be punishable by death. The event went ahead all the same. In 1789 the mayor summoned a troop of dragoons, but their officer declined to intervene, on the ground that the proceedings were peaceable. Intervention by the Society for the Prevention of Cruelty to Animals started in 1833, with the despatch of an observer, who was roughly handled by the crowd. Three years later, more officials turned up, and were assaulted. At the ensuing trial of eight labourers, they pleaded that 'valuable common rights were preserved in the town by the act of bull running'; nevertheless, the practice was declared to be illegal. Even so, considerable efforts were needed to bring it to an end. A force of 200 special constables proved ineffective in 1837. The following year dragoons and metropolitan policemen reinforced the specials. Two bulls were impounded, but a third ran, after being smuggled in 'by a certain noble lord', presumably the Earl Warren of the day. Attempts to stop it failed: 'The metropolitan police, with greater valour than discretion, formed in a compact phalanx on the bridge; but the bull, followed by the bullards, dashed through them as an eagle might through a cobweb.'[80] In 1839 there was a further confrontation, and this time a young bull was smuggled in by one of the special constables, but it was the last to run. The town worthies were weary of the struggle and also of the cost to the ratepayers. For many years the bull-runnings were affectionately remembered, helped by a song which became a kind of local anthem. With 'various additions and variations' it could 'still occasionally be heard' until the 1860s. The tune is based on that of a Scots contra-dance, 'The Penny Wedding', but the words have a populist, rather than a popular, ring.

Song of the Stamford Bullards

Come all you bonny boys
Who love to bait the bonny bull,
Who take delight in noise,
And you shall have your belly full.
On Stamford Town's bull-running day,
We'll show you such right gallant play,
You never saw the like, you'll say,
As you have seen at Stamford.

Earl Warren was the man
That first began this gallant sport;
In the castle he did stand,
And saw the bonny bulls that fought;
The butchers with their bull-dogs came,
These sturdy stubborn bulls to tame,
But more with madness did inflame,
Enrag'd they ran through Stamford.

Delighted with the sport,
The meadows there he freely gave,
Where these bonny bulls had fought,
The butchers now do hold and have;
By charter they are strictly bound,
That every year a bull be found;
Come daub your face you dirty clown,
And stump away to Stamford.

Come, take him by the tail boys,
Bridge, bridge him if you can;
Prog him with a nail boys;
Never let him quiet stand.
Through every street and lane in town
We'll chevy chase him up and down;
You sturdy strawyards⁸ ten miles round,
Come stump away to Stamford.

ᵍ labourers

Bring with you a prog stick,
Boldly mount then on his back;
Bring with you a dog Dick,
Who will also help to bark.
This is the rebel's riot feast,
Humanity must be debas'd,
And every man must do his best
To bait the bull in Stamford.[81]

Hunting

It was often felt that the suppression of cock-fighting, bull-baiting, and bull-running, which had big proletarian followings, was an attempt to discipline the lower orders. Attendance at such events on the part of the poor was a result of idleness. The well-to-do, some of whom supported the cruel old sports, were not idle, but leisured, and could transfer their allegiance to fox-hunting, fishing, or shooting, which remained unscathed. Horses might be ridden to death in steeplechases and stags hunted to death in parks, while RSPCA spokesmen defended both sports, and failed to protest when Queen Victoria patronized stag and otter hunts.

Steeplechasing (cross-country racing on horseback from one convenient landmark, usually a steeple, to another) and fox-hunting were justified as good schooling for cavalry officers, provided they were not 'killed in the training'. Wellington said that Leicestershire fox-hunters were the best of his officers at Waterloo. In addition, fox-hunting could claim to be keeping down a pest (though it has been known for centuries that foxes were carefully preserved just for the chase). Deer-hunting was originally considered to be socially superior, as was hare-coursing, but, as Keith Thomas has pointed out, 'Fox-hunting . . . had gained steadily in popularity with the gentry during the sixteenth and seventeenth centuries, particularly when deer grew scarcer and hare-coursing was impeded by enclosures.'[82] Both sports received a measure of support from ordinary people, especially hare-coursing, which continues to this day. Current opposition by anti-blood-sports campaigners has plenty of precedents, including that of Thomas More's Utopians, who pitied the hare, and of William Blake, who wrote: 'Each outcry of the hunted Hare / A fibre from the Brain does tear.' (He also believed that 'The Game Cock clip'd & arm'd for fight / Does the Rising Sun affright'.)[83] Those coursing the hare usually felt great admiration for their quarry, and expressed the excitement of the chase in ballads, starting with the now lost 'Songe of the Hunting and Killinge of the Hare' (1577).[84] When a ballad of 1660, 'The Hunting of the Hare',[85] was included in a radio programme for schools in

1974, Robin Pedley, Professor of Education at Southampton University, wrote to protest: 'The singing of jolly hunting songs is an insensitive practice which is abhorrent to an increasing number of teachers.' A BBC spokesman replied that the song was chosen as 'part of the British folk heritage', but conceded that 'the root question of whether old songs should be dropped when we no longer approve of their sentiments will continue to be a matter for serious consideration when planning future programmes.'[86] Notwithstanding such debates, songs of hare-hunting have continued in oral tradition alongside the huge number on fox-hunting.

'The Fox Chase; or The Huntsman's Harmony, by The Duke of Buckingham's Hounds, To an excellent new Tune much in Request' (see illustration)[87] was first printed in black letter sometime between 1689 and 1709. The nobleman in question was George Villiers, second duke of Buckingham (1627–88), who kept a pack of hounds at Helmsley in North Yorkshire. The ballad not only survived in oral tradition for almost three hundred years, but set the pattern for many other pieces which chronicle, sometimes at great length and in tedious detail, the triumphant pursuit of the fox. Others, like Henry Fielding's ballad-opera song of 1734, was lyrical about the chase in general:

> The dusky night rides down the sky,
> And ushers in the morn;
> The hounds all join in glorious cry,
> The huntsman winds his horn.[88]

Here a husband prefers the joys of hunting to the company of his wife. In another song called 'Doctor Mack' or 'Parson Hogg', dating from the early nineteenth century, the eponymous clergyman cannot resist the call of the hunt:

> It happened he had a pair to wed;
> Bold Reynard passed in view, sir.
> He drew the surplice over his head
> And bade the pair adieu, sir.
> They both did pray that he might stay,
> For they were not half bound, sir.
> He said that night to bed they might
> To tally ho the hounds, sir.[89]

The same theme, which is, no doubt, hardly a caricature of some of the hunting parsons of the nineteenth century, recurs in 'The Hunting Day', by William Williams (1805–90). Williams, who was the honorary secretary of the North Warwickshire Hunt, wrote the song in 1860 for the entertainment of his friends, and had it printed in Birmingham. It circulated widely, and is sung with variations to this day in various parts of the country. The chorus typifies the general mood of the song:

> We'll all go a-hunting today,
> All nature looks smiling and gay.
> So we'll join the gay throng that goes laughing along
> And we'll all go a-hunting today.[90]

Particular hounds, like Old Snowball of the Holme Valley Beagles in Yorkshire, had their own celebratory songs.[91] So did particular hunts, such as the Exmoor and the Quorn; and so did huntsmen, of whom the most famous was John Peel of Caldbeck (1777–1854), though Joe Bowman of nearby Ullswater (1879–1924) vies in popularity, at least in the Lake District.[92]

Although hunting songs are widespread in oral tradition, they are found mainly, not surprisingly, in the hunting areas of England and Ireland, where they are sung at hunt suppers and promoted by the sporting fraternity. Hunting, by its nature, has little appeal to town-dwellers, and indeed, recent campaigns for its abolition have come mainly from the towns. It remains the preserve of the well-to-do, except in the north of England, where beagles and fell-packs are followed mainly on foot, and working-class participation is considerable. New hunting songs, alongside and also adapting the older tradition, have continued to emerge down to the present day.

In general, hunting songs tend to be limited to the delights of the sport; none the less, many express admiration for the endurance and cunning of the fox, while voicing triumph at his demise:

> He led us a chase six hours in full cry;
> Tally ho, hark away, now soon he must die.
> We will cut off his brush with a hallooing noise,
> And we'll drink a good success to all fox hunting boys.[93]

Moreover, there is decided sympathy for bold Reynard in a number of songs which antedate the modern agitation against fox-hunting which Keith Thomas sees as beginning with an article published in 1869. In John Masefield's anti-hunting poem *Reynard the Fox* (1919), the quarry features in the third person, but in several songs it speaks for itself:

> Most Gentlemen take delight,
> In hunting bold Reynard the Fox,
> Near to Gaffer Gilding I lay.
> I fed upon rat geese and ducks.

> 'Tis near to Gaffer Gilding I lay,
> Not thinking so soon I should die,
> I was chas'd by a fresh pack of hounds,
> Caus'd me from my country to fly.

Ignoring considerations of verisimilitude, the fox even recounts its own death:

> It was in Stone fields they kill'd me
> Where the blood thirsty hounds did me follow
> They tore my old jacket to pieces
> And there gave the huntsman's loud halloo.
>
> But since old Reynard you have kill'd
> You may go to the Dolphin and dine
> And put his fore paw in a bumper
> And drink my Lord's health in good wine.[94]

In another song, a class-conscious animal, this time a vixen, engages in a dialogue with a huntsman, and concludes with this reflection:

> I wish in my heart I was under the ground,
> Where lords, dukes and gallants they never could be found—
> Now I'll drink thy good health, with all my old heart,
> In a bumper of wine, my boys, a gallon or quart.[95]

Of the old blood sports, hunting the otter (until recently), the stag (until now), and the fox (also until now) survived because they involved wild, rather than captive, animals; because they seldom involved large crowds, gambling, disorder, or damage (except for that caused by the passage of the hunt, which was regarded as legitimate); because they were rural, rather than urban; and above all, because although they had a working-class following, they were organized by and for country gentlemen and prosperous farmers. All this contrasts strongly with bull-baiting and cock-fighting, and also with old-style football and prize-fighting, in which men were pitted against each other.

Football

Several traditional football games survive, of which one, at Haxey in Lincolnshire, might possibly have developed from an earlier bull-running custom. They normally have few rules, indeterminate-sized teams, and wide territories and time-scales. At Ashbourne in Derbyshire, for example, a game is played on Shrove Tuesday and Ash Wednesday from 2 to 10 p.m. The goals are three miles apart, and the teams, Up'ards and Down'ards, consist potentially of all the men living respectively north and south of the Henmore brook. This song about the game was written by a local entertainer in 1821:

> The ball is turned up, and the Bull-Ring's the place,
> As fierce as a bull-dog is every man's face;
> Whilst kicking and shouting and bawling they run,
> Until every stitch in the ball comes undone.
> There's Faulkner and Smith, Bodge, Hand, and some more,
> Who hide it and hug it, and kick it so sore,
> And invite a good whopping at every man's door,
> In the neat little town of Ashborne.[96]

Popular football like this has survived, sometimes only after a tenacious struggle, in certain villages and small towns; but it was once reasonably common, not only in England, but also in Wales and Scotland. In many places it was suppressed only with great difficulty. In Derby, for example, soldiers and police were brought in the 1840s, much as in Stamford a few years earlier, to bring to an end the bull-running.

The appeal of such sport, apart from the sheer joy of muddy, violent physical exercise, lay in ritualized local rivalries, a sense of occasion and celebration, and a feeling that the people were in control, if only for a brief time. In several cases, such as at West Haddon in 1765 (see Chapter 1), the participants became involved in political action, such as the destruction of enclosure fencing. As with fairs, those opposed objected to such popular licence, to damage, disorder, and drunkenness, and also to the disruption of the normal patterns of business. Occasionally there was aristocratic support for a time-honoured, 'manly' sport. The duke of Northumberland provided a meadow in 1827–8 after the game was driven off the streets of Alnwick, thereby helping to ensure its survival to the present day. Today's attitudes to Association Football, both for and against, have many similarities with those to the street football of the past.

Prize-fighting

Wrestling and prize-fighting also had aristocratic backers as well as the support of ordinary people. Wrestling was concentrated in several main centres, the north-west, the south-west, and the south Midlands, whereas prize-fighting was more widespread. Both took place in connection with fairs or wakes, under the aegis of publicans or as separate tournaments or even single bouts. Prize-fighting drew larger crowds, with the attendant problems, and was sometimes banned by the magistrates on the grounds of breach of the peace or unlawful assembly. For this reason, fights were sometimes held close to county boundaries so that they could be moved from one jurisdiction to another in order to escape a possible ban.

Outstanding fights were extensively chronicled in street ballads, which served in the first instance as reportage, but were later reprinted, and sometimes entered oral tradition as a form of historical record. Other pieces, which might be valedictory, were devoted to a particular fighter and his career. John Harkness of Preston issued at least eleven sheets on prize-fights,[97] in addition to four on wrestling and five on foot-racing. Many were issued soon after the events described, and provided round-by-round commentary and inter-round summaries of the action. In late 1845 alone, Harkness printed seven sheets on fights and fighters, beginning with 'Bendigo, Champion of England' subtitled 'A New Song of the Great Fight between Bendigo and Caunt . . . which took place at Witchwood, on Tuesday, September 9th, 1845':

> So we'll drink success to Bendigo, who showed such gallant play,
> For by his skill he won the mill and bore the prize away.

Immediately afterwards he issued an alternative view of the same contest, presumably for sale to supporters of the defeated pugilist, under the title 'The Unfair Fight between Caunt and Bendigo'. A little later, Harkness published 'Young Tyler and Robinson Huzza', which, although it opens 'Come all young fellows that delight in any game, / Come listen to these lines which I have lately penn'd', dates from before 1832. This, incidentally, is one of the few boxing songs to have entered oral tradition: Cecil Sharp found a version in Somerset in 1906 with the improved opening: 'Come all you young fellows that delight in a little game, / Come listen unto me and I will tell you plain.'[98]

After a pause, no doubt to avoid glutting the market, Harkness printed 'The Great Fight which took place between Young Molyneux and Hammerlane on the 9th of June, 1840', which was followed on consecutive sheets by 'Bendigo and Deaf Burke', 'Crib and Molyneux', and 'The Death of Simon Byrne'. The last two refer respectively to fights of 1811 and 1830, and Harkness was taking advantage of interest aroused by current happenings to reprint classic contests of the past. Such practices could be multiplied many times, with different printers and at different periods.

Prize-fighting first became popular in England in the late seventeenth century, when Maximilien Misson, a French Protestant exiled in London, wrote: 'Tout ce qui s'appelle *Fighting* . . . est une chose délicieuse à un Anglais.' From the middle of the eighteenth century until about 1830, interest was enormous. Lord Byron took lessons in boxing from Gentleman

Jackson. Mendoza, Jem Belcher, and Tom Cribb were household names. Hazlitt wrote a celebrated essay called 'The Fight' (1822) on a contest between Bill Neate and Tom Hickman at Hungerford, the result of which was despatched to London by carrier pigeon. The fancy, or sporting fraternity, included members of the aristocracy, the gentry, and the clergy. There was also mass support, with the Cribb–Molyneux fight of 1811 attracting 15,000 spectators and the Spring–Langan fight of 1824 at Worcester, 30,000.

As well as bare-fisted punching, certain wrestling holds were also allowed. Fights were often lengthy. A round lasted until one contestant was knocked down, and the bout ended only when he could no longer come up to the scratch, a line drawn on the ground, for the next round. The masculine pronoun is appropriate, for the sport, as regards both participants and spectators, was almost exclusively a male preserve. Women did fight occasionally, though. At Elmstead, near Chelmsford, there was a 'pitched battle' (meaning a formal, rather than an informal, encounter) between two women,

being stripped, without caps, and hair tied close, to it they set, and for forty-five minutes maintained a most desperate conflict. One of them, an adept in the science, beat her antagonist in a most shocking manner and would certainly have killed her, but for the interference of the spectators. To the vanquished heroine her husband was bottle-holder, and with a degree of barbarity that would have disgraced a savage, we are informed he instigated his fair rib to the fight.[99]

An Irish ballad celebrates an undated contest in America between Jane Murphy and an unnamed German woman. Even so, these 'manly-hearted females' would have been watched largely by men, though the ballad's concluding invocation is to both sexes:

> So Erin's sons and daughters fair fill up the flowing glass
> And toast to brave J. Murphy valiant lass
> She trashed the German's daughter with strength and sinew keen
> She wears her female champion belt clasped round her jacket green.[100]

Severe injuries were common, and fatalities by no means unusual. Later, bare-fisted fighting was made illegal, and the formation of urban and county police forces made it easier for magistrates to prevent contests. The decline of the sport was regretted by some. George Borrow wrote of Crib, Tom Spring, Broughton, Stack and Ben Caunt: 'Let no one sneer at the bruisers of England. What were the gladiators of Rome, or the bull-fighters of Spain, in its palmiest days, compared to England's bruisers?'[101]

By the 1850s the popularity of pugilism was declining. Hooliganism at contests was driving away the respectable, and there were scandals over the fixing of fights. Even so, the sport still attracted the masses to a degree at least comparable with Association Football in recent times. According to Tom Langley, 'Tom Sayers, the greatest and practically the last prize-fighter, was responsible for a tremendous upsurge of prize-ring popularity but after his last fight the decline of the ring was so rapid that within ten years it was stone dead.'[102] Sayers (1826–65), once a beach attendant at Brighton and a bricklayer, moved to Camden Town and started a career as a fighter in 1849. He was defeated only once, by Langham, in 1853. Several of his fights were recorded in ballads, such as 'Lines on the Great Fight between Tom Sayers, Champion of England, and Bob Brettle, of Birmingham' (1859).[103] He last fought in 1860, against the Irish-American J. C. Heenan, for £200 a side and the championship of the world. There was intense interest on both sides of the Atlantic, and despite extensive newspaper coverage the event was also treated in several ballads:

> Such ribbing and such up and down
> Lor, how the swells did shout,
> Their ribs did nicely rattle,
> And their daylight near knocked out,
> Tom Sayers let into Heenan,
> Heenan let into Tom,
> While the Fancy bawled and shouted,
> Lads, my jolly lads, go on.
>
> At length bounced in the peelers,
> And around the ring did jog,
> So these heroes were surrounded
> By a lot of Hampshire hogs,
> Who caused them to cut their stick,
> And from the fight refrain,
> That they were both determined
> In the ring to meet again.[104]

When boxing was revived in the 1880s under sanitized rules, its coverage by the cheap press seems to have precluded the production of street ballads. As late as 1963, however, a radio programme entitled 'The Fight Game'[105] commented at length and in depth not on a particular contest, but on the sport in general, through the powerful combination of songs, sound effects, and recorded speech, developed by Ewan MacColl, Peggy Seeger, and Charles Parker, known as radio ballads.

As with old-style prize-fighting, a host of sporting events were chronicled in ballad and song. The balloon ascents which drew large crowds in the late eighteenth and early nineteenth centuries were duly commemorated, and the balloonists, such as Sadler and Green, celebrated.

Even a parachute descent at South Shields inspired a ballad, 'Shipley's Drop frae the Cloods', as late as 1890.[106]

Rowing and Running

Rowing, especially in the north-east, was another popular sport and hence a topic for song. 'The Skimmer Lads'[107] concerns the Thames, but one of the chief centres of the sport was the Tyne, where rowing races flourished on a professional basis from the 1840s to the 1880s. Working-class involvement on a large scale was precluded after 1866, when new rules were drawn up which excluded not only the professional rower, but any 'mechanic, artisan or labourer'. Even so, it was some twenty years before rowing was eclipsed on Tyneside by professional football, and a whole range of local song-writers—Geordie Ridley, Joe Wilson, Ned Corvan, John Taylor, J. P. Robson, and William Dunbar—contributed to its literature.

Professional running also lingered in the north of England, where it is still not entirely dead, and in Scotland, where it is still very much alive. The great vogue in recent years for long-distance charity races with mass participation has been caught in Keith Gregson's ballad of 1981 entitled 'The Great Fun Run from Newcastle to Shields', which was not only broadcast but printed and sold in the streets (see illustration).[108]

Cricket

The ancient sport of cricket (the word, in the form 'creckett', was first used in a document of 1598) still attracts not only immense interest, but also mass participation. It has produced a huge literature, but only a few ballads. These include: 'Dungiven Cricket Match'[109] from Northern Ireland and 'The Kentish Cricketer'[110] from the south of England. 'The Game of Cricket'[111] was printed in Durham, and 'Cricketing's All the Rage' mentions the same city:

> Durham City has been dull so long,
> No bustle at all to show:
> But now the rage of all the throng
> Is at cricketing to go.
> Long-Field, Long-Stop, Bowl or Bat,
> All different posts engage;
> Ball struck—not caught—a notch for that,
> O cricketing's all the rage!

The piece appears, somewhat incongruously, on the same sheet as 'Fall, Tyrants, Fall', an encomium on the 1848 revolutions. It concludes:

> After the noble game is done,
> Arm in arm the victors go,
> Praising much the champion
> Who struck the longest blow.
> A few walk off to Keepier Wood,
> Love does their hours engage:
> At least so it is understood,
> Though cricketing's all the rage.[112]

The heart of cricket remains the village green, or, in the case of Radnage in the Chilterns, the common, where the local team was renowned for its red, white, and blue caps, and also for its song, which was in particular demand after a win. Horace Harman, a local schoolmaster, heard it in a taproom in the 1920s, but it must date from before 1864 and the introduction of over-arm bowling. The tune is 'A-begging we will go'.

THE CRICKET SONG

Come all ye jolly cricketers, whoever you may be;
I'll have you pay attention and listen unto me.
For to cricket we will go, will go,
To cricket we will go.

We'll go out on the common, boys, and there we'll choose our ground:
But first we'll choose our umpire, and then we'll choose our men.

Well played, my pretty partner, be sure to bat upright;
And when she comes with a hop-hop-hop we'll cut her out of sight.

Well played, my pretty partner, see how she tips the bail;
And if you keep them to that length I'm sure we shall not fail.

Well thrown, my pretty partner, see how she nips the wind;
And when she goes by the bowler we'll all back up behind.

And now the game is ended, boys, we'll merrily drink and sing
Good health unto our cricketers and glory to our queen.

And now the game is ended, boys, and we have won the ball,
The very next time we come this way we'll give this house a call.[113]

6

THE SEXES

Relationships between men and women, sexual and otherwise, are a major—perhaps the major—preoccupation in balladry, as no doubt, in literature in general. Songs and ballads of this kind often closely reflect the social conditions prevailing when they originate. They may cease to circulate when the climate changes, or alternatively, continue long afterwards, providing that they continue to hold significance for singers and listeners.

Rough Music

Certain irregularities in marriage, especially violence by one partner towards the other or blatant adultery, were signalized in popular disapproval by ceremonies variously known as 'rough music', 'lowbelling' (see illustration), and 'riding for the stang'. Hogarth depicted a skimmity-ride in an illustration for *Hudibras*, and George Walker showed riding the stang in his *Costumes of Yorkshire* (1814). In Dorset the custom persisted at least until 1917, and the skimmington scene has a climactic role in Hardy's *Mayor of Casterbridge* (1886). In the 1930s James Carpenter found men in several counties—Nottinghamshire, Lancashire, Lincolnshire, Staffordshire and Yorkshire—who remembered the partly improvised chants or 'nominies' which accompanied the ritual of procession, effigy, and clamour.[1] Ceremonies of rough music lingered in Sussex until recently. One took place at West Hoathly in 1952. Another, of uncertain date, is evoked in a song recorded five years later by the 84-year-old George Tompsett of Cuckfield:

AT TURNERS HILL

At Turners Hill I do declare a day or two before the fair, (*bis*)
They all thought it a pretty trick to play to them the rough music.) (*bis*)
Right fol lay, right fol lairol liddie fol the day.

When the riot first begun, beating kettle[a] and the drum,
The old ship-bell an the pot-lid too, the mortar and pestle that did go.

Madam then she did came out; warmin' pans an' tongs about.
They summonsed up eleven young men.
The swore to one that was not there, and so those young men they got clear.

Then up Wall 'ill they did march up, ribbins in their hats they put;
And at the *Ship* they made a stop, and the townie people did flock up.[2]

Such treatment was not meted out exclusively to marital offenders. Political opponents, press-gangs, strike-breakers, and informers could also be on the receiving end. In 1827, for example, an Isle of Wight smuggler-turned-informer was given the treatment at Newport, and as a result packed his bags and went to London:

The grandest sight I ever saw, I vow and do declare,
Was the effigy of C——e and his wife carried round the fair.

In a cart they dragg'd them through the streets, while the music it did play,
While C——e and his wife that cursed rogue, was tied to a gallows high,
While Jack the Executioner, his business did complete,
They brought them near the place they dwell, and tore him to pieces in the street.[3]

Wife-selling

Stanging songs were closely connected with this custom, and are now extinguished with it. Songs dealing with the sale of wives, on the other hand, have survived the end of the practice. They were not, of course, an integral part of it; often they were merely a fictional departure from it. Prose broadsides[4] usually give the names, dates, and places of wife and, more rarely, husband sales. Ballad sheets[5] are vague, deliberately so. They nevertheless reflect intense public interest, and also show something of the ceremony—halter, market, auction, celebration—involved. Thomas

[a] sheep-bell

d'Urfey's 'The Hopeful Bargain'[6] of 1719–20 is perhaps the earliest song on the topic. Late in the eighteenth century came 'The Smithfield Bargain; or, Love in a Halter. A Favourite Comic Song Written by Mr T. Jones',[7] and in the nineteenth a series of street ballads of which one, 'The Carpenter's Wife', is current in Irish oral tradition to this day. The festivities with which it concludes are those of a perfectly normal wedding:

> They sent for a fidler and piper to play,
> They danced and they sung until the peep o' day.
> Then Jack to his hammock with his Betsy did go,
> While the fidler & piper played 'Rosin the Beau'.[8]

Weddings

Wedding celebrations are the subject of rumbustious pieces full of feasting, dancing, and occasionally fighting, like the Irish 'Wedding at Ballyporeen'[9] and the Scots 'Tinkler's Waddin'',[10] both still sung. 'The Collier's Wedding', published by the Newcastle schoolmaster Edward Chicken in 1720, is lively, ribald, and also accurate: John Brand uses it to illustrate nine different points about weddings in his *Observations on the Popular Antiquities of Great Britain* (1777). It is a poem, rather than a song, as the mock-Virgilian opening shows:

> I sing not here of warriors bold
> Of battles lost or victories won . . .
> I choose to sing, in strains much lower,
> Of collier lads, unsung before.[11]

Thomas Wilson's 'The Country Wedding', written probably between 1800 and 1810, chronicles the modest nuptials of weavers Sam and Bess who walk to Manchester for the ceremony and back afterwards. They are preceded by blind Jud the fiddler, hired at a fee of five shillings, who also plays at the celebration:

> Now th' lads they fell to doncin', an' lasses join'd 'em in the' fun,
> Exceptin' Bess, who linger'd an' nudged at Sam, an' whisper'd, 'Come'.
> Blind Jud struck up, 'Off she goes', an' Sam cried, 'On, wi' o' my heart'.
> No doubt Sam donced i' double time, an' Bess, aw'm sure, hoo play'd her part.
>
> The neighbours they coom flockin' in, and happiness did wish the pair.
> An' to conclude the weddin' feast, blind Jud wi' th' fiddle banish'd care;
> Sam paid for o' th' weddin' fees; with cake an' ale they did regale;
> An' to this day, wife Bess agrees, that Sam in love does never fail.[12]

In another Lancashire piece, Johnny Green, the eponymous hero of many ballads, drives with Nan in a horse and cart from Oldham to be

married in Manchester. They, too, have a fiddler, but much of the
narrative concerns their visit to Manchester Museum, where they see:

> There's snakes an watch-bills just loike poikes
> Ot*ᵃ* Hunt an aw th' reformink toikes,
> An thee an me, an Sam o Moiks,
> Once took a blanketeerink.
>
> .   .   .   .
>
> There's Oliver Crumill's bums an balls,
> An Frenchmen's guns they'd tean i' squalls,
> An swords, os lunk os me, on th' walls,
> An bows an arrows too, mon:
> Au didna moind his fearfo words,
> Nor skeletons o men an birds,
> Boh au fair hate seet o greyt lung sowrds
> Sin th' feyght at Peterloo, mon.[13]

In many songs, courtship leads to a formal wedding, but in some,
other procedures follow. 'The Wedding Song', which is still in oral
circulation, seems to hark back to the days before the Hardwick Act of
1753 when a simple declaration by the parties was regarded as binding:
'So to church they went the very next day [after deciding]/ And were
married by asking as I've heard say.'[14] Even more informal, though just
as binding in the eyes of the participants, was the practice of jumping
over a broomstick, which was favoured by the navvy community until
well into the nineteenth century:

> I called for a pint of beer, and bid the old wench drink, sir,
> But whilst she was a-drinking, she too at me did wink, sir.
> Well, then we had some talk, in the back we had a rally,
> Then jumped o'er brush and steel, and agreed we'd both live tally.[15]

Bundling

When procreation was regarded as essential, or even only as desirable, a
woman's becoming pregnant was a good signal for marriage, and, as
Macfarlane remarked, 'The evidence suggests that there was little
emphasis on virginity of brides in traditional English society.'[16] This is not
surprising in view of the custom of 'bundling', the courtship practice by
which lovers lay, dressed or partly dressed, on the same bed. The *Oxford
English Dictionary* gives the earliest use of the verb 'to bundle' in this sense
as 1781 (the noun 1807), but the reality is a great deal older, from Norway
to New England and from Western Europe to Afghanistan, and may date
back to the time when a whole family and its visitors occupied the same

ᵃ That

bed. The custom was far removed from licentiousness. In Wales in the eighteenth century the man retained 'an essential part of his dress', and the woman had 'her under-petticoat fastened at the bottom by a sliding knot'.[17] In America, as an extra precaution, a wooden board was often placed in the bed to divide the pair. Bundling was so carefully controlled on the island of Lewis that, as T. C. Smout pointed out, during the last two decades of the nineteenth century, illegitimacy was running at below 2 per cent.[18] Frankenburg, who found bundling practised in Wales until the 1940s, with or without a ritual bolster between the couple, observed 'that its secrecy makes possible trial and error, and it ensures a choice of partner to the girl or boy concerned at the same time as giving the community and the parents some control over who married whom'.[19] For England the evidence is sparse, even tenuous, though in Suffolk, bundling was current within recent memory. The clergy opposed it, and one remonstrance received this reply: 'But, vicar, you wouldn't buy a horse without getting astride to see how it trotted.' W. H. Barrett (1891–1974) remembered not only this remark, but also this uninhibited song, heard in the taproom of the Ship Inn, Brandon Creek. Unfortunately, the tune was not taken down.

BUNDLING SONG

Now lasses and lads hark to my song,
'Tis bundle together all the night long;
The game is risky, allow me to say;
One can also get damaged rolling in hay.

So when the moon is waxing bright.
Across the fen you make for a light
That brightly shines to beckon you on
To the feather bed she lies upon.

You will find the ladder beside the wall,
Out there for purpose in case you call.
Raise it quietly, not stopping to linger,
Until rung by rung you reach the window.

A gentle tap and window's wide open,
And in you go with no word spoken.
Tread softly, bor, the boards may creak,
To awaken the father who's fast asleep.

Nip into the bed and snuggle down
Beside the warm body in the nightgown.
If her sister is there then rise in a stew—
You can bundle with one but not with two.

Now lusty lads just listen to me:
A bundle's a bundle wherever it be.
There's only one ending for me to sing:
The parson won't bless you as he puts on the ring.[20]

There is further evidence in the shape of songs of night visiting, though here bundling (tacitly approved by parents) cannot always be distinguished from clandestine assignation (though sometimes parental or even marital opposition is made clear). The knock at the window to begin and the dawn parting to end are common to both kinds, and night visiting has inspired some of the finest lyrics in the language. 'Love Song' was recorded from Peter Flanagan of County Fermanagh as recently as 1972. This records a meeting between earthly lovers, but there is a hint, with 'burning rocks' in the last verse, of contamination from a variation on the theme in which it is the lover's ghost which pays a fleeting visit.

LOVE SONG

It was when he came to his true love's window,
He kneelèd low down upon a stone,
And through the pane he whispered slowly,
'Are you asleep, love, are you alone ?'

She raised her head from her snow-white pillow,
And snowy, snowy was her milk-white breast,
Saying, 'Who is that at my bedroom window,
Disturbing me from my long night's rest?'

'I am your lover, do not discover,
But rise up darling and let me in,
For I am tired of my long night's journey,
And likewise, love, I'm wet to the skin.'

It was slowly, slowly she did put on her,
And twice as slowly she let me in.
It was in our arms we embraced each other
Until that long night, love, was nearly in.

When that long night, it was nearly ended,
And the early cocks, they began to crow,
We kissed, shook hands, and alas we parted,
Sayin', 'Goodbye, darling, I must be going.

'Farewell, love, I can stay no longer.
The burning rocks I have to cross.
And it's o'er the hills I will roll in splendour,
From the arms of you, my love.'

Here is a health unto all true lovers,
A health to my love where e'er he be.
This very night I'll be with my darling
For many's a long mile he is from me.[21]

Whether or not practised through such customs as bundling and night visiting, sexual trial and error led to a large number of births out of wedlock. As Peter Laslett has written, 'Illegitimacy has been called a social problem for the last two centuries and a moral problem from time immemorial.' He adds, with reference to the period since the eighteenth century, that 'Nearly all the earlier writings were heavily moralistic in tone.'[22] This is not the case with a large number of the songs on the subject, however. Yet it is true that warnings, partly jocular, are given to women 'never to let a sailor boy an inch above your knee', or to watch out for bachelors wearing navvy boots, pit boots, or cattle smocks:

Remember the chaps that are single and free,
For their hearts do run light and their minds do run young,
So beware of the chaps with the cattle smocks on.[23]

Songs of Broken Faith

It is true, too, that there are bitter songs of broken faith, on both sides. 'The Forlorn Lover', entered in the Stationers' Register on 1 March 1675, is a magnificent piece which has survived orally to this day in versions which, although abbreviated to six or seven verses, nevertheless retain the deeply poignant sense of loss which pervades the original:

But when I did hear my Love askt in the Church,
I went out of my seat and sate in the Porch,
I found I should falsly be left in the lurch,
And thought that my heart would have broken.

But when I did see my Love to Church go
With all her bride-maidens they made such a show,
I laught in conceit but my heart was full low
To see how highly she was regarded.

But when I saw my Love in the Church stand,
Gold ring on her finger well seal'd with a band:
He had so indued her with house and with land,
That nothing but Death can them sunder.[24]

More often it is the woman who is left in the lurch, sometimes with the additional burden of carrying a child. In 'O no, my Love, not I', an early nineteenth-century street ballad which remained in oral tradition in Britain and North America for a hundred years, 'a pretty maid a making of her hay' turns down an offer of marriage, but changes her mind when she finds herself pregnant. She writes to the man concerned, 'But his answer it was back again, O no, my love, not I':

If I were to wed thee folks would think me mad,
What pleasure can I have any more than I've had?
For you are of so low degree and I'm so high.
But his answer it was back again, O no, my love, not I.

The very best thing that I can persuade you to do
Is to take your baby on your back and a begging to go,
And when you are weary you may sit down and cry,
And curse the very hour you said no, my love, no.[25]

The theme of palming off unwanted children dates from at least as early as the Elizabethan jigs, and features in ballads current up to the twentieth century. Two examples among many deal with tricking an absconding father at least into paying for the upkeep of his child. A countrywoman tricks a sailor into accepting his child in the guise of a basket of eggs in the eighteenth-century song of the same name;[26] a hundred years later a chambermaid brings home to a commercial traveller the paternity of a child presented as a Christmas goose.[27] Such songs were warnings to the unwary; the underlying message, though, is not to abstain from sexual activity, but to take part with one's eyes open to the risks involved. Indeed, many songs are positive paeans to sexual pleasure.

Rough music in Warwickshire, or 'lewbelling'. The picture of 1909 from the *Illustrated London News* is captioned: 'Punishment by Effigy: A Lewbelling Band and the Dummies of an Erring Pair. Lewbelling is a custom which, although it has almost died out, is occasionally observed, and such an observation took place recently. The word "lewbelling" seems to be derived from "lewd" and "belling", roaring or bellowing. A "lewbelling" occurs when the morals of a married man or woman have left something to be desired, and neighbours wish to show their disapproval. In the case illustrated, the effigy of the man was made first, and was exposed for three days; the effigy of the woman was exposed for two days. The figures were placed side by side, the woman's arm upon her lover's shoulder. A band of thirty or more youths and boys, beating all kinds of tin utensils, paraded the village for three nights. On the third night, after dark, the effigies were taken down and burnt. The dummies were set up opposite the woman's house. The fear of this form of public exposure of fault is said to act as a great deterrent.' The village in question was Brailes.

Particular and merry Account of a most Entertaining and Curious

SALE OF A WIFE,

Of a pretty young WOMAN, *who was* Sold *to a gallant young Fellow,*
For FIFTEEN Sovereigns, and a Dozen of Wine, this Morning.
Together with the *Wedding* SONG.

AT an early hour a young couple came into the market. The Lady was dressed neat and clean, and so attractive were her rosy cheeks and sparkling eyes, that all the folks in the market soon collected about her, (she being to be sold.)

Well, good folks, says the Lady's spouse here's a rare bargain to dispose off! Here's my pretty sweet Wife, who will try all she can, to please any man, who's willing to take her for life. What have you got to say, Mr Butcher? Oh! says the Butcher she charms my very heart to look at her! here's 17s. for a beginning. That's too little, says Snobby, the Cobler, I will run to my uncle's with some of my customer's shoes, to raise the wind, & give 3s more: Oh-ho, says Frisk, the fiddler, & Friz, the barber, we will join and buy her between us; two shillings a-piece more says they: That won't do, cries Snip the tailor, putting on his spectacles, I have 20s. in my pocket,& I will sell my Dandy collar, stays, busk, sheers, thimble, needles and goose, to raise 1s more. Clear the way, you silly bodies, quoth a Miller, or I'll shave you all with a wooden razor, here's 50s. for my ducky, so mount upon my old mare and let us trot home to the mill together; Botheration, says a Farmer, I'll capsize you all together, here's 3l. for her, 7s more

says a Tallow-Chandler, 2 more bade the Baker, and 10 more the Painter: A gallant Publican hearing the fun, bounced forward with such haste that he upset the Barber & Tailor in the mud, & almost trod the fiddlers' toes off: He instantly paid down Fifteen Pounds, and took them all to an Inn, where they had a capital Dinner and after emptying a dozen of Wine, the happy couple mounted a gig, and set off in full glee.

The Wedding Song.

NOW come jolly neighbours let's dance sing and play,
And away, to the neighbouring wedding away.
All the world is assembled, the young & the old
To see the fair beauty that is to be sold.

So sweet and engaging the Lady did seem,
The market with bidders did presently teem,
A Tailor sung out that his goose he would sell,
To buy the fair Lady—he lov'd her so well.

But a gallant young Publican 15l. did pay
And with the young Lady he marched away.
Then they drank, & carous'd & rejoiced all day
The glass pass'd around and the piper did play

Success to this couple, & to keep up the fun,
May the bumpers fly round at the birth of a son
Long life to them both, in peace & content,
may their days & their nights for ever be spent

(Price One Penny.)

Catnach, Printer, 2, Monmouth-Court:
BILLS, CARDS, etc. Printed on very Reasonable Terms

'Sale of a Wife'. Broadside.

1147

THE
Fright'ned York-shire Damosel,
OR,
Fears Dispers'd by Pleasure.

To the Tune of, *I met with a Country Lass*, &c.

Licensed according to Order.

(1)

WHen first I began to Court,
  and pritty young Maids to Wooe
I could not win the Virgin Fort,
  but by the *Bogulmaroo*.

(2)

I Kiss'd her in Summer time,
  and in the cold Winter too;
At last I took her in the Prime,
  but by the *Bogulmaroo*.

(3)

My Love she was going one Night
  to Bed as she us'd to do,
When on the Stairs she saw a *Spright*
  it was the *Bogulmaroo*.

(4)

She came to my Chamber-door,
  and cou'd not tell what to do;
But straight began to weep full sore,
  for fear of *Bogulmaroo*.

(5)

At last she came boldly in,
  tho' still her poor heart did rue;
For looking back the *Spright* did Grin,
  O cruel *Bogulmaroo*.

(6)

She started and run in haste,
  and close to my Bed-side drew;
Her Eyes she durst not backward cast,
  for fear of *Bogulmaroo*.

(7)

But into my Bed she crept,
  and did her Sorrows renew,
She wrung her hands, and sadly wept,
  for fear of *Bogulmaroo*.

(8)

I turn'd about to the Maid,
  as Lovers are wont to do;
And bid her be no more afraid
  of th' Ugly *Bogulmaroo*.

(9)

I Kiss'd and Embrac'd her then,
  our pleasures they were not few;
We lay abed next day till Ten,
  for fear of *Bogulmaroo*.

(10)

My Love she was all Dismay'd,
  to think of what she had done;
Arise, said I, be not afraid,
  the *Bogulmaroo* is gone.

(11)

I Marry'd her the next day,
  and did her pleasures renew;
Each night we spend in Charming Play,
  for all the *Bogulmaroo*.

(12)

I ne'r said a word of the thing,
  nor never intend to do;
But ev'ry time she Smiles on me,
  I think of *Bogulmaroo*.

Printed and Sold by **J. Millet**, next door to the *Flower-de-Luce*, in *Little-Brittain*: 1689.

'The Fright'ned Yorkshire Damosel'. Street ballad.

'The Ranting Whore's Resolution'. Part of a street ballad.

The ranting Whores resolution;

Wherein you find that her only Treasure
Consisteth in being a Lady of Pleasure.

To the Tune of, *General Monk's March.*

Oh! You presume too hard.
Hey for a Boy or a Girl &c.

Oh! fye upon care,
Why should we despair,
Give me the Lad that will frollick,
There is no disease,
But musick will please,
If it were the stone or the cholick.
The Reins that distills Wine,
So will only be mine,
Or that calls for a Cup of Canary,
That will tipple and sing,
Kiss, caper, and spring,
And calls for his Mob, and his Mary.

Such Sinners as these
My pallat will please,
For this is a Lad that will knock it,
So this is a Lad that will knock it,
Set Beggars to me,
But carry good gilt in his pocket,

I care not from whence
He gets his expence,
So how he comes by his treasure,
So I have the sweets
When he and I meets,
For I am a Lady of pleasure.

I love a young Heir,
Whose fortune is fair,
And frollick in Fishstreet-dinners,
We so boldly doth call,
In private payes all,
These Boyes are the noble beginners,
For what the old Father
In long time did gather,
So soon it is vvne vvithout measure,
He'll lye in my lap,
Like a Bird in a trap,
And call me his Lady of pleasure.

The second Part.

HE svvears gallant Cloaths
And studies new Oaths
And gets pretty words from the players,
He svvaggers and Roars,
He calls the next Oars,
And cryes here's a grace for your fair,
Thus we in delight
From morning till night,
Do annoy to cast away treasure,
It might in my arms
I secure him from harms,
For I am a Lady of pleasure.

When this Gallant's spoke,
I'le another be spoke,
And he hath my protection,
I call him my Love,
My Jewel, my Dove,
And svvear by my reputation,
That I never did know,
What it was till now,
Though I have had men before measure
With such tricks as these
I'le Coxcombe I please,
For I am a Lady of pleasure.

When they are in Jayle,
They vvretchedly rail
And at me they cast all their curses,
Let them laugh that vvin,
I care not a pin,
When I have confuembeo their purses,
I know not their faces,
When Warriers of Woodstreet make
But when they're whole men (secure
I'le know them sure,
For I am a Lady of pleasure.

To the same Tune.

I live by the quick
And not by the sick,
O; such whose estate lies a bleeding,
My must must be bound,
For men that are found,
For I am a Lass of high feeding,
If once they grow poor,
No honvy, no Whore,
And yet they shall wait on my leisure,
I only fulfill,
My fancy and will,
Which shews me a Lady of pleasure.

I laugh when they tell
The stories of Hell
I think there is no such Cavern,
If heaven there be
(As some will tell me)
I am sure it must be in the Tavern,
Where there is no wine,
There is nothing divine,
We think of a grave at my leisure,
Boy fill th'other glass
For I am Lass
That will be a Lady of pleasure.

In freedom and joyes
I spend all my dayes,
For there is no greater blessing,
Than musick and meat,
God wine and the feat,
And nothing to pay for the treating,
Let Soldiers prattle
Go turn up their eyes,
And speak inords by line and by leasure,
I'le neath canvas at last,
Her death comes at last,
Then there lives Lady of pleasure.

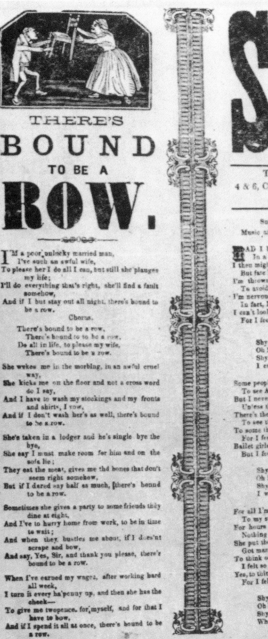

THERE'S BOUND TO BE A ROW.

I'M a poor, unlucky married man,
  I've such an awful wife,
To please her I do all I can, but still she plagues
  my life;
I'll do everything that's right, she'll find a fault
  somehow,
And if I but stay out all night, there's bound to
  be a row.

Chorus.

There's bound to be a row,
  There's bound to be a row,
Do all in life, to please my wife,
  There's bound to be a row.

She wakes me in the morning, in an awful cruel
  way,
She kicks me on the floor and not a cross word
  do I say,
And I have to wash my stockings and my fronts
  and shirts, I vow,
And if I don't wash her's as well, there's bound
  to be a row.

She's taken in a lodger and he's single bye the
  bye,
She say I must make room for him and on the
  sofa lie;
They eat the meat, gives me the bones that don't
  seem right somehow,
But if I dared say half as much, there's bound
  to be a row.

Sometimes she gives a party to some friends they
  dine at eight,
And I've to hurry home from work, to be in time
  to wait;
And when they bustles me about, if I doesn't
  scrape and bow,
And say, Yes, Sir, and thank you please, there's
  bound to be a row.

When I've earned my wages, after working hard
  all week,
I turn it every ha'penny up, and then she has the
  cheek—
To give me twopence, for myself, and for that I
  have to bow,
And if I spend it all at once, there's bound to be
  a row.

SHY! SHY!! DREADFULLY SHY!

T. PEARSON, PRINTER,
4 & 6, Chadderton St., Oldham Road,
MANCHESTER.

Sung by GEORGE LEYBOURNE.
Music at HOPWOOD AND CREW'S, London.

HAD I been a monk or a hermit, that dwelt
  In a cave, where the world could not see;
I then might be quiet, collected, and cool,
  But fate has not will'd it to be.
I'm thrown on the world, with its troubles and
To avoid them I ev'ry day try; [trials,
I'm nervous, fidgety, very reserved,
  In fact, I'm most awfully shy.
I can't look a girl in the face, but I blush,
  For I feel most awfully shy,

Chorus:

Shy, shy, shy, shy.
Oh! I'm so shy—dreadfully shy;
Shy, shy, shy, shy, [so shy.
I can't pass a shy shop, because I'm

Some people go to the Theatre each night,
  To see Actresses dress'd "comme il faut,"
But I never will rest my eyes on the stage,
  Unless the footlights they're put low;
There's the Ballet girls too, so graceful to vie
  To see them is stretched ev'ry eye.
To some this is good, but 'tis not to me,
  For I feel most awfully shy.
Ballet girls movements are all very well,
  But I feel so wretchedly shy.

Shy, shy, shy, shy.
Oh! I'm so shy—dreadfully shy;
Shy, shy, shy, shy, [shy.
I would if I could, but I can't I'm so

For all I'm so shy, I once fell in love,
  To my sweetheart no question could pop,
For hours I would sit, by my loved one and say
Nothing! and then I would stop.
She put the question, I blushing said "yes,"
  Got married—felt I should die,
To think of the future, tears came to my eyes,
  I felt so terribly shy,
Yes, to think of the future, tears came to my eyes,
  For I felt so uncommonly shy.

Shy, shy, shy, shy.
Oh! I'm so shy—dreadfully shy;
Shy, shy, shy, shy, [shy.
When I put on the ring, I was awfully

'There's Bound to be a Row' Street ballad. 'Shy! Shy!! Dreadfully Shy!'

The Map of Mock-begger Hall, with

his scituation in the spacious Countrey called Anywhere.

To THE TUNE OF *It is not your Northerne Nanny;* or,
Sweet is the Lasse that Loves me.

This woodcut from a street ballad of *c.*1685 shows Mrs Holland's brothel in Southwark in the time of Charles I. The building was defended by a moat and drawbridge.

Stick up for the Women,

AND

NINE HOURS A DAY.

AIR:—Act on the Square.

———:o:———

All thro' this good old land of ours,
  Commotion there has been,
And in the poor man's working hours,
  Great changes we have seen;
But while they struggled for their rights
  And to improve their lot,
Our poor white slaves are left at home,
  Neglected and forgot.

CHORUS.

Act on the square, boys, act on the square,
Stick up for the women, for that's only fair,
For a woman's the pride of the land we all say,
Then why should she work more than 9 hours a day

What can a woman have to do ?
  The men will often say,
They only have to cook and stew ;
  And pleasant pass the day ;
But let a man just take her place,
  When baby begins to roar,
He'll find himself in such a mess,
  He'd never try no more.

You would first the children have to dress,
  And breakfast get, you know,
There's Tommy standing on his head,
  While Jack upsets the Po' ;

There's Sally at the water,
  With firewood setting sail,
While Bobby makes an awful noise,
  By twisting pussy's tail.

At one o'clock the 'Hooter' goes,
  The men come home to dine,
And if it is not ready done,
  Look out then for a shine.
At five o'clock he's done his work,
  And then can do the grand,
While you are slaving like a Turk,
  He's singing ' Happy Land.'

You factory girls of England now,
  Who get such little pay,
The roses from your blooming cheeks,
  Hard work has driven away ;
Oft-times to please your masters,
  You are working past your time,
But if your are late they'll shut the gate,
  And make you pay a fine.

Young women then take my advice
  When courting your young man,
Tell him when the knot is tied,
  That this will be your plan—
Eight hours for work, eight hours for sleep,
  And then eight hours for play,
Sundays must be all your own,
  And ' night work ' double pay.

'Stick Up for the Women'. Street ballad.

The VVoman to the Plow
AND
The Man to the Hen-Roost,
OR, A fine way to Cure a Cot-quean.
The Tune is, I have for all good wives a Song.

Part of a street ballad printed betwe
1678 and 1680.

Le mari qui file tandis que la femme porte la

Another version of the world turned upside down, with the roles of the sexes reversed.

Sexual Pursuit

Several, like the well-known 'Lovely Joan',[28] taunt a man for failing to take advantage of a situation, and add salt to the wound by hinting that he is effeminate. 'Quand on tenait la poule il fallait la plumer', says 'L'Occasion manquée',[29] a song mentioned by Gérard de Nerval in the early nineteenth century, but dating back at least to a *pastourelle* of the thirteenth. Conversely, successful male strategy in pursuit of a female is a perennial preoccupation of ballad-makers, as of writers at large. The imagery of the chase is employed in Joseph Martin's piece 'The Huntsman's Delight',[30] the history of which could be paralleled many times over. Starting as a black-letter ballad in the late seventeenth century, it appears in abbreviated form in the eighteenth as a slip-song,[31] in oral tradition in the nineteenth, then, lightly but effectively bowdlerized, as a class-room song in the twentieth, under the title 'The Keeper'.[32]

Another street ballad of the 1680s, 'The Fright'ned Yorkshire Damosel' (see illustration),[33] shows one man's extreme ingenuity in having a woman frightened into his arms by a friend's appearance in the guise of a ghost. This may well be a conceit rather than a true story, but the song, metamorphosed into 'The Foggy Dew', took lasting hold. As recently as the late 1940s a radio performance by Peter Pears of Benjamin Britten's arrangement caused an outcry from listeners, which resulted in a ban by the BBC.[34]

Elaborate stratagems are unnecessary in the many cases in which the parties involved are only too eager for a sexual encounter. The narrator is often the neutral, omniscient third party of fiction, as in 'The Three Jovial Companions',[35] another ballad of the late seventeenth century. Here, three 'merry travellers' spend the day drinking at an inn run by a widow, her cousin, and a maid. The men's bill of 'thirty good shilling and Six pence' is 'Lovingly paid' by sex. The women thank them, and invite them to call again. The mood is pleasant, even sunny, but this is clearly a piece of masculine wishful thinking. It has many analogues. Even when the narrator is ostensibly a woman, as in 'The Bonny Scot; or, The Yielding Lass', one wonders whether the attitude expressed is truly feminine, or whether it is what a male would like it to be:

> He lowly vail'd his Bonnet oft,
> And sweetly kist my Lips so soft,
> Yet still between each honey Kiss,
> He urg'd me gang to further bliss;
> Till I resistless fire did feel,
> Then let alone my Spinning-wheel.

Among the pleasant Cocks of Hay,
Then with my bonny Lad I lay,
What Damsel ever could deny,
A Youth with such a Charming Eye?
The pleasure I cannot reveal,
It far surpast the Spinning-wheel.[36]

With a male narrator, not surprisingly, little doubt lingers. Women are not only readily available, but sometimes aggressively eager, as in 'A Bold Dragoon', which is an oral version of 'The Jolly Trooper', from an eighteenth-century garland. The dragoon rides out of the north and comes to a lady who recognizes him and, in a transparently symbolic gesture, leads his horse to the stable for hay and corn. To the dragoon she offers refreshment, then, without further preliminaries:

She stepped upstairs, she made the bed,
She made it plumb & easy,
And into bed she nimbly jumped
And said, Dragoon, I'm ready.

O he pulled off his armour bright,
He cast it on the table,
And into bed he nimbly jumps,
To kiss whilst he was able.

The words are not without a lyrical element:

They spent the night till break of dawn,
They saw the light full grieving.
O hark! I hear the trumpet sound.
Sweet maid! I must be leaving.

I would the trumpet ne'er might call,
O cruel does it grieve me.
My heart, my very heart will break,
Because, dragoon, you leave me.[37]

The language is chaste. Much more is conveyed by suggestion than statement, by implication than enumeration. The euphemistic use of 'kiss' and 'kissing' is widespread:

If kissing was not lawfull,
The lawyers would not use it,
And if it was not Gospel,
The Parsons would refuse it,

> And if it was not a dainty thing,
> The Ladies would not crave it,
> And if it was not a plentifull thing,
> The poor Girls would not have it.[38]

Sexual Metaphor

Sexual metaphor is widely used, too. The tinker calls at an all-female household to block the holes. A woman follows a cobbler for the sake of his long pegging awl. The coachman's whip, the grenadier's fiddle, the miller's stones, are counterparts to such female symbols as the cuckoo's nest. The last phrase is the title of a song which was widely sung, though seldom printed:

> Oh, give to me the girl that's pretty in the face,
> Give to me the girl that's slender in the waist;
> But give to me the girl that's nimble in the twist,
> For the bottom of her belly is the cuckoo's nest.[39]

Mrs Cecilia Costello (1883–1976) of Birmingham learnt this from an Irish aunt at the age of 7, though it was many years before she realized its import. A similar fragment of the song was popular with English morris men, who used it and other fragments to accompany their dancing.

The terminology of trades exercised particular fascination for those seeking metaphor. Weaving was an especially popular source. One piece tells of a woman with a loom under her apron on which a weaver works the Rose and Crown and Diamond Twill patterns. Her loom becomes sprung, so there is a pause, after which 'As my shuttle went to and fro / I wove her the pattern called the Touch and Go.'[40] Another obliging volunteer comes forward in 'The Bury New Loom', which was first printed in 1804 by Swindells of Manchester. The terminology used would have been familiar only to those in the trade. 'Lams' are foot treadles which operate the jacks (levers used to raise the harness controlling the warp thread). 'Healds' are loops of cord or wire through which the warp threads pass, and a 'lathe' is a supporting stand on a loom.

> As I walked between Bolton and Bury,
> It was on a Moon shiny night,
> I met with a buxom young weaver,
> Whose company gave me delight:
> She says, my young fellow come, tell me
> If your level and rule are in tune?
> Come, give me your answer correct,
> Can you get up and square my new loom?

I said, Dear lassie, believe me,
I am a good joiner by trade,
And many a good loom and shuttle,
Before in my time I have made;
Your short lams and jacks and long lam
I quickly can put them in tune,
My rule is now in good order
To get up and square a new loom.

She took me and showed me her new loom,
The down on her warp did appear.
The lam jacks and healds put in motion,
I levelled her loom to a hair.
My shuttle ran well in her lathe,
My treadle it did work up and down.
My level stood close to her breast-beam,
The time I was squaring her loom.[41]

Such pieces have a strength and a confidence combined with a refreshing lack of self-consciousness. The sexual act, even the casual sexual act, is treated with joy and with dignity, and not without delicacy.

Coarse and Obscene Songs

The writing and outlook here contrast with the contrivance which mars many frankly obscene pieces. In the final analysis the difference between the (acceptably) erotic and the (unacceptably) obscene may lie simply in the mind of the beholder, with one person's eroticism being another's obscenity. Circumstances are also important, and what is permissible in a barrack-room or in rugby-club showers is not necessarily acceptable in a suburban drawing-room. Style and treatment are also important factors. Another divide separates those who use such material and those who merely observe its use. Francis Place seems to have been obsessed with the obscene songs against which he campaigned for many years. Writing of the 1780s, when his father was a London publican, he saw a distinct connection between such songs and sexual laxity:

Want of chastity in girls was common. The songs which were ordinarily sung by their relatives and by young women and the lewd plays and interludes they occasionally saw were all calculated to produce mischief in this direction. . . . Some of these songs sung by the respectable tradesmen who spent their evenings in my father's parlour, were very gross, yet I have known the parlour door thrown open wide, that whoever was in the bar and the Tap room might hear every word. They were sung with considerable humour by men who were much excited; every one within hearing was silently listening, and at the conclusion of the song expressed their delight by clapping their hands and rapping the tables.[42]

Place explains elsewhere that these songs came from printed ballad-sheets, 'bawled about the streets, and hung against the walls. It will seem incredible that such songs should be allowed but it was so. There is not one of them that I have not heard myself sung in the streets, as well as at Chair Clubs, Cock & Hen Clubs & Free & Easy's.'[43] He is referring here to the collection of thirty-three songs,[44] some fragmentary and some given only by title, which he submitted along with his verbal evidence to the Parliamentary Select Committee on Education of 1835. He testified that:

The ballads sung about the streets, the books openly sold, cannot be adequately described. I have given you in writing, the words of some common ballad which you would not think fit to have uttered in this Committee. At that time [the 1780s] songs were of the most indecent kind; no one would mention them in any society now; they were publicly sung and sold in the streets and markets, and bought by maid-servants.[45]

Some of this material is not obscene at all, for, like 'Jack Hall' (see Chapter 4), it deals with crime and criminals. For the rest, 'songs which cannot be described from their nastiness', according to Place, are jovially coarse, rather than unpleasantly obscene. He remembered, for example, two verses of 'A Hole to put poor Robin in':

> One night as I came from the play
> I met a fair maid by the way
> She had rosy cheeks and a dimpled chin
> And a hole to put poor Robin in.

> A bed and blanket I have got
> A dish a kettle and a pot
> Besides a charming pretty thing
> A hole to put poor Robin in.[46]

The full text appeared, among other places no doubt, in *The Man of War's Garland* of 1796 under the title of 'Poor Robin':

> As I was coming from the play,
> I met a fair maid by the way,
> She had a charming pretty thing,
> And a hole to put poor Robin in.

> I took this fair maid in my arms,
> And soon enjoy'd her lovely charms.
> So close to me then she did cling,
> She'd a hole to put Robin in.

I laid this fair maid on the grass,
And there I pleas'd my pretty lass,
By playing with her pretty thing,
In her hole I put Robin in.

She had a charming slender waist,
As ever lord or duke embrac'd,
She'd rosy cheeks and a double chin,
And a hole to put poor Robin in.

No pretender is my name.
Among the girls I have the fame,
For whether I do lose or win,
I'm sure to put poor Robin in.

I married this girl and brought her home,
And then I had a wife of my own,
I thought it was a pretty thing
I'd a hole to put poor Robin in.

Now I goes whistling to my plough,
To card and spin my wife knows how;
A merry life we do begin,
I've a hole to put poor Robin in.

Altho' my house it is but small,
It serves for parlour kitchen and all.
I'm joyful still in every thing,
I've a hole to put poor Robin in.

A bed and blankets I have got,
A dish a spoon a kettle and pot;
I am as happy as the king,
I've a hole to put poor Robin in.

What care I for Holland smocks,
What care I for powder'd locks,
In the dark my wife she's like a queen,
She's a hole to put poor Robin in.[47]

At least one of Place's songs, 'a description of two poor whores who had seen better days',[48] is positively anti-erotic. The same might be said for another, of which he writes:

Two women used to sing a song opposite a public house the sign of the Crooked Billet at the back of St Clements Church in the Strand. It was an open space, between Holywell Street and Wych Street. The song was a description of a married man who had a lecherous wife, it described his being a pale fellow reduced by her to a skeleton. I can only remember the last two lines

'And for which I' am sure she'l go to Hell
For she makes me fuck her in church time.[49]

It is interesting to find women singing this, for much coarse song is sung only by men and is male-orientated. There is some evidence of women's singing such songs in a single-sex setting, but they appear to have adopted items from the male repertoire rather than evolving their own. Not surprisingly, feminists are now seeking songs in which women take the initiative, but these are not necessarily obscene. Some, perhaps like that of Place's two women, show up the sexual shortcomings of men, and this is a venerable theme.

Sexual Inadequacy

'A Pleasant New Ballad; being A Merry Discourse between a Country Lass and a Young Taylor; shewing Hoe the Taylor lost his plight and pleasure His yard not being by the Standard Measure'[50] was published in the 1670s or 1680s. It may be a male rerun of the well-worn anti-tailor tradition, rather than a genuinely anti-male song. There is ambiguity in 'A New Song called the Farmer's Delight', dating from the early nineteenth century. Is the farmer's inability to thrash the jolly widow's corn a true confession of male inadequacy, or a contribution to the male myth of female insatiability?

> With her I agreed to do the deed,
> To thrash it every swoople O.
> The second stroke my flail it broke,
> My swoople and my couple O.
>
> My swoople was oak altho' it broke
> I think it might be mended O.
> Stiff and strong, stout and long,
> It broke before it bended O.
>
> She hiss'd she scoff'd she jeer'd she mock'd
> The jade had no discretion O.
> De'il take her tale [tail], she tired my flail,
> I was forced to quit my thrashing O.[51]

Yet there is no mistaking the message in 'The Wanton Seed', printed in the early nineteenth century and remaining in oral tradition for over a hundred years: namely, that the sown meadow remains barren because of the man's shortcomings. 'When forty weeks was gone and past' is a formula which normally precedes the announcement of a pregnancy, but here the text continues:

She came unto me with a slender waist;
She came unto me making this complaint,
That she wanted some more of the chiefest grain.[52]

It is worth remarking in passing on the delicacy with which the point is made. Other songs are more direct. 'O dear O' widely appeared on ballad-sheets—there were five different editions in Birmingham alone—and in the age of high Victorian hypocrisy treated with astonishing frankness the subject of a husband's impotence.

O Dear O

As I walked out one summer's morning
To view the trees and leaves a-springing
I saw two birds upon a tree
Chirping their notes and sweetly singing.
O! dear O! What shall I do?
My husband's got no courage in him, O! dear O!

I saw two maidens standing by.
One of them her hands was wringing,
And all her conversation was
My husband's got no courage in him.

All sorts of meat I did provide,
All sorts of drink that is fit for him;
Both oyster pie and rhubarb too,
But nothing can put courage in him.

My husband he can dance or sing,
Do anything that's fit for him,
But he cannot do the think I want
For alas he's got no courage in him.

My husband is admired wherever he goes,
And everyone looks well upon him,
With his handsome foot and well shaped toes,
But still he's got no courage in him.

Seven long years I've made his bed,
Six of them I've laid beside him;
And this morning I rose with my youthful bloom
That shows he's got no courage in him.

Every night when to bed he goes
I throw one leg right over him,
And my hand I clap between his thighs
But I can't put any courage in him.

If he does not shortly try,
A cuckold I am sure to make him,
For let me do whate'er I will
I really can't put courage in him.

I wish that he was dead and gone,
In the grave I quick would lay him,
And then I'd try another one
That has got a little courage in him.

Come all fair maids where'er you be,
Don't have a man before you try him.
Do not have to sing with me,
My husband's got no courage in him.[53]

The song turned up in the early twentieth century with three singers, all
men, which is perhaps surprising. It would be even more surprising if it
had not been sung by women too, especially since some other complaints
regarding husbands' sexual deficiencies were indeed sung by both sexes.
There is no evidence as to the singers of the eighteenth-century piece 'An
Excellent New Ballad, Concerning a Bridegroom and his Bride who were
lately Married at *Borrowstounness*, giving a full and true Account of the
Behaviour, and of the Bridegrooms running away from the Bride the same
Night, without Beding with her',[54] but in the text both sexes seem equally
appalled at the man's action.

Marital Discord

Marriage between people of widely different ages was condemned by both sexes. 'Jockeys Complaints for Want of his Jenny',[55] printed between 1656 and 1682, expresses the bitter regret of a man who has forsaken his young sweetheart to marry an old woman. Conversely, 'The Complaint of a Widdow against an Old Man', dating from between 1585 and 1616, looks unhesitatingly towards youth:

> Shall I wed an aged man, that groaneth of the Gout,
> And lead my lyfe in miserye, within doores and without?
> No! I will haue a Batcheler, of lyvely bloud and bone,
> To cheare me in my latter dayes, or els I will haue non.[56]

Resentment of old partners by the young is very common in songs sung by both men and women. 'Sally's Love for a Young Man' was printed in the eighteenth century, but recorded from both men and women in the twentieth:

> I've often heard of an old man
> But now I'm catch at last;
> I wish some other had got him
> Before the knot was cast.
> I wish that death had seized him,
> And ta'en him at a call,
> That I might have had a young [man]
> To roll me from the wall.[57]

Class and Marriage

The discrepancies in age and in sexual activity between Sally and her old husband have arisen because of parental insistence on the match, which in turn is motivated by economic considerations: 'for the sake of money and land'. The intervention of parents in the choice of a mate is frequently opposed in songs, whether, as here, it promotes a mismatch or whether it opposes a desired union. A Scots father in the classic 'Lady Maisry'[58] burns his daughter at the stake because she declines to renounce the English lord whose child she is bearing. Because she has a different alliance in mind, a mother turns away her son's lover, the eponymous 'Lass of Roch Royal',[59] and the woman and her baby both perish in the sea. The implacable hostility here seems to be because of the woman's humble origins, and in many songs lovers obstinately seek to marry across barriers of class and condition, while parents do their utmost to oppose. A ballad current in the seventeenth and eighteenth centuries shows how a weaver overrides his father's objections to marry a servant maid; a nineteenth-century version replaces her by a factory maid.[60] In a similar way a plough-boy is updated to a factory boy;[61] in both cases wealthy parents resisting their daughter's desire to marry the boy arrange for him to be press-ganged to sea, but she manages to buy his discharge. Songs with this kind of theme are numerous.

Conversely, class loyalty in the choice of a mate is strongly expressed on many occasions. Thomas Lanfiere, the author of 'The Clothiers' Delight', also wrote 'The Taunton Maid's Delight, or Hey for the honest Woosted-Comber', which begins:

> You pretty Maids where e're you are, come listen unto me,
> And briefly to you I'l[l] declare in every degree,
> My choice in choosing of a mate to you I will unfould,
> A Woorsted-Comber is the man that I love better than Gold:
> *They hey for the Woosted-Comber brave, I love him as my life,*
> *[If] ever I a Husband have, I will be a Comber wife.*[62]

'The West-Country Lawyer; or, The Witty Maid's Good Fortune' also dates from the seventeenth century, though it was current until the twentieth. In it a 'pretty maid' rejects a lawyer's invitation to make her 'a lady for ever' on the ground that

> I'd rather be a poor man's wife
> Sit at my wheel a-spinning
> Than I would be a lawyer's wife
> They are the worst of women.[63]

Another song which lasted for 250 years comes to a different conclusion: in 'Beautifull Nancy: or, The Witty Lass of London', printed between 1682 and 1696, a countrywoman rejects an alderman's sexual and financial offers but accepts his proposal of marriage:

> She lives now in Triumph and Splendour,
> Nay likewise has pleasure at will,
> For Honesty, Lasses, commend her;
> It is the best Policy still.[64]

Here, a poor woman triumphs over a wealthy man by spirit and superior wit. On other occasions, workers score over employers by seducing their wives. The curiously titled 'Old Mother Flip Flop against a Wash-tub',[65] an eighteenth-century slip-song, tells how in the absence of a farmer his wife is seduced by a farm-labourer. In a ballad of similar date, 'The Crafty London 'Prentice; or, Bow-Bells',[66] an apprentice is badly treated not by his master, but by his master's wife. He discovers that she secretly frequents a 'crack-shop' (brothel) 'to act her wanton sport', and, in effect, blackmails her to his sexual and monetary advantage. Conversely, another apprentice declines an offer of marriage from his mistress on the grounds that he is promised to her chambermaid. Furious at being rejected, the mistress causes him eventually to be hanged, by slipping a gold ring into his pocket, then accusing him of stealing it. The loyalty of 'The Sheffield Apprentice'[67] (such is the title of the song, which was published in 1794) to his own kind is the general rule. As we have seen, plough-boys, shepherds, and labouring men are attracted to milkmaids and servants, and vice versa. The miner, too, is widely celebrated as a romantic figure. In a song borrowed from shepherds, who in turn took it from sailors, we hear:

> The colliers are the best of boys, their work lies under ground,
> And when they to the ale-house go they value not a crown;
> They spend their money freely and pay before they go,
> They work under ground while the stormy winds do blow.

It is in the same piece, 'The Brave Collier Lads',[68] that a woman before accepting a collier's advances checks that he belongs to 'the brave union boys'. 'Collier lads get gold and silver', says another song, but 'Factory lads get nowt but brass.'[69] Even so, in a different piece, Mary endures ten months' confinement in a cellar on bread and water until her father changes his mind and allows her to marry a factory boy. Again, a spinner about to wed a factory girl gives this warning to others who might (literally) run away from their responsibilities:

> Always use them tenderly when you are so inclined,
> And they will please you to the heart, according to your mind,
> But should you prove obstropelus, and make their bellies swell,
> Then weekly wages you must pay unto the factory girl.
>
> If you attempt to run away and cannot pay the brass,
> Maidens they will beat you as neatly as you can cast.
> The overseer will send you unto the tread mill
> And make you pay or else consent to wed the factory girl.[70]

A printer in turn rejects a cutter, a seamstress, a cook, and a chambermaid, and decides to marry Sally, 'since none like a spinner my fancy can please'.[71] A power-loom weaver fights a fellow worker for the hand of a 'Dashing Steam Loom Weaver',[72] and a couple from the Springfield Road in Belfast sing in their happiness:

> Now we'll be getting married for she has named the day
> And happy we'll be together as we go along our way
> We'll have a tiny little house and a garden for to till
> And we'll bring our children up like us to work in the cotton mill.[73]

Infidelity and Incompatibility

Infidelity and incompatibility in marriage provide a great deal of material for songs. Adultery is among the commonest of themes. Women, it appears, readily succumb to the attractions of the travelling tinker, tailor, drover, or even parson. There are versions all over Europe, especially in the sixteenth and seventeenth centuries, of the story in which a wife pretends illness and sends her husband five miles to fetch her a bottle of the 'Water of Absalon'. Having seen the parson slip into the house, a friend of the husband's warns him and carries him back in a sack. He is thus not only able to discover and forestall the intended adultery, but to mulct the parson into the bargain, merely by threatening to geld him.[74] In a twentieth-century version (where, incidentally, the Water of Absalon is replaced by a bottle of whisky), the conclusion is different:

> He banished his wife the very same day,
> Gelded the parson and sent him away.[75]

It must be said that the parson does not fare well in popular literature; all too often he pays the price of being identified with the squire and the landowner. Even Nonconformist clergymen do not escape the reputation for sexual appetite which goes back to their medieval predecessors. 'The Saint turn'd Sinner; or, The Dissenting Parson's Text under the Quaker's Petticoats'[76] is self-explanatory. In 'The Methodist Parson Or, the Flitch of Bacon'[77] a preacher passes off as his Bible the lumps of bacon which he is obtaining (together with other favours, we infer) from a farmer's wife, until he is challenged by the husband. In 'The Ranting Parson' however, it is a farmer's wife herself who exacts a penalty for forwardness. She pretends to accept the ranter's proposition, and tells him to undress and get into bed first. When he has done so, she brings in a hive of bees and locks them in with the parson, whose discomfiture is typical of the subgenre:

> All smart[ing] and sore with stings he ran home to his wife in his shirt,
> Such a figure of fun for to see, all besmear'd with the mud and the dirt.
> Next morning the farmer came home, as I for truth have been told,
> In one of the ranter's side pockets found thirty bright sovereigns in gold.[78]

Sympathy lies here, as in many other pieces, with the husband who, sometimes despite his wife and sometimes in league with her, repels those who seek her favours. The unreasonably suspicious husband is the subject of a modern folk-tale, here put into song by Bernard Wrigley:

OUR BILL

Our Bill had a concrete mixer.
He was coming home last night;
When he came down t'street and he saw his house
There's a sports car parked outside.

He thought here's me going out to work
While my wife's at home on t' job,
So he swore he'd get her lover boy
And smash him up his gob.

Then he thought, now look here, Billy, lad,
Use what's under your crop.
So he ups with his concrete mixer,
Fills the car right up to t'top.

He gets back in his cab
And sits as quiet as a mouse,
And he sees the bloke coming to his car,
But he come from next door's house.

Well, Bill starts up his engine;
He'd never felt such a prat.
He was down that road and a mile away
In twenty seconds flat.

But if Bill had stayed a bit longer
He'd have seen his wife so sweet
Giving a kiss to her lover boy
As he pedalled down the street.

So now his wife she gets her oats
And Bill he feels a berk
For thinking his wife was having it off
While he was out at work.[79]

Such joyous celebration of successful adultery is widely found. The cuckold is a stock figure of fun, now as for centuries; and the seducer is often admired. Sympathy goes against the cuckold, but the song is still

male-orientated in that it celebrates the triumph of a man. This attitude is
of long standing. 'The Wanton Wife of Castle Gate', issued probably in
1693, is a curious piece in which the male narrator first laments that his
'best beloved will fancy me no more', then recommends sexual opportun-
ism: 'But if you meet a bonny lass with black and rowling eyes, / You must
kiss her and embrace her you may know the reason why.' Next he moves to
the woman of the title, who embodies such opportunity:

> There lives a Wife in Castle Gate but I'le not declare her name;
> She is both brisk and buxome, and fitted for the Game;
> She can knife it she can trip it, as she treads along the Plain;
> Till she meets some jolly Boat-man that will turn her back again.
>
> Her husband is a quiet man and an honest man is he;
> And for to wear the Horns, sir, contented he must be:
> He may wind them at his leisure and do the best he can,
> For his wife will have her pleasure with a jolly Boat-man.

The narrator then either reverts to thinking of his love, or turns his mind to
a new love:

> O, my Mally, my honey, O can thou fancy me?
> Then let us to bed haste where we will merry be,
> For good Gold and Silver for thee I'le take care,
> And for a large pair of Horns for thy Husband to wear.

The conclusion may be merely a concession to conventional morality,
since it is at variance not only with the words, but also with the weight of
the ballad as a whole:

> You young men and Batchelers that hears this pretty Jest,
> Be not of the Opinion this couple did profess;
> But be kind to your wives and your sweethearts alway:
> And God will protect you by night and day.[80]

The tragic consequences of adultery are explored in other pieces. The
three people involved all meet their deaths in the violent 'Little Musgrave
and Lady Barnard',[81] which was well enough known to be quoted
in Beaumont and Fletcher's *Knight of the Burning Pestle* (c.1611), but
remained in oral tradition in North America until the mid-twentieth
century. A case involving a more bourgeois milieu was that of Rose
Marshall (née Anderson) of Perth, who was repudiated and then divorced
by her merchant husband in 1803 on the grounds of her alleged adultery
with the raffish Lord Elgin (seventh of the title, and later vendor to the
British Museum of the Elgin Marbles). Local people sympathized with the
woman, and so did the writer of a song which remained current in the area

for at least a century. 'Who that has been reared in Perthshire', asked
Robert Ford in 1899, 'has not heard of the ballad of "Rosey Anderson",
which, fifty years ago, was sung at all the markets and fairs in the Valley of
Strathmore, and ever to greedy and delighted ears?' After moving to
London, Rosy Anderson was driven to seek help in the Bedlam hospital,
and she 'became sufficiently abandoned as to be compelled to seek for a
living in the streets'.[82]

Prostitution

It was common for seduced and sacked servant girls to be forced into
prostitution, less so for the well-to-do. Destitution, as in the case of Rosy
Anderson, was often the decisive factor. Perversely, perhaps, many of the
ballads on the subject are addressed to men and give warnings, sometimes
jocular, sometimes serious. Countrymen in town or at fairs, as we have
seen, were thought to be particularly at risk. One verse of 'Whores eight o'
Penny' (1744) sums up the dangers:

> She took me up an Alley, all for to use my pleasure;
> She tipt me with both itch and pox, it being cold weather.
> She pick'd my purse and served me worse than e're I was by any.
> O! how the whore did hug and squeeze until she nip'd my money.
> *Honest Women there is few, Jilts there is many.*
> *At every corner of the street there's Whores eight o' Penny.*[83]

A few pieces put the viewpoint of the prostitutes themselves. 'The
Ranting Whore's Resolution' (see illustration),[84] printed in 1672, is open
and even cynical. 'The Kissing Lasses of Yarmouth', of perhaps a century
later, is rather more subdued. The tune intended seems to have been that
of one of Place's songs, 'Gee ho dobbin'.

THE KISSING LASSES OF YARMOUTH

Come listen a while and a store [story] I'll tell,
Of lasses of pleasure that near hand to [do] dwell.
To tell our abode we are not asham'd,
You'll find us at Yarmouth come but to a lane.
Well done, lasses, O brave lasses,
Hi ho for such lasses my fancy to please.

You're welcome, gentlemen, pray now walk in,
We're from half a crown to a noggin of gin.
We are not so stiff as the lasses in town;
When trading is dead the price must come down.

But now the sailors have taken a prize,
We'll do our endeavours our wages to rise.
It's best to provide for our friends in good time
And to make our hay while the sun it doth shine.

The rest is just as frank, in connection with both the rewards and the hazards:

Says Phoebe to Phillis we'll follow the game,
Altho' we are told it will bring us to shame.
Tho' the case is hard I really must own,
Why should not the lasses make use of their own?

To Bridewell of late poor Phillis was sent,
And there for a while was forc'd to beat hemp,
But now she is free she swears by the mass
She'll not work with her hands while she can live by her arse.

At the end, it appears that some have taken to prostitution in order to keep themselves in the absence of their husbands:

Says Bet to her spouse, You took all your pay,
You left me no credit when you went away.
I being industrious have acted my part
And got a good living by my grandmother's mark.

Therefore, dear husband, no longer complain,
And since you are return'd I'll be honest again.
So now turn and kiss me and to end all strife
Be you a kind husband and I'll be a fond wife.[85]

'The Whores' Downfall' tells of Madam Carr and Jenny the journey-woman. Trade is good, with sailors paying half-a-crown and lawyers half a guinea, but hard times come, and Jenny wishes to make a change:

Madam, let's go home, and not rove no longer.
Here we trudge the streets both with cold and hunger.
Here we starve and pine, see my joints are shaking,
Not one cross of coin this night have we taken.[86]

She resolves to leave. A quarrel ensues, and both women are taken to 'the workhouse quod' and set to beating hemp.

'The Magdalene's Lament', from Scotland, relates, or rather hints at, how a woman became a prostitute after a gang rape, then, after a period of affluence, landed in a house of correction where she was whipped. She longs for a way out of her predicament and for a conventional life-style:

But if I were at libertie,
As I hope to be soon,
I hope to be a married wife
Whan a' thir days are done.[87]

The song is said to have belonged to the repertoire of 'Mussel Mou'd' Charlie Leslie, an Aberdeenshire ballad-singer who died in 1792 at the age of 105.

The 'Poor Whores' Complaint' is the fullest and soberest statement of its kind that I have seen in ballad form. It is difficult to date. Holloway and Black suggest 'possibly seventeenth-century', but I believe that, like several other pieces on prostitutes quoted here, it dates from the late eighteenth century, when the growth of towns and the incidence of war helped to bring about a great increase in prostitution. Few if any accounts of the lot of prostitutes have the realism and force of this crude printed ballad-sheet.

Come listen a while and you shall hear,
How the poor Whores fares in the winter
They've hardly got any rags to hide their ware
Indeed tis a despret thing Sir.
With their draggel tales thats nine inches deep,
And hardly a shooe or a stocking,
Yet if a Cull[b] they by chance should meet,
At him they will be bobing.[88]

Prostitution continued long after the eighteenth century, of course, and so did ballads dealing with it, but the voice heard is most often that of the man, gratified, cheated, or infected, seldom that of the woman actively and spiritedly commenting on her lot.

[b] man

More Marital Strife—and Concord

In returning, like the poor Magdalene, to married life, we encounter a
huge number of ballads in which the opposing standpoints of wives and
husbands are presented like mirror images. 'Be careful in Choosing a
Wife',[89] warns of the supposed deceit, ill temper, and slatternliness of
certain women. 'Advice to Bachelors' tells of a man who prefers hanging to
marriage. Early versions are lacking, but James Hopkinson quotes one
which he heard sung in the Nottingham cabinet-maker's shop where he
served his apprenticeship in the 1830s. 'This is an innocent example of
what were sung by the men', he wrote; 'but some were so bad that they
were not fit to *think about* much less to mention and only wish my ears had
never heard them.'[90]

The titles of 'The Man who wish'd he'd Never got Married'[91] and
'The Unfortunate Wife'[92] speak for themselves. The latter had a particularly long history, from broadside of 1794[93] to music-hall song of 1857[94] to
children's rhyme of the twentieth century.[95] It may have been a riposte
originally to 'The Careless Bachelor', a piece of ?1775 in which a married
man looks back to the delights of a single life.

> When I was a Bachelor, O then, O then,
> I could smoke my pipe,
> And carouse all the night;
> The world it went rowling and bowling,
> And the world it went very well with me, O then.
>
> I marry'd a wife, O then, O then,
> I marry'd a wife, O then;
> I marry'd a wife, and she plagued my life,
> Oh! the world it went worser and worser,
> And the world it went very bad, &c.[96]

Wives were frequently taken to task for their alleged inefficiency in
performing the household tasks. The ironically titled 'Thrifty Housewife',
for example, gives a catalogue of complaints. The context is that of a small
farm, but it must have had an appeal to townsfolk, for the song was printed
on broadsides in York, among other places.

> She sweeps the chamber once a week,
> So cleanly and tidy is she,
> When she goes out to work she falls asleep,
> She is such a thrifty wife to me.

She milks the cow in the chamber pot,
So cleanly and tidy is she,
And she strains the milk in the tail of her s——k,
She is rather too nasty for me.

My wife is called the queen of sluts,
So cleanly and tidy is she,
She roasted a hen both feathers and guts,
A delicate morsel for me.

Other offences include cheeses not turned, beef improperly salted so that it becomes full of maggots, and a lack of cleanliness in person and household. The piece concludes:

Each night I have trouble to put her to bed,
For as drunk as a sow is she,
For seven long years I've wished her dead,
So d——l come take her from me.[97]

The devil indeed comes for a termagant in 'The Farmer's Curst Wife', but she wreaks such havoc in hell that he is obliged to return her to her husband. Robert Burns based his own 'Kellyburnbraes' (1792) on the ballad, which circulated widely in England, Ireland, Scotland, and North America, and is still current.[98] It is one of a number of pieces in which the battle between the sexes takes allegorical or symbolic form. 'Marrow-bones',[99] for example, is ostensibly the tale of a woman's attempt to blind and drown her husband, which ends in her own death. Yet the mood is jovial, and the real conflict is one of wits. The unimaginative might take it literally, and there were some protests as recently as the 1970s when the song was sung in schools. Similarly, 'The Holly Twig'[100] tells of a husband beating his wife until she becomes lame and blind, at which point the devil takes her away, leaving him to rejoice at being rid of her. The song was printed as early as 1760, sung by Grimaldi in the 1820s, and known until recent years on both sides of the Atlantic. Once more, the mood is jolly, and it would be hard to take the words literally. Nevertheless, one is uneasy about the considerable number of songs which appear to celebrate husbands' violence towards wives. 'A Stitch in Time', by Mike Waterson, gives one wife's answer:

A STITCH IN TIME

Oh there was a woman and she lived on her own,
She slaved on her own and she skivvied on her own;
She'd two little girls and two little boys
And she lived all alone with her husband.

For her husband he was a hunk of a man,
A chunk of a man and a drunk of a man;
He was a hunk of a drunk and a skunk of a man,
Such a boozing, bruising husband.

For he would come home drunk each night,
He thrashed her black, he thrashed her white;
He thrashed her, too, within an inch of her life,
Then he slept like a log, did her husband.

One night she gathered her tears all round her shame,
She thought of the bruising and cried with the pain,
Oh, you'll not do that ever again,
I won't live with a drunken husband.

But as he lay and snored in bed
A strange old thought came into her head.
She went for the needle, went for the thread,
And went straight to her sleeping husband.

And she started to stitch with a girlish thrill,
With a woman's heart and a seamstress' skill;
She bibbed and tucked with an iron will
All around her sleeping husband.

Oh, the top sheet, the bottom sheet, too,
The blanket stitched to the mattress through;
She stitched and stitched for the whole night through,
Then she waited for the dawn and her husband.

And when the husband woke with a pain in his head
He found that he could not move in bed.
'Sweet Christ, I've lost the use of me legs!'
But this wife just smiled at her husband.

For in her hand she held the frying pan;
With a flutter in her heart she gave him a lam.
He could not move, but he cried, 'God damn!'
'Don't you swear,' she cries to her husband.

Then she thrashed him black, she thrashed him blue
With the frying pan and the colander, too;
With the rolling pin just a stroke or two,
Such a battered and bleeding husband.

She says, 'If you ever come home drunk any more
I'll stitch you in, I'll thrash you more,
Then pack my bag and I'll be out of the door:
I'll not live with a drunken husband'.

So isn't it true what small can do
With a thread and a thought and a stitch or two?
He's wiped his slate and his boozing's through,
It's goodbye to a drunken husband.[101]

7

POLITICS

A POWERFUL body of political protest in the form of song and ballad stretches a thousand years from the Normans to nationalism and nuclear power today. For the most part, and not surprisingly, it is critical of established authority, sometimes with a regressive, more often with a progressive, intent.

During the reign of James I rents rose, and with them the cost of living. Many retainers were dismissed, though there was an increase in ostentation among the wealthy. Ballads such as 'Pitties Lamentation for the cruelty of this age'[1] bemoaned the decline in hospitality. So did 'Times Alteration; Or, The Old Man's rehearsall, what brave days he knew, A great while agone, when his Old Cap was new', by Martin Parker, which looks back two hundred years to a semi-feudal golden age:

> A man might then behold
> At Christmas, in each hall,
> Good fires to curbe the cold,
> And meat for great and small;
> The neighbours were friendly bidden,
> And all had welcome true;
> The poore from the gates were not chidden
> *When this old cap was new.*
>
> Blacke-jacke to every man
> Were fill'd with wine and beere;
> No pewter pot not kanne
> In those dayes did appeare:
> Good cheare in a noble-man's house
> Was counted a seemly shew;
> We wanted no brawne nor sowse
> *When this old cap was new.*
>
> We tooke not such delight
> In cups of silver fine;
> None under the degree of a knight
> In plate drunke beere or wine:

> Now each mechanicall man
> Hath a cup-boord of plate, for a shew,
> Which was a rare thing then
> *When this old cap was new.*[2]

The 'mechanicall' men had little cause for satisfaction; on the contrary, they expressed themselves with searing bitterness in 'The Poore Man Payes for All', of 1630, which takes the form of a relation of a dream:

> Me thought I saw how wealthy men
> Did grind the poore men's faces,
> And greedily did prey on them,
> Not pittying their cases:
> They make them toyle and labour sore
> For wages too-too small;
> The rich men in the taverns rore,
> *But poore men pay for all.*
>
> Me thought I saw an usurer old
> Walke in his fox-fur'd gowne,
> Whose wealth and eminence controld
> The most men in the towne;
> His wealth he by extortion got,
> And rose by others' fall;
> He had what his hands earned not,
> *But poore men pay for all.*
>
> .   .   .   .
>
> Me thought I was i' th' countrey,
> Where poore men take great paines,
> And labour hard continually,
> Onely for rich men's gaines:
> Like th'israelite in Egypt,
> The poore are kept in thrall;
> The task-masters are playing kept,
> *But poore men pay for all.*[3]

Hard times, distress, unemployment: these were perennial themes in ballads. One seventeenth-century fragment remained popular in Lincoln-shire at harvest homes and Christmas suppers for some two hundred years:

> Oh dear my good masters, pray what shall we do,
> In this year sixteen hundred and seventy-two?
> For since Queen Elizabeth mounted the throne,
> Sure time like the present scarce ever were known.[4]

'All Things be dear but Poor Mens Labour'[5] runs one title of 1675 which is echoed in 'The Troubles of this World; or, Nothing Cheap but Poor Mens Labour'[6] of about 1692. A century later, 'The Complaints of the Poor' is in the same vein:

> The poor working men are to be pitied good lack,
> They are loaded with work till their bones they do crack,
> They may work till they drop, and be taken up dead,
> They can hardly get cheese to eat with their bread.[7]

The list of those contributing to the plight of the poor includes bakers, millers, butchers, and also 'badgers'—dealers who bought up supplies in the hope of causing prices to rise, so that they could sell at a profit (see also Chapter 2).

It was not only the poorest who suffered, but also tradesmen and artisans. 'The Trades-men's Lamentation'[8] of 1688 is a dialogue between a weaver and a glover on 'the Dullness of their Trades'. 'General Distress' (to the tune of 'Gee ho Dobbin', for which, see page 228) probably dates from the late eighteenth century.

> You surely have heard of great General Distress,
> Who has march'd through this land which once plenty did bless,
> If this beggerly gentleman means long to stop,
> I fear every tradesman must shut up his shop.
> *O Old England, wonderful England, plentiful England,*
> *What is this world come to?*
>
> A tradesman looks nothing without a grand show,
> And shuffling and scheming is all the go,
> To sack what they can and like birds hop the twig,
> For bankruptcy's now all the fashion and rig.
>
> The goods are sold off much below the trade price,
> And no one harbour more cats than catch mice,
> An honest man can't live which makes him look cross,
> For you must buy and sell now and live by the loss.
>
> The face of the hungry looks ragged and thin,
> And their bones are just ready to start through their skin,
> And trade is so slack that unless some relief,
> We shall eat one another instead of roast beef.[9]

Taxation

The levels of prices and taxes frequently inspired comment. Once in a while the abolition of a burden produced a delighted response, as in 'England's Joy, For the Taking off of The Chimney-Money':

Now happy Times are coming on, let's pray that they may last;
For now the Chimney Tax is gone, our chiefest care is past:
We'll in our country Cottage sing, and push the Iugg about;
We'll drink an Health unto our King, till all our Liquor's out.[10]

The king in question was William III. During his journey from Torbay to London in 1688, he had, writes Macaulay, 'been importuned by the common people to relieve them of the intolerable burden of the hearth money'. Largely on William's initiative, the tax, which had been imposed by Charles II, was abolished in 1689. Again according to Macaulay, it had 'pressed heavily on the poor, and lightly on the rich. A peasant, all of whose property was not worth twenty pounds, had to pay several shillings, while the mansion of an opulent nobleman in Lincoln's Inn Fields or Saint James's Square was seldom assessed at two guineas.'[11] The hearth tax was replaced in 1696 by the window tax, but the grateful balladeer of 1689 was not to know that this would happen.

The imposition of taxes, more often than their abolition, is chronicled in ballads. In July 1785 the celebrated Dr Crotch heard 'a political ballad on Mr Pitt's taxes' sung in the streets of Oxford. He took down only the tune, but the words have survived on a printed sheet. Pitt was the leader of a minority government from December 1783 until March 1784. When he was returned with a majority after a general election, he set about improving the financial position of the country: as a result of the Seven Years War and the American War of Independence the national debt had risen to a staggering £250 million. His first budget, in June 1784, introduced a wide range of new taxes, and was greeted by a ballad with the chorus, 'Sing tanta ra rara, tax all'.[12] In his second budget, the following year, 'the levy on employers of manservants was increased, that on salt was tidied up, and new taxes were laid on post horses, on gloves, on the employers of female servants, on pawnbrokers' licences and—most controversially—on retail shops'.[13]

THE BUDGET, A NEW SONG

Good people draw near, and the Budget you'll hear,
Of a man that is wonderful wise; for who is so fit,
As our young Master Pit, to raise a poor nation's supplies.

Now all servants male, and shops in retail,
May hang down their heads in dismay, since Billy's declar'd,
They must both be prepar'd, a tax in his Budget to pay.

If salt you wou'd eat, to relish your meat,
For the flavour to make it go down, he wisely has said,
A tax must be paid, to ease the distress of the Crown.

If in business you thrive, and post-horses drive,
Or gloves on your hands you should wear, for either, or both,
You must pay, howe'er loth, so doth Billy's Budget declare.

Our friends Two to One,[a] who've many undone,
O'er the poor they have long had a sway; but o'ertaken at last,
For their rog'ry past, and a licence to cheat they must pay.

But what is the worst, and most to be curst,
Of all taxes young Billy has laid, is for 'scaping the whore,
And condemning the poor, the poor virgin for being a maid.

It is very well known, in London fair town,
A maid is a thing that's but rare; then why should he, pray,
Condemn those to pay, who've a burden they like not to bear.

Since, 'twixt you and me, we all must agree,
No tax should be laid on an oddity, here's a pox to the man,
Who'd adopt such a plan, as a tax on a maiden's commodity.

But now if by chance, Master P—— should advance,
Midst a few of these injured fair, some with mops, some with brooms,
And soap well perfum'd, they wou'd make him repent it most dear.

Then a tub, being brought in, to scrub they'd begin,
From his belly quite round to his back, then with one accord,
Crying is this your reward, for taxing of Dolly's Old Hat.[14]

Ballad-writers and readers continued to take a keen interest in Pitt's
fiscal measures. 'The Burthen of Taxes', published in 1794, refers to
George III:

> Yet bluff Mr Million,
> Thinks P—— his postillion

[a] pawnbrokers

> Is driving on wonderful well,
> But how can it be,
> Is a mystery to me,
> I think he is driving to hell.[15]

Two of the 'ballad chronicles' by William Mackay of Birmingham were devoted respectively to 'The Budget' (1797) and 'Billy Pitt's Progression in Taxation' (1798).[16] The introduction in 1799 of tax at two shillings in the pound on incomes of over £60 per annum led to a wide range of ballad responses, which shows the breadth of audience which such sheets commanded. One offered a patriotic welcome to the sharing of burdens:

> From the peer so down to the mechanical man,
> They must all come beneath our master's plan,
> And curtail their expences to pay their share,
> To preserve their rights & their liberties dear.[17]

Another, probably published a little later, which also attacked forestallers and regraters, believed that the poor were the losers:

> From the TAX UPON INCOME, invented by Pitt,
> Though the Great Ones contrive to lose nothing by it,
> Yet we who have little are sure to be hit,
> GOOD LORD DELIVER US![18]

A third gleefully reflected that the rich would have to pay:

> Ye quidnuncs so queer who thro' politics trudge it,
> And mumble each crust of the minister's budget,
> Among the various ways he has found out to link 'em,
> Don't you think he did the job in the Tax upon Income?
> Lord how the great folks must come down with the clinkum,
> When the gemman he goes round for the Tax upon Income.[19]

When income tax, having been abolished in 1816, was reintroduced by Sir Robert Peel in 1842, the popular response was once more favourable. As one S. Lane of Norwich put it,

> What's the use of your grumbling all you that have money
> And swearing Point Blank that you have not got any;
> Come Fork out the Tin, for I'm sure you can't grudge it,
> This Tax on the Income is the best in the Budget.[20]

Taxation in general remained unpopular. One ballad, 'John Bull and the New Taxes', first issued in 1841, remained in circulation for over a century, turning up in Galway in 1930 and in Glasgow forty years later.[21] Passing off old songs as new was a time-honoured practice, but so too was the creation of genuinely new songs, albeit often on traditional lines. 'Farewel and adieu to the year ninety three / I hope this new year better times we shall see' is the opening of 'A Short Sketch of the Times, A New Song for the Year 1794'.[22] 'The Odds and Ends of the Year 1830' provides a series of questions and answers, including:

> What do you think of the bold Captain Swing?
> I think through the country he has done a wicked thing,
> He has caused great destruction in England and France
> If Justice overtakes him on nothing he'll dance.

> What do you think of bold Henry Hunt?
> I think he is a man that will speak his mind blunt,
> He is chosen M.P. he is clever and cute,
> He will polish up the Commons like a Wellington boot.

> What do you think of Ireland's Dan?
> I think that O'Connell is a valiant man,
> For the Union of Erin he loudly does call,
> And he says he is determined to agitate them all.[23]

Some political commentaries in ballad form were successively updated. 'Noble Sportsmen' (see illustration),[24] which was probably issued in the late 1840s, has an earlier version which refers to the Chartist uprising of 1839:

> J. Frost thro' Wales a hunting went, he knew not how to ride,
> He had a well bred Chartist horse, but got on the wrong side,
> It is allowed if he had kept the reins tight in his hand,
> He'd not been so easily hunted off unto Van Dieman's Land.[25]

A later version, entitled 'A New Hunting Song for 1854',[26] deals largely with the outbreak of the Crimean War.

Royalty

Royalty was a favourite subject for ballad-writers. Comment could be fierce, and likewise the reaction of its recipients. Henry I was offended by one Luke de Barra, and said: 'This man, being a wit, a poet, and a minstrel, composed many indecent songs against me, and sung them openly to the great entertainment of my enemies; and since it has pleased God to deliver him into my hands, I will punish him, to deter others from the like petulance.'[22] The satirist was sentenced to have his eyes put out, and died from wounds received while struggling with the executioner.

Shakespeare in *King Lear* quotes a welcome to Queen Elizabeth on her accession. The piece, by William Birch, is entitled 'A songe betwene the

Quenes majestie and Englande', and takes the form of a dialogue between
E. (England) and B. (Bessy, or Queen Elizabeth).

> *E.* Come over the born bessy come over the born bessy
> Swete bessy come over to me
> And I shall the take and my dere lady make
> Before all other that ever I see.
>
> *B.* My thinke I hear a voice at whom I do rejoyce
> And aunswer the now I shall
> Tel me I say what art thou that bids me com away
> And soo earnestly doost me call.
>
> *E.* I am thy lover faire hath chose thee to my heir
> And my name is mery Englande
> Therefore come away and make no more delaye
> Swete bessie give me thy hande.
>
> *B.* Here is my hand my dere lover Englande
> I am thine both with mind and hart
> For ever to endure thou maiest be sure
> Untill death do us two depart.[28]

Other accessions were received no less enthusiastically. 'The Royal
Patient Traveller' (1660),[29] by Henry Jones of Oxford, celebrates Charles
II's escapes from the Parliamentarians and his restoration to the throne.
'The Subjects' Satisfaction' is 'a new Song of the Proclaiming King
William and Queen Mary, on 13th. of this Instant February' (1688).[30]
When William IV mounted the throne in 1830, his nautical exploits were
given sycophantic coverage on ballad-sheets.[31] Even radically inclined
printers saluted the accession of Victoria seven years later, though some
made unwarranted assumptions as to her intentions. One makes her say:
'That poor-law bill, with many more, / Shall be trampled to the floor— /
The rich must keep the helpless poor, / While I am Queen of England'.[32]
In another, an unemployed Belfast weaver expresses these sentiments:

> Since the young Queen Victoria is now on the throne
> I hope we won't grieve for the time that's to come,
> Our trade it will flourish in Ireland again,
> So here's to the young Queen and long may she reign.[33]

Victoria's marriage and the births and subsequent alliances of her many
children were also grist for the balladeer, whose attitude was often sharply
critical and sometimes scurrilous. 'In 'Married at Last', Victoria is
depicted as sex-hungry and Albert as carpet-bagging:

I am a damsel gay and free,
The world may say what it likes of me,
I am the Queen of all the land,
And I can't do without a man;
Prince Albert is the man for me,
He is devilish fond of skilligalee,
There is nothing like a wedded life,
I can't forget my wedding life.

Prince Albert came to marry me,
From mother's land of Germany,
Stark naked miles for me he'd run,
For I've got money though he's got none,
Thirty thousand is not much I'm sure,
Old Farmer Bull must find some more,
Since I got married I will make it right,
And fry the sausages day and night.[34]

Like Albert's, the allowances paid to other members of the royal family were distinctly unpopular. 'The Princess Royal's Dowry' (1859) expresses resentment both at the dowry of £40,000 and the annual allowance of £8,000 which were to be paid:

Lord Palmerston he did declare
He'd quickly tax the nation
To support the Princess Royal
In her proper rank and station.
They'll tax the deaf, the lame, the blind,
To help to pay expenses;
With a double tax on all the girls
That's flounced up to the hainches.

.   .   .   .   .   .

They're going to tax the farmer lads
That harrows, ploughs, and ditches,
They'll lay a tax on powdered wigs,
And all the livery breeches,
They'll tax us all, both old and young,
To support these idle drones, sir,
That does nothing else but suck
The marrow from our bones, sir.[35]

Royal marriages have frequently given rise to scandals of one kind or another. The abdication of Edward VIII took place on 10 December 1936; yet, at a school Christmas party in Swansea before the end of the same term, 'when the tune played happened to be "Hark the Herald Angels

Sing", a mistress found herself having to restrain her small children from singing this lyric, known to all of them:

> Hark the herald angels sing,
> Mrs Simpson's pinched our king.
> Peace on earth and mercy mild,
> I wonder if she'll have a child.'[36]

The name of one personage from a much earlier royal drama survives in a children's rhyme of which Flora Thompson quotes a version in *Lark Rise*:

> Queen, Queen Caroline
> Dipped her head in turpentine.
> Why did she look so fine?
> Because she wore a crinoline.[37]

George IV's move in 1820 to dissolve his marriage with Caroline of Brunswick and to deprive her by Act of Parliament of the title of queen encountered considerable popular opposition. Among the ballads supporting Caroline were such pieces as 'Italian Liars witnesses against our Queen', 'The King at Sea and the Queen on Shore', and 'The Queen shall enjoy her own again'.[38] The bill was abandoned by the House of Lords. Caroline was excluded from George IV's coronation in 1821, and died shortly afterwards.

Parliament

Parliamentary proceedings frequently attracted the attention of balladeers, sometimes at their peril. Before and during the Civil War and the Commonwealth (not to speak of afterwards) the ballad-writers whose work circulated in print and in manuscript were usually proponents of the Royalist cause. As C. H. Firth has remarked, 'The Puritans were hardly capable of answering their adversaries in kind. They neither wrote ballads, nor sang them. Their maxim was "if a man be merry, let him sing psalms", and they disapproved of the amorous ditties, romances, and satirical songs loved by the common people.'[39]

Examples of the last genre mentioned are the ballads on the destruction of crosses at Cheapside in 1643 and at Charing Cross four years later. These were two of the twelve crosses erected at places where the body of Queen Eleanor had rested in 1290 on its journey from Nottinghamshire to London for burial at Westminster Abbey. The Puritans considered them papist, and ordered the two in London to be pulled down. Each had its ballad, sharp, mocking, witty, angry—in short, in the best vein of political song. 'The Downfall of Charing-Cross' concludes:

Methinks the common-council shou'd
Of it have taken pity,
'Cause, good old cross, it always stood
So firmly in the city.
Since crosses you so much disdain,
Faith, if I were you,
For fear the king should rule again,
I'd pull down Tiburn too.[40]

The king's execution was itself commemorated in ballads, but those published during the Commonwealth limited themselves to fairly conventional valediction. 'The King's Last Farewell to the World', for example, which was published with official imprimatur in 1648, begins:

Through fear of sharpe & bitter paine,
by cutting off my dayes,
No pleasure in my Crown I take,
Nor in my Royall Rayes.[a]
I shall discend my grived heart,
(for none my life can save)
Unto the dismall gates of death,
to moulder in the Grave.[41]

There were some ballads on the Parliamentary side, if only from the unrespectable wing. Gerard Winstanley's 'Diggers' Song' of 1649, which remained in manuscript (see illustration) for almost 250 years before being printed, is one of the finest expressions of revolutionary fervour in English, though its tune belongs to the same family as that of 'Jack Hall':

With spades & hoes & plowes: stand up now stand up now
wth spades & hoes &c.
Yo[r] freedome to uphold seeing Cavaleirs are bold
to kill you if they could & rights from you to hold
Stand up now diggers all.[42]

Winstanley, who was fined £11. 9s. 1d. and had his four cows confiscated for digging on St George's Hill in Surrey, also wrote a highly political 'Diggers Christmass-Caroll'[43] attacking kings, priests, and lawyers.

The Commonwealth's response to hostile ballads was to suppress them. In February 1647 the House of Commons set up a committee to look into the suppression of 'the publishing in the streets, by ballad-singers, of pamphlets and ballads scandalous to the Parliament'. this led to *An Ordinance against unlicensed or scandalous Pamphlets, and for the better Regulating of Printing* (30 September 1647), which forbade the publication

[b] array

of any unlicensed 'Book, Pamphlet, Treatise, Ballad, Libel, Sheet or sheets of News'. The penalties for the maker, writer, or composer of such material were a fine of forty shillings or up to forty days imprisonment in default; for a printer, twenty shillings or twenty days; and for a bookseller or stationer, ten shillings or ten days. A 'Hawker, Pedler or Ballad-singer' was to 'forfeit and lose all his Books, Pamphlets and printed Papers exposed to sale, and also to be whipt as a Common Rogue'. Enough infringements must have occurred to justify further action, for a parliamentary Act in September 1649 increased some of the penalties and extended liability. An author's fine, for example, went up to ten pounds, and a printer was liable to have his press seized and broken up. Many towns introduced their own by-laws and edicts. The flow of printed ballads was effectively stopped, though material continued to circulate orally and in manuscript form. Some of this surfaced into print at the Restoration, when the new freedom was used to extol the monarchy and to vilify Cromwell and the Commonwealth. It was also exploited, as we have seen, to issue ballads criticizing the political and social conditions of the time.

During the eighteenth century, ballads frequently played a part in political campaigns, such as the one directed against Walpole's excise proposals of 1733.[44] Candidates in elections had songs printed and sung to further their cause. The name of John Baker Holroyd (1735–1821), a candidate in two bitterly contested elections (one a by-election) in Coventry in 1780, is repeated in one piece with a frequency which would be unremarkable with a brand name in a television commercial today. The tune was 'Hearts of Oak':

> Then for Holroyd we'll vote, and for Holroyd we'll sing,
> He's a Friend to our Country, our Rights, and our King;
> As a Soldier he'll fight in our Country's Cause,
> As a Member he'll stand by our Rights and our Laws:
> *True blue is our colour, true blue are our Men,*
> *Then always be ready, steady Boys steady,*
> *To vote for a Holroyd again and again.*[45]

John Wilkes was helped in what we should now call his 'publicity' by pieces such as 'A New Song on Alderman Wilkes, Member of Parliament for Middlesex. Sung by the true Sons of Liberty', probably in 1770, with the chorus:

> Wilkes still shall bear the sway,
> Nothing shall him dismay,
> Now he has got the day,
> Brave English boys'.[46]

THE
IRISH
EMIGRANT.

NOBLE
SPORTSMEN.

William Pratt, Printer, 82, Digbeth, Birmingham.
Cheapest Song Warehouse in England.

I'm sitting on the stile Mary,
　Where we sat side by side,
On a bright may morning long ago,
　When first you were my bride,
The corn was springing fresh and green
　The lark sang loud and high,
　　And was on your lip, Mary,
　　　The love light in your eye.

The place is little changed, Mary,
　The day's as bright as then,
The lark's loud song is in my ear,
　And the corn is green again !
　　The soft clasp of your hand,
And your breath warm on my cheek,
And I still keep listening for the words
　You never more may speak.

'Tis but a step down yonder lane,
　And the little church stands near,
The church where we were wed, Mary,
　I see its spire from here ;
But the grave-yard lies between, Mary,
　And my step might break your rest,
For I've laid you, darling, down to sleep
　With your baby on your breast.

I'm very lonely now, Mary,
　For the poor find no new friends ;
But oh ! they love the better still
　The few our father sends.
And you were all I had, Mary,
　My blessing and my pride ;
There's nothing left to care for now,
　Since my poor Mary died.

I'm bidding you a long farewell,
　My Mary kind and true,
But I'll not forget you darling,
　In the land I'm going to.
They say there's bread and work for all,
　And the sun shines always there,
But I'll not forget old Ireland,
　Where it fifty times as fair.

All you that are low spirited I think it won't be wrong
To sing to you a verse or two of the new hunting song,
This is a hunting season—the sport it has begun,
And heroes they will have the fun with their fine dogs and gun.

CHORUS.

A-hunting they will go, will go, and a-hunting they will go,
And lay out schemes and try all means to keep the poor man low.

'Tis of one of our brave huntsmen, my song I will commence,
Brave Buonaparte I will begin—the war a man of sense,
From Corsica he did set off to hunt upon a chance,
He hunted till he became the Emperor of France.

And Nelson for his hunting he got the nation's praise,
He was the greatest huntsman that hunted on the seas,
He with his warlike terror a-hunting bore the sway,
A Frenchman's ball proved his downfall in Trafalgar Bay.

And Wellington at Waterloo he had the best of luck,
He hunted from a lieutenant till he became a duke,
Men that did fight well for him, and did him honours gain,
He tried all that he could do to have their pensions ta'en.

Feargus O'Connor round the country a-hunting did go,
Calling meetings in every town to tell the truth you know,
The tyrants tried to keep him down, but that was all in vain,
The people swear they'll back him up and have their rights again.

Prince Albert to this country came a-hunting for a wife,
He got one whom he said he loved far dearer than his own life,
Oh ! yes, he got the blooming Queen to dandle on his knee,
With thirty thousand pounds a year paid from this country.

They are hunting the beggars through the country every day,
And hawkers if they do not a heavy license pay,
They won't allow the poor to beg—it's against the law to steal,
For one there's the Bastile, and the other the Jail.

Now to conclude my hunting song—I hope you will agree
The poor they are starving—the rich will have their spree,
And to complain it is a crime, so poor you must remain,
The parson says, "contented be and you will heaven gain."

69

'The Irish Emigrant'/'Noble Sportsmen'. Street ballad.

THEY ARE ALL SLIDING IN
Bobby's Sliding Scale

AIR.—" Cheating."

THE Tories are a sliding
    The Country all around,
And Bobby has a sliding scale,
    To slide about the Town.
The Corn Bill has caused a pretty row,
    With every class of men,
And sliding Bobby says the price
    Shall stand at Three Pounds Ten,

CHORUS.

And they are all sliding,
The Tories are all sliding in
Bobby's sliding scale.

Unto the Queen at Brighton,
    They sent Bobby's sliding scale ;
She slided down at Windsor,
    Till she got a Prince of Wales.
May she and Albert happy dwell,
    In spite of wind and weather
And with delight, both day and night,
    Slide jovially on together.

Old Arthur was a sliding,
    All with the Tory crew,
He can slide from Piccadilly
    To the plains of Waterloo.
One day as he was sliding,
    A great dispute arose,
So bang he slided on his rump,
    And fell upon his nose.

Neddy Natchbull goes a sliding,
    Some times on good intent,   [Gates,
He goes sliding through the Turn-pike
    When the is down in Kent.
The noble Duke of B————m
    Goes sliding for a heat,
And he wont allow his men to slide,
    To get much food to eat.

Then there's old Charley W————ce,
    Can either slide or hop,
He went sliding out of Bristol once,
    Over the chimney pots,
Old Jemmy B————w he can slide,
    With Harry G————n round,
And F————t swears that he can slide,
    From here to Epsom Downs.

W————d can slide to Brentford,
    So clever in a trice,
R————e can slide through Westminster,
    On mud instead of ice.
S————y, down through Lancashire,
    Can slide both late and soon,
While B————t down into Wiltshire slides,
    A raking for the moon.

Johnny R————l says he will never slide,
    As you may understand,
If he can be protected by
    A little bit of lamb—
He will slide into the Commons,
    To ease the people's woes,
And he will have a slide at Bobby,
    Till he hits him on the nose.

Now in England, Scotland, Ireland,
    The Isle of Man, and Wales,
The Tories think they have got them fine,
    Into a sliding scale.
They slide the poor man up and down,
    Until he drops his head,
May the Devil slide the rogues away
    And let us have cheap bread.

BIRT, Printer, 39, Great St. Andrew Street,
Seven Dials.

A street ballad of 1842.

A New Song on the Great Demonstration, which is to be made on Kersal Moor, September 24th, 1838.

YOU Reformers of Eng'and and Ireland attend,
To this song I have made which has lately been penn'd
Concerning a meeting which now has took p ace,
Our rights for to gain and to better our case
The time it is co ne, boys, the work has begun
To be free. or forever be slaves.

You Lancashire lad's, this day is the time
Reformers will now both their hands and hearts join,
For Freedom and Liberty's now is the cry,
To ro longer be slaves but like Freemen to die.
So let us be steady, determined and ready,
When met boys upon Kersal Moor,

The rich man he lives in his luxury at ease,
The poor man's degraded, death stares him i'th face,
The rich knows not now what to eat, drink, or wear,
The poor's clothed in rags, what does the rich care,
But our motto shall be, 'huzza for liberty,'
Now we're met boys upon Kersal Moor.

From Macclesfield, Stockport, and Oldham they've come
Ashton, Rochdale, and Middleton with music & drums
Bury, Bolton and Leith, it is a grand show,
Reformers all marching, Then dance in a row.
With banners so free and loud shouts of huzzas
New Reformers join on Kersal Moor.

The Manchester lads now they lead on in front,
As they did in the days of brave HENRY HUNT,
Annual Parliaments, Suffrage, determined to gain,
The greatest Reformer of the age.

The Ballot without these we slaves must remain
Determined to be either bondsmen, or free,
United upon Kersal Moor,

The Birmingham lads and the lads of the North.
Have showed us great courage their valour and worth
Will the brave men of Lancashire now behind lag,
All that do their heads ought to be stuck in a bag.
But no's! all the cry, we will fight till we die,
For Liberty on Kersal Moor.

There is Fielden, brave Attwood, and Oastler so free
Fletcher, Stephens. O'Connor, who all do agree
Re'orm it is needful, Reform we will have,
For Freedom's the cry of the honest and brave.
Be loyal and true boys, think on Peterloo,
Remember this on Kersal Moor.

You Fema'es of England all join the true cause
Your liberty's rights, brave freedom and laws.
That in after ages our children may say,
Our forefathers struggled, fought for liberty.
And join the throng now we bravely move on,
To the Meeting held on Kersal Moor.

So up and be doing—in one Union join,
That the bright star of freedom may brightly shine,
And liberty's about resound from shore to shore,
That Britons are free and will be slaves no more,
Huzza for Reform, we shall weather the storm
At this meeting upon Kersal Moor.

J. Wheeler, Printer Whittle street Manchester.

The manuscript alterations suggest that this sheet was to be issued in amended form to advertise a further Chartist meeting in Nottinghamshire.

written by Embleton

THE POOR LAW CATECHISM

Question. What is your Name?

Answer. They call me Pauper.

Q. Who gave you that Name?

A. The Board of Guardians; to whom I applied in the time of trouble and distress, when I first became a child of want, a Member of the Workhouse, and an inheritor of all the insults that poverty is heir to.

Q. What did the Board of Guardians do for you?

A. They did promise and vow two things: firstly, that I should be treated like a convicted felon, being deprived of liberty and fed on prison fare; and lastly, that I should be an object of oppression all the days of my life.

Q. Rehearse the Articles of thy Belief?

A. I believe in the cruelty of Lord Harry Brougham, the author and fosterer of the present Poor Laws. I also believe that these Laws have caused the death of tens of thousands by cruelty, starvation, and neglect.

Q. How many Commandments have you, and such as you are to keep?

A. Ten.

Q. Which be they?

A. The same which the Poor Law Commissioners spake in Somerset House, saying—We are thy Lords and Masters, who cause thee to be confined in Bastiles, and separated thee from the wife of thy bosom and the children of thy love:

1. Thou shalt obey no laws but ours.

2. Thou shalt not make for thyself any substitute for skilly, nor the likeness of tea, nor any other kind of food or drink, except as is allowed in the workhouse; for we are jealous men, punishing with severity any transgression against our laws; and shouldst thou disobey in this, we shall teach you a lesson that shall last thee all the days of thy life.

3. Thou shalt labour hard, and for nothing; none of thy earnings shall be thine own, therefore we say thou shalt labour in vain.

4. Remember the Sabbath day, Six days thou shalt work hard, and have little to eat; but the seventh day is the sabbath, in which we cannot make you work, and so we give you liberty for an hour or two, to save the parish the expence of your Sunday dinner.

5. Honour the Poor Laws, the Commissioners, the Guardians, and the Beadles; thou shalt take no offence at what they say or do, else thy days shall be made more miserable in the Workhouse wherein thou livest.

6. Thou shalt commit murder, by deserting thy starving children, for we will give thee no assistance to get them food.

7. Thou shalt learn to forget all the dear ties of nature—for we will separate thee from the wife of thy bosom, and the children of thy love.

8. Thou shalt rob thyself of the society and enjoyment of her whom thou hast sworn to protect while life shall last.

9. Thou shalt bear false witness whenever a pauper dies; and should the Coroner or Jury ask you how you live, tell them you live like Lords, and are as happy as Princes.

10. Thou shalt covet the labourer's food, his clothing, his friends, and all the comforts which thou once had, yet shalt thou long in vain, for remember, O Pauper! that the motto of every workhouse is "He who enters here, leaves all hope and comfort behind."

LINES

ON THE DEATH OF AN OLD PAUPER,

WHO WAS

Sentenced to Imprisonment for not Working at the Union Pump.

Oh! Englishmen, come drop a tear or two,
While I relate a thrilling tale of woe;
Of one, who age demanded all the care,
And love, that aged pilgrims ought to share.
This poor old man whose limbs refused to bear,
The weight of more than eighty years of care,
Was brought before a parson, worse than Turk,
And sent to gaol because he could not work.
(Weep, Sons of Britain! mourn your sire's disgrace
Weep, English mothers! hug your rising race,
And pray to him who gave your children breath,
They may not live to die this old man's death.)
In a dark dungeon, he was close confined,
No friend to comfort or to soothe his mind;
No child to cheer his lonesome dying bed,
But soon he rested with the silent dead.
O, ye who roll in chariots proud and gay;
Ye legal murderers there will come a day
When you shall leave your riches all behind,
A dwelling with the ever lost to find;
And your great Master, He whose name is good,
Will hold you guilty of your brother's blood.

BIRT, Printer, 39, Great St. Andrew Street, Seven Dials, London.

1840

'The Poor Law Catechism'.

Sale of ballads supporting John Wilkes outside the Fleet Prison, London, c.1770.

'You noble diggers all stand up now'. Part of the manuscript of Gerard Winstanley's song.

Four years later there followed both 'A New Touch of the Times or Success to True-blew' (see illustration)[47] and 'Wilkes and Granby'.[48] A contemporary print shows three women outside the Fleet prison selling ballads on 'Wilkes and Liberty'. The central figure wears a card with the inscription 'Squire Wilkes again and again'; a boy is chalking the number 45 (that of the celebrated issue of the *North Briton* for which Wilkes was arrested in 1763); and even a girl's doll carries the word 'Freedom' (see illustration).

Nor was it only the opposition which used ballads. During the general election of 1784 the *Morning Herald* reported that 'ministers have actually sent down three coach-loads of ballad-singers to Yorkshire'.[49] A covered wagon with their supplies of pamphlets and ballads went with them. Ten years later, according to William Gardiner, 'Ballad-singers were paid, and stationed at the end of streets, to chaunt the downfall of the Jacobins, and the glorious administration of Mr Pitt.'[50]

Parliamentary proceedings themselves frequently featured in ballads. Successive campaigns for the reform of the franchise mustered popular support in this way. The Reform Bill of 1831, which became law the following year, was supported in a stream of pieces, such as 'Reform and King William for Ever'.[51] Yet if hopes were high, so too was disenchantment:

> They said Reform would do us good,
> It has not yet, I wish it would.
> For thousands they are in want of food,
> May starve and be content yet.
> The farmers and the tradesmen cry,
> They'll bring us all to poverty,
> In England we can no longer stay,
> We must go to America.

Thus 'A True Statement of the Present Times', which looks back wistfully to the past, and sees only the levelling power of death as any consolation in the future:

> In good old times I've heard 'tis true,
> A poor man kept a pig and cow,
> With commons and places to keep them on,
> A poor man might live happy then,
> But now they are all taken in,
> And the rich do reap the gain,
> Workhouses and jails they now have made,
> To send them there 'tis quite a trade.

.   .   .   .

> But the time will come we shall be no more,
> The rich will be equal to the poor
> No more they'll in their coaches ride,
> For death he will pull down their pride,
> And the day draws nigh at hand,
> When we at the bar must stand,
> Then every man will be judged indeed,
> According to the lives they lead.[52]

The fire which largely destroyed the Houses of Parliament in 1834 was treated as a sensational news item by some ballad-printers, but at least one, the radically inclined Willey of Cheltenham, took the opportunity to make political capital:

> Some said that Swing had come to town,
> To stay the Winter season,
> Some said it was an accident,
> And others said 'twas treason.
> And one old man declared aloud,
> His name was Peter Pompey,
> That Guy Faux was in St James's Park,
> Riding on a donkey.
>
> .   .   .   .
>
> For many centuries has these
> Gothic structures stood the weather,
> But oh, alas! their time is come,
> They fell and died together,
> This dreadful loss will shortly fill
> The Nations with alarms,
> The 'Agony Bill, and Poor Law Bill',
> Died in each other's arms.[53]

The so-called Agony Bill,[54] introduced in 1833 by Sir Andrew Agnew, sought to make illegal on Sundays gaming, betting, hunting, bull-baiting, holding fairs or wakes, and indulging in 'any pastime of public indecorum, inconvenience or nuisance'. It was defeated by six votes. On the other hand, the Poor Law Amendment Act (sometimes known as the New Starvation Law) was passed, in 1834. The English system of parish relief went back to Elizabethan times. A compulsory poor rate was first levied in 1572, and the system which grew from it was regulated in Acts of 1597 and 1601. According to Henry Fielding, the Poor Law Act of 1601 'gave a new turn to the minds of the mobility. They found themselves no longer obliged to depend on the charity of their neighbours, nor on their own

industry for a maintenance. They now looked upon themselves as joint
proprietors in the land, and celebrated their independency in songs of
triumph; witness the old ballad which was in all their mouths: "Hang
sorrow, cast away care; The parish is bound to find us." '55 The reference
is to a ballad by Richard Climsall entitled 'Hang sorrow, let's cast away
care' (1668).56 This turned up a few years later in Playford's *Musical
Companion* as a round:

> A Fig for care, why should we spare? the Parish is bound to save us;
> For thou and I and all must dye, and leave the world behind us:
> The Clerk shall sing, the Bells shall ring, and the old wives wind us:
> Sir John shall lay our bones in Clay, where no body means to find us.57

The Amendment Act of 1834 empowered the Poor Law Commissioners to group parishes into unions where workhouses (which also became
known as unions) would be built. The able-bodied might receive no relief
except within the workhouse, where conditions were to be deliberately
made harsh. Married paupers were to be kept apart. The new system was
quickly implemented in the south of England, but was resolutely, even
violently, opposed in the east and the north. The new 'Bastilles', as they
were dubbed, were set on fire or pulled down, and it took up to ten years
before they were established in some northern towns. According to E. J.
Hobsbawm, the act 'created more embittered unhappiness than any
statute of modern British history'.58 It also created, or at least exacerbated,
the fear and detestation of the workhouse which are a leitmotiv of
Victorian literature.

A welter of ballads contributed to the opposition. In October 1834 two
men were arrested at Sculcoats in Yorkshire for 'singing and vending a
ludicrous and inflammatory burlesque upon the New Poor Law Bill'. As a
result, 'their stock-in-trade was burnt by order of the Magistrates, and
they were discharged on promising never to do the like again'.59 Two years
later Dr Kay, the Assistant Commissioner, reported from Norwich,
without giving the source of the funds, that 'every market day about a
dozen blind men are now employed to recite ballads to the poor people on
the market hill, the substance of which is the horrors of the Poor Law
Commissioners' proceedings'.60 A good deal of such material has
survived. 'The grain is well housèd, with plenty in store, / Yet villains
are griping and grinding the poor,' says the writer of 'A Dialogue and
Song on the Starvation Poor Law Bill', in an unconscious echo of the
seventeenth-century 'Clothiers' Delight'. Of the separation of pauper
children from their parents in the workhouse he says: 'This puts me in
mind of Herod the King, / When the Messiah was born, quite evil his

sting.'[61] After a searing description of the penal-style system, Edward
Lamborn of Uffington in 'The New Poor Law and the Farmers' Glory'[62]
promises, again in a biblical vein, that the legislators responsible will go to
hell. With bitter irony, his ballad is written to the tune of 'Home, sweet
Home'.

Nothing is known of Lamborn apart from his name, but the Bradford
balladeer Reuben Holder is better documented (see Introduction). He
wrote a piece on the Bradford anti-Poor Law riot,[63] and another entitled
'The New Starvation Law examined':

> Come you men and women unto me attend,
> And listen and see what for you I have penn'd;
> And if you do buy it, and carefully read,
> 'Twill make your hearts within you to bleed.
>
> The lions at London, with their cruel paw,
> You know they have pass'd a Starvation Law;
> These tigers and wolves should be chained in a den,
> Without power to worry poor women and men.
>
> Like the fox in the farm-yard they slily do creep;
> These hard-hearted wretches, how dare they sleep,
> To think they should pass such a law in our day,
> To bate and to stop the poor widow's pay.
>
> And if they don't like their pay to be stopp'd,
> 'Gainst their own will into th 'Bastile they're popp'd;
> They home must break up, and never return,
> But leave their relations and children to mourn.
>
> .   .   .   .
>
> When a man and his wife for sixty long years
> Have toiled together through troubles and fears,
> And brought up a family with prudence and care,
> To be sent to the Bastile it's very unfair.
>
> And in the Bastile each woman and man
> Is parted asunder,—is this a good plan?
> A word of sweet comfort they cannot express,
> For unto each other they ne'er have access.
>
> Of their uniform, too, you something shall hear,—
> In strong Fearnaught jackets the men do appear;
> In coarse Grogram gowns the women do shine,
> And a ninepenny cap,—now won't they be fine?

On fifteenpence halfpenny they keep them a week;
Had Commissioners this we should have them to seek,
They'd not come to Yorkshire to visit us here,
And of such vile vermin we soon should be clear.

After speaking of the governor, the poorhouse schoolmaster, and the parson, Holder concludes:

Ye hard-working men, wherever you be,
I'd have you watch closely these men, d'ye see;
I think they're contriving, the country all o'er,
To see what's the worst they can do for the poor.

But if that their incomes you wish for to touch,
They'll vapour, and grumble, and talk very much,
The Corn Laws uphold, the poor will oppress,
And send them to th'Bastile in th' day of distress.[64]

Popular Movements

Holder's reference reminds us that another great ballad controversy raged around the passing of the Corn Law of 1815 and the later campaign against it which led to 'Bobby's Sliding Scale' (see illustration)[65] of 1842 and its abolition in 1846. However, as one might expect, extra-Parliamentary popular movements also preoccupied the ballad-writers. Opposition to Midland enclosures in 1607 included a 'libel' thrown into the parish church at Caistor, Northamptonshire, entitled 'The Poor Man's Friend and the Gentleman's Plague', which begins:

You gentlemen that rack your rentes, and throwe downe Land for corne,
The tyme will com that som will sigh, that ever they were borne.
Small care you have for to maintayne trueth or godlines.
You seek your gayne and still the poore oppresse.
Yee throw downe townes and houses to, and seek for honors more.
When we your tenantes arre constraynde to beg from doore to doore.
Redres we will have, or we will knowe whye no.
We will adventure lief & goods and so the matter shall goe.[66]

At about the same time the draining of the fens in East Anglia was being strongly opposed in legal actions, and also by the making of 'libellous songs to disparage the work', such as 'The Powtes [Fowlers'] Complaint':

The feather'd fowls have wings, to fly to other nations;
But we have no such things, to help our transportations;
We must give place (oh grievous case) to horned beasts and cattle,
Except that we can all agree to drive them out by battle.

Wherefore let us intreat our antient water nurses,
To shew their power so great as t'help to drain their purses;
And send us good old Captain Flood to lead us out to battle,
Then two-penny Jack, with skales on's back, will drive out all the cattle.

This noble Captain yet was never known to fail us,
But did the conquest get of all that did assail us;
His furious rage none could assuage; but, to the world's great wonder,
He bears down banks, and breaks their cranks and whirlygigs asunder.[67]

These were manuscript or oral pieces. By contrast, the ballad war of the 1790s was largely conducted in print. Burke's reference in his *Reflections on the French Revolution* (1790) to the 'Swinish Multitude' was seized upon and repeatedly used against him. There was 'The Swinish Multitude's Address to Mr Burke' ('Sold by R. Lee, at the TREE OF LIBERTY, No. 2, St Ann's Court, Dean-Street, Soho; where may be had variety of Cheap Patriotic Publications')[68] and 'Burke's Address to the "Swinish Multitude"'

> Ye vile Swinish Herd, in the Sty of Taxation,
> What would ye be after? disturbing the Nation?
> Give over your grunting—Be off—To your Sty!
> Nor dare to look out, if a King passes by:
> *Get ye down! down! down! Keep ye down!*[69]

'The Tree of Liberty, A New Song, Respectfully Addressed to the Swinish Multitude, by their Fellow Citizen, William England',[70] issued probably in 1794, praises the American and French revolutions and refers approvingly to the execution of Louis XVI. There is also a footnote to 'those Patriotic Worthies, Margarot, Muir, Skirving, Palmer, Gerald, &c. now suffering Exile in the Cause of Parliamentary Reform'. These men who, rather than Bruce and Bannockburn, were the subjects of Burns's 'Scots wha hae' were sentenced to terms of seven or fourteen years' transportation by the Scottish courts in 1793 and 1794 for their political activities. When one of them, Joseph Gerrald, urged in his own defence that Jesus Christ had been a reformer, Braxfield, one of the judges, made the celebrated rejoinder: 'Muckle he made o' that; *he* was hanget.' In 1795 a further sheet ironically gave 'Wholsome Advice to the Swinish Multitude':

> You lower class of human race, you working part I mean,
> How dare you so audacious be to read the works of Pain,
> The Rights of Man—that cursed book—which such confusion brings,
> You'd better learn the art of war, and fight for George our King.
> *But you must delve in politics, how dare you thus intrude,*
> *Full well you do deserve the name of swinish multitude.*

There's the laborer and mechanic too, the cobler in his stall,
Forsooth must read the Rights of Man, and Common Sense and all!
For shame, I desire ye wretched crew don't be such meddling fools,
But be contented in your sphere, and mind King Charles's rules.[71]

The Rights of Man (1791–2) by Tom Paine was itself a reply to Burke's
Reflections. A parody of the national anthem was issued in November 1792
to support the book's arguments and to oppose the war with France:

God save—'The Rights of Man!'
Give him a heart to scan
Blessings so dear;
Let them be spread around,
Wherever Man is found,
And with the welcome sound,
Ravish his ear!

.   .   .   .   .   .

Let us with France agree,
And bid the World be free—
Leading the way.
Let Tyrants all conspire,
Fearless of sword and fire,
Freedom shall ne'er retire,
Freedom shall sway![72]

On the other hand, Paine was attacked in several sheets, such as 'Tom
Pain's Life' (with the chorus of '*Sing Tanta-ra-ra-ra Rogue* PAIN'), 'The
Reformer of England',[73] and 'A New and Loyal Song, intitled Down with
Tom Paine' (to the tune of 'Gee ho Dobbin'):

Come all honest Britons assist me to sing;
Long Life and good Health let us drink to the King
So take off your Hats now, and give him a Cheer,
Then down with the Paineites if any be here,
GOD *save* GEORGE *our* KING,
Let us for ever sing—down with Tom Paine.[74]

The same tune was used a generation or so later for a bitterly ironic
piece, 'The Peterloo Massacre' (see Introduction), by Michael Wilson
(*c.*1763–1840), a Manchester poet and furniture dealer who was 'at heart a
Jacobin' and 'occasionally avowed his political opinions so strongly that his
family were for some time in great fear of his being apprehended'. His was
one of a number of ballads inspired by the Peterloo massacre of 16 August
1819. Some gloried in the action taken by the yeomanry. 'The Answer to
Peter-Loo', for example, begins:

On the sixteenth day of August, eighteen hundred and nineteen,
All in the town of Manchester the REBELLY CREW were seen,
They call themselves reformers, and by Hunt the traitor true,
To attend a treason meeting on the plains of Peter-Loo.

Those hearers at their patron's call came flocking into town,
Both Male and Female Radical, and many a gapeing clown,
Some came without their breakfast, which made their bellies rue;
But got a warm baggin^c on the plains of Peter-Loo.

The events are described in a gleeful and gloating manner, but the writer
stops short of admitting that casualties were caused:

When the Yeoman did advance the mob began to fly,
Some thousands of old hats and clogs behind them there did lie;
They soon pulled down their Treason Flags, and numbers of them flew;
And Hunt they took a prisoner on the plains of Peter-Loo.

Now Hunt is taken prisoner and sent to Lancaster gaol,
With seven of his foremost men, their sorrows to bewail;
His mistress sent to the hospital her face for to renew,
For she got it closely shaven on the plains of Peter-Loo.[75]

On the other side, 'The Mask of Anarchy' was no doubt pre-eminent;
but Shelley's burning anger is expressed in a poem written from distant
Italy. Popular ballads came from nearer at hand. One of them, simply
entitled 'Manchester Meeting',[76] was clearly printed before the event, as
with execution sheets, for sale to people attending on the day. The writer
clearly expected a peaceful protest, for he reports the gathering of 'weaver
lads' from Stockport, Middleton, Oldham, and Ashton, congratulates
Hunt and Wolseley on their speeches, and concludes with the hope that
trade will revive. 'A new song On Peterloo Meeting'[77] is only too well
aware of the real happenings of the day. It has the feeling of a lament, and
is set, no doubt with deliberate care, to the tune 'Parker's Widow' (Parker
being a seaman executed after the Nore mutiny of 1797). In 'The Meeting
at Peterloo', sorrow gives way to anger, and also to hope:

O God above look down on us for thou art just and true,
And those that can no mercy show, thy vengeance is their due.
Now quit this hateful, mournful scene, look forward with this hope,
That every murderer in this land may swing upon a rope.

But soon Reform shall spread around, for sand the tide won't stay,
May all the filth in our land right soon be washed away;
And may sweet harmony from hence in this our land be found,
May we be blest with plenty in all the country round.[78]

^c meal

'The Manchester Massacre',[79] which appeared in *The Radical Reformers'*
New Song Book, breathes lofty defiance, to the tune of 'Scots wha hae'.
Finally, John Stafford, a weaver from Ashton-under-Lyne, who seems
from internal evidence to have been present, wrote two ballads: 'Peterloo'
and 'Another Song concerning Peterloo'.[80] The latter, to the well-known
local tune of 'Joan o' Greenfield', is in the vernacular.

> But as soon as we geet'n as far as Blue Pig,
> A middle aged woman we met at full trig,
> You'd better turn back, unless youn tay your pikes,
> For Manchester's fill'd with o' sorts of scrikes,
> Yooman Cavalry are drunken, if they are not aul be sunk'n,
> And they're killing folk at every street end.
>
> I said to this woman, you tell a strange tale,
> Is that Manchester law! I vow and declare,
> Manchester law mon, and ne'er tall of that,
> For justices and constables are all of one mack[d],
> For what they cannot kill fairly, they tane to th' New Bailey,
> And th' Infirmary's filled wi' lame folk.

The former is in standard English.

PETERLOO

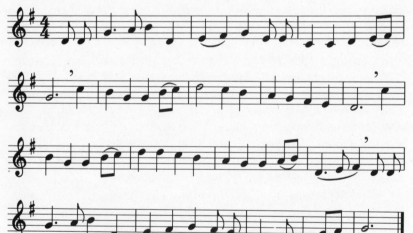

> On the Sixteenth day of August, it was held at Peterloo,
> A just and lawful meeting we knew it to be true,
> With flags and caps of liberty they did assemble there,
> Both in peace and good order, the reformers did appear.

[d] make

The stage was erected and reformers stood all round,
A space was only left between for tyrants and blood hounds,
The constables and vampires they came to rule the day,
Stand steady men, stand steady and their truncheons play'd away.

Your flags and caps of liberty we'll entirely take away,
We'll cut all down before us and show you tyrants play,
For we know you are unarmed, and we'll murder all we can,
Both men, women and children, in spite of 'Rights of Man'.

From Smedley cottage to the hustings, it was crowded all the way.
The patriots joined hand in hand, the band did sweetly play,
Not the least thoughts of murder that did commence that day,
Until that cruel action on Peterloo did sway.

The brave champion of reform, when the hustings mounted on,
He fill'd them all with joy, for to see that valiant man,
To see that gallant hero, with courage bold so fair,
He won the heart of every working-man was there.

The patriots agreed that the champion took the chair,
When he saw female reformers, he smil'd at them being there,
But before he had address'd them all, there came that hellish crew
To murder all poor people that were come to Peterloo.

With their glittering swords and carbines to kill unarmed men
They are worse than Algerines, when strangers meet with them
For they've murdered their own neighbours, that striv'd to fill their purse,
And now they're half-naked must be trampled down with horse.

They form'd themselves four deep, three times over made a charge,
But reformers they stood firm, so they could not play at large
Until a space was opened occupied by their own crew,
For to murder all poor people that were come to Peterloo.

From the outside to the hustings, those ruffians cut away,
I've a charge against you Mr. Hunt, one of the crew did say,
I am ready now to join you, I'm just at your command,
So they took him to the New Bailey, as before it had been plan'd.

Some flags and caps of liberty, these ruffians did destroy,
But still a valiant female her colour she did fly,
Till she could no longer hold it, amongst that murdering crew
So she fell down amongst the rest on the plains of Peterloo.

A poor woman struggling with an infant in her arms,
One of the crew came riding up for to destroy her charms,
She said spare my little creature but that butcher cut her too,
And left her with her infant bleeding on the Plains of Peterloo.

An old woman hearing this story, and believing it was true,
She went to seek her son that was gone to Peterloo,
And as she went along the street, a ruffian she did meet.
She knew him from a child,—she had liv'd in the same street.

This old woman spoke right kindly, and she call'd him by his name,
I know you will not hurt me, Thomas Shelberdine, she said,
But to fulfil his orders like the rest of the same crew,
He cut her down that instant as they did at Peterloo.

So now you special constables, I'll give you all your due,
For backing those proceedings that were done at Peterloo,
Both landlords and shopkeepers, your doors I'll pass by,
If you had no swords or carabines, you made your truncheons fly.

So come all you brave patriots wherever that you be,
You must all unite together to gain your liberty,
And not forget those tyrants, but with justice them pursue,
And all such cruel murderers that went to Peterloo.

'Green upon the Cape', the tune which Stafford had in mind for this song, may be a variant title for 'The Plains of Waterloo' (which was no doubt also intended for 'The Answer to Peter-Loo'). Another air from the same battle was 'With Wellington we'll go', and this was employed with conscious irony for a Peterloo song which 'was much sung in and about Manchester' after the event, and persisted in oral tradition until the 1890s, but only in fragmentary form. 'Although I have met with several people who remember the song being sung, yet I cannot get a complete version of it,' wrote Frank Kidson, who published what he did obtain in his *Traditional Tunes* (1891):

> *With Henry Hunt we'll go, my boys, with Henry Hunt we'll go;*
> *We'll mount the cap of liberty in spite of Nadin Joe.*
> 'Twas on the sixteen day of August, eighteen hundred and nineteen,
> A meeting held in Peter Street was glorious to be seen;
> Joe Nadin^ᶜ and his big bull-dogs, which you might plainly see,
> And on the other side stood the bloody cavalry.[81]

The same metre did duty for 'Battle of Spitaloo', a derisive piece on the breaking up by troops and police ('the red and the blue') of a Newcastle Chartist meeting in 1839.

> On the thirtieth day of July, the Chartists did combine,
> That they would hold a meeting at Newcastle upon Tyne;

ᶜ Deputy Constable of Manchester

In spite of Mayor or Magistrates, they would come up to a man,
But when the Police them attack'd, they took to their heels and ran.
At the Battle of Spitaloo, my boys, at the Battle of Spitaloo—
The Chartists' colours were taken at the Battle of Spitaloo.[82]

The Chartist national convention which is mentioned in this song assembled in London in February 1839, moved to Birmingham in May, and dissolved itself in September after issuing, then rescinding, a call for a general strike. Its arrival in Birmingham was greeted by a stirring ballad, 'Death or Liberty', to the tune of 'Merry Little Soldier':

Britons awake, no longer slumber,
'Tis but to will it, and be free;
Arise, Unite, swell out your number,
Break the chains of slavery!
Let proud tyrants see, you're determined to be free;
Strike the blow, lay tyrants low.
In your ranks have no dissention.
Hail the National Convention.
On to Victory, to Death or Liberty![83]

Various demonstrations and meetings in support of the convention alarmed the magistrates, who swore in hundreds of special constables and sent to London for reinforcements. The London police violently dispersed a meeting in the Bull Ring on 4 July, and the 'Chartist Riots' ensued, starting on 15 July. William Lovett and John Collins declared that 'the people of Birmingham were the best judges of their own rights to meet in the Bull Ring, and the best judges of their own power and resources to obtain justice', for which they were convicted of seditious libel, and sentenced to a year's imprisonment. Their release from Warwick gaol in July 1840 was celebrated by a meeting of 30,000 people and 'A New Song in Praise of W. Lovett & J. Collins'.[84]

Welcoming political figures back from imprisonment became a regular function of ballad-writers, but in the case of John Frost and the other leaders of the Newport rising, rather melancholy pieces were produced on their trial and sentences in a manner typical of the genre. In 'The Trial, Lamentation and Farewell, of the Unfortunate John Frost', which seems to have been issued after the guilty verdict of 9 January 1840 and before the death sentence (later commuted to transportation for life) of 19 January, Frost is made to utter entirely uncharacteristic sentiments:

Oh, in Newport Town I once did dwell,
I harmony and peace,
Where with my wife and children dear,
All blessings did increase,

Until treachery and rebellion,
My spirits did inflame,
Caused me from virtue's paths to stray,
And bring myself to shame.[85]

'The Last Farewell to England of Frost, Williams, and Jones'[86] is a lachrymose valediction, though it does mention the 'tens of thousands' who petitioned for a free pardon. For Frost's true sentiments it is necessary to read his book *The Horrors of Convict Life* (1856), since few of the ballads on him are sympathetic. Chartist ballads in general are not numerous, possibly because the Chartists preferred more respectable anthems and conventional verse forms.

Modern Political Songs

The political song nevertheless continued to flourish. The 1930s produced songs and parodies on unemployment (as we saw in Chapter 3) and the social and political scene. 'When the red revolution comes', to the tune of 'John Brown's Body', had verses such as 'We'll make Anthony Eden wear a fifty-shilling suit' and 'We'll stick a mast in Churchill and float him down the Thames',[87] thus exemplifying the dictum of a writer of 1861: 'We must own that the ballad-singer handles the names and doings of those who sit in high places with a familiarity scarcely equalled by Mr Punch himself.'[88] Even those in lower places did not necessarily escape. Harry Pollitt, secretary of the Communist party, was the subject of 'Harry was a Bolshie'. He is murdered 'by reactionary cads', goes to heaven, and asks to see 'Comrade God'. He plays the 'Internationale' on his harp, and brings the angels out on strike since he does not like the hymns. He is sent to hell, and becomes people's commissar there:

The moral of this story is very plain to tell:
If you want to be a Communist you'll have to go to hell.[89]

The song was written 'for a lark' by a student called Erin Williams at a National Unemployed Workers' Movement camp in 1935, and became widely known, in several variants. It was sung by soldiers during the Second World War, and I heard it myself from Boy Scouts on a cross-Channel packet in the 1950s.

Another favourite of the 1930s was 'Red Fly the Banners, O', a political remake of one of the best-known English folk-songs, 'Green grow the Rushes, O'. This, too, has many variants, which shows how widespread it was. The second verse, for example, can be the splendidly dialectical 'Two, two, the opposites, interpenetrating, O'. The whole thing is a curious mixture of international-style socialism and the homely British variety.

RED FLY THE BANNERS, O

I'll sing you one, O.
Red fly the banners, O.
What is your one, O?
One is workers' unity
And ever more shall be, so.

I'll sing you two, O.
Red fly the banners, O.
What are your two, O?
Two, two, the hands of man,
Toiling for his living, O.
One is workers' unity
And ever more shall be, so.

Three . . . Three, three, the rights of man.
Four . . . Four for the four great teachers.
Five . . . Five for the years of the Five Year Plan.
Six . . . Six for the Tolpuddle Martyrs.
Seven . . . Seven for the hours of the working day.
Eight . . . Eight for the Eight Route Army.
Nine . . . Nine for the days of the General Strike.
Ten . . . Ten for the days that shook the world.
Eleven . . . Eleven for the eleven republics.
Twelve . . . Twelve for the works of Lenin.[90]

One of the significant phenomena in post-war Britain has been the re-emergence of Welsh and Scots nationalism. The Free Wales Army in the 1960s used a tune well known in England for:

Tramp, tramp, tramp, the boys are marching,
To join up the F.W.A.
Underneath the Union Jack,
We never will be free,
So let's lift high our Ddraig goch*∫*—
For liberty.[91]

This is one of many Welsh nationalist songs in the English language. Others, often inspired by Irish models, deal with civil disobedience ('Trefechan Bridge'[92]) or direct action ('Remember Cwm Tryweryn'[93] and 'The Abergele Martyrs'[94]) or embody general defiance ('We are not conquered yet'[95]) and derision:

We're looking up England's arsehole,
It's the prettiest view we know.
          —'Anglomanian Anthem'

Guy Fawkes was a hell of a bloke
He thought it would be quite a joke
To send the MPs up in smoke.
God save the King of England.
          —'A Tribute to Guy Fawkes'

∫ red dragon

Let's be kind to Anglo-Saxons
To our neighbours let's be nice
Welshmen, put aside all hatred
Learn to love the bloody Sais*g*.
　—'Let's be kind to Anglo-Saxons'[96]

The Scots, too, have a long and distinguished tradition of nationalist song, of which one example must suffice. On Christmas Day 1951 the Stone of Scone was removed from Westminster Abbey, taken to Scotland, and hidden. Immense publicity ensued, and a great hue and cry. Numerous suspects were interrogated by the police, without success. There is a story that one man, weary of questioning, eventually said that he would reveal who had stolen the stone. Detectives leaned forward eagerly to hear the identity of the culprit: 'Edward I' was the name given. A whole crop of songs, by such writers as T. S. Law, Sidney Goodsir Smith, Norman McCaig, and Morris Blythman, were published anonymously in a booklet entitled *Song o' the Stane*. There was also a piece by the singer John McEvoy, called 'The Wee Magic Stane'.

THE WEE MAGIC STANE

Oh the Dean o' Westminster wis a powerful man,
He held 'a the strings of the state in his hand.
But with all this great business it flattered him nane,
Till some rogues ran away wi' his wee magic stane.
Wi' a too ra li oora li oora li ay.

Noo the stane had grat pow'rs that could dae such a thing
And withoot it, it seemed, we'd be wantin' a king,
So he called in the polis and gave this decree—
'Go an' hunt oot the Stane and return it tae me'.

g English

So the polis went beetlin' up tae the North
They huntit the Clyde and they huntit the Forth
But the wild folk up yonder just kiddit them a'
Fur they didnae believe it was magic at a'.

Noo the Provost o' Glesca, Sir Victor by name,
Was awfy pit oot when he heard o' the Stane
So he offered the statues that staun' in the Square
That the high churches' masons might mak a few mair.

When the Dean o' Westminster wi' this was acquaint,
He sent for Sir Victor and made him a saint,
'Now it's no use you sending your statues down heah',
Said the Dean, 'but you've given me a jolly good ideah'.

So he quarried a stane o' the very same stuff
An' he dressed it a' up till it looked like enough
Then he sent for the press and announced that the stane
Had been found and returned to Westminster again.

When the reivers found oot what Westminster had done,
They went aboot diggin' up stanes by the ton
And fur each wan they feenished they entered the claim
That this was the true and original stane.

Noo the cream o' the joke still remains tae be tellt,
Fut the bloke that was turnin' them aff on the belt
At the peak o' production was so sorely pressed
That the real yin got bunged in alang wi' the rest.

So if ever ye come on a stane wi' a ring
Jist sit yersel' doon and appoint yersel' king
Fur there's nane wud be able to challenge yir claim
That ye'd croont yersel' king on the Destiny Stane.[97]

Similarly derisive songs emerged in Scotland during the CND protests
of the early 1960s against the stationing of Polaris submarines in the
Clyde. 'Ban Polaris—Hallelujah'[98] was sung to the tune of 'John Brown's
body', while 'Yankee Doodle' served for:

Chase the Yankees oot the Clyde
Away wi' Uncle Sammy,
Chase the Yankees oot the Clyde
An' send them hame tae mammy.[99]

Other pieces drew on the Scottish music-hall tradition, and others still on
children's songs. 'Ding Dong Dollar' was based on 'Oh ye canny shove yer

granny aff a bus', which derived its tune from 'She's coming round the mountain':

> O ye canny spend a dollar when ye're deid,
> O ye canny spend a dollar when ye're deid;
> Singing ding, dong, dollar, everybody holler,
> Ye canny spend a dollar when ye're deid.[100]

These songs were widely sold in sixpenny booklets. They travelled to America, where they were taken up by Pete Seeger. Samuel Marshak, the translator of Burns and Shakespeare, produced Russian versions.

Other songs opposing the military use of nuclear power are considered in Chapter 8. Protest against the civil nuclear industry has also produced songs. Concern about the environment in general and the dangers of nuclear power in particular, has grown enormously in recent years. The disaster at Chernobyl in 1986 profoundly affected public opinion, though it came too late to be considered in the long-running public enquiry on the proposal to build a PWR reactor at Sizewell in Suffolk. The Layfield Report has found in favour of the Central Electricity Generating Board's proposal, to the disgust of its opponents. The board's huge resources allowed it to mount a skilful television advertising campaign, whereas Greenpeace's reply was deemed political, and disallowed. Opponents, however, have made use of songs like 'Still in the Memory',[101] by Leon Rosselson, and 'The Sizewell ABC', by Tim Laycock.

THE SIZEWELL ABC

A is for the atoms which we love to split,
B is for the bomb—you're all living near it.
C is for the cost which will be very high,
D is the danger we always deny.
So merrily, so merry are we,
No smoothies on earth like the CEGB.
We spend public money for all we are worth,
And our latest reactor could cost you the earth.

E's the exhibition so glossy and true,
F is the fools that we're making of you.
G is the government, our plans they adore;
H is for Harrisburg which we ignore.

Now I's the inquiry we've rigged up for you,
J is for jobs—they'll be only a few.
K is for kilowatts made expensively.
But low level fall-out we throw in for free.

M is for Magnox too old and too tame,
N is for nuclear, it's out favourite game.
O is the outfall that warms up the tide
And P's the plutonium we make on the side.

Q is for queer goings on by the sea,
R is for radioactivity.
S is the swimming pool we'll build for you
When the truth has been told and our plans are forced through.

U is the underground bunkers you'll need,
V is for very strange business indeed.
W's the wool we've pulled over your eyes
And X marks the spot where your town used to lie.

Now Y and Z just don't fit what I play,
They're practically useless but won't go away.
In fact just like Sizewell, I hope you'll agree,
One 'A' is enough, there's no need for a 'B'.[102]

8

WAR AND PEACE

THE Falklands war of 1982 was too short in duration and too limited in scope to give rise to a body of verse and song comparable with that produced, say, in the First World War. One man involved, David Tinker, might have proved to be a latter-day Wilfred Owen; but he was killed (like Owen himself) late in the conflict, and his war poems perished with him, though his letters and earlier poems survived to be published by his father as *A Message from the Falklands* (1982). At least two songs were written later by non-combatant opponents of the war. Dave Rogers's 'The Malvinas' begins as a traditional-style lament, to the tune of the 'The Young Trooper Cut Down in his Prime' (which deals with the ravages not of war but of venereal disease):

> As I passed through Portsmouth I heard a yound woman
> Lamenting her husband, one morning in May;
> For his body lies cold in the far South Atlantic;
> Down at the bottom of San Carlos Bay.

Then the piece turns to bitter political comment and strongly anti-war sentiments:

> Once more the old cry is for queen and for country.
> Like Suez and Cyprus we've heard it before.
> How long will they cling to that damn' scrap of empire?
> How many more lives will be wasted in war?[1]

Roger Woddis's poem 'Sick Parade', later set to music by Peter Coe, springs from the presence of the wounded and the spectre of the dead at the victory celebrations. Referring to the singing of 'Rule Britannia' and the like, it says:

> None of the songs that were chorused
> Nor any brave words that were said
> Could banish the ghost from the banquet
> Or silence the voice of the dead.[2]

Battle

The work of writers such as Rogers and Woddis was dedicated to opposing a war, but ballads with favourable comments on battles, campaigns, and wars were part of the stock-in-trade of singers for centuries. The defeat of the Spanish Armada in 1588 occasioned twenty-four pieces,[3] of which only four have survived, three of them by 'the Balletting Silke Weaver of Norwich', Thomas Deloney (?1563–1600). 'The Queen's Old Soldiers',[4] from about the same time, celebrates the achievements of Drake, Raleigh, and a long list of other military men, including some engaged in 'the Irish Wars'. The tune later came to be called 'The Fine Old English Gentleman' (see Chapter 2). 'Lord Willoughby'[5] tells the story of an unspecified battle in which 1,500 Englishmen, led by Peregrine Bertie, Lord Willoughby of Eresby, defeat a Spanish army of 40,000 men. C. H. Firth believes the battle in question to be that of Nieuport, which took place in Holland in 1601.[6] The ballad, which was probably not written before 1624, fails to mention that the English soldiers were serving in a Dutch army.

> The fifteen[th] day of *July*, with glistering speare and shield,
> A famous fight in *Flanders* was foughten in the field:
> The most couragious officers was *English* captains three;
> But the bravest man in Battel was brave Lord *Willoughby*.

The ballad's popularity is attested by a series of broadside reprints, which continued until the eighteenth century. The career of another commander, John Churchill, duke of Marlborough, was celebrated in a similar manner. 'The Soldiers Lamentation for the Loss of their General',[7] published in 1712, refers to his dismissal by Queen Anne the previous year, and reviews his many victories. 'Lord Marlborough' is another valediction, this time put into the mouth of the dying general himself. His patriotic fervour is undimmed; as he recalls past campaigns, and in particular the battle of Ramillies, he says: 'Fight on, my boys, for fair England, / We'll conquer or we'll die.'[8] No text is extant earlier than nineteenth-century broadsides, which is perhaps why Marlborough is made to spurn riches (whereas he was lavishly rewarded, not least by Blenheim Palace, for his successes). The pathos, patriotism, and nobility of the piece must have been attractive to singers and their listeners, for several versions (with sumptuous tunes, incidentally) survived orally until recent times. Oddly enough, Marlborough has been remembered by the French, too, in 'Malbrouck s'en va-t-en guerre'.

It was quite common for battles to be celebrated in ballads, and these were usually a mixture of reportage and myth-making. A single battle might occasion several different pieces. The battle of Dettingen (1743), for example, the last in which a reigning British monarch (George II) personally commanded on the field, features in at least two broadsides and a song, 'The Rose of Dettingen',[9] which was cherished until recent times by one of the regiments involved, the 12th (Suffolk).

Many such pieces proved ephemeral, such as two on the Jacobites' defeat at Culloden and one of their retreat from Preston in 1745. Duke William was not to pass even into English oral tradition as a hero. On the other hand a powerful body of Jacobite songs[10] has remained widely known in Scotland to this day.

Even English commanders popular in their own time had no guarantee of immortality in ballads. John Manners, marquis of Granby, was loved by his men because of his concern for their welfare, combined with his courage, honesty, and intolerance of corruption. He is remembered for galloping so furiously after the French during the battle of Warburg (1760) that his wig flew off, revealing his pate and giving rise to the phrase 'going for them bald-headed', which has remained in the language. His likeness is still to be seen on inn signs, partly, it is said, because he paid off his NCOs with a gratuity which enabled them to set up as innkeepers. 'The Marquis of Granby's March'[11] is a paean of praise to him, and he is mentioned as the 'soldier's friend' in ballads on the battles of Minden (1759) and Warburg.[12] These were presumably written in England from accounts published in newspapers or furnished by returning eye-witnesses. There is evidence, though, that ballads in a similar vein were written by soldiers themselves. One Todd, a pioneer corporal, noted in his diary on July 1761 after the battle of Vellinghausen that 'this Instant a Song is Composed of the Action whereof I got a copy of it from our Serjeant Major Roe'. He then gives the full text of 'A New Song in praise of Lord Granby & his Brave Veterans who Boldly Engaged the Enemy and gain'd a Compleat Victory, July 15th & 16th 1761':

> Sound Praises of fame in the Name of Granby
> Great Wonders is done in High Germany
> Upon the 15th of July the French gave attack
> Our Left wing repuls'd them & soon drove them back.
> *Chorus ye Sons of Britania and sing,*
> *Success to Great Granby & Long Live the King.*
>
> Next Morning by two we Briskly begun
> Over Blood being restless wou'd not let them a Lone
> A Brigade with Colours we took prisoner
> With pieces of Cannon whilst they were in fear

They are always Boasting of Courage I say
But upon our Approach they hasten away
For when Granby Appears they are always in fear
Crying out Mon Dieu Quarter Anglateer

So swiftly he rode while their Bullets they did send
Oh Brittain thank Heaven for such a kind friend
Both Country & Soldiers write & agree
In Sounding the praise of Great Granby

He ne'er so the Army One day for to want
If Gold could it purchase tho' ever so scant
Gave us Beer gave us Brandy & all we disired
We thank you Lord Granby was all he required.[13]

Although Todd was not the writer of this song, its sentiments are his, as can be seen from his account of the battle. The song lacks picturesque detail like that of the 'White spotted Dog' observed 'running backwards & forwards from the Enemy a good while untill he was Kill'd', and the crispness of observation in passages such as this: 'As we were retreating back through a deal of Bushes, & thick wood, a Stout, Clean Granidier Lay surrounded with Bushes with one of his thighs shatter'd to pieces by one of our Cannon Balls & made great Lamentation.' The song fails, too, to mention the large number of casualties on both sides, but it accords with the exultation in victory felt by the men involved: 'Thus Ended this Memorable Battle of Fellinghausen or Battle of the wood much to the Honour of our Commander & the Defferent Corps Engaged therein as Each Soldier minding no fatigues but Mirth & Jollity Appear'd in Every mans Countenance.' Todd repeatedly praises Granby: on the evening of the first day he 'Wrapt'd himself in his great Coat & Lay down upon the ground amongst us which greatly Encouraged our men althoug we were in the greatest wants of alsorts of Necessarys at this time & Expecting to Engage every Moment'. During the second day: 'our Noble Commander the Marquis of Granby . . . was in all places Encouraging us during the Action which caused his brave Veterans to drive the Enemy of.' Finally, on 18 July, he wrote: 'Lord Granby out of His own generosity Order'd a Bullock to Each Regiment of the English that was Engaged the 15th Instant & half a Loaf of Bread with Half a pint of [word missing] to Each man.'[14]

Granby's contemporary, Wolfe, was even more widely celebrated in song, but it seems that a little time was needed for the full impact of his death to register. 'The Siege of Quebec' (1759)[15] records his death, together with that of Monkton, but gives pride of place to Brigadier Townsend, Wolfe's subordinate. As it began to sink in, the magnitude of

the victory made a powerful impression, however, as did Wolfe's death in
the hour of his triumph. Stories circulated of his request for news of the
battle as his eyesight failed after his third and fatal wound, and his remark
that since the French were giving way, he was content to die. These,
together with an account of his parting for the campaign from his fiancée
(Katherine Lowther), feature in a ballad beginning 'Cheer up your hearts
young men let nothing fright you',[16] which was published and several times
reprinted in North America, though not apparently in Britain. On the
same sheet is a poem on Wolfe's death by Tom Paine which did find its
way to Britain. During the War of Independence it was adapted to fit the
deaths of the American generals Warren (killed at Bunker's Hill) and
Montgomery (who died, ironically, while leading an assault on Quebec).
The poem's highly literary style can be judged from the opening lines:

> In a sad mouldering cave where the wretched retreat
> Britannia sat wasted with care.
> She mourn'd for her Wolfe and exclaim'd against fate,
> And gave herself up to despair.

Another piece, this time by an anonymous hand, sets out to link Wolfe
with antique virtue, but is unfortunate in its choice of reference:

> When ancient Romans did lament,
> And Nero's death gave discontent
> Well may England then complain,
> Her chiefest glory, Wolfe, is slain.
> *Mourn England, mourn, mourn and complain,*
> *Thy chiefest glory, Wolfe, is slain.*[17]

The chorus, substantially, was later used for a lament on the death of
Nelson, whose culminating achievement, like Wolfe's, came at his death:

> Mourn, England, mourn, O mourn and complain,
> For the death of Lord Nelson who died on the main.

The best known of the Wolfe songs 'Bold General Wolfe', was still
'vastly popular ... throughout England' at the end of the nineteenth
century, according to Baring-Gould,[18] and a version was discovered in
oral circulation in Canada as recently as 1957.[19] The concluding
apostrophe of a broadside text, with its 'soldier's friend' reference (as with
Granby), may give one of the keys to Wolfe's popularity:

> So let all commanders do as I have done before
> Be a soldier's friend, be a soldier's friend
> They'll fight for ever more.[20]

The American War of Independence gave rise to a considerable body of songs, on both sides. One of them, 'The Maiden's Lamentation', was written down in 1778 by Timothy Connor, an American seaman imprisoned at Forton, near Portsmouth:

THE MAIDEN'S LAMENTATION

It was on a summers morning the 14th Day of May
The Norfolk slipt her cable and for Boston sail'd away
The sun it shin'd most glorious to Boston we were bound
Where the Hills and fields were lined with pretty girls alround

There was a youthful Damsel all in her blooming years
Made woeful Lamentations her eyes was full of tears
Twas for her best beloved as you shall understand
Who wanted to travel into some foreign Land

Little she thought of parting with her own hearts delight,
Until he came and told her he must go out and fight
For to defend the Nation the Land that we live in
And as he did salute her these words she did begin

O! marry me sweet William O Marry me I pray
My heart is full of sorrow as very well it may
The cause of all my weeping to you it is well known
O Marry me sweet William and leave me not alone

Suppose that I should meet a Damsel that is charming fair and gay
To whom I'd take a fancy Molly what would you say
Would not you be offended, no, no I'd love her too
I'd step aside sweet William, while she did pleasure you

Well answered Dearest Molly, these words are very kind
They are so sweet and pleasant, they always shall be mine
But when we're all in battle, what will you do there then
When we are all Sailors, and Vallient fighting Men

Where Cannons they are roaring and bullets they do fly
And drums and trumpets sounding to drown the dismal cry
And soldiers by a bleeding a dismal sight to see
A Stay at home Dear Molly and do not follow me

O do not talk of dangers for love I do design
To see the line of battle and there to spend my time
Along with you I'll venter for all New England's pride
And fear no kind of danger while you are by my side.[21]

The song has an extraordinary resonance, standing as it does at the head
of a lengthy line of descent, of which, more shortly. In addition, its theme
of a woman's insistence, or attempted insistence, on accompanying her
man into battle, either on land or at sea, was remarkably widespread. The
notion of the female warrior, sometimes fighting as a woman but often
disguised as a man, produced a plethora of ballads with titles like 'The
Gallant She-Souldier' (c.1655),[22] 'The Famous Woman Drummer'
(1658),[23] 'The Soldier's Delight; or, The She-Voluntier' (1674–9),[24] 'The
Female Warrior' (?1678–89),[25] 'The Maiden Warrior' (1682–96),[26] and
'The Woman Warrior' (1710–12).[27] There were many more in a similar
vein, and, judging by titles like 'La Fille-soldat'[28] the vogue extended to
France, too.

Such songs are a tribute to feminine spirit, resourcefulness, and also
pugnacity, but one wonders whether their underlying rationale might not
have been to popularize and humanize soldiering and warfare. A good part
of their attraction lay in the sexual tension engendered by the thought of a
woman's presence among men in the guise of a man:

> Every night to my quarters I came.
> I was no way ashamed to lie with a man,
> And pulling off my breeches to myself I often smiled:
> To lie with a soldier and a maid all the while.[29]

So reflects the eponymous female drummer in a song which mentions the
siege of Valenciennes (1793), but continued to circulate until the twentieth
century.

Oddly enough, there was indeed a female drummer at Valenciennes.
Her name was Mary Ann Talbot (1778–1808),[30] and it is possible that her
story inspired the song. Other biographical or autobiographical accounts
of soldiering by women concern Hannah Snell (1723–92)[31] and Christian

Davies (1667–1739),[32] both of whom received official pensions. A Thomasine Clark is recorded in 1655 as having served for some five years as a soldier, and 'some time Drummer to the Company'.[33] The last was possibly Dorothy Lawrence, who in a book published in 1919 described herself as 'the only English woman soldier, late Royal Engineers, 51st Division, 179th Tunnelling Company'.[34] She was very different from her predecessors, of whom she was ignorant. In the first place she was 'a lady'. Further, she managed only ten days near the front, in 1915, which were mainly spent in hiding. She did dress in a soldier's uniform ('In my estimation there can be nothing immodest in the appearance of a woman dressed in male attire'), but she took no part in military routine. Her venture had journalistic motives, and was made possible only through the help and connivance of several soldiers: 'Only later I realised how splendidly these men *had* behaved—rough soldiers, away from civilisation, surrounded only by the coarsening influence of war! Yet no one harmed this fool of an English girl!' Dorothy Lawrence was soon discovered and, after a fortnight's confinement in a convent, was sent home, having been obliged to promise not to tell her story until official permission was forthcoming. Perhaps she did have a little of the spirit, if not the toughness and endurance, of her sisters of the past.

The intended military adventure of 'The Maiden's Lamentation' of 1778 moved in the 1790s from Boston to Spithead, then in successive adaptations to Egypt for both the naval and the army battles of the Nile (1798 and 1801), then to Lisbon (1808) for an engagement during the Peninsular War. Later still, the song did duty for the Sikh wars of the 1840s in India and the American Civil War.[35]

'The Brags of Washington',[36] another song of the American Revolution, also fathered numerous progeny. Its tune was used for Wellington's victories in Spain,[37] and was in turn updated for Waterloo:

> With Wellington we'll go, we'll go, with Wellington we'll go,
> For Wellington commanded us on the plains of Waterloo.[38]

With deliberate irony the same thing was parodied after Peterloo (see Chapter 7).

During the French and Napoleonic wars ballads poured in profusion from the ballad presses. Gavin Greig has commented: 'The twenty years that ended with Waterloo have left more traces on our popular minstrelsy than any other period of our history has done.' He adds: 'The historian might find it worth while to study these soldier-songs. He might learn some things that are not to be found in dispatches.'[39]

The battle of Waterloo alone produced numerous pieces. 'The Plains of

Waterloo'[40] (usually beginning 'On the sixteenth day of June, my boys, in Flanders where we lay') gives a detailed narrative of the action, starting two days before. It is said to have been written immediately after the battle by Sergeant Grant of the 92nd regiment (later called the 'Gordon Highlanders'). One broadside prescribes the tune 'Hanoverian March'.[41] Another tune was obtained by Christie[42] from a veteran of Waterloo and the 92nd regiment who died in 1857. The text remains remarkably similar in the different versions but in a variant heard until at least the 1880s at the hiring fairs of north-east Scotland, the last, triumphant verse was amended to run:

> Here's a health to Queen Victoria,
> In peace lang may she reign;
> Likewise the Duke of Wellington,
> That noble son of Erin.
> For though he was a Tory knave,
> His courage aye was true,
> He displayed both skill and valour too
> That day at Waterloo.[43]

Leaving aside this coda, the tone of such pieces is almost always elevated, bellicose, and ultra-patriotic, and it frequently characterizes songs on colonial wars. There were also sentimental songs, on the French, as on other wars. 'Bloody Waterloo'[44] has the theme of a soldier coming unrecognized to his true love on 'the banks of Clyde', and first rather perversely announcing his own death, then his safe return. 'Elwina of Waterloo'[45] tells of a wounded soldier's rescue from the battlefield by 'a maiden most charming'. Both songs end happily in marriage.

A belligerent, even derisive tone appears in such ballads as 'The Devil and Buonaparte',[46] 'The Pitman's Revenge against Buonaparte',[47] and 'Bonaparte's Disasters'[48] (in Russia). The invasion threat is treated in 'Invasion. A New Song', which contemptuously dismisses the landing made in Wales in 1797: 'But the girls of that country met these gasconaders, / And down fell the arms of our desperate invaders.'[49] 'The Boxing Match between John Bull and Bonaparte', on the same theme, concludes:

> Our Tars will at sea, box the Corsican elf,
> They're a match for his Second, the Devil himself;
> From Bonaparte and his host no Invasion we fear,
> John Bull will him box and keep the coast clear.[50]

The sporting metaphor, the arrogant and unrealistic attitude, the unjustifiably light-hearted approach: all these are common currency in British war ballads produced primarily for civilian consumption in many different periods.

The distinction between civilian and military singers and audiences is, of course, often blurred. Sergeant Grant wrote 'The Plains of Waterloo', which was widely printed on ballad-sheets, then sung for at least a hundred years after the battle. Within a few days of another battle, that of the Alma in the Crimea, Corporal John Brown of the Grenadier Guards wrote his song 'The 20th of September, 1854'.[51] This soon reached the streets as a ballad, part of the last great outpouring of the genre. It was one of several on the Alma, of which the best-known is 'The Battle of Alma'[52] by James Maxwell of Tirmeel, Northern Ireland, which became widely popular and has remained in oral tradition to the present day. Other battles—Balaclava, Inkerman, Sebastopol—inspired other ballads. Generals were celebrated, such as Napier, and Florence Nightingale was not forgotten. In all this, the mood remains cheerful and martial. Even the disastrous charge of the Light Brigade aroused enthusiasm in a song published as both sheet music and street ballad, which again remains current orally to this day:

> And they were but six hundred, 'gainst two score thousand foes.
> Hemmed in with furious cannon, and crushed with savage blows,
> Yet fought they there like heroes, for our noble England's fame,
> Oh, glorious charge! heroic deed! what honour crowns thy name.
> Four hundred of those soldiers fell, fighting where they stood,
> And thus that fatal death vale they enriched with English blood.
> Four hundred of those soldiers bequeathed their lives away,
> To the England they had fought for on that wild October day.
> *Oh! 'tis a famous story, proclaim it far and wide,*
> *And let your children's children re-echo it with pride;*
> *How Cardigan the fearless, his name immortal made,*
> *When he crossed that Russian Valley with his famous Light Brigade.*[53]

Criticism of the inept conduct of the war was apparently left in the Crimea to such people as William Russell, *The Times* correspondent, and at home to a few voices opposed to the Government. Yet a letter of 1855, written 'from the Camp' in the Crimea, and commenting on 'the singing of old songs, catches, glees, and choruses, [which] forms a principal feature in the amusements', goes on to suggest an element of protest:

During the long evenings of the past summer our men used to sit in some old redoubt or abandoned trench, and there the song and toast went round, and once or twice I heard some original and extemporaneous verses, *apropos* to the time and place, to our Government at home, to our Generals at headquarters, to the Czar in his palace, and to Johnny Russ in front, which were not only witty and satirical, but highly indicative of poetic genius.[54]

The only example quoted is an improvised addition to 'The British Grenadiers', but one wonders whether the Crimean troops were not singing something along the lines of the soldiers' songs of the First World War, with their resilience, ribaldry, and cynicism.

The semi-official songs of that war, like the sentimental 'Keep the Home Fires burning'[55] or 'Goodbyee',[56] were sung by soldiers and civilians alike. The improvised songs of the march, the barracks and the trenches became known to the general public in bowdlerized versions after the war. A selection from both kinds appeared in 1930 as the Daily Express Community Song Book No. 3, *Songs that Won the War*. The unofficial songs were in a few cases traditional ('Never trust a sailor')[57] or based on traditional models ('The Old Black Bull'[58]); but for the most part they were parodies of hymns ('Raining, Raining, Raining',[59] from 'Holy, Holy, Holy') or popular songs of the day ('I don't want to be a Soldier', from 'On Sunday I walk out with a Soldier'):

> I don't want to be a soldier,
> I don't want to go to war,
> I'd rather stay at home,
> Around the streets to roam,
> And live on the earnings of a well-paid whore.
> I don't want a bayonet up my arse-hole,
> I don't want my ballocks shot way.
> I'd rather stay in England,
> In merry, merry England,
> And fuck my bleeding life away.[60]

Disenchantment

The tradition of songs celebrating battle and war is mingled with a dissident, subversive vein, both military and civil. Conditions of life in the Army and the Navy are bitterly criticized, while people left behind lament the effects of war on their communities, together with the heartbreak to individuals caused by separation and bereavement.

Men joined the armed forces for a variety of reasons: to escape from hunger and poverty, domestic problems or debt; to gratify an impulse; to seek adventure and excitement. In some cases they were persuaded to volunteer. In others, they were forcibly taken for service in time of war. The Navy was usually less popular than the Army, and thus impressment for it was used more widely. During the seventeenth century it seems to have been accepted with resignation, but resistance gradually grew. In his recent book on the Georgian navy, *The Wooden World* (1986), Professor Rodger suggests that 'The press was highly distasteful to all, but it was accepted by every one who had any experience of the subject as an unavoidable necessity.' This squares oddly with his later statement that because of opposition to impressment, 'Riots and fights ashore were commonplace, and pitched battles occurred between incoming merchant-men and the Impress service's cutters or boats.' He contends of 'those fights of which something is known' that 'they appear to have a factor in common': 'In every case the attacks were led or instigated by deserters from the Navy.' This does not apply to the incident which he describes in which a whaler, the *Golden Lyon*, was boarded by a press-gang as she was coming into Liverpool docks. The whalermen overpowered the crew of the press-cutter and dispersed ashore. The conclusion was not happy, though Rodger relates it with considerable satisfaction:

There the incident might have ended as many had done before, but Captain Nightingale of the *Vengeance* was a determined man, and though pressing ashore in Liverpool was reckoned impossible, he organised a raid that night, surprised the men of the *Golden Lyon* renewing their protections at the Custom House, and carried off seventeen of them, firing over the heads of the pursuing mob. Nightingale flogged several of the men who had fired on his boats.[61]

Rodger does not say whether the 'pursuing mob' was composed of naval deserters, nor does he comment on the legality of the punishment ordered by Captain Nightingale for actions taken by men before they were under his command.

The ballad evidence on impressment points in a different direction. According to Bruce and Stokoe, the press-gang on Tyneside 'was a fertile theme for local rhymesters from the earliest period of its operation down to living memory'. They quote a verse which ends, in response to the question, 'Where hes ti been, maw canny hinny?':

> Aw've been ti the norrard,
> Cruising back and forrard,
> But daurna come ashore
> For Bover and his gang.[62]

Captain John Bover died in 1782, 'having for several years previous', as a memorial tablet in Newcastle cathedral points out, 'filled with the highest credit the arduous situation of regulating officer of this port'.

Bruce and Stokoe also quote a song beginning 'Here's the tender coming, / Pressing all the men', together with 'O the lousy cutter'.[63] The words and music of the latter first appeared in *Blackwood's Edinburgh*

Magazine in 1821. The Tynesider Thomas Doubleday, soap-manufac-
turer by trade and radical thinker by inclination, described in a letter under
the curious pen-name of Mr Shufflebotham, how he 'went the other day to
bring my nephew Roger home from school, which he was obligated to
leave on account of a fever that had got among them; and a speat of rain
coming down the river, we stopped at O—— to give the beasts a feed till
the wet was over'. While the landlady was 'righting the table and setting me
down a warm glass of rum and water, and Roger a sup of ale', the travellers
heard 'a callant in the kitchen' singing various songs, including:

> O! the weary cutters—they've ta'en my laddie frae me,
> O! the weary cutters—they've ta'en my laddie frae me;
> They've press'd him far away foreign, with Nelson ayont the salt sea.
> O! the weary cutters—they've ta'en my laddie frae me.[64]

In balladry, press-gangs are almost invariably shown in an unfavourable
light. Indeed, the only exception I know is a group of pieces, the first of
which dates from the late seventeenth century, in which a group of women
dressed as soldiers or sailors press fourteen or twenty tailors. The position
here is abnormal because the victims belong to a deeply unpopular trade.[65]
'The Press'd Man's Lamentation' (see illustration)[66] represents the norm.
The press-gang effectively ceased to be used after 1815 (though it was still
listed as a grievance by the women Chartists of Newcastle in 1839), but
songs expressing fear and loathing of it continued in oral tradition for at
least a century afterwards, so deeply ingrained was the popular attitude.[67]
Such songs no doubt also had an appeal as paradigms for oppressive and
arbitrary treatment in other spheres of life.

Soldiers were often recruited less by force than by trickery, persuasion,
or inveiglement. Ballads on victories in battle undoubtedly helped to
glamourize Army service. Some pieces were deliberately aimed at recruit-
ment. 'Over the Hills and far away' is mentioned as early as 1704 in
Farquhar's play *The Recruiting Officer*, and one of its verses mentions
Marlborough. The fine melody and stirring words must have drawn many
a man into the Army:

> Hark, now the drums beat up again,
> For all true soldier gentlemen,
> Then let us 'list and march, I say,
> Over the hills and far away.
> *Over the hills and o'er the main,*
> *To Flanders, Portugal and Spain,*
> *Queen Anne commands and we'll obey,*
> *Over the hills and far away.*[68]

A similar impulse was at work in 'The Scarlet and the Blue':

Hurrah for the scarlet and the blue, and the helmets a-glittering in the sun,
And the bay'nets flash like lighting to the beating of the big bass drum.
Hurrah for dear old England and her flag that's waving in the sky,
When the captain of the reg'ment says, 'We'll conquer or we'll die'.[69]

This was written in the 1870s by John J. Blockley. Its many adaptations include an IRA version of about 1916 which was also sung by members of the International Brigade during the Spanish Civil War. Another martial song, 'Fighting with the 7th Royal Fusiliers',[70] which dates from the 1890s, is said to have produced at a time of dearth 'such an overwhelming rush of recruits that the authorities could easily, had they so chosen, have raised several additional battalions'.[71]

Army service was welcomed by some as an escape from even more oppressive servitude. Even women rejoiced in going, not as female soldiers, but as soldiers' wives. Six men in every hundred were allowed to marry 'on the strength', and their wives were permitted to live with them in barracks and to accompany them abroad. In 'The Sodger Laddie', a ballad printed in 1781, a Scots woman defiantly celebrates her departure.

THE SODGER LADDIE

Chorus

My yellow mou'd*ᵃ* mistress, I bid you adieu,
For I've been too long in slavery with you,
With washing and scouring I'm seldom in bedy
And now I will go with my sodger laddie,
My sodger laddie, my sodger laddie,
The kisses are sweet of a sodger laddie.

With the crust of your loaf, and dregs of your tea,
You fed your lap doggie far better than me,
With rinning*ᵇ* and spinning, my head was unsteady,
But now I will go with my sodger laddie.

For yarn, for yarn, you always did cry,
And look'd to my pirn*ᶜ*, ay as ye went by;
Now the drums they do beat, and my bundle is ready,
And I'll go along with my sodger laddie.

She is well-informed about the duties and dangers of following the regiment.

I'll always be ready, with needle and soap,
For possing*ᵈ* and patching to serve the whole troop,
I'll be loving and kind, and live like a lady,
When I go abroad with my sodger laddie.

In heat of battles, I'll keep on the flank,
With a stone in a stocking, and give them a clank,
If he be knocked down, though he be my daddy,
I'll bring all his clink to my sodger laddie.

For robbing the dead is no thievish trick,
I'll rifle his breeches, and then his knapsack,
But yet on a friend I'll not be so ready,
If he's been acquaint with my sodger laddie.[72]

Other women, less adventurous, were left behind lamenting. 'Jenny's Complaint', written in 1803 by Robert Anderson (1770–1833) of Carlisle, concerns the enlistment of her sweetheart, Jemmy:

To Carel*ᵉ* he set off wi' wheat;
Them ill reed-cwoated fellows
Suin wil'd him in—then meade him drunk:
He'd better geane to th' gallows.[73]

(The song was given a new lease of life in the 1970s through an adaptation by A. L. Lloyd.)[74]

ᵃ mouthed   *ᵇ* running   *ᶜ* bobbin (of spinning wheel)   *ᵈ* washing   *ᵉ* Carlisle

Once a man had accepted the queen's shilling, he was in fact enlisted, though a medical examination and an attestation or oath of allegiance before a magistrate were required to complete the formalities. A man might change his mind before attesting, either by absconding or by paying the sum of a pound, which was known as 'smart money'. Jemmy had gone too far to turn back:

> My fadder would hae paid the smart,
> And show'd a gowden guinea,
> But, lack-a-day! he'd kiss'd the buik,
> And that'll e'en kill Jenny.

Warnings against the blandishments of recruiting parties are frequently given in the form of song. 'The Black Horse' tells how a weaver is accosted at Galway market by a Sergeant Ackeson and first resists, then succumbs to his invitation to join the Light Dragoons. He looks back regretfully:

> Farewell to my old father, likewise my sisters three,
> And fare you well, dear mother, for your face I'll never see;
> And when I'm going through Armagh town you will run in my mind,
> So fare you well sweet Carlow town and the girl I left behind.[75]

The setting reminds us that Irishmen made an important contribution to the British Army. In 1830 they numbered almost 43,000, or just over 42 per cent of its strength. After the Great Famine, numbers declined. As Spiers says, 'The Irish proportion of the army dropped to 27.9 per cent in 1870, 15.6 per cent in 1888, and 9.1 per cent in 1912.'[76] Even so, it remained significant.

Some ballads went far beyond mere expressions of regret over joining up. 'The Countryman's Reply to the Recruiting Sergeant', for example, systematically scrutinizes and rejects the claims made. 'Lots o' glory? Lots o' gammon', says one pointed line.

> "Lots o' gold, and quick promotion?"
> 'Phew! jest look at William Green;
> He's been *fourteen years* a fightin',
> As they call it, for the queen;
> Now he comes home invalided,
> With a sergeant's rank and pay
> But that he is made a captain,
> Or is rich, I arnt heerd say.
>
> "Lots o' fun and pleasant quarters,
> And a soger's merry life;
> All the tradesmen's—farmers' daughters
> Wantin' to become my wife?"

Well, I think I'll take the shillin';
Put the ribbins in my hat!—
Stop! I'm but a country bumpkin,
Yet not quite so green as *that*.

'*Fun?* a knockin' fellow-creatures
Down like ninepins, and that 'ere;
Stickin' bay'nets through and through 'em,
Burnin', slayin', everywhere;
'*Pleasant quarters?*'—werry pleasant!
Sleepin' on the field o' battle,
Or in hospital, or barricks,
Crammed together jest like cattle.

The conclusion is unequivocal:

Strut away then, master sergeant:
Tell yer lies as on ye go;
Make your drummers louder rattle,
And your fifers harder blow:
I shan't be a 'son o' glory',
But an honest workin' man.
With the strength that God has guv me,
Doin' all the good I can.[77]

'The Recruiting Party', written by H. F. Cook to the tune of 'The Bold
Dragoon', is the complete anti-recruiting song. It was issued in 1846, and
the soldiers dying in India to which it refers must have been engaged in the
Sikh wars. The locality is left blank so that the singer can supply his own.

THE RECRUITING PARTY

Come all you lads of —— and listen to my song,
I hope you will not frown on me, let it be right or wrong;
The soldiers now they are in town making such a bother,
With shillings in their hands taking young men from their mothers.
[*Singing*] *Whack row de dow [dow, fal la la la la,*
And whack row de dow dow, fal la la la la].

Four serjeants are in front with swords in their hands,
And quickly followed after by the military band;
Then the privates are in the rear with their colours flying,
While thousands of poor soldiers in India are dying.

If you do enlist, mind what I say, to headquarters you'll be sent,
With a suit of grand clothes on your back, and drill'd till you're content;
With eyes right and left, and stand at easy, keep yourselves in order,
And if you don't attend to them, you'll be kept on bread and water.

When you come from the guardhouse you'll have queer notions in your heart,
To be confined I'll not stop here, I quickly will desert,
To bring you back a file of men will quickly follow after,
With the iron ruffles on your hands march'd back to your own quarters.

Next morning a court martial then will be held on you,
You will be trembling in your shoes, but it is too late to rue;—
A cat o' nine tails is your doom, tied up to the triangle,
So better you had staid at home 'turning your mother's mangle!'

And when that you are growing old, and not fit for guard,
You'll be dismissed from the ranks with a blank discharge;
Then you come home not fit for work, and relations are all dead,
Then up and down the town you must go a begging for your bread.

So all young men take my advice, and do not go and 'list,—
Don't be entrapped by serjeants with shiners in their fist,
But mind your work and stay at home with your sisters and brothers,
And strive to be a credit to your fathers and your mothers.[77]

Those who ignored such warnings, and entered the Army or the Navy, often bitterly regretted the step they had taken. Ballads complaining at the lot of the soldier or sailor attempted to warn off potential recruits. In one printed sheet, 'The Harness', of 1810, which deals (unusually) with conditions on a troop-ship before moving to service life in the Cape, the narrator utters a heartfelt wish:

> If providence ordains it,
> My discharge I could obtain,
> The devils all crimp sergeants
> I would never go again.[79]

In a manuscript song, 'The Indian Compensation', Private John Whitworth reflects:

> There are country chaps and Townsmen too
> Perhaps join the army
> Recruiting sergeants at each fair
> Will c[h]arm them with their blarney
> Your Regiment now in India is
> And that a glorious station
> You wont wear half your clothing out
> And they will give you compensation
>
> The men thats going home this year
> And has their time complited
> Will spread the news among their friends
> In India how they are treated
> The would be soldiers that I'll swear
> Wont leave their situations
> When they have heard the proper version of
> Our India compensation.[80]

Another disincentive was the use of corporal punishment, which persisted in the Army until 1881. Even then, there were those unhappy with its abolition: Queen Victoria, for example, expressed anxiety that no substitute punishment could be found. Frank Peel in *The Risings of the Luddites* (1880) gives an account of the punishment of a soldier sentenced to receive 300 lashes for refusing to fire on 'his brothers' who were attacking Cartwright's Mill in 1812. In fact, after 25 lashes the rest of the flogging (inflicted publicly, in front of the mill) was remitted at the request of Cartwright. Even 25 lashes was agonizing, and the description raises further doubts about Mary Anne Talbot's dismissive accounts:

Stepping forward and measuring the distance for an instant the man raises the whip, it whistles swiftly through the air and descends on the white back of the soldier on which a broad red line appears, while underneath the muscles quiver visibly. Again and again the whip is raised and descends, and by and by the onlookers are shocked to observe that the skin is broken, the blood begins to trickle

slowly down, and the sight becomes sickening. The women in the crowd, for there
are many present, turn their eyes from the sight, and even stout-hearted men
cannot forbear to express their pity for the poor wretch, who with pale face and
firmly compressed lips, suffers the dreadful blows.[81]

A series of scandals kept the public campaign against flogging on the
boil. There was the punishment of Alexander Somerville at Birmingham
in 1832, for writing to a newspaper to say that he and his comrades in the
Scots Greys would 'never, never, never' have 'raised an arm' against 'the
liberties of our country'.[82] Money was raised to buy Somerville out of the
Army. Private John White of the 7th Hussars was not so fortunate: he died
after a flogging in 1846, and thus inspired a national outcry and a crop of
ballads.[83] Private Robert Slim also died after a flogging in 1867.[84] Several
campaigns against flogging produced ballads with titles like 'Never Flog
our Soldiers' (see illustration)[85] and 'Lay of the Lash' (oddly coupled on
the same sheet with the national anthem):

> Be tied to the halberds, or grating, and whipped,
> WHY should the soldier, or sailor—back stripped—
> While the 'officer'—acting, perhaps, very much worse—
> Is secured from the Lash, by the strength of the purse?
> By the strength of the purse! for to what, but to that,
> Does he owe his commission, 'signed, sealed', and all that?
> So raise the stern cry, nor till death let it fall:—
> 'The Lash be for none—or the Lash be for all!'[86]

The perennial answer to grievance was desertion, though if this were
unsuccessful, it of course brought further punishments—flogging, confinement, even execution—in its wake. 'A warning for all Souldiers that
will not venture their lyves in her Maiestye's cause and their Countrie's
right; wherein is declared the lamentation of *William Wrench*, who, for
running away from his captaine, with other two more, were executed for
the same fact, in severall places about *London*, upon the viii. day of
September last, 1600' is one compendiously titled sheet, supposedly by
Wrench, 'Made with his owne hand, after his condemnation, in *Newgate*'.[87]
Similar in tone, though with a happy ending, is 'A Warning to Deserters',[88]
published in the eighteenth century. It tells how Hugh Stenson, a 17-year-
old soldier from Ashbourne in Derbyshire (the details may indicate a true
story or have been invented for verisimilitude) deserts his regiment in
Ireland so as to return to his sweetheart, Molly Green, of Whitchurch,
Shropshire. He is betrayed to the authorities, returned to Ireland, court-
martialled, and sentenced to death. He hears of the duke of Devonshire's
arrival in Ireland, and writes to him for a pardon. The duke (who, despite

his title, had extensive estates in Derbyshire) responds to the appeal from 'his countryman', and orders his discharge. The moral of the tale is:

> You soldiers, all, where'er you be,
> I beg a warning take by me,
> And never from your colours fly,
> Lest for deserting you must die.

The elements of desertion, betrayal, and pardon occur in other ballads. The 'Trois Déserteurs'[89] of a French piece who have taken French leave (their expression is, incidentally, 'filer à l'anglaise') are reprieved on the scaffold by their general. In England 'The New Deserter'[90] is variously forgiven by General Wolfe, the Duke of York, King George, and Prince Albert. The notion might well owe something to George III's comment on a sentence of 1,500 lashes awarded to a private of the 54th that 'no sentence of corporal punishment should exceed 1,000 lashes',[91] though this also puts into perspective the ballad's wishful thinking. Its hold was nevertheless tenacious. As recently as 1960 John Arden included an adapted version in his play *Serjeant Musgrave's Dance*. As Arden shows, desertion was likely to be a much more desperate matter. This, too, is reflected in defiant songs like 'The Rambling Royal'[92] (whose motives like those of Stenson, are personal) and 'The Rambler from Clare'[93] whose motives are political; indeed, he joins the United Irishmen, the secret society which was the chief organizer of the Irish rebellion of 1798).

Other Irishmen in the British Army express their revulsion at fighting. 'The Kerry Recruit'[94] in the Crimea treats in a jocular fashion his 'hot breakfast of powder and ball' and the 'big Russian bullet (that) ran off with my thigh', but a compatriot of his reacts differently in a song entitled 'Aherlow'.

AHERLOW

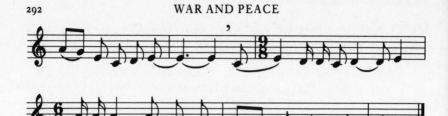

Ah, my name is Patrick Sheehan, and my years are thirty-four.
Tipperary is my native place, not far from Galtymore.
I came of honest parents, but now they're lying low,
And many a pleasant day I spent in the Glens of Aherlow.

Bereft of home and kith and kin and plenty all around,
I starved within my cabin, and I slept upon the ground.
Aye, and cruel as my lot was, I ne'er did hardship know,
Till I joined the English army far away from Aherlow.

Rise up there, says the corporal, you lazy Irish hound,
Why don't you see, you sleepy dog, the call of arms sound.
Alas, I had been dreaming of days long, long ago,
Till I awoke before Sebastopool and not in Aherlow.

I groped to find my musket, how dark I thought the night.
O blessed God, it was not dark, it was the broad daylight.
And when I found that I was blind and me tears began to flow,
And I longed for even a pauper's grave in the glens of Aherlow.

O blessed Virgin Mary, I might end the mournful tale,
A poor blind prisoner here I am in Dublin's dreary jail.
Struck blind within the trenches, where I never feared the foe,
And never will I see again my home, sweet Aherlow.[95]

This song, sung in 1979 by Peter Flanagan of Ballymenone, was written
in 1857 by the Irish Nationalist Charles Kickham (1828–82) with the
deliberate intention of discouraging enlistment. It was based on a
newspaper account of the arrest and imprisonment for begging of Patrick
Sheehan, a blind veteran of the Crimean War. The treatment of returning
servicemen was a frequent cause for complaint. 'The Maunding Soldier,
or, The Fruits of Warre is Beggary' is specifically intended as a request for
money:

It is not Bread nor Cheese,
Nor Barrell Lees, nor any scraps of meat like these,
But I doe beg of you
A shilling or two, sweet Sir, your Purses strings undoo.[96]

THE
Preſſed Man's
LAMENTATION.

FArewell our Daddies and our Mammies,
  Our friends & relations we muſt bid adieu,
For the Preſs-gang they have preſs'd us,
  For to fight our daring Foe :
Now the bloody War's beginning,
  Many thouſands will be ſlain,
And it more than ten to one.
  If any of us return again.

To hear the cries in every city,
  Likewiſe in every market Town.
'Twill make your heart to bleed with pity,
  For to hear the preſs'd men moan :
Now we are preſs'd and put in Priſon,
  Where for a ſeaſon we muſt ſtay,
Till the bloody war calls for us,
  For to croſs the raging ſea.

It grieves us ſore to leave our parents,
  Likewiſe our wives and children dear ;
To hear them round the priſons crying,
  From our eyes brings floods of tears,
It muſt be a dreadful meeting,
  When we quit the britiſh ſhore.
When we go to the field of battle,
  Where the thundering cannons roar.

Now, good people, give attention,
  To theſe lines which here are penn'd,
And the wars may ſoon be over,
  That we may ſoon return again,
To be a comfort to our wives,
  And enjoy our children dear,
But in the wars there is great danger,
  Many of us will be killed I fear.

'The Pressed Man's
Lamentation'. Street ballad.

NEVER FLOG
Our Soldiers.

Tune.—" Willie, we have miss'd you."

IF I was Queen of England, I would find a better plan,
   I would never flog our soldiers, who guard our native land,
They guard us night and day, and from dangers keep free;
When God defends the right, they fight for you and me.
They bid us stand at ease, while fighting hand to hand :
Oh, never flog our soldiers, who guard our native land !

The night my Willie 'listed, we both were torn apart,
I thought I'd ne'er more see him, and that would break my heart.
My sorrows then began, and I was left alone,—
The tortures of the army, by him could not be borne !
I have heard my Willie say, the sight he could not stand,
Oh, never flog our soldiers, who guard our native land !

Oh, now he's gone for ever, I thought we ne'er would part,
I will wear this little treasure, for ever near my heart ;
I gaze on it so dear, it looks like his blythesome way,
He told me not to fear, he'd come back some other day.
Ah ! what is that I hear ! the door opens with his hand,
Oh, never flog our soldiers, who guard our native land,

Now you have come to see me, you are wearing your red coat ;
I think now that you love me, and that keeps up my hope ;
But if you should be late, and then you don't get in,
They'll flog you like the rest of men, that serve our British Queen ;
But if they flog you now you have offer'd me your hand,
You shall never be a soldier, to guard our native land !

Now good night ! God bless you ! for I'll be left alone,
Come let me now impress you, that I'll make you a home.
We'll live happy day by day, and our sorrows then set free,
Oh do not longer stay, for the flogging troubles me ;
They will take you going back, for desertion bind your hands,
And flog you like our soldiers, who guard our native land,

The night my Willie 'listed, how merry he did seem,
To think he had the honour, to serve our British Queen,
Never thinking of the lash that was lying in his way,
To torture him so cruelly if e'er he went astray.
If the lash it is not burnt, and banished from their hands,
He shall never be a soldier, to guard our native land.

You would not
LEAVE YOUR
NORAH ?

YOU would not leave your Norah ?
   To pine alone behind,
The wide, wide world before her,
   And no one to be kind.
The times are hard and trying,
   But, Dennis, perhaps they'll mend,
You would not leave your Norah ?
   You yet may want a friend.

Yes, Norah, dear, I am going.
   And yet it breaks my heart,
To see your eyes are flowing
   With tears because we part.
'Tis sad to leave old Erin,
   A stranger's home to share,
But sadder still, I'm fearing,
   With none to love me there.
          You would not, &c.

Then, Dennis, take me with you,
   You know not half I do,
There no one to forbid you,
   I've saved a pound or two.
I'll soothe you in every sorrow.
   If first the priest you'll tell :
Yes, Norah dear, to-morrow,
   Then Erin, fare-thee-well.
          I could not, &c.

London : Printed at the " Catnach Press," by W. S. FORTEY, Monmouth Court, Seven Dials.

'Never Flog Our Soldiers'/'You would not leave your Norah?' Street ballad.

An Appeal
BY
UNEMPLOYED
Ex-Service Men.

Please purchase a Copy and thus Help.

Some thousands in England are starving,
  And all through no fault of their own,
The troubles of poverty sharing,
  And only to them it is known.
It's hard when the cupboard is empty,
  And through the streets the poor men
    must roam,
And all the week through with nothing to do,
  Yet with poor hungry children at home.

Then pity the Ex-Service workmen,
  Who starve all the week through,
They don't want to shirk any kind of hard
    work,
  But, alas, they can't get it to do!

A man who is fond of his children,
  To keep them alive does his best,
So to him it must be bewildering,
  Yet brings sorrow to both parents' breast,
To see his dear little ones starving,
  In the midst of deep poverty hurled,
For no one can tell what they must feel
  So friendless and alone in the world.

The workman must live by his labour,
  And that he needs have day by day,
And altho' he may have feeling neighbours
  They have nothing they can give away.
For no one knows where the shoe pinches,
  But those who the pain have to bear,
With no work to do, all the week through,
  And just nothing but sorrow and care.

There are many in towns and in cities,
  Who are walking the streets all foot sore,
They surely deserve all your pity,
  As dejected they pass by your door.
At factories and workshops they're calling
  But they're told the same words every day,
There's no orders in hand, all over the land,
  So no wages the masters can pay.

It used to be called happy England,
  But where is its happiness now?
When people are slaving in thousands,
  At the factory, the loom and the plough.
In this country there's millions of money,
  But those who have got it take care,
Their sovereigns they nurse and they keep a
    full purse,
  So the poor man can't get a share.

Then do what you can to assist them,
  For they're all flesh and blood like your-
    selves.
Their poverty sadly oppresses them
  With no food at all on the shelves.
The help that your fellow-man's needing,
  Should be given the country all through,
So help the poor man, the best way you can,
  Who *would* work if he had it to do.

W. C. SUCH, Printer and Publisher,
183 & 185, Union Street, Borough, London, S.E. 1.

[COPYRIGHT]

'An Appeal by Unemployed ex-Service Men'. Street ballad.

Sapper Dorothy Lawrence from her own book, 1919.

A contemporary engraving of Hannah Snell, 1750.

The soldier-narrator lists his service, which includes taking part in the battle of Breda (1637), and offers, if bona fides are needed, to show his wounds. The demobilization of the Parliamentary army in 1660 inspired a further ballad, entitled 'The Lamentation of a Bad Market: or, The Disbanded Souldier', with the wistful refrain of 'Alas poor souldier, whither wilt thou march?' The veteran, after reviewing the eighteen years of campaigning during which 'This fauchion by my side has kill'd more men, I'le swear it, / Than Ajax ever did, alas! he ne'er came near it', determines to retire:

> Into the countrey places I resolve to goe,
> Amongst those sun-burnt faces, I'le goe to plough or keep a cow,
> 'Tis that my masters now again must do.[97]

The advent of peace was often unwelcome to fighting men, since it could often lead to destitution. 'The Soldiers Complaint' begins:

> Brother Soldier do you hear of the news,
> There's Peace both by Land and Sea,
> No more the old Blades must be us'd,
> Some of Us disbanded must be.
>
> Says the Colonel i am sorry for it,
> Says the Major my heart it does ach,
> Says the Captain I dont at all know,
> What Course in this World to take.

The lieutenant proposes to 'court some rich Widow', and the ensign to go from door to door crying 'pots and kettles to mend'. The ordinary soldiers are divided between going 'to the Highway' as robbers or returning to their trades, but they at least express satisfaction at their release:

> Says the Soldier long time I have been
> I marched thro' Rear, File, and Rank
> But now I discharged must be,
> I return them abundance of thanks.[98]

The ballad, which seems to date from the Seven Years War, was adapted during the short peace of 1801–2 to suit a naval context, and was retitled 'Distressed Men of War'.[99] The surgeon is to become a quack doctor, the midshipman a shoeblack, and the simple sailor once more a highway robber. The printer of this sheet, Joshua Davenport, issued at the same time 'Sailor's Complaint' in which Jack has been discharged but cannot obtain the prize-money and arrears of wages to which he is entitled:

Dear shipmate I've been here a month,
And cannot get mine, for the truth
On board of a man of war I went,
When I was a frolicsome youth,
My king and my country to serve,
I fought like a sailor so bold,
Now that the wars are all over
I really cannot get my gold.

To a navy officer each day I did go,
I've been both hungry and dry
My money I then did demand,
You cannot have it they cry;
My life I have ventur'd for gold,
My king and my country to serve.
Now the wars are all over,
Brave sailors may perish and starve.[100]

Difficulties were even greater during the depression which followed the
peace of 1815. Those returning from military service to unemployment
felt a deep sense of betrayal, not for the first time, and not for the last. 'The
Tradesman's Complaint', from the Newcastle printer John Marshall,
says:

For many a battle then we have been in,
On board of a ship, thro' France and thro' Spain,
But we settled the job when at WATERLOO,
And now we're come home, and have nothing to do.

When there would be a peace, we did understand,
That the rich and the poor would go hand in hand.
But if you are starving, they'll give no relief,
You may eat what you will, instead of roast beef.[101]

A century later, after the First World War, 'An Appeal by Unemployed
Ex-Service Men',[102] was being sold in the streets of London for precisely
the same reasons.

At least those who returned were fortunate enough to survive. For the
relatives of those that did not, the outlook was often bleak. At the best of
times, those left behind by serving soldiers and sailors were likely to face
hardship. 'The Soldiers' Wives' Complaint',[103] dating from the wars with
France, speaks of families being forced into the workhouse. The same
theme is taken up on a sheet more or less intended for begging which was
published during the Crimean War under the title of 'Protect the Soldiers
Wives and Children':

It is wretched to go to a workhouse,
While your husbands do bleed in the wars
And 'tis hard for the wives and the children
Of a true British soldier to starve.[104]

'The Soldier's Wife's Lament' refers to the same war:

Many a widow is now lamenting,
Down each cheek rolls many a tear,
And many an orphan is relenting
The loss of those they loved so dear.
They weep in agony and pain,
In grief and sorrow they deplore,
Whose gallant husbands nobly perished
On the distant Russian shore.[105]

A profound weariness with war frequently emerges. 'A New Song called Briton's Lamentation' views the conflict over American independence with horror:

I viewed the camps and deep intrenchments where the fruitful gardens stood,
I saw the ground that fought the battle all strew'd with bones and stain'd with
  blood.

Nothing else but devastation is the prospect here away,
May heavens stop this devastation in the fruitful North America.[106]

At the same time, prints were widely sold showing a ragged family amid a scene of ruin. They bore the legend 'Oh, I wish that the wars were all over', which was also the title of a succession of songs. Their heartfelt longing for peace is deeply genuine, but passive. There was also active opposition to the American War, as to many subsequent wars. Fenner Brockway reports in his autobiography, *Towards Tomorrow* (1977), on the Glasgow anti-war campaign of 1914:

My visit revealed that opposition to the war in Scotland was based not on 'Thou shalt not kill' but on working-class wrongs and international working-class solidarity. The leaders—Maclean, Maxton, Shinwell, Kirkwood—deliberately courted imprisonment and deportation not as conscientious objectors but for sedition in urging strikes and boycotts. They were living in a different world from the English pacifist opposition to the war. Thousands of workers marched in procession through the streets singing Maxton's song to the tune of 'Hallelujah, I'm a Bum':

HENRY DUBB

O I'm Henry Dubb and I won't go to war
Because I don't know what they're all fighting for

To hell with the Kaiser, to hell with the Tsar,
To hell with Lord Derby and also GR*ƒ*

I work at munitions, I'm a slave down at Weir's;
If I leave my job they'll give me two years

To hell with the sheriff, to hell with his crew;
To hell with Lloyd George and Henderson too

I don't like the factor, his rent I won't pay.
Three cheers for John Wheatley, I'm striking today

To hell with the landlord. I'm not one to grouse,
But to hell both with him and his bloody old house.[107]

James Maxton (1885–1946) and the rest opposed what they regarded as a
capitalist war in which working men of different nations would be killing
each other for the benefit of a different class. Maxton was later
imprisoned, together with John Maclean, though this neither diminished
his popularity on Clydeside nor prevented his subsequent election as an
Independent Labour Party MP. Others, like David Kirkwood, were less
uncompromising. Despite the view that 'I hated war. I believed that the
peoples of the world hated war', he worked in a munitions factory: 'I
resolved that my skill as an engineer must be devoted to my country. I was
too proud of the battles of the past to stand aside and see Scotland
conquered. Only those who remember 1914 can understand the struggle
of mind and the conflict of loyalties which so many of us experienced.'[108]

Not until the campaigns of the 1960s and onwards against nuclear
weapons were anti-war movements of such strength seen again. From
the first CND march from Trafalgar Square to Aldermaston at Easter
1958, song was an essential concomitant. On the march, at vigils,

ƒ George Rex (King George V)

during social events, songs lifted the spirits and hammered home the message. 'Strontium Ninety'[109] dates from 1958, as does 'The H-Bomb's Thunder', with its chorus:

> Men and women, stand together,
> Do not heed the men of war.
> Make your minds up, now or never,
> Ban the Bomb for evermore.[110]

The Scots anti-nuclear songs of the same time, as we saw in Chapter 7, inclined more to the vernacular and the irreverent. This has remained largely the case in the CND revival of the 1980s. In *The Anti-Nuclear Songbook* (1982) 'The H-Bomb's Thunder' still has pride of place, but it is followed by a motley collection of parodies with dubious scansion—of hymns ('O Little Town of Windscale,'[111] and 'God rest ye, merry protesters'[112]), music-hall pieces ('Oh I do love to live beside reactors'[113] and 'Trident, Trident, What an insane idea'[114]) and even nursery songs:

> No cruise missiles wanted here today,
> No cruise missiles wanted here today,
> For if one cruise missile should accidentally stray
> There'd be no more people left around to say . . .[115]

The intention is propagandist, not aesthetic. The writing is aimed at the present, not the future. The result is that in some cases great issues are given a lively and humanizing presentation; in others they are trivialized and made banal. The same was true of the parodies of the striking farm-workers in the 1870s and of soldiers in 1914–18. Some of the anti-nuclear songs are parodies of parodies. 'When this nuclear war is over', for example, stems from 'When this bloody war is over', which derives from 'Take it to the Lord in prayer':

> When this nuclear war is over, no more sheltering for me.
> In my new protective clothing, oh how happy I shall be.[116]

There are also reflective, lyrical songs, such as Ian Campbell's 'The Sun is Burning', which was written in 1963. Here the utter horror of nuclear warfare is reinforced by its intrusion into the peaceful daily round of normal life.

THE SUN IS BURNING

The sun is burning in the sky
Strands of cloud are gently drifting by.
In the park the dreamy bees
Are droning in the flowers among the trees;
And the sun burns in the sky.

Now the sun is in the west
Little kids lie down to take their rest,
And the couples in the park
Are holding hands and waiting for the dark;
And the sun is in the west.

Now the sun is sinking low;
Children playing know it's time to go.
High above a spot appears,
A little blossom blooms and then drops near;
And the sun is sinking low.

Now the sun has come to earth,
Shrouded in a mushroom cloud of death.
Death comes in a blinding flash
Of hellish heat and leaves a smear of ash;
And the sun has come to earth.

Now the sun has disappeared,
All is darkness, anger, pain and fear.
Twisted, sightless wrecks of men
Go groping on their knees and cry in pain;
And the sun has disappeared.

ABBREVIATIONS

BOOKS were published in London unless otherwise stated. Full details of records and cassettes, cited in short form in the notes, can be found in the Discography. The following abbreviations have been used:

Bagford   J. W. Ebsworth (ed.), *The Bagford Ballads* (2 vols, Hertford, 1878). The original collection is in the British Library.

BDL   Bodleian Library.

BL   British Library.

CL   County Library.

Euing   *The Euing Collection of English Broadside Ballads* (Glasgow, 1971). The Euing collection is in Glasgow University Library.

Firth   C. H. Firth collection, in the Bodleian Library or Sheffield University Library, as indicated.

Harding   W. H. N. Harding collection, Bodleian Library.

Johnson   John Johnson collection, Bodleian Library.

Kidson   Frank Kidson broadside collection, 10 vols, Mitchell Library, Glasgow.

Madden   Sir Frederic Madden Collection, Cambridge University Library. The library has a card index by title to the collection.

Pepys   Hyder E. Rollins (ed.), *The Pepys Ballads* (8 vols, Cambridge, Mass., 1929–32). The Pepys ballads are in the library of Magdalene College, Cambridge. For a recent facsimile publication of the entire collection, see W. G. Day (ed.), *Pepys Ballads* (5 vols, Cambridge, 1987).

PL   Public Library.

RL   Reference Library.

RO   Record Office.

Roxburghe   William Chappell and J. W. Ebsworth (eds), *The Roxburghe Ballads* (9 vols, Hertford, 1871–99). The Roxburghe collection is in the British Library.

Sharp   *Cecil Sharp's Collection of English Folk Songs* (2 vols, 1974). Sharp's original manuscripts are in the library of Clare College, Cambridge.

Shirburn   Andrew Clark (ed.), *The Shirburn Ballads, 1585–1616* (Oxford, 1907). Original manuscript in the library of the earl of Macclesfield, Shirburn Castle, Oxfordshire.

UL   University Library.

VWML   Vaughan Williams Memorial Library, Cecil Sharp House, London.

NOTES

Introduction

1. John Selden, *Table Talk* (1689), ed. S. H. Reynolds (Oxford, 1892), p. 105.
2. Joseph Ritson, *Dissertation on Ancient Songs* (1877 edn), p. 86.
3. John Fairley, 'History as Lived by the Men Who Were There', *Listener*, 25 Sept. 1986, pp. 8–9 and 18.
4. H. Bett, *English Myths and Traditions* (1952), p. 106.
5. Roger J. McHugh, 'The Famine in Irish Oral Tradition', in Thomas Desmond Williams and A. Dudley Edwards, *The Great Famine* (Dublin, 1956), pp. 391 and 435–6.
6. William Chappell, *Popular Music of the Olden Time* (1859), p. 678.
7. Carl Philip Moritz, *Journeys of a German in England* (1783), trans. Reginald Nettel (1965), p. 57.
8. BL, Francis Place MS, Add. MS 27825, fol. 151, song 14.
9. Printed by J. Pitts, 6 Great St Andrew Street, Seven Dials, London [1824–44], in Trinity College, Cambridge, Macaulay's Ballad Scrapbook, MS o.15.67.
10. Frank Peel, *The Risings of the Luddites* (1880), pp. 119–20.
11. Frank Peel, *Spen Valley Past and Present* (Heckmondwike, 1893), pp. 258–9; on record *Fine Old Yorkshire*.
12. Peel, *Risings*, p. 119.
13. Thomas Babington Macaulay, *The History of England from the Accession of James the Second* (1848–61), ed. C. H. Firth (6 vols, 1913), vol. 1, p. 410. On Macaulay's use of ballads, see C. H. Firth, *A Commentary on Macaulay's History of England* (1938), pp. 97–105.
14. Macaulay, *History* (ed. Firth), vol. 1, pp. 410–12.
15. Macaulay's (two) Civil War ballads, originally published in 1824, were reprinted in *Knight's Penny Magazine*, 2 (1846), 221–4.
16. Street ballad printed by R. Tibbutt, Haymarket, Leicester [1826]; in Trinity College, Cambridge, Macaulay's Ballad Scrapbook; repr. in *The Leicestershire Historian*, 2, no. 11 (1980–1), 24–5.
17. G. O. Trevelyan, *Macaulay's Life and Letters* (2 vols, 1908; orig. 1878), vol. 2, pp. 405–6.
18. Letter to T. F. Ellis, 12 Jul. 1841, in *Letters of Thomas Babington Macaulay*, ed. Thomas Pinney (6 vols, Cambridge, 1974–81), vol. 3, p. 383.
19. Letter to Fanny Macaulay, Nov. 1847, ibid., vol. 5, p. 133.
20. W. W. Wilkins, *Political Ballads of the Seventeenth and Eighteenth Centuries* (2 vols, 1860), vol. 1, p. ix.
21. C. H. Firth, 'The Ballad History of the Reigns of Henry VII and Henry VIII', p. 21. For full details of this and other 'Ballad History' articles by Firth, see Select Bibliography.
22. The part of Firth's collection in Sheffield UL is listed in Peter W. Carnell, *Ballads in the Charles Harding Firth Collection* (Sheffield, 1979). The contents of the 32 volumes of his collection in the BDL are not catalogued.

23. Dorothy George quotes ballads in *London Life in the Eighteenth Century* (Harmondsworth, 1966; orig. 1925), pp. 200, 257, and 384; and in *England in Transition* (Harmondsworth, 1953; orig. 1931), pp. 50–2, 27, and 28.

24. E. P. Thompson quotes ballads in *The Making of the English Working Class* (1966) on pp. 292–3, 299, 306, 308, 310, 440, 462, 547, 555, 559, and 563.

25. Robert Brécy, *Florilège de la Chanson Révolutionnaire de 1789 au Front Populaire*, p. 9 (my trans.).

26. Roberto Leydi, *Canti Sociali Italiani*, p. 241 (my trans.).

27. N. A. M. Rodgers, *The Wooden World*, pp. 11 and 12.

28. Ibid., pp. 98 and 135–6.

29. Cyprian Blagden, 'Notes on the Ballad Market in the Second Half of the Seventeenth Century', *Studies in Bibliography*, 6 (Charlottesville, Va., 1954), 161–80; R. S. Thomson, 'The Development of the Broadside Ballad Trade and its Influence upon the Transmission of English Folksongs' (Cambridge Univ. Ph.D. thesis, 1974).

30. *Re* Harkness sheets, see Madden, vol. 18, fols 600 and 613.

31. For ballads entered, see Rollins, *An Analytical Index*.

32. Anon., 'Street Ballads', *National Review*, 13 (1861), 399–400.

33. I have a photocopy of the bill, which was communicated by Mr J. H. Stonehouse of Pocklington, Yorkshire.

34. Anon., 'Old Jemmy Catnach', *London, Provincial, and Colonial Press News*, 17 Jan. 1867, pp. 22–3. See also Steve Roud and Paul Smith, *A Catalogue of Songs and Song Books Printed and Published by James Catnach 1832* (West Stockwith and Addiscombe, 1985).

35. G. J. Holyoake, *Sixty Years of an Agitator's Life* (2 vols, 1893), vol. 1, p. 32.

36. See Roy Palmer, *Street Ballads in Birmingham* (forthcoming).

37. C. J. Hunt, *The Book Trade in Northumberland and Durham to 1860* (1975), p. 85.

38. See Dorothy Thompson, *The Chartists* (1984), pp. 232–3. See also Harry Boardman and Roy Palmer (eds), *Manchester Ballads* (Manchester, 1983), introduction.

39. See Thompson, *The Chartists*, p. 233. I am also indebted to Owen Ashton for information about Willey.

40. In Public RO, HO45/OS 2410 AE Part 5, 1848, Miscellaneous Bundle.

41. Letter from J. MacGachen, Corse Hill, Tewkesbury, to G. Cornwell Lewis, MP (same source).

42. The originals of Willey's broadsides are in Madden, vol. 23.

43. W. E. Adams, *Memoirs of a Social Atom* (2 vols, 1903), vol. 1, pp. 142–3.

44. Letter to John Reeves from 'Friend to Church & State', 12 Dec. 1792; in BL, Correspondence of the Association for Preserving Liberty and Property, Add. MS 16922, fol. 45.

45. Letters to John Reeves from Britannicus, 5 Dec. 1792; in BL, Add. MS 16920, fol. 119.

46. Letter to John Reeves from Fidelia, 4 Dec. 1792, in BL, Add. MS 16920, fol. 119.

47. Report of 28 Dec. 1792; in BL, Add. MS 16923, fol. 45.

48. T. Harpley, 25 Dec. 1792; in BL, Add. MS 16923, fols 85–6. I am indebted to Marilyn Morris for the references in nn. 44–8.

49. BL, Francis Place Papers, Add. MS 27825, fol. 144.

50. Rollins, *Analytical Index*, no. 1003.

51. Street ballad no. 465, printed by Harkness, Preston; in Madden, vol. 18, fol. 1001. Written in 1845 and inscribed on a tombstone in Ely Cathedral.

52. On bellmen's ballads, see L. Shepard, *History of Street Literature*, pp. 118–20.

53. Author's collection.
54. A. Hewitson, *History of Preston* (Preston, 1883), p. 179.
55. Charles Dickens, in *Household Words*, 1853, p. 347.
56. *Preston Guardian*, 8 Nov., 1853, p. 4. See also below, ch. 3.
57. John Masefield, *Wanderings* (1943), p. 16.
58. William Wordsworth, *The Prelude* (1805 text; Oxford, 1970), book 7, lines 195–6 and 209.
59. Douglas Jerrold, *Heads of the People* (1840), p. 294.
60. Anon., 'Street Ballads', pp. 407 and 411.
61. Thomas Middleton, *The World Tost at Tennis* (1620).
62. In H. L. Collmann (ed.), *Ballads and Broadsides*, no. 39.
63. In R. Lemon, *Catalogue of a Collection of Broadsides*, no. 71.
64. Ibid., no. 72.
65. On Elderton, see Hyder E. Rollins, 'William Elderton: Elizabethan Actor and Ballad Writer', *Studies in Philology*, 17 (1920), 119–245.
66. On Deloney, see F. O. Mann, *The Works of Thomas Deloney* (Oxford, 1912).
67. On Parker, see Chappell, *Popular Music*, pp. 418–20, 434–9, and 291–3.
68. 'A True Subject's Wish', 'Britaines Honour', and 'Good Newes from the North', in BDL, Wood Collection, 401, fols 141, 132, and 134.
69. Charlotte Sophia Burne, *Shropshire Folk-lore* (1883), p. 534.
70. G. M. Trevelyan, 'Border Ballads', p. 94.
71. 'The Forest Gate Fire', sung by Samuel Webber (1874–1973), who was born in Poplar; recorded in Birmingham by Roy Palmer, 1971; in *Folk Review*, 5, no. 4 (Feb. 1976), 19.
72. Michael MacDonagh, 'The Ballads of the People' *The Nineteenth Century*, 54 (Sept. 1903), 458–71 (p. 464).
73. J. Harland and T. T. Wilkinson, 'An Essay on Songs and Ballads', *Transactions of the Historical Society of Lancashire and Cheshire*, NS 11, (1870), 116–17.
74. 'The Farewell to Hounslow of Col. W— and the 7th Hussars/'The Shoemaker and the Snob', in BDL, Firth, Military Ballads and Songs, c14, p. 356.
75. Quoted in Anon., 'Street Ballads', pp. 408–9; facs. of original in Charles Hindley (ed.), *Curiosities*, p. 103.
76. Anon., 'Street Ballads', p. 408.
77. On Holder, see William Scruton, 'An Eccentic Rhymester', *Yorkshire Daily Observer*, 12 Feb. 1902. Some 20 sheets by Holder, including most of those mentioned, are in Bradford PL, Scruton Collection, Broadsides, no. 2.
78. A copy of *Saint Monday* (1790) is in Birmingham RL, no. 239216, as is 'A Collection of Poems by George Davis, Broadsides and Manuscript, *c.*1790–1819', no. 413435.
79. W. H. G. Armitage, 'Joseph Mather: Poet of the Filesmiths', *Notes and Queries*, 195 (1950), 320–5.
80. See *The Songs of Joseph Mather*, ed. J. Wilson (Sheffield, 1862). The first edition of Mather's works is *A Collection of Songs, Poems, Satires etc, written by Joseph Mather, of Sheffield* (Sheffield, 1811). I am indebted to John Baxter for communicating his unpublished typescript, entitled 'Joseph Mather, Radical' (1974).
81. Street ballad without imprint in Sheffield City Library, MP1415; printed in Wilson (ed.), *The Songs*, no. 44.
82. Ibid., no. 38.
83. Some of her songs are reprinted in Keith Gregson (ed.), *Cumbrian Songs and Ballads*.
84. See Keith Gregson, 'The Cumberland Bard'.

85. See Palmer, *Birmingham Street Ballads*.
86. J. Morfitt, quoted in S. J. Pratt, *Harvest Home* (3 vols, 1805), vol. 1, p. 274.
87. John Harland (ed.), *Songs of the Wilsons*, pp. 26–7.
88. Peter Bailey (ed.), *Music Hall: The Business of Pleasure* (Milton Keynes, 1986), p. xv.
89. Laurence Senelick, 'Politics as Entertainment', p. 151.
90. See Keith Gregson, *Corvan. A Victorian Entertainer*.
91. 'The Auchengeich Disaster', in Norman Buchan (ed.), *101 Scottish Songs*, p. 130; on record *Bonny Pit Laddie*.
92. W. H. Armstrong (ed.), *Song Book containing 25 Popular Songs by the late Thomas Armstrong* (Chester-le-Street, 1930). See also Huw Benyon and Derrick Little (eds), *The Work of Tommy Armstrong* (Consett, 1987).
93. Surprisingly, there is no monograph on MacColl or his work, but a chapter is devoted to him in Ian Watson, *Song and Democratic Culture in Britain*.

Chapter 1: The Country

1. 'Robin Hood and Guy of Gisborne', in Joseph Ritson (ed.), *Robin Hood: A Collection of all the ancient Poems, Songs and Ballads* (East Ardsley, 1972; orig. 1795), p. 83.
2. J. W. Goethe, *Italian Journey*, trans. W. H. Auden and Elizabeth Mayer (Harmondsworth, 1982), p. 310. See also Flemming G. Anderson, *Commonplace and Creativity: The Role of Formulaic Diction in Anglo-Scottish Balladry* (Odense, 1985).
3. *Shirburn*, pp. 360–4.
4. Street ballad issued *c.* 1685–8, in *Roxburghe*, vol. 7, p. 29.
5. John Broadwood (ed.), *Old English Songs*, no. 5; for a version noted in 1908, see *Sharp*, no. 250.
6. 'Turnip Hoeing', in Roy Palmer (ed.), *English Country Songbook*, no. 10; on record *When the Frost*.
7. A. G. Street, *Farmer's Glory* (1963) orig. 1935), p. 62.
8. J. Arthur Gibbs, *A Cotswold Village* (1934; orig. 1898), p. 63.
9. George Orwell, 'Hop-Picking', written 1931; printed in *Collected Essays*, ed. Sonia Orwell and Ian Angus (Harmondsworth, 1984; orig. 1945), vol. 1, pp. 75–97.
10. W. H. Hudson, *A Shepherd's Life* (1924; orig. 1910), p. 123.
11. Ibid., pp. 60–1.
12. 'The Shepherd's Song', sung by Willie Scott; recorded by Francis Collinson, 1953, School of Scottish Studies Archive, no. SA 1953/254; published in *Tocher*, no. 25 (1977), 38–9; on record *Shepherd's Song*, sung by Willie Scott himself.
13. In Thomas Hughes, *The Scouring of the White Horse* (1859; orig. 1858), pp. 234–5; on record *Green Fields*.
14. Roy Palmer (ed.), *Painful Plough*, no. 14; on record of same title.
15. 'Once I was a Shepherd Boy', in *Sharp*, no. 255.
16. Flora Thompson, *Lark Rise to Candleford* (1954; orig. 1939, as *Lark Rise*), ch. 3.
17. 'A Happy Man: A Hard Life—the Story of Arthur Lane (1884–1975)', ed. Roy Palmer from recordings made by Philip Donnellan and Charles Parker, *Oral History Journal*, 8 (1980), 30–5.
18. Raymond Williams, *The Country and the City* (1973), p. 263.
19. Fred Kitchen, *Brother to the Ox* (1942; orig. 1940), p. 60.
20. Palmer (ed.), *English Country Songbook*, no. 94; on record *Our Side*.
21. 'The Pretty Factory Boy', street ballad no. 353, printed by Harkness, Preston [*c.* 1843]; in Madden, vol. 18, fol. 889.

22. 'I am a Pretty Wench', in Alfred Williams, *Folk-Songs of the Upper Thames*, p. 123.
23. 'The Saucy Ploughboy', street ballad printed by Ryle and Company, Monmouth Court, Bloomsbury [1838–34]; facs. in Palmer (ed.), *Painful Plough*, p. 30.
24. 'The Nutting Girl', in Palmer (ed.), *English Country Songbook*, no. 72; on record *Broomfield Wager*.
25. Street ballad without imprint; in Harding, Quarto Sheets, no. 3356.
26. Communicated by Maurice Ogg (1946–80) of Coleby, Lincolnshire, who learned it from Albert Robinson of Winteringham; on record *Song of a Shropshire Farm Worker* and cassette *Songs of a Hampshire Man*.
27. Edwin Grey, *Cottage Life in a Hertfordshire Village* (St Albans [?1934]), pp. 61–2.
28. Palmer (ed.), *English Country Songbook*, no. 23.
29. Street ballad printed for 'E. Brooksby, *at the* Sign of the Golden-ball, in *Pye-corner*', London (*c.*1700); in *Euing*, no. 159B.
30. Palmer (ed.), *English Country Songbook*, no. 18; on record *Songs of a Shropshire Farm Worker*.
31. Street ballad printed by W. Wright, Smithfield, Birmingham [1827–9]; in BDL, Douce, vol. 10, p. 321. The sheet is damaged, and missing words and letters have been added in square brackets. I am indebted for this reference to Frank Purslow. The tune, sung by Daniel Wigg, Preston Candover, Hants., was noted by George Gardiner, Jul. 1907; in VWML, Gardiner MSS, Hp. 756; printed in Frank Purslow, *The Foggy Dew* (1974), p. 95.
32. *Notes and Queries*, 2nd ser., 9 (1860), 64.
33. Ibid., 10 (1860), 125.
34. Street ballad printed 'for the Assignes of Thomas Symcocke' (*c.*1624); in *Roxburghe*, vol. 2, p. 582.
35. William Cobbett, *Rural Rides* (1830), ed. George Woodcock (Harmondsworth, 1967), pp. 226–7; written 20 Oct. 1825.
36. John Clare, *The Parish*, ed. Eric Robinson (Harmondsworth, 1986), pp. 33–4; written 1820–7.
37. Street ballad printed by J. Catnach, Seven Dials, London [1813–38], in Johnson, Street Ballads, Box 2.
38. Street ballad printed by Fordyce, 48 Dean Street, Newcastle [1829–37]; in Bradford PL, Broadsides, no. 2, p. 27.
39. Street ballad no. 742, printed by Harkness, Preston [1854]; in Madden, vol. 18, fol. 1275; repr. with tune in Palmer (ed.), *Painful Plough*, no. 3; on record of same title.
40. 'Fifty Years Ago', sung by George Fradley (1910–85), Sudbury, Derbyshire; recorded and communicated by Mike Yates. The song is an updated version of 'I am One of the Olden Time, or, Fifty Year Ago', which was written in the 1860s by the music-hall performer Harry Clifton. Cassette *One of the Best*.
41. Sung by John Collinson (born 1862), blacksmith, of Casterton, Westmorland; noted (text only) by Anne Gilchrist, 1909; printed in Anne G. Gilchrist, 'Some Old Westmorland Folk-Singers', *Journal of the Lakeland Dialect Society*, no. 4 (Nov. 1942). A tune, noted from Collinson in 1905 by Percy Grainger, is in the Grainger MSS; see Jane O'Brien, *The Grainger English Folk Song Collection* (Nedland, Australia, 1985), no. 38.
42. See J. F. C. Harrison, *The Common People* (1984), p. 229.
43. William Cobbett, *Political Register*, 16 Oct. 1824, p. 132.
44. See E. P. Thompson, 'The Crime of Anonymity', in Douglas Hay et al., *Albion's Fatal Tree* (1975), pp. 275ff.

45. W. E. Tate, *The English Village Community and the Enclosure Movements* (1967), p. 89.
46. J. Harvey Bloom, *Folk Lore, Old Customs and Superstitions in Shakespeare Land* (1930), p. 129.
47. *The Northampton Mercury*, 19 Aug. 1765.
48. Quoted in L. Marion Springhall, *Labouring Life in Norfolk Villages* (1936), p. 80.
49. 'The Coney Warren', in Roy Palmer (ed.), *A Ballad History*, no. 23.
50. Street ballad printed by Tupman, High Street [Nottingham, 1837], in Nottingham UL, Ballads, 1, pt 2, no. 18. For Derby there are six ballads opposing the enclosure of Nun's Green, in L. Jewitt (ed.), *Ballads and Songs of Derbyshire*, pp. 188–203. John Freeth's 'The Cottager's Complaint', in Palmer (ed.), *Ballad History*, p. 68, campaigned against the enclosure of Sutton Coldfield.
51. 'Enclosure', 'The Village Minstrel', and 'Remembrances', are in John Clare, *Selected Poems*, ed. J. W. and Anne Tibble (1973), pp. 115, 50, and 225.
52. See 'A New Song on the Birmingham Election', street ballad printed by Taylor and Company, Birmingham [1837]; in Birmingham RL, Folder of Political Broadsides; repr. in Roy Palmer (ed.), *Birmingham Ballads*, no. 17.
53. E. J. Hobsbawm and George Rude, *Captain Swing* (Harmondsworth, 1973), Appendixes 1 and 2. See also Hudson, *Shepherd's Life*, pp. 209–11; and M. Sturge Gretton, *Some English Rural Problems* (1922), pp. 68–9.
54. T. Roach, 'The Riots of 1830', *Hampshire Notes and Queries*, 13 (1896), 97–8. I am indebted to Bob Bushaway for this reference. The 1906 version of 'The Owslebury Lads' was sung by James Staff of Winchester, Hants., and noted by George Gardiner, in VWML, Hammond MSS, H. 204; printed in Palmer (ed.), *Painful Plough*, no. 8; on record of same title.
55. For example, 'The Nottingham Poacher', in Palmer (ed.), *English Country Songbook*, no. 50, on record *George Dunn*; 'The Sheepstealer', in Palmer (ed.), *Painful Plough*, no. 12, on record *Manchester Angel*; 'Copy of Verses on the Fatal Fishing Affray at Cockermouth', in J. M. Denwood, *Cumbrian Nights* (1930), facing p. 80.
56. *James Hawker's Journal. A Victorian Poacher*, ed. Garth Christian (1961), pp. 77, 95, and 2. See also David Smith and Barry Lount, *The Life of a Victorian Poacher, James Hawker* (Fleckney, 1982).
57. G. M. Trevelyan, *English Social History* (Harmondsworth, 1967; orig. 1911), vol. 1, p. 185.
58. J. L. and Barbara Hammond, *The Village Labourer* (2 vols, 1948; orig. 1911), vol. 1, p. 185.
59. Harry Hopkins, *The Long Affray. The Poaching Wars, 1760–1914* (1985).
60. Palmer (ed.), *English Country Songbook*, no. 49.
61. Street ballad no. 9, printed by Thomas Ford, New Square, Chesterfield [?1830–?9]; in Derby PL, Derbyshire collection, pressmark 8607; the tune intended was probably 'The Mill, Mill, O', in Frank Kidson (ed.), *Traditional Tunes*, pp. 131–3. On Bill Brown, see also *York Courant*, 3 Apr. 1770, and Roy Palmer, 'The Death of Bill Brown', *English Dance and Song*, 41 (1979), 9–10.
62. Street ballad printed by Henson, Northampton [1837]; in Harding, Quarto Street Ballads, no. 3689; repr. in Palmer (ed.), *Ballad History*, no. 49.
63. Street ballad no. 203, printed by Harkness, Preston [1843]; in Madden, vol. 18, fol. 738; see also Hopkins, *Long Affray*, p. 205.
64. Street ballad no. 488, printed by Harkness, Preston [1846]; in Madden, vol. 18, fol. 1634.
65. Hopkins, *Long Affray*, p. 208.
66. Street ballad printed by T. Pearson, Manchester [1861–72, though the events to

which it refers took place in 1843]; in BDL, Firth, c 19, p. 56; see Hopkins, *Long Affray*, pp. 207–9.

67. Sung by Joseph Taylor, Saxby-All-Saints, Lincolnshire; noted by Percy Grainger, 1906; in *Journal of the Folk Song Society*, no. 12 (1908), 186; repr. in Patrick O'Shaughnessy (ed.), *More Folk Songs from Lincolnshire*, no. 13; on record *Unto Brigg Fair*.

68. Sung by Fred Whiting, Kenton, Suffolk; recorded by Mike Yates, 23 Jan. 1984; in *English Dance and Song*, 46 (1984), 18; on record *Who Owns*.

69. *James Hawker's Journal*, pp. 33 and 35.

70. Bob Bushaway, *By Rite: Custom, Ceremony and Community in England, 1700–1800* (1982).

71. Quoted in Henry Best, 'Rural Economy in Yorkshire in 1641, Being the Farming and Account Books of Henry Best', *Transactions of the Surtees Society* (Durham, 1857), 136.

72. Isaac Bickerstaffe, *Love in a Village* (1762), quoted in William Hone, *The Every-Day and Table Book* (1838; orig. 1827), vol. 3, cols 177–8.

73. F. Scarlett Potter, 'The Duologues given in Character by the Warwickshire Peasantry', *Long Ago*, 2 (1873–4), 130.

74. Marmaduke C. F. Morris, *Yorkshire Reminiscences* (1922), p. 53.

75. See, for example, Clare, *Selected Poems*, p. 42; Thomas Hardy, 'The Dorsetshire Labourer', *Longman's Magazine*, Jul. 1883, pp. 255–68; *idem, Far from the Madding Crowd* (1874), ch. 6; *idem, The Mayor of Casterbridge* (1886), ch. 23; Melvyn Bragg, *The Hired Man* (1969).

76. See, for example, Arthur Lane, 'A Happy Man', p. 32; Melvyn Bragg, *Speak for England* (1976), pp. 184–7; S. Harrison, *Yorkshire Farming Memories* (York, 1981), p. 4, and cassette of same title; Charles Kightly, *Country Voices: Life and Lore in Farm and Village* (1984), pp. 23–33 and 150–1; Kitchen, *Brother to the Ox*, ch. 6, 'Martlemas Fair'.

77. Unpublished; communicated by Dave Hillery.

78. Robert Chambers, *Popular Rhymes of Scotland* (London and Edinburgh, 1870), p. 260. See also E. M. Wright, *Rustic Speech and Folklore* (Oxford, 1913), p. 306.

79. Robert Ford, *Vagabond Songs*, p. 202.

80. Palmer (ed.), *English Country Songbook*, no. 34; on record *I Wish*.

81. *Reports on Agriculture* (1843), p. 91.

82. Street ballad no. 667, printed by Harkness, Preston [1850]; in Madden, vol. 18, fol. 1202.

83. Street ballad printed by H. P. Such, 177 Union Street, Borough, London [1876–85]; in Harding, Quarto Street Ballads, no. 2686; the tune intended, 'Tommy Make Room for Your Uncle', can be found in Harold Scott (ed.), *An English Song Book*, p. 140.

84. Street ballad no. 187C, printed by H. Such, 177 Union Street, London [1863–85]; in BL, Baring-Gould Collection, LR 271 a 2, vol. 5, p. 77.

85. J. Skinner, *Facts and Opinions concerning Statute Hirings* (1861), pp. 6–7.

86. Street ballad no. 335; 'Sold by J. Livsey, 45, Hanover-Street, Shudehill, Manchester' [1833–50], in Harding, Quarto Street Ballads, no. 40.

87. Street ballad no. 511, printed by Harkness, Preston [1847]; in Madden, vol. 18, fol. 1046; repr. in part in Palmer (ed.), *Painful Plough*, no. 4; on record *Country Hirings*; for fragments from oral tradition, see *Lincolnshire Magazine*, 1 (1932–4), 141, and 3 (1936–8), 154.

88. Unpublished.

89. The most complete collection is John Ord, *The Bothy Songs*. See also David

Buchan, *The Ballad and the Folk*, ch. 19; David Kerr Cameron, *The Ballad and the Plough* (1978), and *idem, Cornkister Days* (1984); Hamish Henderson, 'The Bothy Ballads', *Journal of Peasant Studies*, 2 (1975), 497–501 (this is an extract from Henderson's notes to the record *Bothy Ballads*); Bob Munro, 'The Bothy Ballads: The Social Context and Meaning of the Farm Servants' Songs of North-eastern Scotland', *History Workshop Journal*, no. 3 (1977), 184–93; and the records *Bothy Ballads* and *Frosty Ploughshare*.

90. John R. Allen, *Farmer's Boy* (1985; orig. 1935), p. 96.
91. Cameron, *Ballad and the Plough*, p. 38.
92. Ord, *Bothy Songs*, pp. 209–11.
93. Hamish Henderson, 'The Ballad, the Folk and the Oral Tradition', p. 104.
94. E. W. Bowling, *A Bedfordshire Parson* (1885), p. 75.
95. *The Autobiography of Joseph Arch*, ed. John Gerard O'Leary (1966; orig. 1898, as *Joseph Arch: The Story of his Life*), p. 23.
96. In Edward Jenkins, 'The Story of the South Warwickshire Labourers' Union', *Good Words* (1872), 347.
97. G. D. H. Cole and Raymond Postgate, *The Common People, 1746–1946* (1961; orig. 1946), p. 402.
98. Palmer (ed.), *Painful Plough*, no. 18.
99. In Howard Evans, *Songs for Singing at Agricultural Labourers' Meetings* (London and Leamington, n.d.), pp. 22, 9–10, 13–14, and 8–9.
100. Street ballad printed by H. P. Such; in Kidson, vol. 10, p. 164.
101. *Autobiography of Joseph Arch*, pp. 25–6.
102. Written by Jay Wallis; sung by Leslie Sarony on the 78 rpm Imperial Record no. 2032. I am indebted to Adrian May for a tape copy.
103. See Orwell's novel *A Clergyman's Daughter* (1935), ch. 2, pt 3.
104. Marion Shoard, *The Theft of the Countryside* (1980). See also *idem, This Land is Our Land* (1987).
105. Written by Anton Lagzdins (born 1954), Dec. 1982.

Chapter 2: The Town

1. Street ballad printed by W. Wright, Moor Street, Birmingham [1822–6 or 1831–5]; in Birmingham RL, Songs, p. 47; the original is in 64 short lines, without a break; the chorus has been added with the tune 'Fine Old English Gentleman', in Robert Leach and Roy Palmer (eds), *Folk Music in School* (Cambridge, 1978), p. 94. Versions of the song are on the records *Oldham's Burning, Fine Old Yorkshire*, and *Mike Waterson*.
2. 'Hodge in London', street ballad no. 91, printed by W. and T. Fordyce, 48 Dean Street, Newcastle [1839–45]; in Sheffield UL, Firth, B190.
3. 'Yorkshireman in London', in *Holroyd's Collection of Yorkshire Ballads*, pp. 224–5. The earliest version I have seen is in *A Garland of New Songs*, issued by J. Marshall, Old Flesh-Market, Newcastle [1811–29]; see Frances M. Thomson, *Newcastle Chapbooks in Newcastle upon Tyne University Library* (Newcastle upon Tyne, 1969), no. 139. A tune from oral tradition is in Patrick Shuldham-Shaw and Emily B. Lyle (eds), *The Greig-Duncan Folk Song Collection*, vol. 2 (1983), no. 298.
4. 'Birmingham Boy in London', street ballad printed by J. Pitts, 6 Great St Andrew Street, Seven Dials, London [1820–44]; in Madden, vol. 8, fol. 140; repr. in John Holloway and Joan Black (eds), *Later English Broadside Ballads*, vol. 2, no. 21.
5. 'Rough Joe in Search of a Wife', by Thomas Wilson (died 1852); in John Harland (ed.), *The Songs of the Wilsons*, pp. 43–5.

6. 'Jock Hawk's Adventures in Glasgow', in Ord, *Bothy Songs*, pp. 228–9; repr. with tune in Roy Palmer (ed.), *Everyman's Book of British Ballads*, no. 73; on record *Scotia*.

7. Street ballad without imprint, in BL, York Publications, 1870 c 2, p. 130.

8. Quoted by J. J. Tobias, *Crime and Industrial Society in the Nineteenth Century* (Harmondsworth, 1972; orig. 1967), p. 105.

9. Sung by Walter Pardon (born 1915), Knapton, Norfolk; recorded by Bill Leader, 1974; in Palmer (ed.), *English Country Songbook*, no. 109; on record *Our Side*.

10. 'Pat Molloy', sung by Peter Flanagan, Ballymenone, Co. Fermanagh; recorded by Henry Glassie, 1974; in Henry Glassie, *Passing the Time*, pp. 693–4.

11. 'Macdonald's First Visit to Glasgow', sung by Flora MacNeill on the record *Streets of Glasgow*.

12. Street ballad in Magdalene College Cambridge, Pepys Ballads, vol. 1, p. 188.

13. Street ballad printed by Booth, Selby [1830s]; in BDL, Firth, Broadside Ballads, b 34, p. 169.

14. In John Ashton (ed.), *Modern Street Ballads*, p. 20.

15. 'Somersetshire', sung by Miss Jessie Howman (born 1884), Stow-on-the-Wold, Gloucestershire; recorded by Roy Palmer, 11 Aug. 1966; unpublished.

16. Street ballad printed by T. Birt, 39 Great St Andrew Strett, Seven Dials, London [mid-1840s]; in BDL, Firth, Ballads: Sports and Pastimes, c 19, p. 149.

17. Street ballad without imprint [1790s]; in Chetham's Library, Manchester, Halliwell-Phillips Collection, no. 52. Another copy, from Madden, is repr. in Holloway and Black (eds), *Later English*, vol. 1, no. 49.

18. Street Ballad printed by J. Pitts, 6 Great St Andrew Street, Seven Dials, London [1820s]; in Madden, vol. 9, fol. 403; repr. in Holloway and Black (eds), *Later English*, vol. 2, no. 119.

19. Street ballad without imprint; in Madden, vol. 9, fol. 347, repr. in Holloway and Black (eds), *Later English*, vol. 2, no. 120.

20. Street ballad printed by J. Catnach, 2 and 3 Monmouth Court, Seven Dials, London [1813–38]; in Kidson, vol. 8, p. 119.

21. Street ballad printed by H. Disley, 57 High Street, St Giles, London [1870s]; in Johnson, Street Ballads, Box 3.

22. Street ballad no. 2, printed by Barr, 8 Bridge Street, Lady Bridge, Leeds: in VWML, Cecil Sharp Broadside Collection.

23. *Miscellaneous Songs relating to Sheffield*, appended to *The Songs of Joseph Mather*, ed. John Wilson (Sheffield, 1862), pp. 66–8. Cf. 'Saturday-Night at Birmingham', street ballad printed by D. Wrighton, 7 Edmund Street, Birmingham [1811]; in Harding, Quarto Street Ballads, no. 3426.

24. Street ballad no. 308, printed by T. Pearson, 6 Chadderton Street, Off Oldham Road, Manchester [c. 1861–72]; in Kidson, vol. 10, p. 55; repr. in Boardman and Palmer (eds), *Manchester Ballads*, no. 27; on record *Lancashire Mon*. Cf. 'Oldham on a Saturday Night', street ballad without imprint; in Kidson, vol. 10, p. 119; also on record *Lancashire Mon*.

25. Street ballad without imprint, in Oldham Library, Oldham Collection, p. 93. Cf. 'Manchester at Twelve o'Clock', street ballad printed by J. Wheeler, Whittle Street, Oldham Road, Manchester [1838–45]; in BL, A Collection of Ballads printed at Various Places in the Provinces, 1876 e 3; repr. in Boardman and Palmer (eds), *Manchester Ballads*, no. 15.

26. Street ballad printed by Cadman, 152 Great Ancoats Street, Manchester [1857]; in Kidson, vol. 9, p. 163; repr. in Palmer (ed.), *A Touch*, p. 67.

27. Street ballad printed by J. Davenport, 6 George's Court, St John's Lane, West

Smithfield, London [1800–2]; in Madden, vol. 4, fol. 536; repr. in Holloway and Black (eds), *Later English*, vol. 1, no. 36.

28. See, for example, 'Jack of All Trades Visit to Bristol', street ballad printed by H. Shepherd, 6 Broad Weir, Bristol, in Bristol Central Library; 'Birmingham Jack of All Trades', street ballad printed by Wright, Smithfield, Birmingham [1827–31], in Madden, vol. 21, fol. 743; repr. in Palmer (ed.), *Birmingham Ballads*, no. 11, on record *Wide Midlands*; and 'Roving Jack of All Trades', street ballad without imprint, in Liverpool RO, A Collection of Broadsides, p. 25.

29. Street ballad printed by J. Brereton, Exchange Street, Dublin, in VWML, Cecil Sharp Broadside collection; oral text published with tune in C. O. Lochlainn (ed.), *Irish Street Ballads*, no. 40.

30. 'The New Navigation', written by John Freeth in 1769; repr. in Palmer (ed.), *A Touch*, p. 28; on record *Brummagem Ballads*.

31. *The Times*, 27 Oct. 1809; repr. in Roy Palmer (ed.), *Strike the Bell*, p. 19.

32. Palmer (ed.), *Strike the Bell*, nos 7 and 14.

33. Sturge Gretton, *Some English Rural Problems*, p. 61.

34. Quoted by Palmer (ed.), *A Touch*, p. 37.

35. Harland (ed.), *Songs of the Wilsons*, pp. 61–4. A slightly different version was printed as a street ballad by J. Wheeler, Manchester; in Madden, vol. 18, fol. 485; repr. in Palmer (ed.), *A Touch*, p. 34, and Boardman and Palmer (eds), *Manchester Ballads*, no. 10; on record *Steam Ballads*.

36. 'I Can't Find Brummagen', written by James Dobbs (1781–1837) in 1828; repr. in Palmer (ed.), *A Touch*, p. 78, and *idem* (ed.), *Birmingham Ballads*, no. 12; on records *Brummagem Ballads* and *Wide Midlands*.

37. Street ballad printed by Swindells, Manchester [1830]; in Manchester Central Library; repr. in Boardman and Palmer (eds), *Manchester Ballads*, no. 9.

38. *London Singer's Magazine* (n.d.), pp. 12–13; repr. in Palmer (ed.), *A Touch*, p. 62.

39. Street ballad no. 285; printed by Harkness, Preston [1844, but probably written some years earlier]; in Manchester Central Library; repr. in Boardman and Palmer (eds), *Manchester Ballads*, no. 14. The sheet is damaged, and missing words and letters have been added in square brackets. Cf. 'Liverpool is an Altered Town', street ballad no. 475, printed by Harkness, Preston, in Madden, vol. 18, fol. 1011; repr. in Palmer (ed.), *A Touch*, p. 73.

40. Street ballad printed by H. Paul, 22 Brick Lane, Spitalfields, London [1840–5], in Madden, vol. 14, fol. 428.

41. John Burnett, *A History of the Cost of Living* (Harmondsworth, 1969), p. 262.

42. Street ballad without imprint [1774], in BDL, Firth, Ballads and Poems, 1714–1800, b 22, p. 107.

43. Street ballad without imprint (1800); in Manchester Central Library, BR F 824.04.

44. Street ballad printed by Marshall, Newcastle [1811–15]; in Harding, Quarto Street Ballads, no. 1242.

45. Street ballad without imprint [1801]; in Bristol Central Library.

46. Street ballad printed by Edmunds, place cropped (1809); in Birmingham RL, Broadsides 119932, p. 41.

47. John Burnett, *Plenty and Want* (Harmondsworth, 1968; orig. 1966), p. 99.

48. *Harvest Songster*, printed by Pitts, London [c.1825]; in Birmingham RL, no. 401061; repr. in Palmer (ed.), *A Touch*, p. 175.

49. Street ballad 'Printed by T. King, Birmingham, and sold by Mr Green at his Music Stall near the Turnpike, City-road [London], and at 27 Fatherstone-street, City-road, where an extensive collection of old and new songs, harp and violin

strings, fancy stationery, &c. may be had' [?1850s]; in Johnson, Street Ballads, Box 10.

50. Street ballad printed by J. Wheeler, Whittle Street, Manchester [1838–45]; in BL, A Collection of Ballads, 1876 e 3, p. 130.

51. First published in *The Harmonist's Preceptor or Universal Vocalist containing all the new songs* [*c.*1837]; quoted in Palmer (ed.), *A Touch*, p. 156.

52. Street ballad printed by J. V. Quick, 42 Bowling Green Lane, Clerkenwell, London [1831 or 1832]; communicated by Norman Longmate from a collection of ballads in BL; published in Palmer (ed.), *A Touch*, p. 156.

53. William Derricourt, *Old Convict Days*, ed. G. L. Becke (1899), p. 8.

54. Street ballad printed by H. Disley, 57 High Street, St Giles, London [1871]; in BL, Baring-Gould Collection, LR 271 a 2, vol. 1–1, p. 145.

55. Geoffrey Brace (ed.), *Something to Sing* (Cambridge, 1964), p. 49; on record *Streets of Song*.

56. Written by G. S. Miles in 1972; printed in Roy Palmer, *The Folklore of Warwickshire* (1976), pp. 152–3.

57. Learnt by the Oldham Tinkers 'from an Oldham business man, Laurie Cassidy', and sung by them on the record *Oldham's Burning*.

58. Written by John Pole in 1974; printed in Sam Richards and Tish Stubbs (eds), *The English Folksinger*, p. 177; on record of same title.

59. Written by Adam McNaughtan in 1968; printed in Norman Buchan and Peter Hall (eds), *The Scottish Folksinger*, p. 23.

Chapter 3: Industry

1. James Hogg, *The Jacobite Relics of Scotland* (2 vols, Edinburgh, 1819), vol. 1, p. 32.

2. 5 p.m. programme, BBC Radio 4, 13 Jan. 1986.

3. See record *Waulking Songs*.

4. BBC Sound Archive recording of 1937–9 and 1954.

5. Quoted in Theodore Zeldin, *France, 1848–1945: Taste and Corruption* (Oxford, 1980), p. 303.

6. A. K. Hamilton Jenkin, *The Cornish Miner* (Newton Abbot, 1972; orig. 1927), pp. 102–3.

7. 'Mad Maudlin to find out Tom of Bedlam', in *Pills to Purge Melancholy*, vol. 2 (1700), p. 192. See also Robert Graves, Jack Lindsay, and Peter Warlock, *Loving Mad Tom* (1927).

8. A. L. Beier, *Masterless Men* (1985), p. xix.

9. Street ballad '*Printed for* P. Brooksby, *at the* Golden-Ball, *in* Pye-corner' [London, 1672–95]; in *Bagford*, vol. 1, pp. 216–18; original in 4-line stanzas; tune from *Choice Ayres and Songs*, book 5 (1684), in Claude M. Simpson, *The British Broadside Ballad and its Music* (New Brunswick, N.J., 1966), p. 41. An oral version was recorded in 1952 by Seamus Ennis under the title of 'A-begging I will go', BBC Sound Archive no. 18136; on record *Lancashire Mon*.

10. *Folk Music*, 1, no. 6 (1964), 29; on record *Manchester Angel*.

11. Beier, *Masterless Men*, p. 3.

12. Street ballad without imprint; in Sheffield UL, Firth, A21; repr. in Palmer (ed.), *A Touch*, p. 130.

13. Street ballad no. 76, printed by T. Ford, Irongate, Chesterfield [?1830–?9]; in Derby PL, Derbyshire Collection, pressmark 8607.

14. Street ballad without imprint; in BDL, Firth, Broadside Ballads, b 34, p. 203. The tune is not expressly indicated, but should clearly be 'The Shamrock Shore', of

which a version noted by Frank Kidson from an anonymous street singer in Leeds has been given in *Journal of the Folk Song Society*, no. 9 (1906), 255.

15. *Folk Scene*, no. 7 (1965), 14.
16. 'Twankydillo', in Palmer (ed.), *English Country Songbook*, no. 5.
17. 'The Blacksmith', street ballad without imprint; in Kidson, vol. 3, p. 94.
18. *Miscellaneous Songs*, pp. 88–94 and 112–13, in Wilson (ed.), *The Songs of Joseph Mather*. 'The Jovial Cutlers' is rep. in Roy Palmer (ed.), *Poverty Knock*, no. 1.
19. *Songs of Joseph Mather*, no. 1; original in 8-line stanzas; v. 3 deficient in original.
20. Roy Palmer, *The Minstrel of Quarry Bank. Reminiscences and Songs of George Dunn (1887–1975)* (Dudley, 1984), p. 13.
21. Corngreaves Ironworks Prayer, 27 Feb. 1863, communicated by H. W. Gwilliam.
22. MS communicated by Frank Billington of Halesowen.
23. Robert H. Sherard, 'The White Slaves of England. No. 2, The Nailmakers of Bromsgrove', *Pearson's Magazine*, 1896, p. 167.
24. Recorded by A. L. Lloyd in 1971, and quoted in Leach and Palmer (eds), *Folk Music in School*, pp. 8–9.
25. See record *Save Shotton*; one song, 'The Men who Make the Steel', is in Palmer (ed.), *Ballad History*, no. 82.
26. John Stagg, 'Some Old North Country Songs', *Early English Musical Magazine*, Mar. 1891, p. 40; on record *Bonnie Pit Laddie*.
27. Ord, *Bothy Songs*, p. 42.
28. Burns, *Poems and Songs*, ed. James Kinsley (1971), no. 366.
29. Fragmentary garland, without date or imprint; in Harding, Chapbooks, A3, no. 25, pp. 3–4.
30. See Michael Pollard, *The Hardest Work under Heaven: The Life and Death of the British Coal Miner* (1984), p. 104.
31. Street ballad without imprint (1777); in Johnson, Street Ballads, Box 31.
32. On record *Country Hirings*.
33. Street ballad without imprint; in Sheffield UL, Firth, A11.
34. Street ballad without imprint; in Sheffield UL, Firth, A34.
35. Street ballad printed by J. Ford, 7 Mill Lane, Sheffield; in Johnson, Street Ballads, Box 13.
36. Street ballads printed by D. Thomas, Wallcroft, Lancashire; in Sheffield UL, Firth, A24A.
37. Street ballad without imprint; in volume of broadsides formerly belonging to Sabine Baring-Gould, and now in the National Library of Wales.
38. Street ballad without imprint; in Harding, Quarto Street Ballads, no. 649.
39. Sung by Rab Morrison of Woolmet Colliery, Midlothian; recorded by Hamish Henderson, and printed in his article 'A Colliery Disaster Ballad', *Scottish Studies*, 7 (1963), 92–100.
40. Several different families of songs on the disaster include 'The Blantyre Disaster', beginning 'By Clyde's bonny banks', in A. L. Lloyd, *Come All Ye Bold Miners*, pp. 179–81; 'The Blantyre Disaster', beginning ''Twas eighteen and seventy', sung by George Hamilton, Edinburgh, recorded by Hamish Henderson, 1962, preserved in the archives of the School of Scottish Studies, SA 1962/15/B23, and published in *A Collection of Scots songs* (Edinburgh, 1972); 'Fearful Colliery Explosion in Scotland', street ballad without imprint, in BL, Crampton Ballads, 11621 h 11, vol. 8, 297; and 'Appalling Colliery Accident in Scotland', street ballad without imprint, in Kidson, vol. 1, p. 120.
41. Armstrong (ed.), *Song Book*, p. 1; on record *Tommy Armstrong*.
42. See Roger de V. Renwick, *English Folk Poetry*, ch. 5.

43. Lloyd, *Come All Ye Bold Miners*, p. 191; on record *Jack of All Trades*.
44. Bradford broadsides covering the period 1804–25 are in the York Minster Library, Hailstone Collection, G. 1. The text of the 1825 sheet appears under the title 'The Bishop Blase Festival', in *Holroyd's Yorkshire Ballads*, pp. 74–6.
45. MS of John Bath in a scrap-book preserved by Lord Foley, which is now in Kidderminster PL; printed in Len Smith, *The Carpet Weaver's Lament*, pp. 19–21.
46. Street ballad printed for F. Coles, T. Vere, J. Wright, and J. Clarke (1674–9); in *Roxburghe*, vol. 7, pp. 7–9.
47. William Gardiner, *Music and Friends* (3 vols, 1838–53), vol. 2, pp. 586–7.
48. Cobbett, *Rural Rides*, p. 341.
49. Street ballad no. 363, printed by Harkness, Preston [1844]; in Madden, vol. 18, fol. 899.
50. Street ballad without imprint, in Manchester Central Library; repr. in Boardman and Palmer (eds), *Manchester Ballads*, no. 5; on record *Iron Muse*.
51. In Roy Palmer (ed.), *The Rambling Soldier*, pp. 33–7.
52. In John Harland and T. T. Wilkinson, *Ballads and Songs of Lancashire*, pp. 193–5; on record *Deep Lancashire*.
53. 'The Weaver and the Factory Maid', in Palmer (ed.), *A Touch*, p. 133; on record *Iron Muse*.
54. T. S. Ashton, *An Economic History of England: The Eighteenth Century* (1972 edn), pp. 203–4.
55. 'The Knocker-up', in Palmer (ed.), *Poverty Knock*, p. 13.
56. Sung by Kathleen Lyons, Batley; recorded by A. E. Green, 1965; in Michael Dawney (ed.), *English Occupational Songs* (1974), p. 24.
57. In Harland and Wilkinson, *Ballads and Songs*, pp. 188–9; on record *Golden Stream*.
58. In Harland and Wilkinson, *Ballads and Songs*, pp. 202–4.
59. *Oxford English Dictionary*, under 'Luddite'.
60. Roy Palmer, *The Folklore of Leicestershire and Rutland* (Wymondham, 1985), pp. 90–2.
61. Byron's speech to the House of Lords on 27 Feb. 1912 is repr. under the title of 'The Frame Breakers' in Mary Palmer, *Writing and Action* (1938), pp. 210–15. I am indebted to Dorothy Thompson for this reference.
62. Public RO, H.O. 42/119; printed with tune in Palmer (ed.), *A Touch*, pp. 286–7; on record *Bitter*.
63. Street ballad without imprint; in Derby PL, Derby Broadsides, pressmark 8672; repr. in Palmer (ed.), *A Touch*, pp. 289–90.
64. In Frank Peel, *The Risings of the Luddites*, p. 47, tune, 'The Gallant Poachers', sung by George Dunn, Quarry Bank, Staffs.; recorded by Roy Palmer, 1971; in Roy Palmer, 'George Dunn: Twenty-one Songs and Fragments', *Folk Music Journal*, 2, no. 4 (1973), 276; on record *Champions*.
65. Robert Reid, *Land of Lost Content. The Luddite Revolt, 1812* (1986), p. 275.
66. On record *On the One Road*.
67. Betty Messenger, *Picking up the Linen Threads, a Study in Industrial Folklore* (Austin, Tex., 1978), p. 48.
68. Quoted in T. C. Smout, *A Century of the Scottish People, 1830–1930* (1986), p. 93.
69. Messenger, *Picking up the Linen Threads*, p. 68.
70. 'The Keelmen's Stick', street ballad printed by W. Stephenson, Gateshead [1822]; in Johnson, Street Ballads, Box 11.
71. 'The Miners' Binding', street ballad printed by Pollock, North Shields [1822]; repr. in Lloyd, *Bold Miners*, pp. 217–18.
72. Palmer (ed.), *Poverty Knock*, no. 18.

73. Ibid., no. 19.
74. 'The Jute Mill Song', in Nigel Gatherer (ed.), *Songs and Ballads of Dundee*, no. 38.
75. Ibid., no. 44.
76. Heard on TV programme 'Citizen Murdoch', *Panorama*, BBC 1, 19 Jan. 1987.
77. Text from the singing of Bob Blair in Norman Buchan, 'Folk and Protest', pp. 175-6.
78. See Smith, *Carpet Weavers' Lament.*
79. See Lloyd, *Bold Miners.*
80. Palmer (ed.), *A Touch*, p. 309.
81. Charles Dickens, 'Locked-out', *Household Words* 1853, pp. 345-8; 'Ten Per Cent', repr. from the Dickens article in Palmer (ed.), *Ballad History*, no. 59; the original sheet is in Madden, vol. 18.
82. 'The Cotton Lords of Preston', street ballad with imprint, but probably issued by Harkness, Preston; in Madden, vol. 18, fol. 1312; repr. in Palmer (ed.), *A Touch*, p. 313.
83. *Preston Guardian*, 8 Nov. 1853, p. 4. For a detailed study of the strike, see H. I. Dutton and J. E. King, *Ten Per Cent and No Surrender. The Preston Strike, 1853-1854* (Cambridge, 1981).
84. Street ballad printed by Disley, High Street, St Giles, London; in BDL, Firth, Ballads, Political and Social, c 16, p. 260.
85. Written by Harry K. McClintoch ('Haywire Mac'), *I.W.W. Songs*, p. 9.
86. E. Trory, *Between the Wars* (Brighton, 1974), p. 121.
87. 'The Bureau' in Gatherer (ed.), *Songs and Ballads*, pp. 93-5.
88. 'The Dream', in Robin Morton (ed.), *Folksongs sung in Ulster*, no. 25.
89. *New City Songster*, no. 20 (Apr. 1985), 12-13 and 16-17.
90. Written in 1985 by Peter Coe; on record of same title.

Chapter 4: Crime

1. B.-L. de Muralt, *Lettres sur les Anglais et les Français et sur les Voyages* (1725) (my trans.).
2. E. P. Thompson, *The Making of the English Working Class* (1963), p. 61.
3. Jonathan Swift, *Poems*, ed. H. Williams (Oxford, 1937), vol. 2, p. 399.
4. James Hopkinson, *The Memoirs of a Victorian Cabinet Maker*, ed. J. B. Goodman (1968), p. 9.
5. Philip Massinger, *The Bondman* (1624), Act v, Scene iii.
6. Herbert L. Collman (ed.), *Ballads and Broadsides*, no. 67.
7. In Joseph Ritson, *Ancient Songs, from the Time of King Henry the Third, to the Revolution* (1792), p. 150.
8. Now lost, but listed in Rollins, *Analytical Index*, no. 1617.
9. Collman (ed.), *Ballads and Broadsides*, no. 54.
10. Roy Palmer (ed.), *Everyman's Book of British Ballads*, no. 48; on record *Wild Rover.*
11. Cecil Sharp, *Folk Songs from Somerset* (5 vols, 1904-9), vol. 2, no. 31. See also *Sharp*, no. 239, and B. H. Bronson, 'Samuel Hall's Family Tree', in *idem*, *The Ballad as Song*, pp. 18-36. On records *Fair Game* and *Country Life.*
12. The tune is prescribed, but not printed for 'The Moderator's Dream', in *Pills to Purge Melancholy*, vol. 2 (1719 edn), p. 182; however, the tune given, but not named, for 'A Song' in ibid., vol. 6 (1720), is probably 'Chimney Sweep'.
13. Francis Place, Specimens of Songs and Fragments, in BL, Place MSS, Add. MS 27825, fol. 150, no. 14.
14. *Punch*, 16-17 (17 Mar. 1849), p. 114.

15. George Petrie, *The Complete Collection of Irish Music*, ed. Charles Villiers Stanford (3 vols, 1905), no. 747.

16. C. A. Federer (ed.), *Yorkshire Chapbooks*, p. 8.

17. 'The Dunghill Cock', in W. H. Logan, *A Pedlar's Pack of Ballads and Songs*, pp. 118–21; on record *Garners Gay*.

18. *Gentleman's Magazine*, 7 Apr. 1739.

19. 'Distressed Men of War', street ballad printed by J. Davenport, 6 St George's Court, London [1802]; repr. in Roy Palmer (ed.), *The Oxford Book of Sea Songs*, no. 79.

20. Macaulay, *History of England*, vol. 1, pp. 373–4.

21. J. Cobley, *The Convicts, 1788–1792* (Sydney, 1965), p. 222.

22. 'Sylvia's Trial of Her Sweetheart', street ballad printed by L. Lund, York; in BL, York Publications, 1870 c 2, p. 9.

23. See Ritson (ed.), and J. C. Holt, *Robin Hood* (1982).

24. A song entitled 'The Great Train Robbery' is in Palmer (ed.), *Ballad History*, no. 81.

25. See John and Alan Lomax, *Cowboy Songs and Other Frontier Ballads* (New York, 1938).

26. See Hugh Anderson, *The Story of Australian Folksong* (New York, 1962), R. E. Edwards, *The Overlander Song Book*; and Warren Fahey (ed.), *Eureka. The Songs that Made Australia*, together with the records *Great Australian* and *Ned Kelly*.

27. Quoted above; in oral tradition as 'Turpin Hero'; in Palmer (ed.), *English Country Songbook*, no. 45.

28. Richard Jefferies, 'The Labourer's Daily Life', in *The Toilers of the Field* (1981; orig. 1892), p. 59.

29. Quoted in W. Roughead, *Burke and Hare* (Edinburgh, 1921), p. 3.

30. Peter Linebaugh, 'The Tyburn Riots against the Surgeons', in Hay et al., *Albion's Fatal Tree*, p. 85.

31. Samuel Richardson, *Letters Written to and for Particular Friends* (1928; orig. 1741), p. 219.

32. 'The Surgeon's Warning' (1798), in *The Poetical Works of Robert Southey* (Paris, 1829), pp. 664–5.

33. 'Mary's Ghost', in Thomas Hood, *Whims and Oddities* (2nd ser., 1844).

34. R. E. Leader, *Reminiscences of Sheffield* (1876), p. 350.

35. Ibid., pp. 351 and 348.

36. 'The Resurrection Men', street ballad printed by Stephenson, Gateshead [1821–38]; in BDL, Harding, Quarto Street Ballads, no. 3266.

37. *The Journal of Sir Walter Scott*, vol. 2 (1890), p. 225.

38. See Roughead, *Burke and Hare* (1948 edn), Appendix 9. A number of the ballads listed are preserved in the National Library of Scotland and Edinburgh City Library, including 'William Burk's Execution', a street ballad without imprint (in both). 'A Timely Hint to Anatomical Practitioners and their Associates—the Resurrectionists. A New Song—Tune, Macpherson's Farewell', another street ballad without imprint, is also in Edinburgh City Library.

39. Written (save for traditional chorus) and sung by the late Angus Russell, Kilwinning, Ayrshire; recorded by Peter Cooke, 1970, School of Scottish Studies, SA 1970/180/A3; published in *Tocher*, no. 5 (1972), 140–1.

40. Grey, *Cottage Life*, pp. 43–4.

41. *The Journals of George Sturt, 1890–1927*, ed. E. D. Mackerness (2 vols, Cambridge, 1967), vol. 1, p. 121.

42. *Trials and Sentence on Mrs. Dyer for the Wholesale Murder of Children. At Reading,*

booklet without imprint [1896], in BDL, Firth, Ballads: Crime and Punishment, c 17.

43. R. Altick, *Victorian Studies in Scarlet* (1972), p. 54. Altick says that the ballad mentioned is printed in F. T. Jesse, *The Trial of Samuel Herbert Dougal* (Edinburgh, 1928), but this is not the case. A search at Essex RO, including the issues of *The Essex Weekly News* for June and July 1903, has failed to turn up the ballad or its mention in the press. Perhaps Dougal's reference is to another local newspaper.

44. P. Collins, *Dickens and Crime* (1962).

45. Altick, *Victorian Studies*, p. 288.

46. 'Mary Ashford's Tragedy', street ballad printed by T. Bloomer, Birmingham [1817]; in Birmingham RL, Ballads 256712, p. 58; repr. in Palmer (ed.), *Birmingham Ballads*, no. 6.

47. Altick, *Victorian Studies*, p. 288.

48. See Thomas Gretton, *Murders and Moralities: English Catchpenny Prints, 1800–1860* (1980).

49. Street ballad printed by J. Catnach, 2 and 3 Monmouth Court, Seven Dials, London; in Hindley (ed.), *Curiosities*, vol. 2, p. 189.

50. Henry Mayhew, *London Labour and the London Poor* (4 vols, 1861–2), vol. 2, pp. 237–8, and vol. 3, pp. 206–7.

51. Street ballad printed by Harkness, Preston; in Hindley (ed.), *Curiosities*, vol. 2, p. 195.

52. 'Horrid Murder of a Gentleman in a Railway Carriage', street ballad without imprint; in Hindley (ed.), *Curiosities*, p. 209.

53. 'The Execution of James Bloomfield Rush', street ballad printed by Harkness, Preston; in Hindley (ed.), *Curiosities*, p. 196.

54. Altick, *Victorian Studies*, p. 288.

55. 'Maria Marten', sung by George Hall, Hooton Roberts, Yorkshire; noted by R. A. Gatty, 1907, in Birmingham RL, MS no. 661164; printed in Palmer (ed.), *English Country Songbook*, no. 61.

56. Sir Samuel Romilly, in Parliamentary Debates 1/XV/366, House of Commons, 9 Feb. 1810.

57. A. G. L. Shaw, *Convicts and the Colonies* (1971), p. 25.

58. The edition printed by Corcoran of Dublin is repr. by J. H. Jennings in *Virginia Historical Magazine*, Apr. 1948, pp. 180–94.

59. Quoted in Shaw, *Convicts*, pp. 138–9.

60. John Frost, *The Horrors of Convict Life* (1856).

61. Marcus Clarke, *His Natural Life* (Harmondsworth, 1970; orig. 1870); William Derricourt, *Old Convict Days*.

62. Birmingham edition printed by T. Bloomer; in Madden, vol. 21, fol. 754.

63. Street ballad printed by J. Pitts, 14 Great St Andrew Street, Seven Dials, London [1802–19, though the song must date from before 1776]; in private collection. A later edition by the same printer is given in Palmer (ed.), *Ballad History*, no. 26, together with a tune of 1907 from oral tradition. Cf. record *Crown of Horn*.

64. Palmer (ed.), *English Country Songbook*, no. 48; on records *Songs from Suffolk* and *Broomfield Wager*.

65. Street ballad without imprint; in Madden, vol. 5, fol. 896; repr. in Holloway and Black (ed.), *Later English*, vol. 1, no. 63.

66. Street ballad without imprint; in BDL, Firth, c 17, p. 205.

67. Street ballad printed by H. F. Sefton, Broad Street, Worcester; in Birmingham RL.

68. 'Botany Bay', beginning 'Farewell to old England', in Anderson, *Australian Folksong*, pp. 4–5.
69. Street ballad printed by T. Batchelar, 14 Hackney Road Crescent, London [1828–32]; in Madden. For an oral version, see *Sharp*, no. 236B.
70. Shaw, *Convicts*, p. 158.
71. Street ballad printed by W. Wright, Moor Street, Birmingham [1831–5, but probably dating from 1828]; in Madden, vol. 21, fol. 781; tune, 'The Convict of Van Dieman's Land', from P. W. Joyce, *Old Irish Folk Music and Songs* (Dublin, 1909), p. 102. See also Roy Palmer, 'The Origin of "Van Dieman's Land" and "Young Henry the Poacher": a Hypothesis', *Folk Music Journal*, 3, no. 2 (1976), 161–4.
72. O. Lochlainn (ed.), *Irish Street Ballads*, no. 21.
73. Ord, *Bothy Songs*, pp. 384–8.
74. Street ballad printed by Jackson and Son, Moor Street, Birmingham [1839–51, but probably dating from 1829]; in Madden, vol. 21, fol. 565; repr. in Palmer (ed.), *Birmingham Ballads*, no. 14.
75. Street ballad printed by W. Wright, Moor Street, Birmingham [1831–5]; in Madden, vol. 21, fol. 781.
76. Palmer (ed.), *Everyman's Book of British Ballads*, no. 59.
77. Anderson, *Australian Folksong*, p. 12.
78. Street ballad printed by T. Dodds, 43 Head of the Side, Newcastle (1842); in Mitchell Library, Sydney.
79. *The Antiquary*, 11 (1885), 209. A version with 5 verses is in J. H. Turner, *The Annals of Wakefield House of Correction* (1904).
80. I. C. Ellis, *Records of Nineteenth Century Leicester* (1935), p. 203.
81. Henry Mayhew and J. Binny, *The Criminal Prisons of London* (1862), p. 303.
82. Street ballad printed by J. Pitts, 6 Great St Andrew Street, Seven Dials, London [?1819]; in BDL, Harding, Quarto Street Ballads, no. 2690; repr. in Palmer (ed.), *Ballad History*, no. 40.
83. Street ballad printed by J. Pitts, 6 Great St Andrew Street, Seven Dials, London [1820–44]; in BL, Baring-Gould Broadsides, LR 271 a 2, vol. 3, p. 195.
84. 'Botany Bay', beginning 'Let us drink a good health', in Edwards, *Overlander Song Book*, pp. 13–14.
85. 'New Bayley Tread-Mill', street ballad printed by A. Swindells, Manchester [?1824]; in Oldham CL, Oldham Collection, p. 92; repr. in Boardman and Palmer (eds), *Manchester Ballads*, no. 7.
86. Quoted in Michael Ignatieff, *A Just Measure of Pain. The Penitentiary in the Industrial Revolution* (1978), p. 177.
87. 'Gaol Song', sung by W. Davy, Beaminster, Dorset; noted by H. E. D. Hammond, 1906; in R. Vaughan Williams and A. L. Lloyd (eds), *The Penguin Book of English Folk Songs*, p. 39; on record *Selection*.
88. 'Bellevue Gaol', street ballad without imprint; in BDL, Harding, Quarto Street Ballads, no. 237. Another version is in Boardman and Palmer (eds), *Manchester Ballads*, no. 26.
89. 'Kirkdale Gaol', street ballad without imprint; in Harding, Quarto Street Ballads, no. 2000.
90. 'A New Song on Wakefield Gaol', street ballad no. 582; printed by J. Harkness, 121 Church Street, Preston [1849]; in Madden, vol. 18, fol. 1117; repr. in Palmer (ed.), *A Touch*, p. 250.
91. 'Warwick Gaol', street ballad printed by Jackson and Son, Birmingham [1839–?51]; in National Library of Wales, Harvey Broadsides, H378.

92. 'County Gaol', two street ballads, one printed by Such of London, and the other without imprint; in Harding, Quarto Street Ballads, nos 729 and 731.
93. Street ballads without imprint; in Kidson, vol. 1, p. 108. An oral version is quoted in Kitchen, *Brother to the Ox*, p. 97.
94. *Song Book*, ed. W. H. Armstrong, pp. 12–13; repr. in Palmer (ed.), *A Touch*, p. 257; on record *Tommy Armstrong*.
95. *Sunday Times*, 5 Nov. 1975.
96. F. P., writing in *English Dance and Song*, 47, no. 3 (1985), 30.
97. On record *I Wish*.

Chapter 5: Pastime

1. Wordsworth, *The Prelude*, book 7.
2. Ben Jonson, *Bartholomew Fair* (1614), II, iv, and III, v.
3. Street ballad 'Imprinted at London for E. W.' [1614]; in *Pepys*, vol. 1, no. 8.
4. *Pills to Purge Melancholy*, vol. 4 (1719–20), pp. 169–70.
5. Street ballad printed for A. M[ilbourne] [*c.*1682]; in *Bagford*, vol. 1, p. 22.
6. 'The Wonders of Bartholomew Fair', street ballad printed by J. Pitts, 14 Great St Andrew Street, Seven Dials, London (1808–14); in Johnson, Street Ballads, Box 7, no. 328.
7. Street ballad printed by Jennings, Water Lane, Fleet Street, London (1809); in author's collection; tune, 'Galloping Randy Dandy O', in *The Bellman*, 28 Jul. 1917, p. 100.
8. My calculations, from lists in John Richardson, *The Local Historian's Encyclopedia* (New Barnet, 1974).
9. Mark Judd, '"The Oddest Combination of Town and Country": Popular Culture and the London Fairs, 1800–60', in *Leisure in Britain, 1780–1914*, ed. John K. Walton and James Walvin (Manchester, 1983), p. 12.
10. *Sharp*, no. 1.
11. Sabine Baring-Gould, *Songs of the West* (1905 edn), no. 16.
12. Palmer (ed.), *English Country Songbook*, no. 113.
13. On record *Unto Brigg Fair*.
14. Street ballad printed by Hoggett, Durham, in Newcastle UL; repr. in Roy Palmer and Jon Raven (eds), *The Rigs of the Fair*, no. 2.
15. BL, Garlands, 11621 b 6.
16. Robert W. Malcolmson, *Popular Recreations in English Society, 1700–1850* (Cambridge, 1973), p. 78.
17. 'Nelly the Milk Maid', street ballad printed by Thornton, Kenilworth; in BDL, Firth, Ballads and Broadsides, b 33, p. 47; repr. in Roy Palmer, 'Some Warwickshire Ballads', *Warwickshire History*, 6, no. 5 (1986) 152.
18. 'Young Ramble Away. A New Song', street ballad printed by Wood, New Meeting Street, Birmingham [1802–27]; in Birmingham RL, Broadsides, 119932, no. 99; cf. Palmer (ed.), *Birmingham Ballads*, no. 23.
19. Allan, *Farmer's Boy*, pp. 12–13.
20. 'Weyhill Fair', in *Notes and Queries*, 7th ser., 5 (1888), 352.
21. 'Howden Fair', ibid., p. 345.
22. Harland and Wilkinson, *Ballads and Songs*, pp. 52–5; on record *Lancashire Mon.*
23. Street ballad printed by Ordoyno, Nottingham; in Madden, vol. 20, fol. 68; repr. in Palmer (ed.), *A Touch*, p. 102; on record *To See*.
24. Street ballad without imprint [?1850s]; in BDL, Firth, Ballads: Sports and Pastimes, c 19, p. 187; repr. in Palmer, 'Warwickshire Ballads', p. 150.

25. John Evelyn, *Diary*, 24 Jan. 1684.
26. Street ballad printed by J. Pitts, 14 Great St Andrew Street, Seven Dials, London [1815]; in BDL, Firth, c 19, p. 143.
27. 'A Description of the Fair in this Town, and of all the Fairs in England', in a garland entitled *The Linnet*, printed by W. Eyres, Warrington; in Harding, Garlands, A. 8, no. 43.
28. Street ballad printed by Wood, Birmingham [1802–27]; in Birmingham RL, 119932, no. 10.
29. Street ballad without imprint [?1850s]; in Kidson, vol. 2, p. 44.
30. Street ballad printed by H. P. Such, 177 Union Street, London SE [1863–85]; in BL, Baring-Gould Broadsides, LR 271 a 2, vol. 1–1, p. 206.
31. Street ballad printed by W. Ford, York Street, Sheffield [1830–58]; in BL, Baring-Gould Broadsides, LR 271 a 2, vol. 1–1, p. 168; cf. Palmer and Raven (eds), *Rigs*, no. 1; on record *English Sporting*; tune in Frank Kidson, *A Garland of English Folk Songs* [1926], p. 4.
32. Written by C. John Trythall in 1912; printed in Clive Gunnell, *The Tavistock Goosie Fair* (St Teath, 1978); cf. Palmer and Raven (eds), *Rigs*, no. 4; on record *Young Hunting*.
33. Written by Bert Lee and R. P. Weston, and issued on a Panachord Record (25400–B) in 1932; oral version in Palmer (ed.), *Ballad History*, no. 77; on record *Deep Lancashire*.
34. 'Bloxwich Wake', in E. J. Homeshaw, *The Story of Bloxwich* (Bloxwich, 1955), pp. 222–4.
35. Voltaire, letter to an unknown correspondent, first published posthumously in *Mélanges Littéraires* (1829) (my trans.).
36. *The Autobiography of Francis Place (1771–1854)*, ed. Mary Thale (Cambridge, 1972), p. xxvi.
37. Dickens, *Sketches by Boz* (1839), ch. 12.
38. Street ballad printed by W. Dever, 18 Great St Andrew Street, Seven Dials, London [?1850]; in BDL, Firth, c 19, p. 138.
39. 'The Crystal Palace', in Johnson, Street Ballads, Box 10; 'Exhibition of All Nations', in BDL, Firth, c 19, p. 196; 'The National Exhibition' and 'Uncle Ned's Visit to the Exhibition', in Madden, vol. 23, fols 96 and 261.
40. Street ballad printed by H. P. Such, 177 Union Street, London SE [1863–85]; in BL, Crampton, 11621 h 11, vol. 4, p. 90.
41. Street ballad printed by Disley, Arthur Street, Oxford Street, London [1860–78]; in BDL, Firth, c 19, p. 178.
42. See 'Johnny Green's Description of Tinker's Gardens', by Alexander Wilson (1804–46), in Harland (ed.), *Songs of the Wilsons*, pp. 52–6 (cf. Boardman and Palmer (eds), *Manchester Ballads*, no. 12); and 'Comic Song. Trentham Park', street ballad printed by Hill and Halden, Stafford, in BL, Crampton, vol. 4, p. 179.
43. 'Rothesay, O', in Norman Buchan (ed.), *101 Scottish songs*, p. 104.
44. Ford, *Vagabond Songs*, p. 1.
45. Palmer (ed.), *Ballad History*, no. 78.
46. Chappell, *Popular Music*, pp. 41–3.
47. Palmer (ed.), *Ballad History*, no. 78.
48. 'A Drop of Good Beer', street ballad printed by Pratt, Birmingham [1845–61, but dating from 1830]; in BL, A Collection of Ballads printed in Birmingham, 18976 e 2; repr. in Palmer (ed.), *A Touch*, p. 168; on record, together with songs listed in nn. 45–7, *The Tale*.

49. Madden, vol. 18, fols. 629, 638, 644, 646–7, 656–7, 705, 744, etc.
50. Street ballad printed by Bonner and Henson, Bristol; in Madden, vol. 23, fol. 130; repr. in Palmer (ed.), *A Touch*, p. 172.
51. Street ballad printed by H. Disley, 57 High Street, Oxford Street, London [1860–78]; in BL, Crampton, vol. 2, p. 11.
52. Philip Stubbes, *Anatomie of Abuses*, ed. F. K. Furnivall (2 vols in 1, 1877–82; written 1583), pp. 180–1.
53. Gardiner, *Music and Friends*, vol. 3, pp. 32–3.
54. Street ballad without imprint; in BDL, Firth, c 19, p. 64.
55. Burne, *Shropshire Folk-Lore*, p. 563.
56. Chappell, *Popular Music*, p. 600.
57. 'Bonny Grey', in Palmer (ed.), *English Country Songbook*, no. 122; on record *English Sporting*.
58. Street ballad without imprint; in BDL, Douce, vol. 3, f. 109.
59. Matthew Hodgart, *The Faber Book of Ballads* (1965), p. 257.
60. Robert Graves, *English and Scottish Ballads* (1957), no. 36.
61. Samuel Butler, *Alps and Sanctuaries* (1891), pp. 305–8.
62. Joshua Vernal, 'The Author of "Wednesbury Cocking"', *Birmingham Daily Post*, 24 Aug. 1859.
63. J. F. Ede, *History of Wednesbury* (Wednesbury, 1962), pp. 153–4.
64. Street ballad without imprint; in BL, A Collection of Ballads printed at Various Places in the Provinces, 1876 e 3, p. 469.
65. See Palmer, *Birmingham Street Ballads*.
66. See, for example, *Listener*, 26 Feb. 1976; *The Times*, 5 May 1983; *Guardian*, 18 June 1985.
67. Joseph Strutt, *The Sports and Pastimes of the People of England*, ed. William Hone (1833; orig. 1801), pp. 257 and 277.
68. 'Perry's Croft Bull Bait', in Jon Raven, *The Urban and Industrial Songs of the Black Country and Birmingham*, pp. 117–18.
69. 'The Wedgbury Cockers', in Homeshaw, *Story of Bloxwich*, pp. 220–1.
70. Street ballad printed by T. Wood, Birmingham [1802–27]; in Birmingham RL, 119932, no. 138.
71. Street ballad printed by J. Russell, Birmingham [1815–39]; in Madden, vol. 23.
72. 'An Account of the Birmingham Association taking a Bull from a Country Wake, in the environs of the town, and marching it as a prisoner to the dungeon in Peck Lane', in William Mackay, *Ballad Chronicles*, no. 13; cf. ibid., no. 12, 'Wyndham's Opinion of Bull Baiting'. Both were written in 1798.
73. Abraham Smith, *A Scriptural and Moral Catechism* (Birmingham, [?1834]), pp. 10–11.
74. Street ballad without imprint; in BDL, Firth, c 19, p. 175.
75. Street ballad printed by Pitts, Great St Andrew Street, Seven Dials, London [1802–44, but probably 1817–27]; in Johnson, Street Ballads, Box 31.
76. Place, *Autobiography*, p. 70.
77. Street ballad printed by R. Raikes and W. Dicey, Northampton [*c.*1764]; in Derby PL, Derbyshire Anthology, MS 8225.
78. George H. Burton, *Stamford Bull-Running* (Stamford, 1927), p. 3.
79. *Stamford Mercury*, 18 Nov. 1785.
80. R. Chambers, *The Book of Days* (2 vols, n.d.), vol. 2, p. 575.
81. Burton, *Stamford Bull-Running*, pp. 4–5.
82. Keith Thomas, *Man and the Natural World. Changing Attitudes in England, 1500–1800* (1983), p. 164.

83. William Blake, 'Auguries of Innocence' [c.1803], in *Poems and Prophecies* (1927 edn), p. 333.

84. Rollins, *Analytical Index*, no. 1179.

85. Street ballad printed for Francis Grove, on Snow Hill, London [1660]; in *Roxburghe*, vol. 7, p. 87.

86. *Guardian*, 9 and 30 July 1974.

87. Street ballad printed by John White, Newcastle upon Tyne [1711–61]; in Chetham's Library, Manchester, Halliwell-Phillips Collection, no. 217. For an earlier version, of between 1689 and 1709, see *Roxburghe*, vol. 1, p. 320; and for a recent version from oral tradition, see Palmer and Raven (eds), *Rigs*, no. 16; on record *English Sporting*.

88. Chappell, *Popular Music*, pp. 650–2.

89. On record *Fine Hunting*.

90. Alexander Mackay-Smith, *The Songs of Foxhunting*, no. 17. For a recent oral version, see Palmer (ed.), *English Country Songbook*, no. 127; on record *Among the Old Familiar*.

91. See 'Old Snowball', on record *Fine Hunting*; 'The Exmoor Hunt', by Henry Newbolt, in R. W. Patten, *Exmoor Custom and Song* (Dulverton, 1974), pp. 60–2; and 'At Quorndon Old Kennels', in J. C. Masters, *Hunting Songs* (Nottingham, [?1883]), p. 11.

92. See 'John Peel' and 'Joe Bowman', in *Songs of the Fellpacks* (Melbreak, 1971), pp. 2–3 and 55.

93. 'The Huntsman', in Palmer (ed.), *English Country Songbook*, no. 126.

94. 'The Fox-Hunting Song', street ballad printed by J. Pitts, 14 Great St Andrew Street, Seven Dials, London [1802–19]; in Madden, vol. 8, fol. 959; repr. in Holloway and Black (eds), *Later English*, vol. 2, no. 53.

95. 'Chivvy, Chivvy O', in Williams, *Folk-Songs of the Upper Thames*, p. 62.

96. 'Derbyshire Football Song', in *South Yorkshire Notes and Queries*, June 1899, pp. 43–4. Cf. 'Alnwick Football Song', in Palmer and Raven (eds), *Rigs*, no. 18.

97. Madden, vol. 18, fols 953, 954, 962, and 1033–6.

98. 'Young Tyler', in Clare College, Cambridge, Cecil Sharp MSS, no. 1090; repr. in Roy Palmer (ed.), *Room for Company* (Cambridge, 1971), no. 34.

99. Quoted in Clifford Morsley, *News from the English Countryside, 1750–1850* (1979), p. 135.

100. 'A New Song on the American Female Prize Fight', in James N. Healy (ed.), *The Mercier Book of Old Irish Street Ballads*, vol. 3, *The People at Play*, no. 15.

101. George Borrow, *Lavengro* (1851), ch. 26.

102. Tom Langley, *The Life of Tom Sayers* (Leicester, 1973), p. 8.

103. Street ballad without imprint [1859]; in Manchester RL, Ballads Q 398.8 S 9, vol. 1; repr. in Palmer and Raven (eds), *Rigs*, p. 42.

104. 'Sayers' and Heenan's Great Fight for the Championship', street ballad printed by H. Disley, 57 High Street, St Giles, London [1860]; in Hindley (ed.), *Curiosities*, p. 124; on record *Gamblers*.

105. See record of same title.

106. Quoted in Keith Gregson, 'When the Balloons went up', *English Dance and Song*, 41, no. 2 (1979), 10.

107. Street ballad, 'Sold at No. 42, Long Lane', London [?late eighteenth century]; in BDL, Firth, c 19, p. 123. See also Keith Gregson, 'The Songs of Tyneside Boat Racing', *North-East Labour History* (1982), 1–5.

108. Issued as a street ballad in 1981; repr. in *English Dance and Song*, 45, no. 1 (1983), 18.

109. Belfast PL, Sam Henry Collection, no. 669.
110. Street ballad printed by J. Catnach, London; in Harding, Quarto Street Ballads, no. 1983.
111. Street ballad printed by Walker, Durham; in Harding, Quarto Street Ballads, ibid, no. 2274.
112. Street ballad without imprint; in Harding, Quarto Street Ballads, no. 742.
113. Text in Horace Harman, *Buckinghamshire Dialect* (1929), pp. 121–2; published with tune in *Three Traditional Songs from Buckinghamshire* (n.d.), no. 1.

Chapter 6: The Sexes

1. The Carpenter collection is in the Library of Congress, but there is a copy at VWML.
2. Sung by George Tompsett, Cuckfield, Sussex; recorded by Mervyn Plunkett, 1957; text in *Folk Song Research*, 5, nos 2–3 (1986–7), 18; tune from copy of tape communicated by Steve Roud.
3. 'Isle of Wight Informer', street ballad without imprint [1827]; in Madden, vol. 22.
4. See 'Sale of a Wife', printed by W. Boag, Newcastle (1828), and 'A true and concise Account of a Woman selling her Husband', printed by W. Stephenson, Gateshead (1824); in John Rylands UL of Manchester, Crawford Broadsides, nos 1656 and 1631.
5. See 'Sale of a Wife', street ballad printed by Livsey, Manchester [1833–50]; in Manchester RL, Ballads, Q 821.04 B 3, p. 44.
6. *Pills to Purge Melancholy* (1719–20 edn), vol. 5, pp. 258–60.
7. *The Vauxhall Songster*, printed by T. Evans, Long Lane, London [1790s], no. 9; in BL, 1876 e 20, p. 71.
8. Street ballad printed by H. Such, 177 Union Street, Boro, London [1863–85]; in Harding, Quarto Street Ballads, no. 546; on record *Shamrock*.
9. Healy, *People at Play*, no. 1.
10. Ford, *Vagabond Songs*, pp. 1–4.
11. Robert Colls, *The Collier's Rant*, pp. 58–64.
12. Harland (ed.), *Songs of the Wilsons*, pp. 38–40.
13. 'Johnny Green's Wedding, and Description of Manchester Old Church', street ballad printed by Swindells, Manchester [1821–46]; in Madden, vol. 21, fol. 163.
14. Bob Copper, *A Song for Every Season*, p. 270; record of same title.
15. 'Navvy on the Line', street ballad no. 572, printed by Harkness, Preston [1849]; in Madden, vol. 18, fol. 1107; repr. in Palmer (ed.), *A Touch*, pp. 40–1.
16. Alan Macfarlane, 'Illegitimacy and Illegitimates in English History', in *Bastardy and its Comparative History*, ed. Peter Laslett, Karla Oosterveen, and Richard M. Smith (1980), ch. 2, p. 75.
17. Lawrence Stone, *The Family, Sex and Marriage in England, 1500–1800* (Harmondsworth, 1979), p. 384.
18. T. C. Smout, *A Century of the Scottish People, 1830–1950* (1986), p. 171.
19. Ronald Frankenburg, *Communities in Britain. Social Life in Town and Country* (Harmondsworth, 1966), p. 61.
20. Enid Porter, *Cambridgeshire Customs and Folklore* (1969), p. 5.
21. Recorded by Henry Glassie, 1972; printed in Henry Glassie, *Passing the Time*, pp. 684–5 and 832.
22. Peter Laslett, Introduction to Laslett et al. (ed.), *Bastardy*, p. 1.
23. 'The Kettle [Cattle] Smock', in Clare College, Cambridge, Sharp MSS, no. 1166.
24. Street ballad without imprint; in *Euing*, no. 112; original in 7-line stanzas; for a traditional version, see *Sharp*, no. 59.

25. 'O no, my Love, not I', street ballad printed by Kendrew, York [1803–51]; in BL, York Publications, 1870 c 2, p. 482; oral version, *Sharp*, no. 175.
26. 'The Basket of Eggs', in Roy Palmer (ed.), *Folk Songs Collected by Ralph Vaughan Williams*, no. 84.
27. 'The Christmas Goose', sung by Arthur Howard (1902–82) of Hazlehead, Penistone, Yorkshire; recorded by Ian Russell, 1981, published in *English Dance and Song*, 43, no. 4 (1981), 7; on record *Merry Mountain*.
28. Palmer (ed.), *English Country Songbook*, no. 64.
29. Henri Davenson, *Le Livre des Chansons*, no. 70.
30. Street ballad printed for W. Thackeray and T. Passinger [*c.*1680]; in Magdalene College, Cambridge, Pepys Ballads, vol. 2, p. 271.
31. 'The Frolicksome Keeper', street ballad without imprint; in BDL, Firth, Ballads and Broadsides, b 33, p. 32.
32. *Sharp*, no. 271.
33. Street ballad printed and sold by J. Millet, next door to the Flower-de-Luce, in Little Britain, London (1689); in Magdalene College, Cambridge, Pepys Ballads, vol. 5, p. 250.
34. V. de Sola Pinto and A. E. Rodway, *The Common Muse*, p. 624.
35. Street ballad printed by C. Bates, at the Sun and Bible in Pye Corner, London [*c.*1685]; in *Bagford*, vol. 1, pp. 51–3.
36. Street ballad printed for C. Brooksby, at the Golden Ball in Pye Corner, London [*c.*1685]; in *Bagford*, vol. 1, 19–21.
37. 'A Bold Dragoon', sung by an old labourer on Dartmoor; noted by W. Crossing, 1878, in Plymouth PL, Baring-Gould MSS, no. 65; published in Bertrand Harris Bronson, *The Singing Tradition of Child's Popular Ballads*, p. 518; on record *Songs of Seduction*. The song appears as 'The Jolly Trooper', in *The Lover's Garland*, BL 11621 c 5.
38. 'The Hog-Tub', street ballad without imprint; in BDL, Firth, b 33, p. 36.
39. Sung by Cecilia Costello (1883–1976), Birmingham; recorded by Roy Palmer, 1971, in *Folk Review*, July 1975, p. 13); for full version, see Palmer (ed.), *English Country Songbook*, no. 91.
40. 'The Weaver'. I have heard this version sung by A. L. Lloyd, but have not seen it in print. A variant is in Edith Fowke (ed.), *The Penguin Book of Canadian Folk Songs*, no. 61.
41. Street ballad without imprint, but issued by Harkness, Preston [1844]; in Madden, vol. 18, fol. 746; on record *Deep Lancashire*.
42. Place, *Autobiography*, pp. 57–8.
43. *Parliamentary Report on Education* (1835), p. 69.
44. The Place songs are among his MSS in BL, Add. MS 27825, fols 146–64.
45. *Parliamentary Report*, p. 70.
46. Place songs, BL, Add. MS 27825, fol. 151, no. 16.
47. Harding, Garlands, A 15 (19), pp. 7–8.
48. Place songs, BL, Add. MS 27825, fols 150–1, no. 13.
49. Ibid., fol. 148, no. 5.
50. Street ballad printed for P. Brooksby, at the Golden Ball, West Smithfield, London [*c.*1670–82]; in *Roxburghe*, vol. 1, pp. 604–6.
51. Street ballad printed by Todd, Thirsk, Yorkshire [*c.*1800]; in BL, 1870 c 2, p. 51.
52. Street ballad printed by T. Bloomer, Birmingham [1817–27]; in Birmingham RL, Ballads, 256712, no. 14; oral version in Frank Purslow (ed.), *The Wanton Seed* (1968), p. 115.
53. Street ballad printed by W. Jackson and Son, Birmingham [1839–*c.*51]; in BL,

Crampton, 11621 h 11, vol. 3, p. 106; tune sung by George Wyatt, West Harptree, Somerset; noted by Cecil Sharp, 1904, in Clare College, Cambridge, Sharp MSS, no. 385. The chorus has been added with the tune.

54. Street ballad without imprint; in National Library of Scotland, Lauriston Castle Collection, Ry. III a 10 (8).

55. Street ballad printed for T. Vere, at the Angel without Newgate, London [1656–82]; in BDL, Rawlinson Collection, Quarto 566.

56. *Shirburn*, no. 66.

57. Street ballad without imprint; in Johnson, Street Ballads, Box 32; on record *George Dunn*.

58. Bronson, *Singing Tradition*, pp. 171–3.

59. Ibid., pp. 197–9.

60. See Roy Palmer, 'The Weaver in Love'.

61. See 'The Pretty Ploughboy', in Palmer (ed.), *English Country Songbook*, no. 94.

62. Street ballad printed for P. Brooksby at the Golden Ball in West Smithfield, London; in Harvard UL, Houghton Library, English Broadside Ballads, vol. 2, no. 65H.

63. Street ballad dating from before 1693; in *Roxburghe*, vol. 7, p. 428; oral version, *Sharp*, no. 118.

64. Street ballad printed for P. Brooksby, J. Deacon, J. Blare, J. Back [1682–96]; in John Rylands UL of Manchester, Crawford Collection, no. 20; oral version, Palmer (ed.), *Folk Songs*, no. 103.

65. Street ballad without imprint; in VWML, Sharp Broadsides; oral version, Palmer (ed.), *English Country Songbook*, no. 39.

66. Street ballad without imprint; in Madden, vol. 26, fol. 28; oral version, Palmer (ed.), *Everyman's Book of British Ballads*, no. 119.

67. In *Three Excellent New Songs* (1794); in Harding, Garlands, A 1, no. 12; oral version, Palmer (ed.), *Everyman's Book of British Ballads*, no. 37.

68. Street ballad printed by W. Harris, 179 Deritend, Birmingham [1828–61]; in BL, Baring-Gould Broadsides, LR 271 a 2, vol. 1–1, p. 170.

69. Harry and Lesley Boardman (eds), *Folk Songs and Ballads of Lancashire*, p. 18.

70. 'Mary and the Handsome Factory Boy' and 'The Factory Girl', street ballads nos 329 and 353, printed by Harkness, Preston [1845]; in Madden, vol. 18, fols 865 and 889.

71. 'The Jolly Cotton Spinner', street ballad printed for A. Gilpin, 17 Oldhall Street; in Madden, vol. 5, fol. 891.

72. Street ballad no. 381. printed by J. O. Bebbington, 31 Oldham Road, Manchester [1856–61]; in Manchester RL, Ballads, Q 398.8 S 9, vol. 2, p. 356.

73. 'The Cotton Mill Song', on record *Songs, Ballads*.

74. 'Tom Tram in the West', in Charles Read Baskervill, *The Elizabethan Jig*, p. 310.

75. 'Little Dickie Milburn', in Purslow, *The Foggy Dew*, p. 52.

76. Rainer Wehse, *Schwanklied und Flugblatt in Grossbritannien* (Frankfurt, 1979), no. 476.

77. Street ballad printed by J. Pitts, 6 Great St Andrew Street, Seven Dials, London [1819–44]; in Nottingham UL, Ballads, A45; on record *Champions*.

78. Street ballad printed by J. Whiting, 131 Moor Street, Birmingham [1833–5]; in Harding, Quarto Street Ballads, no. 3230; oral version, Palmer (ed.), *Folk Songs*, no. 89.

79. Written by Bernard Wrigley in 1970; printed in Bernard Wrigley, *Out of his Head* (Daventry, 1976), pp. 4–5.

80. Street ballad printed for Alex. Milbourn, W. Onely, and T. Thackeray at the

Angel in Duck Lane, London (1693); in F. Burlinghame Fawcett (ed.), *Broadside Ballads*, no. 87; original in 8-line stanzas; on record *Yorkshire Garland*.

81. Bronson, *Singing Tradition*, pp. 210–15.
82. Ford, *Vagabond Songs*, p. 186; on record *Dalesman*.
83. In *Darlington Chapbooks*, printed by M. Vesey (Darlington, 1774), in Harding, Garlands, A. 5.
84. Street ballad printed for F. Coles, T. Vere, and J. Wright, London (1672); in *Pepys Ballads*, vol. 3, p. 138.
85. Street ballad without imprint; in Madden, vol. 5, fol. 929; tune, 'Gee ho Dobbin', in Chappell, *Popular Music*, p. 691; the text is also in Place's songs, BL Add. MS 27825, fol. 164, no. 33.
86. Street ballad without imprint; in Madden, vol. 26, fol. 25.
87. J. R. Kinloch, *The Ballad Book* (1827), pp. 8–9; on record *Scotia*.
88. Street ballad without imprint; in Madden, vol. 6, fol. 1573; repr. in Holloway and Black (eds), *Later English*, vol. 1, no. 96.
89. Street ballad printed by J. Wheeler, Manchester [1838–45]; in BL, 1876 e 3.
90. Hopkinson, *Victorian Cabinet Maker*, p. 37; for a full version of the song, see Roy Palmer (ed.), *Love is Pleasing* (Cambridge, 1974), no. 35.
91. Street ballad no. 402, printed by Harkness, Preston [1845]; in Madden, vol. 18, fol. 938.
92. Street ballad printed by W. Ford, York Street, Sheffield [1830–58], with 'Eccles Wakes'; in BL, Baring-Gould Broadsides, LR 271 a 2, vol. 1–1, p. 168.
93. Holloway and Black (eds), *Later English*, vol. 1, no. 71.
94. Quoted from Sam Cowell's *120 Comic Songs*, in *Journal of the Folk Song Society*, no. 3 (1929), 148.
95. Iona and Peter Opie, *The Singing Game* (Oxford, 1985), no. 71.
96. In *The Careless Bachelor's Garland* (?Newcastle, ?1775), in BL, Collection of Newcastle Garlands, 11621 c 5. I am indebted to Iona Opie for a copy of this item.
97. Street ballad printed by J. Kendrew, Colliergate, York [1803–51]; in BL, York Publications, 1870 c 2, p. 97; on record *Yorkshire Garland*.
98. Bronson, *Singing Tradition*, pp. 471–7.
99. Palmer (ed.), *Everyman's Book of British Ballads*, no. 106.
100. Palmer (ed.), *Folk Songs*, no. 67.
101. Written by Mike Waterson, with a tune by Martin Carthy, adapted from 'On Board of a Man of War', in *New City Songster*, no. 20 (1985), 18–19.

Chapter 7: Politics

1. Street ballad printed by I. W. [?1615 or 1616]; in *Pepys*, vol. 1, no. 17.
2. Street ballad printed by the Assigns of Thomas Symcocke [*c.*1620]; in *Roxburghe*, vol. 2, pp. 581–6.
3. Street ballad printed for H. G. [Henry Gosson], London (1630); in *Roxburghe*, vol. 2, pp. 334–8; repr. in Palmer (ed.), *Ballad History*, no. 4.
4. *Notes and Queries*, 4th ser., 5 (1870), 401.
5. Street ballad without imprint, written by L. W. [Lawrence White]; in BDL, Wood Broadsides, E 25 (119); repr. in Pinto and Rodway, *Common Muse*, no. 42.
6. Street ballad printed for P. Brooksby, J. Deacon, J. Blare, J. Back [1682–96]; in *Pepys*, vol. 6, no. 410.
7. Street ballad without imprint; in BL, 1876 e 20.
8. Street ballad printed for J. Deacon at the Angel in Guiltspur-street, without imprint [1688], in *Pepys*, vol. 3, no. 157.

9. Street ballad without imprint, in VWML, Sharp Broadsides.
10. Street ballad printed for A. Milbourn and sold by R. Hayhurst in Little Britain, London; in *Pepys*, vol. 4, no. 238; repr. in Macaulay, *History*, vol. 3, p. 1345.
11. Macaulay, *History*, vol. 3, p. 36, and vol. 1, pp. 288–9.
12. 'The Budget', street ballad without imprint [1784]; in Madden, vol. 4, fol. 232.
13. John Ehrman, *The Younger Pitt*, vol. 1 (1969), p. 250.
14. Street ballad without imprint [1785]; in Madden, vol. 4, fol. 231; original in 6-line stanzas; tune from MS book (1790) belonging to Dr Crotch, in Mitchell Library, Glasgow, Kidson Collection.
15. Street ballad without imprint, bearing MS inscription '1794'; in Madden, vol. 4, fol. 242.
16. Mackay, *Ballad Chronicles*, nos 1 and 2.
17. 'The Income Tax', street ballad without imprint [1799], to the tune of 'Tanta Rara Rogues all'; in Manchester RL, Ballads, BR F 824.02 BA 1.
18. 'The Poor Man's Litany', street ballad printed by Dean and Munday, 35 Threadneedle Street, London; in Harding, Quarto Street Ballads, no. 3091.
19. 'The Tax upon Income', street ballad printed by J. Jennings, Sheffield; in Sheffield City Library, Miscellaneous Papers, 979M.
20. 'A Rare Row about the Income Tax; or, the Cat Let out of the Bag. By S. Lane, St Margaret's, Norwich', street ballad without imprint; in London UL, Broadside Collection, 602, 1.
21. Street ballad printed by W. Pratt, Birmingham [1841]; in BL, A Collection of Ballads printed in Birmingham, 1876 e 2. Irish version: 'A New Song on the Taxes', in O. Lochlainn (ed.), *Irish Street Ballads*, no. 4. Scots version: 'We Never had such Taxes', in Buchan and Hall, *Scottish Folksinger*, p. 10.
22. Street ballad without imprint; in Madden, vol. 6, fol. 704.
23. Street ballad printed by J. Birt, 10 Great St Andrew Street, Seven Dials, London; in Johnson, Street Ballads, Box 1, no. 91.
24. Street ballad printed by W. Pratt, Birmingham; in Norwich City Library, Ballads printed by Catnach and others, Z 821.024; repr. in Palmer (ed.), *A Touch*, pp. 299–301.
25. See version printed as no. 76 by Harkness, Preston [1841]; in Madden, vol. 18, fol. 605.
26. Street ballad without imprint; in Harding, Quarto Street Ballads, no. 2648.
27. Strutt, *Sports and Pastimes*, p. 187.
28. Street ballad 'Imprinted at London by William Pickeringe dwelling under Saynt Magnus Church' [1588]; in Society of Antiquaries, London, Broadside Collection; repr. in Pinto and Rodway, *Common Muse*, no. 4; quoted in Shakespeare, *King Lear*, III. vi.
29. Street ballad printed for the author, Henry Jones; in BDL, Wood Collection, 401, fol. 171b; repr. in Palmer (ed.), *Ballad History*, no. 9.
30. Street ballad printed for J. Deacon in Guiltspur-street, London; in BDL, Wood Collection, E. 25, 114.
31. See John Ashton (ed.), *Modern Street Ballads*, pp. 228–33.
32. Ibid., p. 274.
33. 'A New Song called the Downfall of Trade', a street ballad without imprint; in Birmingham UL, Selbourne Collection, Irish Ballads.
34. Street ballad printed by H. Paul, 22 Brick Lane, Spitalfields, London [1840–5]; in Derby PL, Derbyshire Ballads of the Eighteenth and Nineteenth Centuries; repr. in Palmer (ed.), *Ballad History*, no. 52.
35. W. Henderson (ed.), *Victorian Street Ballads*, p. 155.

36. First couplet in Iona and Peter Opia, *The Lore and Language of Schoolchildren* (1977 edn), p. 26; second couplet communicated by Iona Opie.

37. Ibid., pp. 40–1.

38. Street ballads printed by John Fairburn, Broadway, Ludgate Hill, London; in BL, Songs and Poems, 1871 f 16, pp. 34, 33, and 32.

39. C. H. Firth, 'The Ballad History of the Reign of Charles I', p. 38.

40. Thomas Percy, *Reliques* (1857 edn), pp. 344–5; repr. in Palmer (ed.), *Ballad History*, no. 6. Cf. 'The Downfall of Cheapside-Crosse', *A Collection of Loyal Songs* (1731; orig. 1662), p. 138.

41. Street ballad printed for Robert Ibbotson, London [1648]; repr. in John Ashton, *A Century of Ballads*, pp. 129–33.

42. Worcester College, Oxford, Clarke Papers, vol. xviii, fol. 32; repr. in *Clarke Papers*, ed. C. H. Firth, vol. 2 (1894), pp. 221–4, and in Palmer (ed.), *Ballad History*, no. 7.

43. *The Works of Gerard Winstanley*, ed. George H. Sabine (Ithaca, N.Y., 1941), pp. 667–72.

44. London UL, Broadside Collection, 351, 3. One of the items, 'Britannia Excisa', is repr. in Palmer (ed.), *Ballad History*, no. 18.

45. 'A New Song', street ballad without imprint; in London UL, Broadside Collection, 423, 9.

46. In *Anacreon's Feast*, garland without imprint; in Harding, Garlands, A 9, no. 9.

47. Street ballad without imprint, in BDL, Firth, Ballads and Poems, 1714–1800, b 22, p. 107.

48. In *Wilkes and Granby's Garland* (Darlington, 1774); in Harding, Garlands, A. 5, Darlington Chapbooks, I.

49. Quoted in John Wardroper, *Kings, Lords and Wicked Levellers* (1973), p. 101.

50. Gardiner, *Music and Friends*, vol. 1, p. 222.

51. Street ballad printed by J. Pitts, 6 Great St Andrew Street, Seven Dials, London [1831–44]; in Birmingham UL, Selbourne Collection, English Ballads.

52. Street ballad printed by J. Catnach, 2 and 3 Monmouth Court, Seven Dials, London [1832–8]; in Harding, Quarto Street Ballads, no. 3899.

53. 'Total Destruction of Both Houses of Parliament', a street ballad without imprint, but issued by T. Willey, Cheltenham [1834]; in Madden, vol. 23, fol. 228.

54. 'The Agony Bill', street ballad printed by Catnach [1833]; in Birmingham UL, Selbourne Collection, English Ballads; repr. in Palmer (ed.), *Ballad History*, no. 47.

55. Quoted in *Notes and Queries*, 4th ser., 4 (1869), 276.

56. *Roxburghe*, vol. 1, p. 509.

57. John Playford, *Musical Companion*, book 1 (1673), p. 57.

58. E. J. Hobsbawm, *Industry and Empire* (Harmondsworth, 1969), p. 229.

59. Quoted in Morsley, *News from the English Countryside, 1750–1850*, p. 261.

60. Quoted in A. Brundage, *The Making of the New Poor Law* (1978), p. 123. I am indebted for this reference to Dr Patricia Hollis.

61. Street ballad printed by Taylor, Birmingham; in Madden, vol. 21, fol. 578; repr. in Palmer (ed.), *A Touch*, p. 260.

62. Street ballad printed by T. Ballard, Oxford; in BL, Baring-Gould Broadsides, LR 271 a 2, vol. 1–2, p. 52; repr. in Palmer (ed.), *Ballad History*, no. 48.

63. 'Verses on the Bradford Riot', printed by E. Keighley, Bradford; in Bradford PL, Scruton Collection, Broadsides, no. 2.

64. Street ballad without imprint; in Bradford PL, Scruton Collection, Broadsides, no. 2.

65. Street ballad printed by T. Birt; 39 Great St Andrew Street, Seven Dials, London; in BL, Baring-Gould Broadsides, 271 a 2, vol. 1–1, p. 46.
66. Belvoir Castle MSS, Letters &c., xv (1607–12), fol. 41. The 'libel' is enclosed in a letter of 26 Jul. 1607 from Sir William Pelham to the earl of Rutland. For some reason best known to himself, the present duke of Rutland has ignored several requests for access to these documents, and I have obtained copies by circuitous means.
67. Quoted in Sir William Dugdale, *The History of Imbanking and Draining of Divers Fens and Marshes* (1662), pp. 391–2; repr. in Palmer (ed.), *Ballad History*, no. 2.
68. Street ballad printed by R. Lee, 2 St Ann's Court, Dean Street, Soho; in BL, 1871 f 16.
69. Street ballad without imprint, but bearing the MS date 'Nov. 1792'; in BL, 1871 f 16.
70. Street ballad without imprint; in BL 1871 f 16.
71. Street ballad without imprint; in Madden, vol. 6, fol. 1929; repr. in Holloway and Black (eds), *Later English*, vol. 1, no. 124.
72. Street ballad without imprint, bearing the MS date 'Nov. 1792'; in BL, 1871 f 16.
73. Street ballads without imprint; in BDL, Firth, b 22, p. 86.
74. Street ballad printed by Weir, Horncastle; in BL, A Collection of Broadsides, LR 301 h 6, p. 13.
75. Street ballad without imprint; in Manchester RL; copy communicated by Brian Maidment.
76. Street ballad without imprint; in Accrington Public Library; copy communicated by Harry Boardman; on record *Transpennine*.
77. Street ballad without imprint; in Manchester RL, BR F 824.04 BAL, p. 134; repr. in Palmer (ed.), *A Touch*, p. 296.
78. Street ballad without imprint; in Johnson, Street Ballads, Box 32; repr. in Roy Palmer (ed.), *Rambling Soldier*, pp. 187–8.
79. *The Radical Reformers' New Song Book* (Newcastle, ?1820), pp. 21–2; in Newcastle UL, Chapbooks, no. 509.
80. John Stafford, *Songs Comic and Sentimental* (Ashton-under-Lyne, 1840), pp. 6–8 and 8–10. I am indebted to Sieglinde Huxhorn for copies of these songs. The tune prescribed for 'Peterloo' is 'Green upon the Cape', which may be a variant title for 'Plains of Waterloo', which is in Kidson's *Traditional Tunes*, p. 121.
81. Ibid., p. 163; repr. in Palmer (ed.), *Ballad History*, no. 41.
82. In *The Newcastle Songster*, NS, no. 5, pp. 16–18; in Harding, Chapbooks, no. 457, 13.
83. Street ballad printed by W. Wright, 99 Lichfield Street, Birmingham [1839]; in Madden, vol. 21, fol. 745.
84. Street ballad printed by E. Taylor, 67 Steelhouse Lane, Birmingham [1840]; in Madden, vol. 21, fol. 595; repr. in Palmer (ed.), *Birmingham Ballads*, no. 19.
85. Street ballad printed by W. Bear, Swansea; in John Frost Museum, Newport.
86. Street ballad printed by J. France, Shrewsbury [1840]; in Birmingham RL, Ballads, 5974; repr. in Leach and Palmer (eds), *Folk Music in School*, p. 105.
87. First verse recalled by Dorothy Thompson; second from *A Songbook*, p. 68.
88. Anon., 'Street Ballads', 407.
89. Pinto and Rodway, *Common Muse*, Appendix 3; on record *English Folk Music Anthology*.
90. Recalled by Dorothy Thompson and Alan Rickman, 1986.
91. Dennis O'Neill and Peter Meazey (eds), *Broadsides. Topical Songs of Wales*, no. 17.
92. Ibid., no. 3.

93. Ibid., no. 23.
94. Ibid., no. 1.
95. Ibid., no. 28.
96. 'Anglomaniac Anthem', ibid., no. 19.
97. Buchan (ed.), *101 Scottish Songs*, p. 38.
98. Ailie Munro, *The Folk Music Revival in Scotland*, p. 74.
99. Ibid., p. 72.
100. Ibid., p. 72.
101. Written in 1986; on record *Bringing the News*.
102. Written in 1982; on record *Giant*.

Chapter 8: War and Peace

1. On record *Freedom Peacefully*.
2. On record *It's A Mean Old Scene*.
3. See Palmer (ed.), *Oxford Book of Sea Songs*, no. 6.
4. Thomas and R. H. Evans (eds), *Old Ballads*, vol. 3, p. 193.
5. Street ballad printed for F. Coles, in Vine Street, near Hatton Garden, London; in *Roxburghe*, vol. 4, pp. 8–11.
6. Firth, 'Ballad History of the Later Tudors', p. 110; *idem*, 'Ballad History of the Time of Charles I', p. 21.
7. Street ballad without imprint [1712]; in Chetham's Library, Manchester, Halliwell-Phillips Collection, no. 119.
8. *Sharp*, no. 302.
9. A. Wyatt-Edgell (ed.), *A Collection of Soldiers' Songs*, no. 52.
10. See record *Fate o' Charlie*.
11. Street ballad without imprint; in Johnson, Street Ballads, Box 29; repr. in Palmer (ed.), *Rambling Soldier*, p. 21; on record *Songs of the Redcoats*.
12. 'The Battle of Minden' and 'The Battle of Warburg', street ballads without imprint; in Madden, vol. 4, fols. 101–2.
13. Wigan RO, Edward Hall Collection, Diaries of Corporal Todd, vol. 3, pp. 64–5, D/DZ EHC 164.
14. Ibid., pp. 53–63.
15. Street ballad without imprint; in Johnson, Street Ballads, Box 29.
16. Street ballad without imprint, headed 'The Death of Gen. Wolfe', in O. E. Winslow, *American Broadside Verse*, no. 61. See also W. E. Greenleaf and H. C. Mansfield, *Ballads and Sea-Songs of Newfoundland* (Cambridge, Mass., 1933), p. 96.
17. 'The Death of General Wolfe', street ballad without imprint; in VWML, Sharp Broadsides.
18. Baring-Gould, *Garland*, no. 5.
19. Edith Fowke, Alan Mills, and Helmut Blume, *Canada's Story in Song*, p. 50.
20. Street ballad without imprint; in VWML, Sharp Broadsides; on record *Watersons*.
21. Timothy Connor, *A Sailor's Songbag*, no. 14; tune, 'The Hills and Dales', sung by Moses Mansfield (aged 81), Almshouse Common, Haslemere, Surrey; noted by F. Keel in *Journal of the Folk Song Society*, no. 21 (1918), 17–18; on record *A Selection*.
22. *Roxburghe*, vol. 7, pp. 728–9.
23. Ibid., pp. 730–2.
24. Ibid., pp. 732–3.
25. BDL, Douce, vol. 1, p. 79.
26. *Roxburghe*, vol. 7, pp. 737–9.

27. BDL, Douce, vol. 2, p. 257.
28. Davenson, *Le Livre des Chansons*, no. 54.
29. 'The Female Drummer', MS version of 1912, communicated by Professor E. M. Wilson; cf. Palmer (ed.), *Rambling Soldier*, p. 162.
30. *Life and Surprising Adventures of Mary Anne Talbot* (1809).
31. *The Female Soldier or The Surprising Life and Adventures of Hannah Snell* (1750).
32. *The Life and Adventures of Mrs Christian Davies* (1740).
33. T. F. Thistleton-Dyer, *Old English Social Life as Told by the Parish Registers* (1898), p. 251.
34. *Sapper Dorothy Lawrence* (1919), p. 93.
35. See G. Malcolm Laws, *American Balladry from British Broadsides* (Philadelphia, 1957), nos 8 and 9; and Palmer (ed.), *Rambling Soldier*, p. 196.
36. Street ballad without imprint; in Madden, vol. 4, fol. 167; repr. in Holloway and Black (eds), *Later English*, vol. 1, no. 12.
37. 'Lord Wellington', street ballad printed by Wood [n.p., 1812]; in VWML, Sharp Broadsides; repr. in Palmer (ed.), *Rambling Soldier*, p. 177.
38. Kidson, *Traditional Tunes*, pp. 161–3.
39. Gavin Greig, *Folk Songs of the North-East* (Peterhead, 1914), art. 25, p. 2.
40. Kidson, *Traditional Tunes*, pp. 120–3; one of these tunes is reproduced in ch. 7.
41. Copy printed by Keys of Devonport; in BDL, Firth, c 14, p. 28.
42. W. Christie, *Traditional Ballad Airs*, vol. 1, p. 266.
43. Ord, *Bothy Songs*, p. 301.
44. *Tocher*, no. 25 (1977), no. 28.
45. Palmer (ed.), *Folk Songs*, no. 28.
46. Street ballad printed by Wood, Birmingham [1802–27]; in Birmingham RL, Ballads, 119932, no. 124.
47. John Bell (ed.), *Rhymes of the Northern Bards*, pp. 37–8.
48. Street ballad printed by Kendrew, Colliergate, York [1812]; in BL, York Publications, 1870 c 2, p. 351.
49. Street ballad printed by Evans, 41 Long Lane, London (1801); in BL, York Publications, 1870 c 2, p. 259.
50. Street ballad with imprint cropped [1801]; in BL, York Publications, 1870 c 2, p. 240. Six ballads on the Fishguard invasion of 1797 are listed in J. H. Davies, *A Bibliography of Welsh Ballads Printed in the Eighteenth Century* (1911).
51. Street ballad no. 681, printed by H. P. Such, 177 Union Street, Borough, London [1863–85]; in BL, Crampton, 11621 h 11, vol. 4, p. 32.
52. Street ballad no. 296, printed by J. O. Bebbington, 6 Goulden Street, Oldham Road, Manchester [1856–61]; in Chetham's Library, Manchester, G. R. Axon Collection of Broadsides and Ballads; oral version in Helen Creighton (ed.), *Songs and Ballads from Nova Scotia*, no. 67.
53. 'Oh! 'tis a famous story, or, Balaclava', street ballad printed by W. S. Fortey, 4 Great St Andrew Street, Seven Dials, London; in BL, Baring-Gould Broadsides, LR 271 a 2, vol. 2, p. 60; on record *Our Side*.
54. Quoted in Logan, *Pedlar's Pack*, pp. 109–10.
55. On record of same title. This song is by Ivor Novello.
56. Ibid.
57. John Brophy and Eric Partridge, *The Long Trail*, p. 60.
58. Ibid., p. 38.
59. Ibid., p. 39.
60. Ibid., p. 48; in fact, a bowdlerized version, which has been restored here to its original form.

61. N. A. M. Rodger, *The Wooden World* (1986), pp. 150 and 175–6.
62. J. Collingwood Bruce and John Stokoe, *Northumbrian Minstrelsy*, pp. 125–6.
63. Ibid., pp. 126 and 163.
64. *Blackwood's Edinburgh Magazine*, 10 (Nov. 1821), 441–6.
65. 'The Female Press-Gang', in John Ashton, *Real Sailor Songs* (1891), p. 33.
66. Street ballad without imprint; in Derby PL, Derbyshire Ballads of the Eighteenth and Nineteenth Centuries.
67. See 'The Press Gang', Palmer (ed.), *Valiant Sailor*, no. 7, and record of same title; 'All Things are quite silent', Palmer (ed.), *Folk Songs*, no. 97; and 'The Press Gang, or, In London Fair City', *Sharp*, no. 215.
68. Lewis Winstock, *Songs and Music of the Redcoats* (1970), no. 8; record of same title.
69. Palmer (ed.), *Rambling Soldier*, p. 59.
70. Street ballad without imprint; in Hull PL, Wilberforce Collection.
71. C. R. Stone, *War Songs*, p. xi.
72. *The Universal Scots Songster* (Edinburgh, 1781); repr. in Thomas Crawford, *Society and the Lyric*, pp. 160–1; tune in Thomson, *Orpheus Caledonius* (1733), p. 62.
73. Robert Anderson, *Ballads in the Cumberland Dialect* (1867 edn), pp. 51–2; originally written in 1803.
74. 'The Recruited Collier', in Alasdair Clayre, *100 Folk Songs and New Songs* (1974), p. 22.
75. Belfast PL, Sam Henry Collection, no. 586.
76. Edward M. Spiers, *The Army and Society, 1815–1914* (1980), p. 48.
77. Street ballad without imprint; in BDL, Firth, Military Ballads and Songs, c 14, p. 108.
78. Street ballad no. 446, printed by Harkness, Preston [1846]; in Madden, vol. 18, fol. 982; tune, 'The Bold Dragoon', in John Farmer (ed.), *Scarlet and Blue*, no. 22.
79. Street ballad without imprint; in Madden.
80. National Museums and Galleries on Merseyside, Diary of Private Whitworth of 1/8th Foot (King's Regt). Whitworth served in India during the mutiny and again from 1871 to 1878.
81. Peel, *Risings of the Luddites*, pp. 126–7.
82. Alexander Somerville, *The Autobiography of a Working Man* (1967; orig. 1848), p. 167. Somerville's famous account of his flogging is in ch. 16.
83. Song entitled 'John White', in Palmer (ed.), *Rambling Soldier*, pp. 106–11. See also Harry Hopkins, *The Strange Death of Private White* (1977).
84. *Inquest into the Death of Private Robert Slim by Flogging*, Parliamentary Papers, 41 c. 202 (1867).
85. Street ballad printed by W. S. Fortey, London; in Harding, Quarto Street Ballads, no. 2093.
86. Street ballad printed by H. Disley, 57 High Street, St Giles, London (1860–78); in Harding, Quarto Street Ballads, no. 2626.
87. 'A warning for all Souldiers', in *Shirburn*, no. 47.
88. Street ballad without imprint; in Madden, vol. 6, fol. 1897.
89. Eugène Rolland, *Recueil de Chansons Populaires*, vol. 4, no. 192.
90. Palmer (ed.), *Rambling Soldier*, pp. 114–6.
91. Quoted by J. Laffin, *Tommy Atkins* (1966), p. 114.
92. Palmer (ed.), *Everyman's Book of British Ballads*, no. 53.
93. Patrick Weston Joyce, *Old Irish Folk Music and Songs* (Dublin, 1909), no. 387.
94. Street ballad without imprint; in VWML, Sharp Broadsides; oral version in O Lochlainn (ed.), *Irish Street Ballads*, no. 1.

95. Sung by Peter Flanagan, Ballymenone, Co. Fermanagh; recorded by Henry Glassie, 1979; in Glassie, *Passing the Time,* pp. 687–8 and 834.
96. Street ballad printed in London for F. Grove, on Snow Hill [late 1630s]; in Ashton, *Century of Ballads,* p. 237.
97. Street ballad printed for Charles Gustavus, London (1660); in T. Wright, *Political Ballads published during the Commonwealth,* p. 229.
98. Street ballad without imprint; in BDL, Firth, c 14, no. 5.
99. Street ballad printed by J. Davenport, no. 6, George Court, St John Lane, West Smithfield, London [1800–2]; in Palmer (ed.), *Oxford Book of Sea Songs,* no. 79.
100. Street ballad printed by J. Davenport, no. 6, George Court, St John Lane, West Smithfield, London [1800–2]; in Madden, vol. 6.
101. Street ballad printed by J. Marshall, Newcastle [1811–29]; in Johnson, Street Ballads, Box 13; repr. in Palmer (ed.), *Rambling Soldier,* p. 258.
102. Street ballad printed by W. C. Such, 183 and 185 Union Street, Borough, London [1917–29]; in Johnson, Street Ballads, Box 8.
103. Street ballad without imprint; in BL, York Publications, 1870 c 2, p. 87; repr. in Palmer (ed.), *Rambling Soldier,* p. 249.
104. Street ballad printed by Ryle and Co., 2 and 3 Monmouth Court, Bloomsbury, London [1850s]; in Johnson, Street Ballads, Box 8.
105. Street ballad without imprint; in Harding, Quarto Street Ballads, no. 354.
106. In the garland *Four New Songs,* printed and sold in Scotch Street, Carlisle [1775–83]; in Cumbria CL, Bibliotheca Jacksoniana, Tullie House, Carlisle.
107. Written by James Maxton; text in Fenner Brockway, *Towards Tomorrow* (1977), pp. 37–87; tune communicated by Lord Brockway, 1981.
108. David Kirkwood, *My Life and Revolt* (1935), p. 82.
109. By Karl Dallas; in Peggy Seeger and Ewan MacColl, *Songs for the Sixties,* p. 17.
110. By John Brunner; ibid., p. 30; also in Palmer (ed.), *Ballad History,* no. 80.
111. *The Anti-Nuclear Songbook,* p. 42.
112. Ibid., p. 38.
113. Ibid., p. 8.
114. Ibid., p. 19.
115. Ibid., p. 14; on record *English Folk Music.*
116. On typewritten sheet of songs issued by Harborne CND (1984).
117. Written by Ian Campbell (born 1931) in 1963; on record *Sun is Burning.*

SELECT BIBLIOGRAPHY

Allan, John R. (ed.), *Tyneside Songs*, Menston, 1972; orig. Newcastle, 1862.

Allingham, William, 'Irish Ballad Singers and Irish Ballads', *Ceol*, 3 (1967), 2–20; repr. from *Household Words*, 94 (10 Jan. 1852).

Anon., 'Street Ballads', *National Review*, 13 (1861), 397–419.

The Anti-Nuclear Songbook, Nottingham, 1982.

Ashraf, Mary (ed.), *Political Song and Verse from Britain and Ireland*, 1975.

Ashton, John, *A Century of Ballads Illustrative of the Life, Manners and Habits of the English Nation during the Seventeenth Century*, 1887.

——*Humour, Wit and Satire of the Seventeenth Century*, 1883; repr. New York, 1968.

——(ed.), *Modern Street Ballads*, 1888.

Baring-Gould, Sabine, *Folk Songs of the West Country*, ed. Gordon Hitchcock, Newton Abbot, 1974.

——*A Garland of Country Song*, 1895.

——*Songs of the West*, 1889–91, 1892, 1905.

Baskervill, Charles Read, *The Elizabethan Jig and Related Song Drama*, Chicago, 1929; repr. New York, 1965.

——'English Songs of the Night Visit', *Proceedings of the Modern Languages Association of America*, 36 (1921), 565–614.

Beckett, Arthur, '"Catnachery in Sussex". Bad Ballads of Forgotten Crimes', *Sussex County Magazine*, 1 (1927), 106–13.

Bell, John (ed.), *Rhymes of the Northern Bards*, Newcastle upon Tyne, 1812.

Bell, Robert (ed.), *Ancient Poems, Ballads and Songs of the Peasantry of England*, 1857; but in fact an edition of the book of the same title edited by James Henry Dixon in 1846.

——*Early Ballads illustrative of History Traditions and Customs*, 1877.

Boardman, Harry and Lesley (eds), *Folk Songs and Ballads of Lancashire*, London and New York, 1973.

Boardman, Harry, and Palmer, Roy (eds), *Manchester Ballads*, Manchester, 1983.

Boyes, Georgina, *The Ballad Today. History, Performance and Revival*, Doncaster and Addiscombe, 1985.

Bradley, S. A. J. (ed.), *Sixty Ribald Songs from 'Pills to Purge Melancholy'*, 1968.

Bratton, J. S., *The Victorian Popular Ballad*, 1975.

Brécy, Robert, *Florilège de la Chanson Révolutionnaire de 1789 au Front Populaire*, Paris, 1978.

Broadwood, John (ed.), *Old English Songs*, 1843.

Broadwood, Lucy (ed.), *English County Songs*, 1893.

——*English Traditional Songs and Carols*, 1908.

Bronson, Bertrand Harris, *The Ballad as Song*, Berkeley and Los Angeles, 1969.

——*The Singing Tradition of Child's Popular Ballads*, Princeton, N.J., 1976. This is a selection from his *The Traditional Tunes of the Child Ballads*, 4 vols, Princeton, 1959–72.

Brooks, H. F., 'Rump Songs: an Index with Notes', *Oxford Bibliographical Society Proceedings and Papers*, 5 (1936–9), 283–304.
Brophy, John, and Partridge, Eric, *The Long Trail. Soldiers' Songs and Slang, 1914–18*, 1965; orig. 1931.
Brown, Mary Ellen, *Burns and Tradition*, 1984.
Bruce, J. Collingwood, and Stokoe, John, *Northumbrian Minstrelsy*, 1882.
Buchan, David, *The Ballad and the Folk*, 1972.
——(ed.), *A Scottish Ballad Book*, 1973.
——'History and Harlaw', in *Ballad Studies*, ed. E. B. Lyle, pp. 29–40, Cambridge and Ipswich, 1976.
Buchan, Norman, 'Folk and Protest', in *The People's Past*, ed. Edward J. Cowan, pp. 165–90, Edinburgh, 1980.
——(ed.), *101 Scottish Songs*, Glasgow and London, 1962.
——and Hall, Peter (eds), *The Scottish Folksinger*, London and Glasgow, 1973.
Burns, Robert, *The Merry Muses and Other Burnsian Frolics*, ed. Eric Lemuel Randall, 1966.
——*Poems and Songs*, ed. James Kinsley, 1971.

Chappell, William, *Popular Music of the Olden Time*, 1859; repr. New York, 1965.
Child, F. J., *The English and Scottish Popular Ballads*, 5 vols, Boston and New York, 1898.
Christie, William (ed.), *Traditional Ballad Airs*, 2 vols, Edinburgh, 1876 and 1881.
Collmann, Herbert Leonard (ed.), *Ballads and Broadsides, Chiefly of the Elizabethan Period*, Oxford, 1912.
Colls, Robert, *The Collier's Rant. Song and Culture in the Industrial Village*, 1977.
Connor, Timothy, *A Sailor's Songbag: an American Rebel in an English Prison, 1777–9*, ed. G. G. Carey, Amherst, Mass., 1976.
Copper, Bob, *Early to Rise. A Sussex Boyhood*, 1976.
——*A Song for Every Season*, 1971.
——*Songs and Southern Breezes*, 1973.
Craig, David, 'Songs of the Bleak Age', in his *The Real Foundations: Literature and Social Change*, ch. 3, 1973.
Crawford, Thomas, *Love, Labour and Liberty: the Eighteenth-century Scottish Lyric*, Cheadle Hulme, 1986.
——*Society and the Lyric: a Study of the Song Culture of Eighteenth-Century Scotland*, Edinburgh, 1979.
Creighton, Helen (ed.), *Songs and Ballads from Nova Scotia*, Toronto and Vancouver, 1933; repr. New York, 1966.
Croker, T. Crofton, *Popular Songs Illustrative of the French Invasions*, 1847.

Davenson, Henri, *Le Livre des Chansons*, Neuchâtel and Paris, 1946; orig. Neuchâtel, 1944.
Davison, Peter, *The British Music Hall*, New York, 1971.
Dawney, Michael (ed.), *The Iron Man. English Occupational Songs*, 1974.
Duncan, E. (ed.), *The Minstrelsy of England*, 2 vols, 1905.

Edwards, Ron, *The Overlander Song Book*, London and Adelaide, 1972.
Elbourne, Roger, *Music and Tradition in Early Industrial Lancashire, 1780–1840*, Woodbridge, Suffolk, and Totowa, N.J., 1980.
Evans, Thomas and R. H. (eds), *Old Ballads, Historical and Narrative*, 4 vols, 1810.

Fahey, Warren (ed.), *Eureka. The Songs that Made Australia*, Sydney, 1984.
Fairholt, Frederick W., *Satirical Songs and Poems on Costume: from the 13th to the 19th Century*, 1849.
Fanshawe, C. A. (ed.), *The Book of Battle Songs*, n.d.
Farmer, John S. (ed.), *Merry Songs and Ballads*, 5 vols, 1897.
——*Scarlet and Blue, or, Songs for Soldiers and Sailors*, 1896.
Fawcett, F. Burlington (ed.), *Broadside Ballads of the Restoration Period from the Jersey Collection known as the Osterley Park Ballads*, 1930. Originals now BL, C.39, k.6.
Federer, C. A., *Yorkshire Chapbooks*, 1889.
Firth, C. H. *An American Garland*, Oxford, 1915.
——'The Ballad History of the Reign of James I', *Transactions of the Royal Historical Society*, 3rd ser., 5 (1911), 21–61.
——'The Ballad History of the Reigns of Henry VII and Henry VIII', *Transactions of the Royal Historical Society*, 2 (1908), 21–50.
——'The Ballad History of the Reigns of the Later Tudors', *Transactions of the Royal Historical Society*, 3 (1909), 51–124.
——'The Ballad History of the Reign of Charles I', *Transactions of the Royal Historical Society*, 6 (1912), 19–64.
——'Ballads on the Bishops' Wars, 1638–40', *Scottish Historical Review*, 3 (1906), 257–73.
——'Ballads illustrating the relations of England and Scotland during the Seventeenth Century', *Scottish Historical Review*, 6 (1909), 113–28.
——'Jacobite Songs', *Scottish Historical Review*, 8 (1911), 251–7.
——*Naval Songs and Ballads*, 1908.
Ford, Robert, *Song Histories*, Glasgow and Edinburgh, 1900.
——*Vagabond Songs and Ballads of Scotland*, Paisley, 1904; orig. 2 vols. 1899–1901.
Ford, Worthington C., 'Broadsides, Ballads etc., printed in Massachusetts, 1639–1800', *Massachusetts Historical Society Collections*, 75 (1922).
——'The Isaiah Thomas Collection of Ballads', *Proceedings of the American Antiquarian Society*, Apr. 1923, 34–112.
Fowke, Edith (ed.), *The Penguin Book of Canadian Folk Songs*, Harmondsworth, 1973.
——Mills, Alan, and Blume, Helmut, *Canada's Story in Song*, Toronto, 1965.
Fowler, D. C., 'The Gosport Tragedy: Story of a Ballad', *Southern Folklore Quarterly*, 43 (1979), 157–96.
Frow, Edmund, 'Working Class Consciousness in Radical Poetry in Manchester, 1790–1850', in *Problems of the History and Literature of the Working Class in Britain from the Eighteenth to the Twentieth Century*, ed. Hanna Behrend, pp. 59–65. Berlin, 1982.

Galvin, Patrick, *Irish Songs of Resistance, 1169–1923*, London and New York, 1962.
Gammon, Vic, 'Folk Song Collecting in Sussex and Surrey, 1843–1914', *History Workshop Journal*, Autumn 1980, pp. 61–89.
——'Popular Music in Rural Society: Sussex, 1815–1914', Sussex Univ. D.Phil. thesis, 1985.
——'Song, Sex and Society in England, 1600–1850', *Folk Music Journal*, 4 (1982), 208–45.
Gardham, Steve (ed.), *An East Riding Songster*, Lincoln and Hull, 1982.
Gatherer, Nigel (ed.), *Songs and Ballads of Dundee*, Edinburgh, 1986.
Glassie, Henry, *Passing the Time. Folklore and History of an Irish Community*, Dublin, 1982.
Goldstein, Leba, 'The Foggy Dew', *Folk Review*, Mar. 1976, 10–11.

Greaves, C. Desmond, *The Easter Rising in Song and Ballad*, 1980.

Green, Tony, 'Some Notes on the Popular Song of the West Riding', *Abe*, 3 (June 1965), 17–32.

Gregson, Keith, *Corvan. A Victorian Entertainer and his Songs*, Banbury, 1983.

——(ed.), *Cumbrian Songs and Ballads*, Clapham, Lancaster, 1980.

——'Robert Anderson, The Cumberland Bard. An Anniversary Reflection', *Folk Music Journal*, 4 (1983), 333–65.

Halliwell-Phillips, J. O., *Catalogue of Proclamations, Broadsides, Ballads and Poems*, 1851. (The material listed is in Chetham's Library, Manchester.)

Harland, John (ed.), *The Songs of the Wilsons*, Manchester, n.d. ?1865; orig. 1842.

——and Wilkinson, T. T., *Ballads and Songs of Lancashire*, 3rd edn, Manchester and London, 1882; orig. 1865–6.

——'An Essay on Songs and Ballads', *Transactions of the Historical Society of Lancashire and Cheshire*, 11 (1870–1), 87–118.

Healy, James N. (ed.), *The Mercier Book of Old Irish Street Ballads*, vol. 3, *The People at Play*, Cork, 1969.

Henderson, Hamish, 'The Ballad, the Folk and the Oral Tradition', in *The People's Past*, ed. Edward J. Cowan, pp. 69–107, Edinburgh, 1980.

Henderson, Kathy, with Armstrong, Frankie, and Kerr, Sandra, *My Song is My Own: 100 Women's Songs*, 1979.

Henderson, W. (ed.), *Victorian Street Ballads*, 1937.

Henry, Sam, *Songs of the People. Selections from the Sam Henry Collection*, ed. John Moulden, Belfast, 1979. (The original collection is in the Belfast PL.)

Hewitt, John (ed.), *Rhyming Weavers and other Country Poets of Antrim and Down*, Belfast, 1974.

Hindley, Charles (ed.), *Curiosities of Street Literature*, 1871; 2 vols, 1966.

——*The Life and Times of James Catnach*, 1878.

Hollingworth, Brian (ed.), *Songs of the People. Lancashire Dialect Poetry of the Industrial Revolution*, Manchester, 1977.

Holloway, John, and Black, Joan (eds), *Later English Broadside Ballads*, 2 vols, 1975 and 1979.

Holroyd, Abraham (ed.), *Holroyd's Collection of Yorkshire Ballads*, ed. Charles F. Forshaw, 1892; repr. East Ardsley, 1974.

Howkins, Alun, and Dyck, Ian C., 'Popular Ballads, Rural Radicalism and William Cobbett', *History Workshop Journal*, 23 (1987), 20–38.

Howson, John, *Many a Good Horseman. A Survey of Traditional Music Making in mid-Suffolk*, Rochford, 1985.

I. W. W. Songs, Chicago, 1974; orig. 1909.

James, Louis, *Print and the People, 1819–1851*, 1976.

Jewitt, Llewelyn (ed.), *Ballads and Songs of Derbyshire*, 1867.

Kennedy, Peter (ed.), *Folk Songs from Britain and Ireland*, 1975.

Kidson, Frank (ed.), *Traditional Tunes*, Oxford, 1891; repr. East Ardsley, 1970.

Klingberg, F. J., and Hustvedt, S. B., *The Warning Drum: the British Home Front faces Napoleon; Broadsides of 1803*, Berkeley and Los Angeles, 1944.

Lane, W. C., *Catalogue of English and American Chapbooks and Broadside Ballads in Harvard College Library*, Cambridge, Mass., 1905.

Lemon, Robert, *Catalogue of a Collection of Broadsides in the Possession of the Society of Antiquaries*, 1866.

Lewis, Roy and John, *Politics and Printing in Winchester, 1830–1880*, Richmond, 1980.

Leydi, Roberto, *I Canti Popolari Italiani*, Milan, 1973.

——*Canti Sociali Italiani*, Milan, 1963.

——(ed.), *Il Folk Music Revival*, Palermo, 1972.

Lloyd, A. L., *Come All Ye Bold Miners. Ballads and Songs of the Coalfields*, 1978; orig. 1952.

——*Folk Song in England*, 1967.

——'On an Unpublished Irish Ballad ["Lord Leitrim"]' in *Rebels and their Causes*, ed. Maurice Cornforth, pp. 177–207, 1978.

Logan, W. H., *A Pedlar's Pack of Ballads and Songs*, Edinburgh, 1869.

Lomax, Alan (ed.), *The Penguin Book of American Folk Songs*, Harmondsworth, 1964.

Lomax, J. A. and A., *American Ballads and Folk Songs*, New York, 1934.

MacColl, Ewan (ed.), *Scotland Sings*, 1953.

——*Shuttle and Cage*, 1954.

Mackay, Charles, *The Cavalier Songs and Ballads of England from 1642 to 1684*, 1863.

——*A Collection of Songs and Ballads relative to the London Prentices and Trades*, 1841.

Mackay, William, *Ballad Chronicles*, Birmingham, 1832.

Mackay-Smith, Alexander, *The Songs of Foxhunting*, Millwood, Va., 1974.

Mackerness, E. D., *A Social History of English Music*, 1964.

McGinn, Matt, *McGinn of the Calton*, Glasgow, 1987.

Maguire, John, *Come Day, Go Day, God send Sunday*, ed. Robin Morton, 1973.

Maidment, James, *A Book of Scottish Pasquils*, 1868.

Manifold, John (ed.), *The Penguin Australian Song Book*, 1964.

Menefee, Samuel Pyeatt, *Wives for Sale*, Oxford, 1981.

Meredith, John, and Anderson, Hugh (eds), *Folk Songs of Australia*, Sydney and London, 1967.

Morton, Robin (ed.), *Folksongs sung in Ulster*, Cork, 1970.

Mulcahy, Michael, and Fitzgibbon, Marie (eds), *The Voice of the People. Songs and History of Ireland*, Dublin, 1982.

Munro, Ailie, *The Folk Music Revival in Scotland*, 1984.

Munro, Bob, 'The Bothy Ballads: the Social Context and Meaning of the Farm Servants' Songs of North-eastern Scotland', *History Workshop Journal*, 3 (Spring 1977), 184–93.

Neil, Philip (ed.), *Between Earth and Sky. Poetry and Prose of English Rural Life and Work between the Enclosures and the Great War*, Harmondsworth, 1984.

Nettel, Reginald, 'The Influence of the Industrial Revolution on English Music', *Proceedings of the Royal Musical Association*, 72 (1946), 23–40.

——*A Social History of Traditional Song*, 1969; originally published as *Sing a Song of England*, 1954.

Nettleingham, F. T. (ed.), *Tommy's Tunes*, 1917.

Neuburg, Victor E., *The Batsford Companion to Popular Literature*, 1982.

——*Popular Literature: A History and Guide*, Harmondsworth, 1977.

O Lochlainn, Colm (ed.), *Irish Street Ballads*, Dublin, 1939.

——*More Irish Street Ballads*, Dublin, 1965.

O'Neill, Dennis, and Meazey, Peter (eds), *Broadsides. Topical Songs of Wales*, ?Cardiff, ?1973.

Ord, John, *The Bothy Songs and Ballads of Aberdeen, Banff and Moray, Angus and the Mearns*, Paisley, 1930; repr. Edinburgh, 1973.

O'Shaughnessy, Patrick (ed.), *21 Lincolnshire Folk Songs Collected by Percy Grainger*, 1968.

——*More Folk Songs from Lincolnshire*, 1971.

——*Yellowbelly Ballads*, part 1, Lincoln, 1975.

O'Sullivan, Donal, 'Dublin Slang Songs, with Music', *Dublin Historical Review*, 1, no. 3 (1938), 75–93.

Palmer, Roy (ed), *A Ballad History of England from 1588 to the Present Day*, 1979.

——(ed.) *Birmingham Ballads*, Birmingham, 1979.

——*Birmingham Street Ballads: the Medium, the Muse, the Message, the Music and the Words*, forthcoming.

——'Canti della Rivoluzione Industriale', *Movimento Operaio e Socialista*, NS, Anno 6, no. 2 (1983), 259–81.

——(ed.) *English Country Songbook*, 1986; originally published as *Everyman's Book of English Country Songs*, 1979.

——'Folk Song and the Teaching of History', in *Folk Music in School*, ed. Robert Leach and Roy Palmer, ch. 6, Cambridge, 1978 and 1988.

——(ed.) *Folk Songs collected by Ralph Vaughan Williams*, 1983.

——(ed.) *The Oxford Book of Sea Songs*, Oxford, 1986.

——(ed.) *The Painful Plough. A Portrait of the Agricultural Labourer in the Nineteenth Century from Folk Songs and Ballads and Contemporary Accounts*, Cambridge, 1973.

——(ed.) *Poverty Knock. A Picture of Industrial Life in the Nineteenth Century through Songs, Ballads and Contemporary Accounts*, Cambridge, 1974.

——(ed.) *The Rambling Soldier: Life in the Lower Ranks, 1750–1900, through Soldiers' Songs and Writings*, Harmondsworth, 1977; repr. Gloucester, 1985.

——(ed.) *Strike the Bell: Transport by Road, Canal, Rail and Sea in the Nineteenth Century through Songs, Ballads and Contemporary Accounts*, Cambridge, 1978.

——(ed.) *A Touch on the Times. Songs of Social Change, 1770 to 1914*, Harmondsworth, 1974.

——(ed.) *The Valiant Sailor. Sea Songs and Ballads and Prose Passages illustrating Life on the Lower Deck in Nelson's Navy*, Cambridge, 1973.

——'The Weaver in Love', *Folk Music Journal*, 3, no. 3 (1977), 261–74.

——and Raven, Jon, (eds), *The Rigs of the Fair. Popular Sports and Pastimes in the Nineteenth Century through Songs, Ballads and Contemporary Accounts*, Cambridge, 1976.

——Bishop, Pamela, and Thomson, Katharine (eds), *Songs of the Midlands*, East Ardsley, 1972.

Pegg, Bob, *Folk*, 1976.

Percival, Milton O., *Political Ballads illustrating the Administration of Sir Robert Walpole*, Oxford, 1916.

Pettitt, Thomas, 'The Later English Ballad Tradition: "The Outlandish Knight" and "Maria Marten"', in *The Ballad as Narrative*, ed. F. G. Andersen, O. Holzapfel, and T. Pettitt, pp. 71–84, Odense, 1982.

Piggott, H. E., *Songs that made History*, 1937.

Pinto, V. de Sola, and Rodway, A. E., *The Common Muse. Popular British Ballad Poetry from the 15th to the 20th Century*, Harmondsworth, 1965; orig. 1957.

Purslow, Frank (ed.), *The Foggy Dew: More English Folk Songs from the Hammond and Gardiner MSS*, 1974.

——*Marrowbones: English Folk Songs from the Hammond and Gardiner MSS*, 1965.

——*The Wanton Seed. More English Folk Songs from the Hammond and Gardiner MSS*, 1968.

Raven, Jon, *The Urban and Industrial Songs of the Black Country and Birmingham*, Wolverhampton, 1977.

Reed, James, *The Border Ballads*, 1975.

Richards, Sam, and Stubbs, Tish (eds), *The English Folk Singer*, Glasgow and London, 1979.

Renwick, Roger de V., *English Folk Poetry: Structure and Meaning*, 1980.

Rimbault, E. F., *Old Ballads illustrating the Great Frost of 1683–4 and the Fairs on the River Thames*, 1844.

Roberts, John S., *The Legendary Ballads of England and Scotland*, 1887.

Rolland, Eugène, *Recueil de Chansons Populaires*, 6 vols, Paris, 1883–90.

Rollins, Hyder E., *An Analytical Index to the Ballad-Entries (1557–1709) in the Registers of the Company of Stationers of London*, Chapel Hill, N.C., 1924; repr. Hatboro, 1967.

——*Cavalier and Puritan: Ballads and Broadsides illustrating the Period of the Great Rebellion, 1640–1660*, New York, 1923.

Roth, H. L., and Jolley, J. T., *War Ballads and Broadsides of Previous Wars, 1779–1795*, Halifax, 1915.

Rump: or an Exact Collection of the Choycest Poems and Songs relating to the Late Times. By the most eminent Wits, from Anno 1639 to Anno 1661, 2 vols, 1662.

Russell, Ian (ed.), *Singer, Song and Scholar*, Sheffield, 1986.

[Sala, George Augustus], 'Bright Chanticleer', *Household Words*, 9 (1855), 204–9.

Salveson, Paul, 'Songs from the Lancashire Seam', *North West Labour History*, 11 (1985–6), 25–38.

Scott, Bill (ed.), *The Second Australian Songbook*, Ringwood, Australia, 1980.

Scott, Harold (ed.), *An English Song Book*, 1925.

Sedley, Stephen (ed.), *The Seeds of Love*, 1967.

Seeger, Charles, 'Folk Music as a Source of Social History', in *The Cultural Approach to History*, ed. C. F. Ware, pp. 316–23, New York, 1940.

——'Folk Music in the Schools of a Highly Industrialised Society', *Journal of the International Folk Music Council*, 5 (1953), 40–4.

Seeger, Peggy, and MacColl, Ewan, *The Singing Island. A Collection of English and Scots Folk Songs*, 1960.

——*Songs for the Sixties*, 1961.

Seeger, Pete, and Reiser, Bob., *Carry it on. A History in Song and Picture of the Working Men and Women of America*, New York, 1985; Poole, 1986.

Senelick, L., 'Politics as Entertainment; Victorian Music Hall Songs', *Victorian Studies*, 19 (1975), 149–80.

Shepard, Leslie, *The History of Street Literature*, Newton Abbot, 1973.

——*John Pitts. Ballad Printer of Seven Dials, London, 1765–1844*, 1969.

Shields, Hugh, 'The Dead Lover's Return in Modern English Ballad Tradition', *Jahrbuch für Volksliedforschung*, 17 (1972), 98–114.

——*Shamrock, Rose and Thistle. Folk Singing in North Derry*, Belfast, 1981.

Shuldham-Shaw, Patrick, and Lyle, Emily B. (eds), *The Greig-Duncan Folk Song Collection*, 3 vols, Aberdeen, 1981–7.

Simpson, Jacqueline, 'Songs of a Female Student Group, 1949–52', *Folk Music Journal*, 4 (1984), 504–27.

Smith, Len, *The Carpet Weaver's Lament: Songs and Ballads of Kidderminster in the Industrial Revolution*, Kidderminster, 1979.
A Songbook, Red Notes Pamphlet, 1977.
Songs of the Fell Packs, Melbreak, 1971.
Stone, C. R., *War Songs*, 1908.

Thompson, E. P., '"Rough Music": le charivari anglais', *Annales*, 27 (1972) 285–312.
——'Time, Work-Discipline and Industrial Capitalism; *Past and Present*, 38 (Dec. 1967), 56–97.
Thomson, R. S., 'The Frightful Foggy Dew', *Folk Music Journal*, 4, no. 1 (1980), 35–61.
Tomlinson, Walter, 'A Bunch of Street Ballads', *Papers of the Manchester Literary Club*, 12 (1886), 305–16.
T., R., 'Street Songs and their Singers', *St James Magazine*, 13 (1865), 190–201.
Trevelyan, G. M., 'The Border Ballads', in his *A Layman's Love of Letters*, 1954.
——*The Middle Marches*, Newcastle, 1935.

Unwin, Rayner, *The Rural Muse. Studies in the Peasant Poetry of England*, 1954.
Urfey, Thomas d' (ed.), *Pills to Purge Melancholy*, 6 vols, 1719–20.

Vicinus, Martha, *Broadsides of the Industrial North*, Newcastle, n.d.
——*The Industrial Muse. A Study of Nineteenth Century British Working-Class Literature*, 1974.

Watson, Ian, *Song and Democratic Culture in Britain*, 1983.
Wilkins, W. W., *Political Ballads of the Seventeenth and Eighteenth Centuries*, 2 vols, 1860.
Williams, Alfred, Folk-Songs of the Upper Thames, 1923.
Williams, R. Vaughan, and Lloyd, A. L., *The Penguin Book of English Folk Songs*, Harmondsworth, 1959.
Winslow, O. E., *American Broadside Verse*, New Haven, Conn, 1930.
Winstock, Lewis, *Songs and Music of the Redcoats, 1642–1902*, 1970.
Woods, Fred, *Folk Revival. The rediscovery of a National Music*, Poole, 1979.
Wright, Thomas, *Political Ballads published during the Commonwealth*, 1841.
Wyatt-Edgell, A. ed., *A Collection of Soldiers' Songs*, [1871].

Zimmermann, Georges-Denis, *Songs of Irish Rebellion. Political Street Ballads and Rebel Songs, 1780–1900*, Dublin, 1967.

DISCOGRAPHY

RECORDS are 12 inch LPs unless otherwise indicated, and are by various artists unless otherwise specified. Cassettes are designated (C).

Among the Old Familiar Mountains. Paul and Linda Adams, Fellside FE006, 1978.
Amorous Muse, The, Peggy Seeger and Ewan MacColl, Argo ZFB66, 1968.
Bitter and the Sweet, The, Roy Harris, Topic 12TS217, 1972.
Bold Navigators, The, Tradition TSR019, 1975.
Bonny Pit Laddie, The, 12TS271/2 (double album), 1975.
Bothy Ballads: Music from the North-east, Tangent TNGM109, 1971.
Bound to be a Row, Jimmy McBeath, Topic 12T303, 1978.
Bright Golden Store, Walter Pardon, Home-made Music HMM LP301, 1984.
Bringing the News from Nowhere, Leon Rosselson, Fuse CF390, 1986.
Broomfield Wager, The, Topic, 12T252, 1975.
Brummagem Ballads, Broadside BR0119, 1976.
Canny Newcassel, Topic 12TS219, 1972.
Champions of Folly, Roy Harris, Topic 12TS256, 1975.
Coorse and Fine. Songs and Ballads of Dundee, Springthyme SPR1017, 1985.
Country Hirings, Paul and Linda Adams, Fellside SFA053, 1976.
Country Life, A, Walter Pardon, Topic 12TS392, 1982.
Crown of Horn, Martin Carthy, Topic 12TS300, 1976.
Daddy, what did you do in the Strike? Blackthorne, 1984 (C).
Dalesman's Litany, A, Dave Burland, Trailer LER2082, 1971.
Deep Lancashire, Topic 12T188, 1968.
Down the Long Road, Bob Davenport, Topic 12TS274, 1975.
English Folk Music Anthology, An, Folkways FE38553 (double album), 1981.
English Sporting Ballads, Broadside BRO128, 1977.
Fair Game and Foul, Topic 12T195, 1970.
Farewell, Musket, Pike and Drum, Strawhead, Tradition, TSR026, 1977.
Fate o' Charlie. Songs of the Jacobite Rebellions, The, Trailer LER3002, 1969.
Fight Game, The, Argo.
Fine Hunting Day, A. Songs of the Holme Valley Beagles, Leader LEE4056, 1975.
Fine Old Yorkshire Gentleman, The, Bill Price, Folk Heritage FHR038, 1972.
For King and Parliament: Popular Music from the English Civil Wars, 1640–1660, Tarleton's Jig, Nun's Meadow Productions NMP1521, 1986.
Fortunes of War, Strawhead, Tradition TSR032, 1978.
Freedom Peacefully, Roy Bailey, Fuse CF386, 1985.
Frosty Ploughshare, The: Bothy Songs and Ballads, Ian Manuel, Topic 12TS220, 1972.
Galloways, Jez Lowe, Fellside FE049, 1985.
Gamblers and Sporting Blades, Topic TOP71 (EP record), 1962.
Garners Gay, EFDSS LP1006, 1971.
George Dunn, Leader LEE4042, 1973.
Giant at Cerne, Tim Laycock, Dingle DIN320, 1982.

Golden Stream, Harry Boardman, AK Records AK7813, 1978.
Great Australian Legend, Topic 12TS203, 1971.
Green Fields, The Watersons, Topic 12TS415, 1981.
Green Grow the Laurels, Topic 12TS285, 1976.
Iron Muse, The, Topic 12T86, 1956.
It's a Mean Old Scene, Peter Coe, Backshift BASH39, 1985.
I Wish there was no Prisons, Jim Eldon, Stick Records SD002, 1984.
Jack of All Trades, Topic 12T159, 1968.
Jug of This: an Introduction to English Folk Song, A, Sussex Tapes, M11, 1987.
Keep A-runnin', it's the Yetties, the Yetties, Argo ZFB16, 1970.
Keep the Home Fires Burning. The Songs and Music of the 1st World War from Original Recordings, Saydisc SDL358, 1986.
Lancashire Mon, A, Harry Boardman, Topic 12TS236, 1973.
Loving Mad Tom, Leader LER2079, 1972.
Manchester Angel, The, Ewan MacColl, Topic 12T147, 1966.
Merry Mountain Child, Arthur Howard, Hill and Dale HD006, 1981.
Mike Waterson, Topic 12TS332, 1977.
Mixed Traffic, Roger Watson, Greenwich Village GVR210, 1980.
Mornin' All, Bob Arnold, Argo ZFB83, 1972.
Music from the Western Isles, Tangent TNGM110, 1971.
Ned Kelly and All that Gang, Martyn Wyndham-Read, Leader LER2028, 1970.
Oldham's Burning Sands, the Oldham Tinkers, Topic 12TS206, 1971.
On the One Road, The Freemen, Emerald GES1050, 1971.
One of the Best, George Fradley, Veteran Tapes VT114, 1988 (C).
Our Side of the Baulk, Walter Pardon, Leader LED2111, 1977.
Owdham Edge, Topic 12T204, 1970.
Painful Plough, The, Topic IMP-A103, 1972; reissured as FS01, 1992 (C).
Persistence of Memory, Brian Peters, Fellside FE051, 1985.
Postcards Home, Bob Davenport, Topic 12TS318, 1977.
Rambling Soldier, The, Roy Harris. Fellside FE017, 1979; reissued as FECD17, 1996.
Rose, Shamrock and Thistle, Eddie Butcher, Leader LED2070, 1976.
Rough and Wrigley, Bernard Wrigley, Topic 12TS241, 1974.
Saturday Night at Tostock Gardeners' Arms, Vintage Tapes 002, 1984 (C).
Save Shotton, SNP/SHO1 (EP record), 1973.
Scotia, The Clutha, Argo ZFB18, 1971.
Selection from the Penguin Book of English Folk Songs, A. L. Lloyd, Collector JGB001, 1960; reissued as FECD47, 1995.
——various artists, Fellside FE047, 1985.
Shepherd's Song, The, Willie Scott, Topic 12T183, 1968.
Song for Every Season, A, Copper family, Leader LEA4049 (4 LPs), 1971.
Songs and Music of the Redcoats, Argo ZDA142, 1971.
Songs, Ballads and Instrumental Tunes from Ulster, The Irish Country Four, Topic 12TS209, 1971.
Songs from Suffolk, Topic 12TS225, 1973.
Songs from the Book of England, Strawhead, Tradition TSR0356, 1980.
Songs of a Hampshire Man, Bob Mills, People's Stage Tapes 05, 1982 (C).
Songs of a Shropshire Farm Worker, Fred Jordan, Topic 12T150, 1966.
Songs of Courtship, Topic 12T157, 1968.
Songs of Seduction, Topic 12T158, 1968.
Steam Ballads, Broadside BRO121, 1977.
Streets of Glasgow, Topic 12TS226, 1973.

Streets of Song, Topic, 12T41, 1959.

Sun is Burning, The, The Songs of Ian Campbell, Ian Campbell Folk Group, Argo ZFB13, 1971.

Tale of Ale, The, Free Reed FRRD023/4 (two LPs), 1977; reissued as FRCD23, 1993.

Tommy Armstrong of Tyneside, Topic 12T122, 1965.

To See the Play, Fiddler's Dram, Dingle DIN304, 1978.

Transpennine: Songs of Lancashire and Yorkshire, Harry Boardman and David Hillery, Topic 12TS215, 1971.

True and Bold. Songs of the Scottish Miners, Dick Gaughan, Scottish TUC, 1986.

Unto Brigg Fair, Leader LEA4050, 1972.

Valiant Sailor, The. Songs and Ballads of Nelson's Navy, Topic 12TS232, 1973.

Wanton Muse, The, Ewan MacColl, Argo DA85, 1968.

Watersons, The, Topic 12T142, 1966.

Waulking Songs from Barra, Tangent TNGM111, 1972.

When the Frost is on the Pumpkin, Fred Jordan, Topic 12TS233, 1974.

Who Owns the Game? Traditional Songs and Melodeon Tunes from Central Suffolk, Homemade Music LP302, 1984.

Wide Midlands, The, Topic, 12TS210, 1971.

Wild Rover no More, Timmy McBeath, Topic 12T173, 1967.

Yorkshire Garland, A, The Watersons, Topic 12T167, 1966.

Yorkshire Farming Memories, York Castle Museum YCM 4/81, 1981 (C).

Young Hunting, Tony Rose, Trailer LER2013, 1971.

INDEX

OF TITLES, TUNES, AND FIRST LINES

Page references in brackets indicate that a song is cited, though its title is not given in the text at that point

A-begging I/we will go, (87), 195
Abergele Martyrs, The, 266
Account of the Birmingham Loyal Association, An, (175)
Act on the Square, 211
Adulterations, 76
Advice to Bachelors, 231
Advice to Farmers, 40
Affecting Copy of Verses, An, 14
Agony Bill, The, 15, 253
Aherlow, 291
Ah, my name is Patrick Sheehan, 292
A is for the atoms, 270
Albion my Country, 14
All Things be dear, 237
All you that are low spirited, 247
Ancient Song of Bartholomew Fair, 161
Anglomanian Anthem, 266
Another Song concerning Peterloo, 260
Appeal by Unemployed Ex-Service Men, An, 295, 298
Are You Vaccinated?, 81
Arthur a Bradly, 183
As I passed through Portsmouth, 271
As I walked between Bolton and Bury, 215
As I walked out, 220
As I was coming from the play, 217
Assizes they are over now, The, 152
A stands for Alcohol, 172
A stands for Alphabet, 115, 117
At the docks there is a strike, 110
At Turners Hill, 197

Badger's Downfall, The, 73
Ballad of Sam Hall, The, 124
Ballad of the Q4, The, 92
Ban Polaris, 268
Basket of Eggs, The, (204)
Battle of Alma, The, 280
Battle of Spitaloo, 262
Battle of Waterloo, 25
Beautiful Nancy, 223
Be careful in choosing a wife, 231
Beggars' Chorus, The, 86, 87
Bellevue Gaol, (155)

Bendigo and Deaf Burke, 191
Bendigo, Champion of England, 191
Bill Brown, 48
Billy Pitt's Progression, 240
Birmingham Boy in London, (63)
Blackburn Poachers, The 48
Black Horse, The, 286
Blacksmith, The, 32, 89
Bloody Waterloo, 279
Bloxwich Wake, (169)
Bob and Joan, 62
Bobby's Sliding Scale, 248
Bold Dragoon, A, 214
Bold Dragoon, The, 287
Bold General Wolfe, 276
Bold Robin Hood, 14
Bonaparte's Disasters, 279
Bonnie Pit Laddie, The, 92
Bonny Grey (173), 174
Bonny Scot, The, 213
Both men and women listen, 212
Botany Bay ['Come all young men'], 148
Botany Bay ['Farewell to old England'], (148)
Botany Bay ['Let us drink'], (154)
Boxing Match between John Bull and Buonaparte, The, 279
Braes of Killiecrankie, The, 84
Brags of Washington, The, 278
Brave Collier Lads, The, 224
Brigg Fair, 164
Bring us in good Ale, 171
British Grenadiers, The, 281
British Spectator, The, 74
British True Blue, The, 14
Brother soldier do you hear, 297
Budget, The, [1784] 238; [1785] 238; [1797] 240
Bullock Hanker's Medley, The, 176
Bumpkin's Journey, 64
Bundling Song, 201
Bureau, The, (117)
Burke and Hare, 132
Burke's Address, 257
Burthen of Taxes, The, 239

Bury New Loom, The, 215
Bye, Bye, Blackbird, 117

Ça Ira, 17
Campbells are Coming, The, 80
Careless Bachelor, The, 231
Carpenter's Wife, The, 199
Caveat for Cutpurses, A, 160
Cease rude Boreas, 175
Chapter of Kings, 118
Chase the Yankees oot the Clyde, 268
Cheating, 248
Cheer up your hearts, 275
Chimney sweep, 124
Chivvy, Chivvy, O, (189)
Cholera's Coming, The, 80
Christmas Goose, The, (204)
Claughton Wood Poachers, 48
Clothiers' Delight, The, 7, 8, 98, 99, 223, 254
Collier Laddie, 93
Collier's Wedding, The, 199
Collier Sweetheart, (224)
Come all honest Britons, 258
Come all ye seamen bold, 3
Come all you bold fellows, 57
Come all you croppers, 5
Come all you gallant poachers, 149
Come all you jolly cricketers, 196
Come all you lads, 288
Come all you lads and lasses, 177
Come all young men, 149
Come all you poor people, 74
Come all you shepherds, 33
Come all you thoughtless young men, 139
Come all you young fellows, 141, 191
Come cropper lads, 105
Come listen a while, 230
Come one and all, 171
Come over the born, 242
Come, Robin, sit deawn, 27
Come you bird fanciers, 173
Come you men and women, 255
Comical Streets of London, The, 66
Complaint of a Widdow, The, 222
Complaints of the Poor, 237
Conversations of the Rose, 16
Copy of Verses, A, 95
Cotton Lords of Preston, The, (116)
Cotton Mill Song, The, 224
Country Hirings, 153
Countryman's Reply, The, 286
Countryman's Visit to Bartholomew Fair, 161
Country Wedding, The, 199
County Gaol, (156)
County Livery, The, 7
Coventry Fair, 165

Crafty London 'Prentice, The, 223
Crib and Molyneux, 191
Cricketing's All the Rage, 195
Cricket Song, The, 195–6
Croppers' Song, The, 105
Croydon Canal, The, 69
Cry for Bread, A, 24
Crystal Palace, The, 170
Cuckoo's Nest, The, (215)
Cutler's Song, The, 89
Cutlin' Heroes, The, 89

Daddy, what did you do in the strike?, 29, 118
Darlaston Wake Bull-baiting, 175
Darlington Fair, 164
Dashing Steam Loom Weaver, 224
Dawning of the Day, The, 32
Days of Queen Elizabeth, The, 32
Death of General Wolfe, The, 275
Death of Simon Byrne, 191
Death or Liberty, 263
Depressed State of the Times, The, 24
Derbyshire Football Song, (190)
Derry Down, 7
Derry Gaol, 158
Description of the Fair, A (166)
Devil and Buonaparte, The, 279
Dialogue and Song on the Starvation Poor
    Law Bill, A, 254
Diggers Christmass-Caroll, 245
Diggers' Song, 245, (251)
Ding Dong Dollar, 268
Dirty Old Town, 81
Distressed Men of War, (126), 297
Dockers' Strike, The, 109
Doctor Mack, 187
Doings of Drink, The, 172
Donkey wot wouldn't go, 7
Don't be fidgety, 41
Downfall of Charing-Cross, The, 244
Down in the Village, 32
Dozen of Divine Points, A, 160
Dream, The, (117)
Drop of Good Beer, A, (171)
Drumdelgie, 54
Drunkard's Farewell, The, 172
Dublin Jack of All Trades, 69
Dunghill Cock, The, (125), 126
Dungiven Cricket Match, 195
Durham Gaol, 29, 157
Durham Strike, 29
Dusky night rides down the sky, The, 187

Eccles Wake, 167
Elwina of Waterloo, 279

England's Joy, 237
English Rover, The, 68
Evils of the Nation, The, 24
Excellent New Ballad, An, 221
Execution of . . . Rush, The (136)
Exhibition of All the Nations, 170

Factory Girl, The (224)
Fairing of Good Counsel, A, 160
Fall, Tyrants, Fall, 195
Fareweel, ye dungeons, 122
Farewel and adieu, 241
Farewell Address, 152
Farewell our Daddies, 293
Farewell to Your Judges and Juries, 148
Famous Woman Drummer, The, 277
Farmer's Boy, The, 37, 51, 57
Farmer's Curst Wife, The, 232
Farm Labourers of South Warwickshire, The, 57
Fatal English Poor Law Bill, The, 15
Female Convict, The, 151
Female Drummer, The, 14, (277)
Female Sailor, The, 151
Female Transport, The, 151
Female Warrior, The, 277
Ferret and the Coney, The, 160
Fifteenth day of July, The, 272
Fifty Years Ago, (40)
Fig for care, A, 254
Fighting with the 7th Royal Fusiliers, 284
File Hewer's Lamentation, The, 90
Fille-soldat, La, 277
Fine Old English Gentleman, The, (22), 62, 272
Flora, the Lily of the West, 14
Florentine Venus, The, 24
Foggy Dew, The, 213
Forced to be Contented, 16
Forestalling done over, 74
Forest Gate Fire, The, (22)
Forlorn Lover, The, 203
Four o'clock at Sullivan's door, 101
Fox Chase, The, 178, 187
Fox-Hunting Song, The, (189)
Fright'ned Yorkshire Damosel, The, 207, 213

Gallant She-Souldier, The, 277
Game of Cricket, 195
Gaol Song, 155, 157, 158
Gartcosh Commandos, The, 84
Gee ho Dobbin, 27, 228, 237, 258
General Distress, 237
General Ludd, 8
General Ludd's Triumph, 104

Girl I Left Behind Me, The, 107
Gloucestershire Colliers, The, 16
Godlie New Songe, A, 18
Godly Garters, The, 160
God rest ye, merry protesters, 301
God save Great Thomas Paine, 26
God save 'The Rights of Man', 258
Golden Farmer's Last Farewell, The, 137
Golden Glove, The, 14
Golden Vanity, The, 14
Goodbyee, 281
Good Christians who my distress do see, 113
Good people all attention, 130
Good people all draw near, 238
Good People of England, 77
Goose-green Starch and the Devil, 160
Gown of Green, The, 32
Great Agricultural Show, The, 170
Great Fight, The, 191
Great North Run, The, 179, 194
Great Unpaid, The, 57
Great Western Rail Road, The, 16
Green grow the Rushes, O, 264
Green upon the Cape, 262
Gresford Disaster, The, 97
Grimshaw's Factory Fire, 102
Grinders' Hardships, The, 89

Had I been a monk, 209
Hallelujah, I'm a Bum, 117, 299
Hampden Song, 25
Hand-loom v. Power-loom, 102
Handloom Weavers' Lament, 100, 102
Hang care, 8
Hang sorrow, 254
Hanoverian March, 279
Happy Husbandman, The, 31
Happy Land. Comic Version, 170
Hark the Herald Angels [parody], 243-4
Harry was a Bolshie, 264
Harness, The, 289
Hathersage Cocking, The, 173
Have you not heard the news, 116
H-Bomb's Thunder, The, 301
Hearts of Oak, 17, 246
Henry Dubb, 300
Here's a health to the jolly blacksmith, 89
Here's the tender coming, 282
Here's to the maiden, 14
Hiring Day, 52
Hodge in London, (63)
Hog-Tub, The, (214-15)
Hoo happy, we liv'd then, 40
Hole to put poor Robin in, A, 217
Holly Ho, (108)
Holy, Holy, Holy [parody], 281

Home, Sweet Home, 73, 255
Hopeful Bargain, The, 199
Horrid Murder of a Gentleman, (136)
Horsfall's Mill, 5
Howden Fair (165)
How Five and Twenty Shillings was expended, 73
How to get a Living, 66
Humours of Frost Fair, The, 166
Humours of London, The, 66
Humours of the Feast, The, 166–7
Humours of the Fleet, The, 153
Hunting a Loaf, 104
Hunting Day, The, 187
Hunting of the Hare, The, 186
Huntsman, The, (188)
Huntsman's Delight, The, 213

I am a damsel, 243
I am a poor old man, 38
I am a pretty wench, (35)
I came to London, 162
I can't find Birmingham, 71, 82
I don't want to be a soldier, 281
If you want to find Rupert Murdoch, 109
I give me curse, 107
I have for all good wives, 212
I'll sing you one, O, 265
I'm a poor unhappy married man, 208
I'm a shepherd, 33
I met with a Country Lass, 207
I'm sitting on the stile, 247
Income Tax, The, 240
Indian Compensation, The, 289
In former days the labourers, 15
In Manchester New Bayley, 154
In Owdham streets, 68
Internationale, The, 264
Invasion, A New Song, 279
Ips, Gips and Johnson, 7
Irish Emigrant, The, 247
Isle of Wight Informer, (198)
Italian liars witnesses, 244
It is not your Northerne Nanny, 210
It's a Mean Old Scene, 118, 119
It's a ye cockers, 173
It's first when I set out, 88
It was eighteen and seventy, 96
It was on a summer's morning, 276
It was when I came to my true love's window, 202

Jack Donohue, 152
Jack Hall, (3–4), 217, 245
Jack of All Trades, 68
Jack the Chimney Sweep, 4, 9

Jeelie Piece Song, The, 82–3
Jenny's Complaint, 285
Joan's Ale, 14
Jockey's Complaints, 222
Jock Hawk's Adventures in Glasgow, (63)
John Barleycorn, 171
John Brown's Body, 108, 264, 268
John Bull and the New Taxes, 240
Johnny Green's Trip, 70
Joley Weaver, The, 98
Jolly Cotton Spinner, The, (224)
Jolly Fellows that Follow the Plough, 35
Jolly Lad's Trip, The, 148
Jolly Thresherman, The, 37
Jolly Trooper, The, 214
Jone o'Grinfield, 99, 118, 167, 260
Jone o'Grinfield's Ramble, 100
Jone's Ramble, 27
Jovial Cutlers, The, 89
Jovial Foresters, The, 16

Keep the Home Fires Burning, 281
Keelmen's Stick, The, 118
Kellyburn Braes, 232
Kendal Fair, 51
Kentish Cricketer, The, 195
Kerry Recruit, The, 291
Kettle Smock, The (203)
King at Sea, The, 244
King of the Cannibal Islands, The, 110
King's Last Farewell, The, 245
Kirkdale Gaol, (156)
Kissing Lasses of Yarmouth, The, 228

Labourer's Prayer, The, 57
Lacaranto, 31
Lads of St Catherine's 176
Lads of Virginia, The, 141, 147
Lady Maisry, 222
Lamentable Life of Robert Sturman, The, 122
Lamentation of a Bad Market, The, 297
Lament of Two Stocking Makers, 99
Lass of Roch Royal, 222
Last Farewell to England, The, 264
Last Hogmanay at Glesca Fair, 171
Last night I had a dream, 117
Late Colliery Explosion, The, 95
Lay of the Lash, 290
Lee Bridge Cocking, The, 173
Let old and young, 140
Let's be kind to Anglo-Saxons, 267
Life in the streets of London, 67
Lillibulero, 174
Lincolnshire Poacher, 48
Lines on the Dreadful Explosion, 95
Lines on the Great Fight, 193

Lines on the Teetotal Barrel, 24
Lines on the Terrible Explosion, 95
Little Dickie Milburn, (225)
Little Lord John, 23
Little Musgrave, 227
Lock-out, The, 57
Long may old England, 17
London Adulterations, 76
London Sights, The, 65
Lord Marlborough, 272
Lord Willoughby, 272
Lovely Joan, 213
Love Song, 202
Luke Hutton's Lamentation, 122

MacAlpine's Fusiliers, 89
MacDonald's First Visit, (65)
Mademoiselle from Armentières, 85
Mad Maudlin, 86
Magdalene's Lament, The, 230
Maggie May, 158
Maiden's Lamentation, The, 276, 278
Maiden Warrior, The, 277
Malvinas, The, 271
Manchester Massacre, The, 260
Manchester Meeting, 259
Manchester Rambler, The, 29
Manchester's an Altered Town, 72
Manchester's Improving Daily, 71, 167
Man that Waters the Workers' Beer, The, 171
Man who wish'd he'd Never got Married, The, 231
Map of Mock-begger Hall, The, 210
Maria Marten, (55)
Marquis of Granby's March, The, 273
Married at Last, 242
Mary and the Handsome Factory Boy, (224)
Maunding Soldier, The, 292
McPherson's Rant, 122, 131
Meeting at Peterloo, The, 259
Meditations at St Helena, 25
Meddling Parson, The, 28
Medley's Remarks on the Times, 41, 74
Merry Little Soldier, 263
Methodist Parson, The, 225
Misery Farm, 58
Moreton Bay, 152
Murder of Maria Marten, The, 139, (144)
Mutton Pie, 52
My Grandfather's Days, 16
My Master and I, 44, 58
My name is Jack, 9
My yellow mou'd mistress, 285

Nae luck about the house, 154

Nail Maker's Lamentation, The, 91
Napoleon, 7
National Exhibition, The, 170
Navvy Boys, The, 88
Navvy on the Line, (300)
Never Flog our Soldiers, 290, 294
Never Trust a Sailor, 281
New and Loyal Song, A, 258
New Bailey Tread Mill, The, 154
New Ballad of Robin Hood, A, 183
New Ballad . . . Treason, A, 20
New Deserter, The, 291
Newe . . . Ballade, A, 20
New-fashioned Farmer, The, 40
New Gruel Shops, The, 15
New Hunting Song for 1854, A, 241
New Rigs and Humours . . . of the Fair, The, 167
New Poor Law, The, 255
New Song, A, 7
New Song called Bloxwich Wake Bull-baiting, A, 174, 175
New Song called Briton's Lamentation, A, 299
New Song called The Bird Fancier, A, 173
New Song called The Farmer's Delight, A, 219
New Song, entitled No Inclosure, A, 41, 43
New Song, in Praise of the Coal-miners, A, 93
New Song in Praise of W. Lovett & J. Collins, 263
New Song, Made Upon the Lads sent to Botany Bay, A, 148
New Song on Alderman Wilkes, A, 246
New Song [on Holroyd], (246)
New Song on Lord Granby, A, 273
New Song on Peterloo Meeting, A, 259
New Song on the American Female Prize-Fight, A, (192)
New Song on the Birmingham Election, (421)
New Song on the Birth of the Prince of Wales, A, 12
New Song on the Downfall of Trade, A, (242)
New Song on the Great Demonstration, 249
New Song on the Preston Guild, A, 13
New Song on the Times, A, 154
New Song on Wakefield Gaol, A, (156)
New Starvation Law, The, 255
New Statute Song, A, 51
New Touch of the Times, A, 73, 77, 252
Nobleman's Generous Kindness, The, 37
Noble Sportsmen, 241, 247
No cruise missiles, 301
Norfolk-Street Riots, 26
Now come jolly neighbours, 206
Now lasses and lads, 201

Now they say in these go-ahead days, 76
Nutting Girl, The, (35)

Oakey Evictions, The, 29
Oaks Pit Explosion, The, 95
Occasion manquée, L', 213
O Dear O, 220
Odds and Ends of the Year 1830, 241
Of all the brave trades, 89
Of the endes and deathes of two Prisoners, 122
O God above, 259
O hark what dreadful tidings, 72
Oh! fye upon care, 208
Oh I do love to live, 301
Oh, in Newport Town, 263
Oh the Dean of Westminster, 267
Oh there was a woman, 233
Oh! 'tis a famous story, 280
Oh ye canny shove yer granny, 268–70
O I'm Henry Dubb, 300
Old Black Bull, The, 281
Oldham on a Saturday Night, 68
Oldham Weaver, The, 100
Oldham Workshops, 68
Old Mother Flip Flop, 223
Old Ned's a Rare Strong Chap, 61, 68
Old Uncle Ned, 57
O Little Town of Windscale, 301
O my name it is Jack Hall, 3
Once I was a Shepherd Boy, (34)
One night as I came from the play, 217
On Going into the Workhouse, 25
Only doing their job, 29, 117
O no, my Love, 204
On Sunday I walk out with a Soldier, 281
On the Christening of the Prince of Wales, 24
On the Death of a Girl, 24
On the sixteenth day of August, 259, 260
On the sixteenth day of June, 279
O the lousy cutter, 282
O the weary cutters, 283
Our Bill, 226
Over the Hills and Far Away, 283
O, why don't you work? 117
Owdham Streets, 68
Owl of Oldham, The, 82
Owslebury Lads, The, 6, 47
O ye canny spend a dollar, 269

Paddy on the Canal, 69
Paddy on the Railway, 69
Paddy's Song, 157
Pal of mine once said, A, 101
Panges of Love, The, 20
Parker's Widow, 259

Parson Hogg, 187
Past, Present and Future, 15, 41
Pat Molloy, (64)
Penny Wedding, The, 184
People think my life is clean, 60
Peterloo, 260, 331
Peterloo Massacre, The, 27, 258
Pilgrim Blithe and Jolly, A, 90
Pitman's Revenge, The, 279
Pitties Lamentation, 235
Plains of Waterloo, The, 262, 278–9, 280
Pleasant New Ballad, A, 219
Ploughman Laddie, The, 93
Ploughman's Song, The, 35, 36–7
Plowman's Glory, The, 164
Policeman's Holiday, The, 117
Poor Colliers' Widows' Weeping Lamenta-
    tion, 95
Poore Man Payes for All, 236
Poor Jack, 104
Poor Man's Friend, The, 256
Poor Man's Litany, The, (240)
Poor Robin, 217
Poor Shepherds, 34
Poor Unhappy Transported Felon's Sorrow-
    ful Account, The, 145
Poor Whores' Complaint, 230
Powtes Complaint, The, 256
Praise of London, The, 65
Preservative against the Punks' Evil, A, 160
Press'd Man's Lamentation, The, 283, 293
Pretty Ploughboy, The, 35, (223)
Prince dothe sit, A, 31
Princess Royal's Dowry, The, 243
Proper new Ballad, A, 31
Protect the Soldiers' Wives, 298

Queen has sent a Letter, The, 28
Queen shall enjoy, The, 21, 244
Queen, Queen Caroline, 244
Queen's Old Soldiers, The, 272
Queen Victoria, (242)

Raining, raining, raining, 281
Rambler from Clare, The, 291
Ramble through the Agricultural Show, The,
    170
Rambling Miner, The, 88
Rambling Royal, The, 291
Ranting Parson, The, 225
Ranting Whores' Resolution, The, 208, 238
Rare Row about the Income Tax, A, (240)
Rawtenstall Annual Fair, 169
Recruited Collier, The, (285)
Recruiting Party, The, 287
Red Fly the Banners, O, 264, 265

Reform and King William, 252
Reformed Drunkard's Children's Song, The, 172
Reformers of England, The, 258
Remember Cwm Tryweryn, 266
Repentance, 26
Resurrection Men, The, 130
Rigs and Fun of Nottingham Goose Fair, The, 165
Rigs of London Town, The, 64
Roast Beef of Old England, The, 8, 76
Robin Hood and Guy of Gisborne, (30)
Roger in Amaze, 161
Roll, Chariot, 85
Roome for Companie, 160
Rose of Dettingen, 273
Rosey Anderson, 228
Rosin the Beau, 199
Rothesay, O, 171
Rough Joe in Search of a Wife, 28, (63)
Roving Ploughboy, 35
Royal Patient Traveller, The, 242
Rufford Park Poachers, 49
Rule Britannia, 271

Sailor's Complaint, 297
Sailors for my Money, 21, 33
Saint George, 160
Saint turn'd Sinner, The, 225
Sally's Love for a Young man, 222
Sammy Slap, the Bill Sticker, 57
Saturday Night, 67
Sayers' and Heenan's Great Fight, (193)
Says the master to me, 44
Saucy Ploughboy, The, (35)
Scarborough Fair, 164
Scarlet and the Blue, The, 284
Scenes of Manchester I sing, 7, 72
Scots wha hae, 257, 260
See it come down, 82
Shall Trelawney Die? 174
Sheffield Apprentice, The, 224
Shepherd's Song, The, (33)
Shepherds' Song, 33–4
She's coming round the mountain, 269
Shiny Dew, 59
Shipley's Drop, 194
Shop Windows, 66
Short Sketch of the Times, A, 241
Shy! Shy!, 209
Sick Parade, 271
Siege of Quebec, The, 274
Sights of London, The, 66
Sizewell ABC, The, 269
Skimmer Lads, The, 194
Smithfield Bargain, The, 199

Sodger Laddie, The, 284
Soldier's Complaint, The, 297
Soldier's Delight, The, 277
Soldier's Wife's Lament, The, 299
Soldiers' Wives' Complaint, The, 298
Somersetshire, (66)
Some thousands in England, 295
Songe betwene the Queenes majestie and England, 241–2
Songe of the Hunting . . . of the Hare, 186
Song for the Times, A, 14
Song of the Stamford Bullards, 184–6
Song on the Otley Statutes, 24
Sound Praises of fame, 273
So you doubt whom to choose, 7
Spanish Ladies Love, The, 20
Spiritual Bankrupt, The, 25
Spiritual Railway, The, 18
Starlaw Disaster, The, 95
Stick up for the Women, 211
Still in the Memory, 269
Stitch in Time, A, 232
Strawberry Fair, 164
Strike Alphabet, The, 115
Striking Times, 116
Strontium Ninety, 301
Subject's Satisfaction, The, 242
Submissive Petition, The, 94, 113
Sudborough Heroes, 48
Sunday Night, 67
Sun is Burning, The, 301–2
Swaggering Farmers, 40
Sweet Country Life, A, 31–2
Sweet is the Lasse, 219
Swinish Multitude's Address, 257
Sylvia's Trial of her Sweetheart, (126)

Take it to the Lord, 301
Taunton Maid's Delight, The, 223
Tavistock Goosie Fair, 169
Tax upon Income, The, (240)
Teetotal Boy, 172
Temperance Alphabet, The, 172
Ten Per Cent, 116
That monster oppression, 11
There is a place in Horsley, 15
There's a farmer up in Cairnie, 54
There's bound to be a row, 209
There was a jovial Beggar, 86
They closed Newcastle, 179
They're changing dear old Brummagem, 82
They said reform would do us good, 16
Three Jovial Companions, The, 213
Thrifty Housewife, 23
Times Alteration, 39, 235
Tinkler's Waddin, The, 171, 199

To help the folk at medical school, 132
Tom Pain's Life, 258
Toon Improvement Bill, The, 28
Tories are a sliding, The, 248
Tradesman's Complaint, The, 297
Trades-men's Lamentation, The, 237
Tramp, tramp, tramp, 108, 109, 266
Transport, The, 148
Tread Mill, The, 154
Treats of London, The, 66
Tree of Liberty, The, 257
Trefechan Bridge, 266
Trial ... of ... John Frost, The, 263
Tribute to Guy Fawkes, A, 266
Trident, Trident, 301
Trimdon Grange Explosion, The, 28
Trois Déserteurs, Les, 291
Troubles of this World, The, 237
True Description of a Trip to the Fair, A, 166
True Statement of the Present Times, A, 252
Turnit Hoeing, (32)
Twankydillo, (89)
'Twas on the sixteenth day of August, 262
Twentieth of September, 1854, The, 280

Uncle Ned's Visit to the Exhibition, 170
Unfair Fight, The, 191
Unfortunate Wife, The, 231
Union Mill, The, 25

Van Dieman's Land, 48, 149, 151
Verses on Daniel Good, 136
Verses on the New Starvation Poor Law, 24
Victoria Bridge on a Saturday Night, 68, 80

Wakefield Gaol, 156
Wanton Seed, The 219
Wanton Wife of Castlegate, The, 227
Warning for all Souldiers, A, 290
Warning to Deserters, A, 290
Warning to Drunkards, A, 172
Warrikin Fair, 165
Warwick Gaol, (156)
Watkinson and his Thirteens, 11, 26
We are not conquered yet, 266
We are out for higher wages, 108
Weary Farmers, The, 51
Weaver, The, (215)
Weaver and the Factory Maid, The (101)
Weaver in Love, The, (223)
Wedding at Ballyporeen, The, 199
Wedding Song, The, 200
Wednesbury Cocking, The, 174, 175, 183
Wee Magic Stane, 267
Welcome, welcome, brother debtor, 153
We'll all go a-hunting, 188
We'il hang old Bryant, 108

We're so miserable, 58
We're the lads, 117
West Country Lawyer, The, 223
We Will Not Stop Again, 53
Weyhill Fair, (165)
What shall we do with Rupert Murdoch?, 109
When ancient Romans did lament, 275
When first I began to court, 207
When I liv'd at whoam, 61
When shaws be sheen, 30
When the King enjoys, 21
When the red revolution comes, 264
When this bloody war is over, 301
When this nuclear war is over, 301
When this old Hat was New, 37, 38, 41
Whitsun Fair in Birmingham, 25
Wholsome Advice, 257
Who Owns the Game?, 49
Whores' Downfall, The, 229
Whores Eight o' Penny, 228
Who starves kiddies? 117
Widdicombe Fair, 164
William Burk's Execution, 131, 140
Wilkes and Granby, 252
Wilkes and Liberty, 252
Willie, we have missed you, 294
Windmill blown down, The, 160
Windsor Election, 174
Winkey Wam, 57
With Wellington we'll go, 262
Woeful Ballad, A, 122
Woman to the Plow, The, 212
Woman Warrior, The, 277
Wonders of Bartholomew Fair, The, (161)
Word of Advice, A, 172

Yankee Doodle, 218
Ye Gentlemen of England, 74
Yellow belly doffers, The, 107
Yorkshireman in London, 63
You coal miners of England, 93
You drunken fond fuddlers, 24
You freemen all of Nottingham, 43
You gentlemen and tradesmen, 100
You gentlemen that rack your rentes, 256
You lads of this nation, 23
You'll easy tell a doffer, 106
Young Edward slain at Waterloo, 28
Young Henry the Poacher, 15, 48
Young Rambleaway, 164
Young Trooper cut down, The, 271
Young Tyler and Robinson, 191
You noble diggers all, 251
You pretty Maids, 223
You Reformers of England, 249
You surely have heard 237
You would not leave your Norah, 294

GENERAL INDEX

Aberdeen, 164
Adams, W. E., 14
adulteration of food, 76, 77
Agnew, Sir Andrew, 253
agribusiness, 42
Aids, 80
Ainsworth, W. H., 127
Albert, Prince, 242, 243, 248, 291
Aldermaston March, 300
Allison, William, 2
Alma, battle of, 280
Alnwick, 190
Altick, Richard, 134
America (USA), 85, 124, 145, 147, 201, 204, 227, 232, 275, 299
American Civil War, 108, 278
American War of Independence, 25, 238, 257, 275, 276, 300
Anderson, Robert, 26, 285
Anne, Queen, 283
Arch, Joseph, 56–8, 81
Arden, John, 291
Armstrong, Tommy, 11, 28, 96–7, 157
Ashbourne, 182, 189, 290
Ashton, T. S., 101
Ashton-under-Lyne, 259, 260
Australia, 146, 147, 148, 149, 152
Aylesbury, 68

Balaclava, battle of, 280
ballad, vi, vii, viii, 1, 3, 5, 6, 12, 34, 41, 42, 96, 104, 108, 109, 122, 126, 131, 150, 152, 164, 166, 169, 173, 174, 175, 186, 197, 222, 227, 230, 231, 235, 238, 240, 241, 244, 245, 246, 254, 257, 259, 260, 263, 264, 273, 274, 277, 278, 280, 282, 283, 284, 286, 288, 290, 291, 297; (bothy), 53–6; (election), 7, 16, 246–7; (execution), 4, 41, 112–15, 245; (murder), 144, 156; (political), 20, 27; (printed), vii, 1, 3–4, 6–8, 11, 12–25, 28, 40, 48, 52, 53, 58, 63, 64, 65, 66, 67, 68, 72, 74, 80, 81, 86, 94–5, 97, 116, 130, 131, 133, 134, 136, 147, 148, 160, 161, 170, 172, 176, 179, 187, 191, 192, 193, 198, 199, 251, 258, 280, 290; (radio) 193
ballad-printers, 18, 19, 20, 135, 191, 242, 253
ballad-singers, 8, 17, 19, 20, 23, 25, 52, 67, 133–4, 135–6, 160, 164–5, 194, 204, 210, 212, 217, 220, 230, 242, 245, 246, 252, 264
balloon ascents, 193
Banff, 122
Baring-Gould, S., 275
Barrett, W. H., 201
Batley, 101
BBC, 187, 213
Beaumaris, 154
Beaumont and Fletcher, 227
Behan, Dominic, 89
Beier, A. L., 86, 87
Belfast, 106, 107, 224, 242
Benbow, Admiral, 3, 4, 124
Birch, William, 241
Birmingham, 13, 14, 18, 24, 25, 27, 62, 63, 67, 68, 69, 71, 73, 134, 150, 151, 163, 165, 170, 174, 175, 183, 188, 215, 220, 240, 244, 263, 290
Bishop Blaise, 97–8, 109, 165
Blackburn, 102
Black Country, 90–1, 163, 176
Blagden, Cyprian, 12
Blake, William, 186
Blamire, Susanna, 26
Bleasdale, Alan, 2
Blockley, John J., 284
Bloxwich, 169, 175
Blythman, Morris, 267
body-snatchers, 71, 80, 127–33
Bolton, 101, 215
Borrow, George, 192
Botany Bay, 126, 146, 147, 148, 154
Bowman, Joe, 188
Bradford, 24, 97, 118, 255
Bragg, Melvyn, 51
Brand, John, 199
Brécy, Robert, 8
Breda, battle of, 297
Bridgnorth, 172, 174
Brighton, 193
Bristol, 68, 73, 172
Britain, 124, 149, 204, 266, 275
British Coal, vii
Britten, Benjamin, 213
Brixton, 154
Brockway, Fenner, 299

Brome, Richard, 86
Bromley, 164
Bromsgrove, 91, 172
Brooksbank, Mary, 108, 109
brothels, 210, 224
Bruce, J. C., and Stokoe, J., 282
bull-baiting, 25, 27, 166, 168, 174, 175–6,
    181, 186, 189, 253
bull-running, 176, 183–6, 190
bundling, 200–2
Burke and Hare, 131–3, 134
Burne, Charlotte, 22
Burnett, John, 73, 76
Burns, John, 109, 110
Burns, Robert, 26, 93, 122, 232, 257, 269
Bury, 215
bush-rangers, 126, 152
Butler, Samuel, 174
Byng, Admiral, 124
Byron, Lord, 22, 103, 104, 191

Cambridge, 7, 12, 68, 122
Campbell, Ian, 301
Canada, 275
canals, 27, 69, 72
Cardigan, Lord, 48
Carlisle, 26, 285
Carlyle, Thomas, 122
Caroline, Queen 21, 244
Carpenter, James, 197
carpet-weavers, 116
Catnach, James, 13, 14, 22, 23, 66, 206
CEGB, vii, 269–70
chainmakers, 90–1, 108, 114
Chappell, William, 3
Charles I, 21, 210
Charles II, 6, 7, 145, 160, 238
Chartists, 14, 24, 147, 241, 249, 262, 263,
    264, 283
Chaucer, 2
Chelmsford, 134, 192
Cheltenham, 14, 253
Chernobyl, 269
Chicken, Edward, 199
chimney-sweeps, 122–3
Chipping Campden, 14
cholera, 71, 80, 81, 176
Churchill, Winston, 264
Civil War, 7, 244
Clare, John, 34, 39, 40, 42, 51, 53, 73
Clarke, Marcus, 147
class, 222 ff.
CND, 268, 300, 301
Cobbett, William, 39, 40, 41, 53, 56, 99
cock-fighting, 25, 27, 66, 172–5, 181, 186,
    189

Coe, Peter, 118, 271
Cole, G. D. H., and Postgate, Raymond, 57
Coleman, Terry, 89
Collins, John, 263
Combination Acts, 104
Cook, H. F., 287
Cooke, Eliza, 22
Corder, William, 138, 139, 144
Corn Laws, 248, 256
Corvan, Ned, 28, 194
Coventry, 68, 165, 166, 246
Crabbe, George, 174
cricket, 66, 173, 180, 195–6
crime, 4, 14–15, 121 ff.
Crimean War, 241, 280, 291, 292, 298
Crome, John, 26
Cromwell, Oliver, 200, 246
Cromwell, Thomas, 1
croppers, 5, 104–6, 112
Cubitt, William, 154
Culloden, 273

Darlaston, 174, 176
Darlington, 164
Davis, George, 24–5
deer-hunting, 186
Deloney, Thomas, 20–1, 272
Denbigh, 172
Derby, 190
Derby, Lord, 48
Derricourt (or Day), William, 147
Derry, 158, 159
Dettingen, battle of, 273
Dibdin, Charles, 22
Dickens, Charles, 18, 22, 116, 134, 170
Diggers, 124, 245, 251
dockers, 109–10
doctors, 80–1, 105, 126, 127, 128
doffers, 106–7
Doncaster, 156
drinking, 171–2
Dryden, 21
Dublin, 68, 69, 145, 292
Dudley, 111
Dundee, 108
Durham, 28, 29, 195

Eccles, 167, 169
Eden, Anthony, 264
Edinburgh, 1, 27, 127, 130, 131, 133, 164
Edward I, 266
Edward VIII, 243
Elderton, William, 20
Eleanor, Queen, 244
elections, 7, 16, 174, 246–7
Elgin, Lord, 227

Elizabeth I, 236, 241, 242
emigration, 58
enclosure, 15, 27, 34, 39, 40–2, 43, 74, 186,
    190, 256
Engels, Frederick, 72
England, 1, 28, 33, 48, 56, 58, 85, 104, 124,
    146, 152, 163, 174, 188, 190, 232, 242, 248,
    249, 254, 266, 273, 291
Eton, 172
Evelyn, John, 160, 166
executions, 14–15, 20, 121, 131, 135–6, 143
Exeter, 99

Fairley, John 2
fairs, 14, 25, 50, 66, 121, 156, 160–71, 173,
    177, 190, 198, 228, 253; (Bartholomew),
    160–3, 170; (Coventry), 165–6; (Eccles),
    167–8; (Fairlop), 170; (frost), 166; (Glas-
    gow), 171; (Greenwich), 169–70, 177; (hir-
    ing), 50–3, 56, 279; (London), 163–4;
    (Nottingham), 165; (Salisbury), 166;
    (Weyhill), 165
Fakenham, 41
Falklands War, 271
farmers, 37, 38, 39, 44, 50–3, 54–5, 74, 166,
    173, 223
farm-workers, 50, 51, 52, 53, 57–8, 59
Farquhar, George, 283
fashions, 65–6
female convict, 151
female highwayman, 126
female prize-fighters, 192
female soldiers, 277–8
Fermanagh, 174
Fielding, Henry, 22, 187, 253
Firth, C. H., 6, 8, 244, 272
football, 41, 182, 189, 193, 194
foot-racing, 191, 194
Ford, Robert, 228
fox-hunting, 14, 40, 178, 186–9, 253
Freeth, John, 27, 69
Free Wales Army, 266
French Revolution, 17, 257
Frost, John, 147, 241, 263, 264

Galway, 240, 286
game laws, 27, 47, 48, 56
Gardiner, William, 99, 172, 252
Garrick, David, 22
Gaskell, Mrs, 100
Gateshead, 14, 29, 130
Gay, John, 22
George II, 273
George III, 47, 239, 257, 291
George IV, 48, 244
George V, 300

George, Dorothy, 8
Gerrald, Joseph, 257
Glasgow, 59, 63, 64, 82, 151, 170, 240, 268,
    299
Gloucester, 14, 15
Goethe, 30
Goldsmith, Oliver, 22
Grainger, Percy, 49
Granby, Marquis, of, 273–4, 275
Graves, Robert, 174
Great Exhibition, 170
Greenham women, 120
Greenpeace, 269
Gregson, Keith, 194
Greig, Gavin, 278
Gretton, M. Sturge, 69
Grey, Edwin, 133
Grimaldi, 232

Hall, Jack, 3, 4, 122–4
Hammond, J. L. and B., 8, 47
Hardy, Thomas (radical), 26
Hardy, Thomas (novelist), 1
hare-hunting, 186–7
Harkness, John, 12, 13, 18, 72, 116, 172, 191
Harman, Horace, 195
Harpenden, 133
harvesting, 32
Hawker, James, 47, 48, 50, 197
Haydn, 29
haymaking, 32
Hazlitt, William, 192
Heenan, J. C., 180
Helmsley, 187
Henderson, Hamish, 56, 96
Henry I, 241
Henry VIII, 2
highwaymen, 4, 125, 126, 127, 297
Hitchen, 174
Hodgart, Matthew, 174
Hogarth, William, 19, 121, 197
Holbeck, 173
Holloway, J., and Black, J., 230
Holroyd, J. B., 246
Holyoake, G. J., 13
Homer, 30
Hone, William, 14
Hood, Thomas, 129
Hopkins, Harry, 47
Hopkinson, James, 121, 131
hop-pickers, 32, 58
Horseman's Word, 56
horse-racing, 14, 25, 27, 166
Holder, Reuben, 24, 255, 256
Hudson, W. H., 32
Hughes, Robert, 147

Hughes, Thomas, 33, 166
Hugill, Stan, 6
hulks, 146, 148
Hull, 13
Hunt, Henry, 27, 200, 241, 259, 261, 262
Huntington, Gale, 6
hymns, 57, 301

illegitimacy, 164, 203
Inkerman, battle of, 280
IRA, 284
Ireland, 1, 2, 51, 117, 124, 152, 188, 195, 232,
    241, 248, 249, 279, 280, 290
iron and steel trades, 89 ff.
itinerant workers, 87–9

James I, 235
Jefferies, Richard, 127
Jerrold, Douglas, 19, 20
John I, 183
Jones, Paul, 124
Jones, William, 264
Jonson, Ben, 19, 22, 160

keelmen, 28, 108, 114
Kemble, Fanny, 70
Kickham, Charles, 292
Kidd, Captain, 124
Kidderminster, 116
Kidson, Frank, 262
Kingsley, Charles, 122
Kirkwood, David, 299, 300
Kitchen, Fred, 35, 156

labourers, 6, 14, 15, 32, 35, 37, 38, 39, 57, 63,
    117, 184, 185, 194, 223, 258
Labourers' Revolt, 47
Lagzdins, Anton, 59
Lancaster, 259
Lanfiere, Thomas, 99, 223
Laslett, Peter, 203
Law, T. S., 267
Laycock, Tim, 269
Ledbury, 19
Leeds, 7, 62, 67, 269
Leicester, 7, 68, 99, 102, 103, 112, 142, 154,
    163, 172, 173
Lewis, Isle of, 201
Leydi, Roberto, 8
Liverpool, 17, 28, 48, 68, 69, 72, 156, 173, 282
Lloyd, A. L., 97, 285
Lloyd George, David, 300
Locke, John, 160
London, 3, 4, 7, 13, 59, 63, 64, 65, 66, 67, 73,
    76, 82, 84, 86, 94, 108, 109, 122, 127, 128,
    133, 135, 145, 160, 162, 166, 170, 172, 174,
    176, 192, 198, 216, 223, 238, 251, 255, 263,
    298
Lord's Day Observance Society, 171
Lovett, William, 263
Luddites, 4–5, 6, 8, 102–6, 128, 289

Macaulay, Lord, 4, 6, 7–8, 9, 10, 13, 99, 126,
    238
MacColl, Ewan, 29, 81, 118, 193
MacGregor, Ian, 119
Macfarlane, Alan, 200
machine-breaking, 4, 5, 102–6, 108
Mackay, Charles, 22
Mackay, William, 171, 240
Maclean, John, 299, 300
Madden, Frederic, 12
Manchester, 14, 27, 59, 61, 62, 69, 70, 72, 73,
    78, 79, 100, 102, 154, 155, 156, 167, 168,
    199, 200, 209, 215, 258, 259, 260, 262
Margarot, Maurice, 257
Marlborough, Duke of, 283
Marshall, Samuel, 269
Marten, Maria, 138, 139, 144
Masefield, John, 12, 19, 188
match-girls, 108
Mather, Joseph, 11, 25–6, 29, 89
Maxton, James, 299, 300
Mayhew, Henry, 135, 154
McCaig, Norman, 267
McEvoy, John, 267
McGinn, Matt, 92
Mehan, Patrick, 157
Middleton, 259
Middleton, Thomas, 20
Minden, battle of, 273
miners, 35, 85, 92–7, 99, 116, 118, 163
Misson, Maximilien, 191
More, Hannah, 17, 171
More, Thomas, 186
Morgan, John, 23
Moritz, Carl Philip, 3
Muir, Thomas, 26, 257
murder, 28, 133–5, 157
Murdoch, Rupert, 108–9
music hall, 288, 301
mutiny, 2, 259

nailmakers, 90, 91–2
Napoleon, 279
Nash, Thomas, 21
National Coal Board, 119
nationalism, 29, 266–8, 292
navvies, 88, 200
navy, 12
Nelson, Lord, 124, 275
Nenagh, 151

Nerval, Gérard de, 213
Nevison, John, 126, 127
Newcastle, 28, 74, 114, 151, 152, 178, 179, 262, 282, 283, 298
Newport, 263
Nightingale, Florence, 280
night visiting, 202–3
Norwich, 7, 20, 21, 135, 240, 254
Nottingham, 43, 73, 99, 103, 122, 150, 151, 231
nuclear power, 269–70
nuclear weapons, 29
NUWM 264

O'Connell, Daniel, 241
Oldham, 27, 28, 62, 68, 70, 82, 100, 173, 199, 259
opera, 1, 41, 187
oral tradition vii, 1, 2–6, 14, 26, 31, 37, 57, 64, 103, 108, 127, 131, 144, 156, 173, 174, 175, 187, 188, 191, 199, 200, 203, 204, 213, 219, 227, 273, 280, 283
Orwell, George, 32, 58
outlaws, 126
Owen, Wilfred, 271
Oxford, 35, 238, 242

Paine, Thomas, 26, 257, 258, 275
Palmer, Thomas F., 26, 257
Palmerston, Lord, 243
Parker, Charles, 193
Parker, Martin, 21, 33, 39, 235
peace, 297 ff.
Pears, Peter, 213
Pedley, Robin, 187
Peel, Frank, 4, 5, 289
Peel, John, 188
Peel, Sir Robert, 240, 248
Peninsular War, 278
Pepys, Samuel, 1, 160, 172
Percy, Bishop, 20
Perth, 227
Peterhead, 157
Peterloo, 26, 27, 200, 249, 258–62, 278
pickpockets, 63, 161
Pitt, William, 238, 239, 240, 252
Pitts, John, 4, 9, 124, 141
Place, Francis, 4, 17, 124, 170, 183, 216, 217, 218, 219, 228
pleasure gardens, 170
ploughmen, 34–7, 54, 57, 167, 223
Plymouth, 59
Pollitt, Harry, 264
Poor Law, 15, 24, 253–6
Portsmouth, 146, 151, 271, 276

press-gang, 12, 198, 281–3
Preston, 12, 18, 19, 22, 48, 72, 73, 116, 172, 191, 273
prison, 15, 153–9
prize-fighting, 27, 66, 190–3
prostitution, 64, 66, 67, 151, 228–30
protest, 37–40, 41, 280

railways, 69–71, 72
reform, 16, 26, 71, 80, 81, 252, 258, 259, 260, 261
Richardson, Samuel, 128
Ridley, Geordie, 179, 194
riots, 41
Roberts, Robert, 81
Robin Hood, 30, 126, 127, 183
Rochdale, 35
Rodgers, N. A. M., 12, 282
Rogers, Dave, 271, 272
Romilly, Sir Samuel, 145
Ross, G. W., 124, 137
Rosselson, Leon, 269
rough music, 197, 205
rowing, 194
Rowlandson, Thomas, 10, 19, 143, 180
Rowley Regis, 176
royalty, 241–4
RSPCA, 171, 184, 186
Russell, Henry, 22
Russell, William, 280

sailors, 6, 35, 63, 85, 128, 229
Saint Monday, 24–5, 101
Salford, 81
Sayers, Tom, 180, 193
Scotland, 1, 6, 28, 33, 35, 53, 56, 59, 65, 95, 117, 157, 174, 190, 201, 230, 232, 241, 248, 267, 268, 273, 279, 299, 300
Scott, Sir Walter, 131
sea shanties, 6, 85, 109, 161
Sebastopol, battle of, 280
Sedgley, 176
Seeger, Peggy, 193
Seeger, Pete, 269
Selden, John, 1
Seven Years' War, 12, 238
Shakespeare, William, 19, 20, 241, 269
Sharp, Cecil, 124, 191
Shaw, A. G. L., 149
Sheerness, 146
Sheffield, 25, 26, 48, 67, 89, 90, 130
Shelley, 259
shepherds, 32–4, 35, 45, 56, 57
Shields, William, 22
Shinwell, Emmanuel, 290

Shrewsbury, 174
Sikh Wars, 287
Sillitoe, Alan, 165
Sizewell, B., vii, 269, 270
Skirving, William, 26, 257
slums, 81–2
Smith, Abraham, 175
Smith, Capt. Alexander, 124
Smith, Sidney Goodsir, 267
Smout, T. C., 201
smugglers, 50, 198
socialism, 265
soldiers, 35, 271 ff.
Somerville, Alexander, 290
songs, vii, viii, 1, 4, 6, 7, 8, 14, 17, 23, 25, 26,
    53, 54, 57, 84–5, 86, 92, 97, 108, 109, 117,
    118, 134, 147, 157, 164, 165, 169, 174, 187,
    188, 193, 197, 198, 199, 202, 203, 204, 213,
    215, 217, 218, 219, 221, 223, 226, 227, 228,
    232, 235, 240, 241, 244, 254, 256, 271, 273,
    277, 278, 279, 280, 281, 299, 300, 301;
    (bothy), 6, 35; (election), 174; (factory),
    106–7; (folk), vi, 3, 30, 31–2, 264; (Jaco-
    bite), 273; (music hall), 22, 28, 231;
    (nursery), 301; (obscene), 216–19; (politic-
    al), vi, 264 ff.; (protest), 235 ff.
Southey, Robert, 128, 130
South Shields, 179, 194
Spanish Armada, 20
Spanish Civil War, 2, 284
Spiers, Edward M., 286
spinners, 107, 224
Stamford, 176, 183, 184, 185, 186, 190
steelworkers, 84
Sterne, Laurence, 128
Stockport, 259
Stourbridge, 91
Street, A. G., 32
strikes, vii, 18, 19, 29, 57, 91, 96, 98, 104,
    107–10, 114, 115, 116–17, 118, 263, 264,
    266, 299, 301
Strutt, Joseph, 175
Stubbes, Philip, 172
Sturt, George, 134
Sullivan, Dick, 89
Swansea, 243
Swift, Jonathan, 121
Swing, 42, 47, 241, 273

Talbot, Mary Ann, 277, 289
Taunton, 223
taxation, 237–40
teetotalism, 18, 24, 172
Tewkesbury, 14
Thatcher, Margaret, 84, 158
Theodorakis, Mikis, 1

Thomas, Keith, 186, 188
Thompson, E. P., 8, 101, 121
Thompson, Flora, 244
Thomson, R. S., 12
Tillett, Ben, 109, 110
Tiltman, Marjorie Hessell, 163
Tinker, David, 271
Tipton, 176
Tolpuddle Martyrs, 42, 236
trade unions, 44, 56–8, 104, 108, 224
train robbers, 126, 127
treadmill, 15, 142, 153–6
Trevelyan, G. M., 22, 47
Trevelyan, G. O., 7
transportation, 47, 49, 121, 126, 128, 145–53,
    156, 257, 263
turnip-hoeing, 32
Turpin, Dick, 125, 126, 127
Tutbury, 176, 183
Tyburn, 9, 121, 122, 123, 124, 128, 245

unemployment, 34, 75, 117–20, 151, 236,
    264, 295, 298
Urfey, Thomas d', 198–9

Van Diemen's Land, 4, 42, 146, 149–51, 152,
    241
Vellinghausen, battle of, 273
Verdi, Giuseppe, 1
Victoria, Queen, 23, 66, 81, 100, 186, 242,
    248, 279, 289
Villiers, George, 2nd Duke of Buckingham,
    187
Voltaire, 170

Wakefield, 104, 156
Wales, 1, 163, 174, 190, 201, 241, 248, 266,
    279
Walker, George, 197
Wapping, 109
Warburg, battle of, 273
Warrington, 165
Warwick, 156, 263
Waterloo, battle of, 186, 278, 279, 298
Waterson, Mike, 232
weavers, 98–101, 102, 106, 107, 167, 215,
    224, 237, 242, 260
weddings, 199–200
Wednesbury, 174
Wellington, Duke of, 70, 186, 278, 279
Welshpool, 172
wife-selling, 198–9
Wight, Isle of, 198
Wilkes, John, 73, 77, 251
Wilkins, W. W., 8
Willey, Thomas, 14–16, 253

William and Mary, 242
William III, 238, 239
William IV, 81, 242, 252, 273
Williams, Erin, 264
Williams, Raymond, 35
Williams, William, 187
Williams, Zepaniah, 264
Wilson, Alexander, 28, 70
Wilson, Joe, 194
Wilson, Michael, 27, 258
Wilson, Thomas, 28, 63, 199
Winchester, 47
Winstanley, Gerard, 245
Wobblies, 117
Woddis, Roger, 271, 272

Wolfe, General, 274–5, 291
Wolverhampton, 151, 181
Woolwich, 146
Worcester, 165, 192
Wordsworth, William, 19, 160
Work, Henry Clay, 22
workhouse, 16, 25, 252, 254, 298, 299
World War, First, 51, 109, 117, 271, 281, 298, 300
World War, Second, 51, 82, 85, 164, 264
wrestling, 190, 191, 192
Wrigley, Bernard, 225

Yarmouth, 228, 229
York, 4, 105, 122, 125, 126, 127, 128, 231

CANCELLED
THE
NORTHERN COLLEGE
LIBRARY
BARNSLEY

5838